CONSTRUCTING *Meaning*

Integrating Elementary Language Arts

JOYCE BAINBRIDGE EDWARDS
GRACE MALICKY
University of Alberta

with a chapter on drama by Pat Payne

Nelson Canada
I(T)P An International Thomson Publishing Company

Toronto • Albany • Bonn • Boston • Cincinnati • Detroit • London • Madrid • Melbourne
Mexico City • New York • Pacific Grove • Paris • San Francisco • Singapore • Tokyo • Washington

I(T)P™
International Thomson Publishing
The ITP logo is a trademark under licence

Published in 1996 by
Nelson Canada
A division of Thomson Canada Limited
1120 Birchmount Road
Scarborough, Ontario M1K 5G4

Canadian Cataloguing in Publication Data
Edwards, Joyce.
Constructing meaning

Includes bibliographical references and index.
ISBN 0-17-604859-6

1. Language arts (Elementary). I. Malicky, Grace, 1944– . II. Title.

LB1575.8.E38 1995 372.6 C95-932784-3

Team Leader and Publisher	Michael Young
Acquisitions Editor	Charlotte Forbes
Project Coordinator	Joanne Scattolon
Production Editor	Tracy Bordian
Production Coordinator	Brad Horning
Art Director	Liz Harasymczuk
Cover/Interior Design	Peggy Rhodes
Cover Illustration	Cathie Bleck
Composition	Linda Mackey
Input Operator	Elaine Andrews

Printed and bound in Canada
1 2 3 4 (TG) 99 98 97 96

Contents

Preface

Effective elementary language arts programs are those in which reading, writing, listening, and speaking are taught in an integrated manner rather than separately. Integration extends beyond the time designated for language arts to areas across the curriculum, such as social studies, science, and mathematics, and beyond the school as children use language in their daily lives. In effective language arts programs, language is used in meaningful, purposeful ways by children and teachers who understand its holistic, constructive nature.

This textbook is an introduction to teaching elementary language arts from an integrated, holistic, and constructive perspective. It is intended for both preservice and inservice elementary school teachers. The book provides a comprehensive theoretical framework accessible to beginning teachers and a balanced presentation of ideas related to different areas of the language arts. Although the book is divided into chapters on oral language, literature, emergent literacy, reading, writing, and drama, the connections between these areas are emphasized throughout.

Each chapter begins with an overview and objectives for teachers. Terms in boldface type are defined in a glossary at the end of the book. Most chapters include *Inside the Classroom* vignettes to help beginning and preservice teachers to vicariously experience the teaching of the language arts. Included in some chapters are book lists, examples of language activities, and samples of children's reading, writing, and oral language. Each chapter ends with a summary as well as a list of selected references to extend knowledge and understanding.

The first two chapters provide a framework for the remainder of the book. Chapter 1 provides the necessary theoretical understandings for planning an effective language arts program. The nature and context of language learning as well as the nature of teaching and learning in the elementary language arts classroom are considered in Chapter 1. This chapter ends with a statement of beliefs about language that serve as the conceptual framework for the remainder of the book.

Chapter 2 deals with the practical organizational framework and begins with a presentation of principles for planning and organizing language arts programs. The chapter then discusses how materials, time, space, and students can be organized to maximize language learning.

In Chapter 3, the discussion of materials introduced in Chapter 2 is extended and the focus is specifically on children's literature. This chapter provides information on how to select children's literature as well as lists of children's books, placing a heavy emphasis on Canadian content.

Chapters 4 through 9 give specific suggestions for teaching each area of language arts. In Chapter 4, the structure of language is described and perspectives on language acquisition are presented. This is followed by an exploration of how language functions in different social contexts, and how language functions in learning in general. Finally, suggestions are made for enhancing oral language development in classrooms.

Chapter 5 describes components of emergent literacy and shows how children's reading and writing begin in the home. General principles for encouraging emergent literacy as well as specific techniques for use with young children are presented.

Chapters 6 and 7 focus on reading, beginning with a consideration of the nature of reading from both psychological and social perspectives. This leads to suggestions for teaching and learning related to response to literature and critical literacy in Chapter 6. In Chapter 7, specific techniques for developing reading strategies are presented.

Chapters 8 and 9 are devoted to writing. Chapter 8 examines models and forms of writing, the process of composing, and methods for teaching the conventional aspects of print (spelling, handwriting, punctuation, and capitalization). Chapter 9 focuses on the role of writing in learning across the cirriculum. This chapter describes strategies for working with journal writing, learning logs, research reports, and study skills.

All areas of the language arts come together in Chapter 10, which takes a detailed look at drama in elementary school. This chapter begins by discussing what counts as drama and then shows teachers how various drama forms can be used in the classroom.

The final chapter on assessment presents information on standardized tests, but its primary focus is on how to use informal assessment techniques in the classroom. The emphasis is on the assessment of children's needs in oral language, emergent literacy, reading, and writing as an integral part of planning and implementing instruction. A section is also included on reporting to parents.

Acknowledgments

We wish to thank all the children, teachers, undergraduate students, graduate students, and colleagues who have helped us understand the nature of the teaching and learning of language arts during our years as students and teachers. Particular appreciation is expressed to the teachers who took the time to write about their classroom experiences in the *Inside the Classroom* vignettes and to the children who provided samples of their reading, writing, and oral language. We are also grateful to the teachers and children in the schools where we took the photographs and to Charles Norman for helping with the photography.

We wish to acknowledge the significant contribution of Pat Payne who drew on her knowledge of language arts to write the chapter on drama. One of the most complete descriptions of drama available in any language arts textbook, this chapter models integration in action. Pat Campbell's contribution to the section on miscues in the chapter on assessment and Sylvia Pantaleo's contribution to the chapter on children's literature are also gratefully acknowledged.

We appreciate the assistance of Tracey Derwing in providing feedback on the linguistics aspects of Chapter 4, and of graduate students Herb Katz and Carol Leroy, who gave us feedback on other chapters. In addition, we received valuable comments and suggestions from the reviewers selected by Nelson Canada. Thanks to Gary Killen (York University) and Beverley Zakaluk (University of Manitoba), and other reviewers from University of Toronto, University of Lethbridge, Queen's University, University of Victoria, McGill University, Lakehead University, University of Manitoba, Memorial University, University of Western Ontario, and Simon Frazer University.

We are also grateful to Mary Effray and Sonia Rywak who helped us with word processing, formatting, and editing the manuscript. Finally, we wish to thank the editorial staff at Nelson Canada for encouraging us to write this book and for providing advice and support during its development.

Joyce Bainbridge Edwards
Grace Malicky
University of Alberta

For Kay Romeike, a woman of the prairie—JBE

CHAPTER 1

Introduction to Language Learning

Two children share books in the school library.

OBJECTIVES

- to develop a foundational understanding of the nature of language learning
- to understand Halliday's functions of language
- to be aware of the purposeful nature of language
- to know that social, political, and cultural differences cause variations in the way children learn, and the way teachers perceive children
- to be aware of the interactional nature of language and learning
- to develop an understanding of classroom discourse

The Nature of Language Learning

Recently, a class of children were studying the novel *Tuck Everlasting* by Natalie Babbitt (1975). Linda Smith's class was working in groups making maps of Treegap and plotting the travels of the characters Winnie and the Tucks. They were writing letters to Mae Tuck in jail, and other children were taking the role of Mae Tuck and answering those letters. They were making "wanted" posters for Mae, and creating a time line of the story. Some were writing an epitaph for Winnie and others were preparing for an oral storytelling session. These classroom activities demonstrate the range of tasks that can be developed in language arts instruction, and that exemplify good teaching based on sound theory of how children learn and develop language.

In answering his question, "What is language?" Michael Halliday (1969) maintained that the answer lies in purpose. He believes that language is, for children, a rich and adaptable instrument for the realization of their intentions; there is hardly any limit to what they can do with it. Children learn language because there is something they want or need to communicate to another person. Even very young children develop the ability to communicate their intentions, and they develop that ability long before they develop language. They push us, take our hands, guide us, point, and generally let us know, one way or another, that they have a need that has to be met. Sometimes their gestures direct the behaviour of the adults around them; they hold up their hands to be lifted up, and they point when they drop a favourite toy. At other times they play, gurgling and repeating sounds and rhythms they have learned.

Halliday went on to say that children know what language is because they know what it does. In other words, children learn *about* language through using it. Halliday explained that children come to understand the purposes of language from their own experience of language in use. Children do not learn explicitly what a noun is, but they do learn to label. They do not understand what **syntax** is, yet they learn how to string words together into meaningful sentences.

It was Halliday (1975b) who coined the phrase "learning how to mean." Children learn language in order to express meaning to others, and to construct meaning for themselves. It is not until we label something that we can talk about it. It is not until we can talk about something (even to ourselves) that we can change it and come to understand it in a different way. A great deal of our thinking is done through language. It is difficult to imagine what it would be like to think without language, for although we think in feelings and images, we construct our most abstract thoughts through the vehicle of language.

Children learn language in real situations, where something is being accomplished. That something may be the singing of a song at bedtime, the talk a mother engages in while she changes a child's clothing, the conversation that goes on around the dinner table, the choice of a television program, or completing a job in the yard. Frequently, children are directly involved, such as when older siblings ask younger children what they would like to play with (even when they know that the child is not yet capable of answering). At other times the language is going on in the world around the child. The **discourse** that is the most important, however, is the discourse that actively involves the child. We know that interaction is necessary for language development to occur. Watching television and being talked *at* are no substitutes for involvement. Genuine involvement and purposeful talk *with* children are the most important conditions upon which their language development rests.

James Britton (1970, 130) described language learning in a child's life as language for "operations and not dummy runs." Language for operations is language used to get something done—a note to a friend, a shopping list. A dummy run, on the other hand, occurs when a child is required to practice language out of context; an exercise in punctuation, for example, or an exercise in sequencing the events of a story in order to understand more complex pieces of work at a later time. Such dummy runs are sometimes used in schools because they are frequently easy to organize, teach, and evaluate, but research shows that children transfer learning little from them to other communication situations.

Providing a language arts program where children are involved in using language for operations, as opposed to dummy runs, makes enormous demands on teachers. The creation of such tasks is no easy matter. Language arts tasks should be based on the experiences of the children, and the tasks must meet the demands of society (i.e., what society expects children to learn in school). The teacher can provide a variety of experiences to meet the different intentions and needs of the students, but this variety implies selection from a range of activities, and choice in the way the tasks are completed.

Halliday's Functions of Language

Michael Halliday (1969) proposed a model of the functions of language derived from his observations of a young child's language development in the early years. He concluded that children develop seven purposes for language use. These functions are as follows:

1. *Instrumental:* "I want." (language as a means of getting things, satisfying material needs)
2. *Regulatory:* "Do as I tell you." (controlling the behaviour, feelings, or attitudes of others)
3. *Interactional:* "Me and you." (getting along with others, establishing relative status and separateness: "Me against you")
4. *Personal:* "Here I come." (expressing individuality, awareness of self, pride)
5. *Heuristic:* "Tell me why?" (seeking and testing knowledge)
6. *Imaginative:* "Let's pretend." (creating new worlds, making up stories, poems)
7. *Representational:* "I've got something to tell you." (communicating information, descriptions, expressing propositions)

In everyday life we encounter *instrumental language* every time we ask another person to meet our needs. Whether we are asking someone to pass the salt or ordering a meal in a restaurant, we are using the instrumental function of language. Closely related to this is the regulatory function. Sometimes it is difficult to tell these two functions apart since, frequently, when we regulate someone else's behaviour it is in order to meet our own needs. In our lives we encounter regulatory language at every turn; a *no smoking* sign, a handbook on how to make a kite, the requirements for an assignment for a university class. *Interactional language* is simply the language we use to maintain and establish relationships (or to have an argument, which is another way of maintaining a relationship). It is the social chat we engage in over coffee, and the conversations we have with friends and colleagues. *Personal language* is used when we tell about ourselves—our feelings, thoughts, and beliefs. Our personal language lets the listener in on who we are, and often reveals part of our unique identity. ***Heuristic** language* is used when we explore and question, when we wonder and hypothesize. We hear it when a friend says, "I wonder what would happen if…" or when a child says, "Did Grandpa always have no hair?" The imaginative function of language comes into full play when we write stories or poetry, when we daydream, make a wish list, or engage in play with a child. Jokes, riddles, and cartoons are part of this realm. *Representational language* is the language of reports, lectures, documentary programs on television, and textbooks. As teachers and students we become very familiar with this type of language.

The Purposeful Nature of Language

Halliday's work tells us that children do not develop language in a haphazard or purposeless way. On the contrary, children develop language because they have needs that must be fulfilled. There are *no* occasions where we use language purposelessly. Cocktail party chat fulfills a social need because it is a way of getting to know people, of getting along with others. Singing alone in the car is a way of entertaining ourselves, filling in time, and expressing a part of ourselves. Talking to ourselves is a way of focusing our thoughts, "walking" ourselves through a process as a kind of rehearsal, and is usually representational or **heuristic** in nature. Halliday noted that not all functions of language develop equally in children, and that some functions must be actively encouraged and fostered. He added that probably the most useful functions in a classroom are heuristic and personal. However, he showed that the most common functions of language used in many classrooms are representative and regulatory. What is important to keep in mind is that all language use has a purpose behind it.

The Communication Event

When we say something, we know we are speaking to someone. The receiver may be a person sitting next to us, someone on the other end of the telephone in another province, or it may be the self. Most people healthily engage in self-talk. Self-talk helps us in understanding things more clearly, and sometimes, when faced with a difficult task, we talk our way through it. Likewise, when listening to language, we are aware the language is coming *from* someone. It might be a newsreader on television, the author of a book, a brother or sister, or a friend. People also become adept at recognizing that there are different forms of language; that language can be put together in different ways for different purposes. If a person wants to speak to a city council on a matter of urgency, that person will be well prepared and have a thoughtfully worked-out argument. If the same person speaks with a friend about the same issue, the language used will likely be more informal and more emotional. We know the difference between a business letter and a script for a play, or a story in a book. We know the difference between a university transcript and a poem. The form of the language we use is directly related to the function the language is fulfilling.

When teachers create relevant and meaningful tasks, they have to combine both knowledge about the topic they are teaching *and* knowledge of how the form, function, sender, and receiver of a communication event interact. Exhibit 1.1 demonstrates a selection of tasks suitable for helping children to develop their responses to the book *Tuck Everlasting*. The tasks are all in the world of imagination, but when children are engaged with a novel such as this, their work *is* relevant and authentic to them. They quickly make the leap from the real world to the world of story.

When the concepts of form, function, sender, and receiver are part of a teacher's planning, the teacher can use these concepts to transform a more general activity, such as "Describe how you think Mae Tuck felt when she was in jail," included in column A in Exhibit 1.1, into a more contextualized, purposeful task, as described in column B.

Exhibit 1.2 shows how these tasks look when they are analyzed according to function, sender, receiver, and form.

The work of Halliday, Britton, Moffet, and Barnes has provided guidelines for analyzing, understanding, and creating language learning activities. Their work has helped

---

EXHIBIT 1.1

Framing Tasks

A

Tasks framed without reference to form, function, sender, and audience

1. Write a story about a child who has to decide whether or not to drink the water from the spring.
2. Describe how you think Mae Tuck felt when she was in jail.
3. Describe the kinds of things you think the Tuck family did between their reunions at the spring.

B

Tasks framed according to form, function, sender, and audience

1. You have just met the Tuck family at the spring. You find out about the magical properties of the water from overhearing their conversation. You know you can drink the water if you want to. What will you do? When you have made a decision, write a letter to Winnie telling her about your meeting and decision, and why you made that decision.
2. In role as Mae Tuck, imagine you are in jail after the killing of the Man in the Yellow Suit. You have your journal with you. Write in your journal about your thoughts, fears, and hopes at this time in your life. Perhaps one of your sons will be able to read it at a later time.
3. You are a newspaper reporter. You have heard of the Tuck family and you have finally traced Angus Tuck to his home. You have managed to get an interview with him and have found out some of the things the family does between their ten-year reunions. Write an article for the newspaper about this amazing family.

---

many teachers to answer the critical question "How can I help my students to learn?" It has provided teachers with a basis for developing language learning tasks that are meaningful, purposeful, and cohesive. The guiding principles outlined in this chapter can be used in developing learning activities in subject areas such as social studies, science, music, and health. Here are some examples of tasks one music teacher developed for her

EXHIBIT 1.2

Analysis of Learning Tasks

Function	Sender	Receiver	Form
1. Personal	Child	the character Winnie	letter
2. Personal	child in role as Mae Tuck	self or son	journal
3. Representational	child in role as newspaper reporter	newspaper reader	newspaper report

students in Grade 6. The theme was a study of two Romantic composers, Johannes Brahms and Robert Schumann.

1. It is the mid-1800s in Vienna, Austria. You and your friend have just attended an evening concert conducted by Brahms, who insisted on playing that very out-of-date music by Bach and Handel. You were bored to tears. It seems from the gossip that many others felt the same way. The evening, however, wasn't a complete loss as you did enjoy the compositions that Brahms himself wrote. Take yourself to a mini-concert by listening to Bach's *Brandenburg Concerto #2 in F*, the second movement, and Brahms' *Piano Concerto #2 in B Flat Major, Opus 83*, the first movement. The music is on tape for you. After you have listened to the concert, role-play your conversation with your friend as you walk home from the concert. Share with each other what the differences in the music are, and why Bach's music sounds so old-fashioned to you. (based on the heuristic and interactional functions of language)

2. You are the editor of the magazine *Neue Zeitschrift fur Musik* (New Paths for Music). Brahms has asked you to draft an eye-catching advertisement to assist him in selling his sheet music. His bestsellers are his violin sonatas, trios, and string quartets. (based on the representational and regulatory functions of language)

3. Robert Schumann has tried to commit suicide by jumping off a bridge. Fishermen have pulled him out of the river. You are a reporter running along

as Schumann is being carried home. By interviewing one of the fishermen and some of the people in the street, you are trying to determine the circumstances leading up to the near-tragedy. You might even be able to arrange an interview with thirteen-year-old Marie Schumann, the eldest daughter. Use a tape recorder for your interviews, and the books provided for your own research. (based on the interactional, heuristic, and representational functions)

The following activities on Ancient Greece illustrate the range of tasks that can be generated in social studies. By selecting various combinations of form, function, sender, and receiver one can create many possibilities. These tasks are one set of possibilities. Students, when supported and allowed to make choices, will generate many more. These activities were developed for a Grade 6 class.

1. **Instrumental**
   Oral: The Delian League was a group of Greek city-states that banded together to protect each other from aggressive forces. Your class constitutes the members of the city-state of Athens, the largest and strongest member. Chios, also a member of the Delian League, has requested your help in battle against Persian aggressors. In a group debate, decide whether or not you should get involved in the war and help Chios.

   Written: You are an accomplished athlete but you have not been chosen to engage in the special training necessary to compete in the Olympic Games. You are unhappy and wish to participate in the games. Write a letter to the selection committee asking them to intercede on your behalf so that you can participate in the training.

2. **Regulatory**
   Oral: You, as citizens of Athens, are concerned about the civil rights of slaves in Athenian society. In small groups, discuss the present slave regulations and devise a new set of civil rights that will allow slaves the same rights as Athenian citizens. You will present these civil rights to the Assembly.

   Written: You are a rich Athenian citizen and all rich citizens of Athens bought and sold slaves regularly. You have just purchased a slave to help in the running of your household. Make a list of daily household chores for the slave to fulfill while she or he is living with your family.

3. **Interactional**
   Oral: You (the class) are citizens of Troy and are awaiting a message from the town crier (teacher in role) after being summoned for an important meeting. The town crier arrives and says, "There is a giant wooden horse outside of the

city gate, left as a peace offering from Greece. We must decide among ourselves whether or not to accept this horse. We must also decide what to do with it, if we choose to accept it." How will you make this decision? What will you say?

Written: Women in Athenian society were confined to the home and were denied the privileges of men. You are all Athenian women who feel they deserve the same rights as men. Discuss these issues among yourselves and write, for publication in the *Grecian Gazette*, individual editorials arguing the rights you desire.

4. **Personal**
   Oral: You are Athenian slaves waiting to be sold. A reporter (teacher in role) interviews you to determine your emotional reactions to being sold.

   Written: In Athens, many landowners frequently found themselves heavily in debt and often had to resort to selling their own children into slavery. You are a child who has to be sold into slavery. Write a diary entry that illustrates how you are feeling the night before you are to be sold.

5. **Heuristic**
   Oral: Citizens of Ancient Greece believed in a direct democracy where all free adult males were equal and contributing members of the government. Some of you are members of the Athenian Assembly, while the rest are reporters who interview the assembly about why they have chosen a direct democracy rather than electing one leader.

   Written: Imagine that the Olympic Games are coming to your country this year. You are chosen to make the public aware of how the first Olympic Games in Greece were conducted. Write a report that describes these games. Provide information on such things as athletic events, opening and closing ceremonies, and prizes awarded. Your report will be published in the local newspaper.

6. **Imaginative**
   Oral: You are in charge of entertainment at an Athenian banquet. To entertain your guests, you have decided to compose "Who am I?", poetic riddles based on mythical Greek gods. In groups of three, compose and audiotape these riddles.

   Written: One of the mythical Greek gods of Mount Olympus has been killed in a fierce battle. You have been summoned by Zeus, ruler of the Olympic gods, to create a replacement. Write a story about a new god and describe where and how your god originated, what he or she is the god of, and what powers he or she possesses. You may also want to physically describe your god. You will send your story to Zeus.

7. **Representational** (The following task involves modern technology in the context of Ancient Greece.)
   Oral: You are a member of the Athenian Tourist Bureau. Your job is to make a television commercial to entice people to visit Ancient Greece. In small groups, compose and dramatize a television commercial.

   Written: You are the editor for *Ancient Greece Abroad*, a magazine for travellers. Design a brochure for these travellers that illustrates the culture of Ancient Greece; you may want to include aspects such as food, entertainment, and art.

It is important to note that many activities fulfil more than one language function. In number five, for example, the written task meets the representational function as much as it does the heuristic one. In order to complete a representational task, a certain amount of heuristic language must first be used. In number seven above, the activity draws on the heuristic, representational, *and* regulatory functions. The above activities are examples of good language learning tasks that also meet many of the objectives of the specific state or provincial programs of study in social studies. Such objectives include understanding that all people have similar physical, social, and psychological needs, and that Greek values, beliefs, and ideas have strongly affected Western civilization. In particular, these activities help to provide a fuller context for the communication skill objectives of writing a summary of the main points, collecting and organizing information into a short report, and sharing ideas through drama and role play.

Such knowledge also helps teachers to guide the students to shape their own learning tasks. The following example will clarify how this shaping might take place:

Teacher:	How are you feeling about this book?
	(Students reply with their comments, thoughts, and personal opinions)
Teacher:	Have you thought about how you might share this with the class?
Student 1:	*A book report?*
Student 2:	*We could act out a play about it.*
Student 1:	*I wouldn't like to live forever. Can you imagine being the same age forever and all your friends and family dying?*
Student 2:	*Yeah, that would be sad. Going from having lots of friends and maybe even your own children, to being more and more alone, always knowing you'll have to say goodbye and move to another town.*

Teacher: Well you have lots of ideas—a report, a play, [forms]—and feelings about everlasting life [function]. What would be a good way to share your feelings?

Student 1: *A play.*

Student 2: *A journal, like we do our daily journal when we write our feelings ... except we can be the people in the story.*

Teacher: Both good ways [form] to express feelings [function]; one a group activity and one individual.

Student 3: *Let's each do a journal first as one of the characters, and then we can act out some of our ideas from our journal.*

Teacher: So you will write a diary entry [form] *as if* you are one of the characters [sender] about your feelings [functions] of having everlasting life. [N.B. Personal journal receiver is also self.] You can then use the journal entries for your play. Great ideas.

In this scenario, the teacher listened to the children's ideas and helped them to shape the task by asking questions that reflected the teacher's knowledge of form, function, sender, and receiver. Children understand this knowledge of form, function, sender, and receiver, although they are not necessarily aware that they know. The teacher capitalized on this implicit knowledge and made it explicit through her questioning. In this way, the teacher helped the students shape their own learning tasks rather than prescribing activities for them.

In the example of Linda Smith's work with *Tuck Everlasting*, at the beginning of this chapter, we can see the impact of Halliday's model, as Linda attempted to contextualize the activities. Many of the tasks were in the realm of imagination, but they remain contextualized, purposeful, and authentic.

The Social, Cultural, and Political Context of Language Learning

Children learn language in their homes, communities, classrooms, and broader society. The way they interact with other people and the way they respond to language in the classroom reflect the interaction patterns and values in their homes and communities.

Although the children in Linda's classroom come from an urban, middle-class neighbourhood, that does not mean that there are no social or cultural differences among them. Some are males, others are females. Although some are rich, most are not. Some are learning English as their second language and some come from single-parent homes. Other classrooms include children who live in poverty and children from aboriginal and other minority groups.

A major challenge of our public schools is to provide equal educational opportunities for all children. Studies suggest, however, that outcomes of schooling are far from equal. In the United States, Hunter and Harman (1979) found that people with limited **literacy** were often the same ones who suffer from one or more other major social problems—poverty, unemployment, racial or ethnic discrimination, social isolation, and so forth. In Canada, the Southam survey (1987) revealed higher rates of illiteracy in rural than in urban populations and among the poor and minorities than among other Canadians.

We don't know whether low levels of literacy result in poverty and injustice, *or* poverty and injustice result in low levels of literacy. There is accumulating evidence that the latter explanation is more likely than the former (Graff, 1987; Levine, 1986; Hunter and Harman, 1979). It is becoming apparent that schools do not meet the needs of children from poor and minority homes as well as they do those from middle and upper-income homes. In order to meet the needs of all the children in our classrooms, language arts programs need to reflect the knowledge, interaction patterns, and language learning needs children bring with them.

Prior Knowledge

Most teachers are aware of differences in prior experiences that children from different backgrounds bring to language learning classrooms. For example, urban children will likely have far less knowledge about farm animals than will children who live on farms. Among farm children, those on mixed farms will have far more knowledge about farm animals than those on grain farms.

The prior knowledge we develop from past experience does not appear to consist of a series of isolated facts or concepts but is instead a mental framework that influences our expectations and imposes structure on the information we receive. Many theorists (e.g., Rumelhart, 1980) refer to these organized frameworks as **schemata**, which develop through repeated experiences in a particular context. For example, children who are taken to McDonald's by their parents begin to develop a schema for going to a restaurant. They know that it is a place where they get food to eat, that they place an order at a counter, that someone at the counter takes the order, that the person at the counter puts the food on a tray, that the food is paid for, that one takes the food to a table to eat, and so on. When their parents take them to another restaurant where they sit down and someone comes to take their order, the children extend their schema for going to a restaurant to include features of that type of restaurant as well. Eventually, children who are taken to eat at a range of different restaurants will establish a schema that is sufficiently well developed to apply to most restaurants.

Interaction Patterns

In addition to differences in prior knowledge, the ways children and teachers interact with one another in typical language arts classrooms are more familiar to some children than to others. As Cazden (1988, 67) notes:

> *In some of its aspects, the demands of classroom discourse are new to all children. In the classroom, the group is larger than even the largest family gathered at meals, and so getting a turn to talk is much harder. When one does get a turn, acceptable topics for talk are more restricted and more predetermined by someone else.... But beyond these commonalties, some children may be at a special disadvantage. For some children there will be greater cultural discontinuity, greater sociolinguistic interference, between home and school.*

Interaction patterns were the focus of a powerful study by Heath (1983) of children from three communities in the Carolina Piedmont region of the United States who attended school together following desegregation. The teachers and parents wanted to know why the children and teachers frequently couldn't understand one another, and more specifically, why children who never stopped chatting at home rarely talked in class, and why children who were unable to answer simple questions in class could explain a rule for a ball game on the playground. Heath found that the children from the three communities had experienced different ways of learning and using language at home. The experiences of some of the children matched the ways language was learned and used in the school better than those of others. In "Maintown," a middle-class, school-oriented community, the focus of literacy-related activities was on labelling, explaining, and learning how to display knowledge. The children from this community were socialized into the interactional sequences that commonly occur in classrooms. Families in "Roadville," a white working-class community, also focused on labelling and explanations, preparing children for literal comprehension tasks in the classroom. However, these children were unprepared for reading activities involving reasoning or affective responses. In "Trackton," a black working-class community, the children were not taught labels or asked for explanations in their homes but instead were asked to give reasons and personal responses to events.

When children from all three communities arrived at school, the predominant type of questions asked by teachers involved having children name attributes of objects taken out of context, e.g., "What colour is the horse in this picture?" The children from Trackton had not been asked these kinds of questions by their parents and they thought these were dumb questions because their teachers already knew the answers. When teachers incorporated questions similar to those the Trackton children were asked at home, the children participated much more frequently and eventually responded to more school-based questions as well.

Many teachers are not aware of the mismatch between their sociocultural backgrounds and those of the children in their classrooms. When the teachers of the children from Trackton developed this awareness and made adaptations in the language arts program, the children were able to participate much more effectively in classroom talk. As Bernstein (cited in Cazden, 1988, 27) indicates:

> *If the culture of the teacher is to become part of the consciousness of the child, then the culture of the child must first be in the consciousness of the teacher.*

Storytelling

Cultural differences are also evident in the ways people tell stories and in what they think are good stories. This was highlighted in research by Michaels and Cazden who listened to children and teachers during sharing time in kindergarten and Grade 1 classrooms (Cazden, 1988). Sharing time, sometimes called "show and tell," is a common activity in primary classrooms when children are invited to share a **narrative** or personal experience about their lives outside of school. Although the children were given a seemingly ordinary request to "tell us something," Michaels and Cazden found that teachers' reactions to children's narratives revealed specific expectations about what stories should be like. "Good" stories were those with a beginning, a middle, and an end, and all the ideas related to one topic. In one classroom, 96 percent of the stories told by white children met these criteria, but only 34 percent of those told by black children were topic-centred. Instead, many black children provided chains of loosely related actions or events often with the topic left unstated. Teachers tended to react negatively to these episodic types of stories.

> Deena: *I went to the beach Sunday and to McDonald's and to the park and I got this for my birthday (holds up purse). My mother bought it for me and I had two dollars for my birthday and I put it in here and I went to where my friend named Gigi. I went over to my grandmother's house with her and she was on my back and I and we was walking around by my house and she was heavy. She was in the sixth or seventh grade...(Cazden, 1988, 13)*

Deena's teacher stopped her there asking her to "talk about things that are really very important." This was in sharp contrast to the way teachers reacted to children who produced topic-centred stories. For example, when one boy told a story about his father's friend making a paper boat out of a dollar bill, the teacher responded: "A man made a boat out of a dollar bill for you? Wow! That's pretty expensive paper to use!" (Cazden, 1988, 7).

Cazden and Michaels believed that the difference in teachers' reactions was due to the match or mismatch between the narrative styles and themes of the children and the knowledge and expectations of their teachers. In order to explore this further, they presented a selection of both topic-centred and episodic stories to black and white teachers and asked them to comment on how well-formed the stories were. Teachers were also asked to predict the probable academic success of the child who told each story. White teachers frequently rated episodic stories as hard to follow and predicted the children would be low-achieving, while black teachers rated both topic-centred and episodic stories positively. Episodic stories are not only told by people in black communities but are also common in aboriginal groups. It is not that children from these communities cannot tell stories but that the stories they tell do not match their teachers' expectations and receive negative reactions.

The political nature of storytelling is also reflected in judgments made about good literature since someone in a position of power does the choosing for those who have less power. It is not surprising that in North America more of what is defined as good literature is written by males than females and by whites than blacks. Bloome (1991) suggests that less-powerful groups are frequently not entitled to tell their stories, to have their stories be part of the literature, or to tell their stories their way. When the white teachers in Michaels and Cazden's research rejected the stories of black children, they were using their position of power to determine what counts as acceptable narratives even though they were likely unaware that they were doing so. When lobby groups work to keep books involving homosexual families and other controversial topics out of the schools, the political nature of storytelling is more overt.

Gender

In a review of literature on the relationship between schooling and gender, Wilkinson and Marrett (1985) reported that males and females perform differently in different subject areas. For example, girls tend to outperform boys in reading in the early grades, but by the secondary level, boys begin to pull ahead, particularly in mathematics and science. The most common explanations given for the differences between boys and girls in early reading achievement are teachers' expectations (teachers expect that girls will be more successful than boys) and the feminization of elementary schools. Some argue that since most teachers in elementary schools are female, boys have few male role models. However, boys are no more successful in reading in classrooms with male than with female teachers.

It has also been suggested that there is a "poor fit between the culturally prescribed male gender role and the student role that has become institutionalized in American elementary schools" (Brophy, 1985, 118). Boys are expected to be active, exploratory learners in our society but schools value passive, recipient learners. By the time children arrive at school in kindergarten, they have already been socialized into differentiated gender roles through their interactions with adults and older children in their homes and communities. What happens at school to either reinforce or break down traditional gender roles?

The short answer is not very much. Research consistently shows that teachers give more attention to boys than to girls (Brophy, 1985). While some of this attention is managerial and disciplinary in nature, boys engage in more verbal interactions of every type with teachers than do girls. Hence, the widespread belief that females talk more than males is not upheld in elementary school classrooms. Even more interesting is the finding that it doesn't matter whether the teacher is male or female; both interact more with boys than with girls. This is not surprising when one considers that all of us, both males and females, have been exposed to the same gender role socialization pressures and as a result, have come to share essentially the same expectations for how boys and girls will behave. Brophy (1985) argues that if gender inequalities are to be eliminated, we may need different, rather than identical, treatment of males and females in elementary classrooms. Teachers may need to consciously call on boys more frequently in language arts and on girls more frequently in science and mathematics.

Language

Children come to school with varying degrees of proficiency in the English language. Another issue teachers face involves the extent to which children's oral language should form the basis for instruction as compared with having them learn standard English. If, for example, we introduce aboriginal children to reading by using their first language or written language reflecting their **dialect**, they may not be able to handle the standard English that is the currency of success in mainstream society. However, if we do not adjust instruction in relation to the language these children bring to school, they frequently have difficulty learning to read because of the discrepancy between their oral language and the language in the books they are asked to read. Delpit (1988, 287) maintains we do children of colour no service to suggest, even implicitly, that product is not important. Children do need to learn to spell correctly and to use correct grammatical forms in order to gain access to power. As language arts teachers we balance between respecting the language brought by the child to the classroom and the child's needs to communicate through standard English. It is more a matter of when, rather than if, the standard form is introduced.

Language is part of who we are and **literacy** is a matter of belonging, of being someone in a literate society. In the Middle Ages, being literate made an individual better than most people, but today literacy is necessary to be as good as other people. Indeed, progress in school is frequently determined by success in learning to read and write. The decision to pass or fail a child is much more likely to be based on reading, for example, than on running speed or artistic ability. This occurs because in our society literacy is generally viewed as being crucial to success as an adult. Unless we invite children into the "magical circle of the literate" (Bhola, 1981), unless they are able to join the literacy club (Smith, 1988), they are effectively excluded from mainstream society.

How this can happen is reflected in the following example of a 14-year-old boy who was referred for diagnosis and remediation of reading problems. He had spent his early years in a dysfunctional family, had been apprehended by social services and placed in a foster home, and at the time of his referral was living in a young offenders centre because he had committed a minor offence. He was able to identify only a few words but wanted to learn to read. One-to-one tutoring was provided and during the sessions, the struggle he was having with finding a place in society became increasingly evident. He was accepted by the group at the young offenders centre and by his foster parents, but he was getting another message from school. His teachers were finding it difficult to meet his reading needs and he was failing in nearly all subject areas. He could either be invited into mainstream society by supportive, successful school programs *or* he could be excluded through continued school failure. Our challenge is to find ways to include rather than exclude such children from literate society. This raises an important issue about whether language learning programs ought to help children fit into existing sociopolitical structures or whether children should learn to critique these structures.

Critical Literacy

Freire (1970) believes that the goal of **literacy** is not adapting people to fit in but rather helping people become aware of the inequities and contradictions in society in order to bring about change. Rather than adapting to existing structures, Freire's goal is to develop literacy programs that help people change the structures responsible for creating inequities in the first place. A term that has begun to appear in the literature in recent years to reflect this goal is **critical literacy**.

Critical literacy goes beyond teaching children how to read and write to providing them with the tools necessary to become aware of and understand inequalities and injustices in society. Critical literacy also involves helping children formulate a vision of what it might be like to live in the best of all societies and to think about ways to make this vision a reality (Kretovics, 1985). Critical literacy is one way education can foster a more democratic society.

The Nature of Teaching and Learning in the Classroom

Language and Learning

A major concept in education is that most learning is mediated through language. In classrooms, language is the most common vehicle for teaching concepts and principles, for enabling children to recall those concepts, principles, and operations, and for evaluating what a child understands and knows. Both oral language and written language are used in this way, and they are used in every subject in the curriculum. Just as there are no occasions when language is used without purpose, there are no subjects in school where language does not play a major part. Music, health, mathematics, science, social studies, art, and physical education all have subject-specific language—a vocabulary and a way of speaking about that subject that must be learned. But just as important is the language children bring to a subject and through which they process their thinking about that subject.

In the past, learning was equated with the *transmission of information*. Knowledge was what students could recall. It was a quantitative notion, where facts and someone else's knowledge were to be learned and regurgitated. The emphasis was on remembering this material, getting good grades, and following the instructions of those who already possessed the knowledge. It led to practices that emphasized the acquisition of basic skills before understanding.

Today our thoughts about knowledge and learning are different. The emphasis is upon the *construction of meaning* and understanding, rather than the reproduction of already existing knowledge; upon reasoning rather than recall. The focus is on actively making meaning, solving problems, and effecting change. What we *do* with knowledge is as important as possessing that knowledge.

Studies on the role of language in learning have emphasized the need for learners to find meaning in the world through the use of language as a tool of exploration. Vygotsky (1962), Polanyi (1969), Britton (1970), and Halliday (1975a) have all argued for the use of language in a heuristic or exploratory way so that students can make greater personal sense of their learning. The work of James Britton (1970) and James Moffett

(1968) has promoted the understanding that language is a major medium through which learners "re-present" experience and the world to themselves. Language enables the learner to make sense of experience and the world. Through relating new experiences and old ones, they build schemata. What is already known and what is already experienced form the basis for any new knowledge that may develop. Frank Smith (1975, 11) expresses this idea as creating a "theory of the world in the head." Experience is also encoded by sound, smell, sight, taste, touch, and feeling. Most people have scented a smell that immediately reminded them of a place, person, or event in their lives. Likewise, language encodes experience, but it takes us beyond the actual experience to reflect and interpret it. It frees us from the immediate context of our lives so that we can imagine and discuss things we have never actually experienced and things we want to know more about.

Putting knowledge and feelings into words helps people to clarify their thinking and make meaning more precise. The things we can talk about are the things we know best. One way to find out if people really understand something is to have them explain it to someone else. Putting thoughts into language forces clarity and enables sounder understanding. Teachers face this each time they stand in front of a class of children and teach. If they truly understand what they are teaching, their explanations will be clear. If they do not understand the subject, they are not as likely to be clear in their explanations and effective in their communication. Likewise, when children are asked to write in a science journal about what happened in a particular science activity and why, they will probably write clearly if they understand the activity, but will likely have difficulty if their understanding is vague. At this point they may need to talk to other children or the teacher in order to more fully understand the activity. This will be explored more in Chapter 8.

Language across the Curriculum

Language across the curriculum was a movement founded in the United Kingdom in the 1960s by James Britton and his colleagues at the London Institute for Education. More recently the concepts of this movement have become known simply as language for learning. The research and publications of the London Institute group led to the government commission and publication in 1975 of A *Language for Life*, also called the Bullock Report. This publication states that all genuine learning involves discovery, that language has a heuristic function, and that to exploit the process of discovery through language in all its uses is the surest means of enabling children to master their native language. The Bullock Report and these beliefs had a great deal of influence in educational discussions but very little impact on actual teaching. It was not until the late 1980s that most teachers came to understand the importance of language across the curriculum, and the ways in which this concept could be implemented.

Children and teachers learn together.

Talking for Learning

In the past, a quiet classroom was valued as a good classroom, and a teacher who managed a quiet class was respected as an effective teacher. Today, we understand more fully the role of talking in learning and recognize that an active and effective classroom is often a classroom with a lot of talk. The role of speaking and listening in learning includes both speaking and listening to others and to self. Sometimes the talk is an internal dialogue. It is usually more effective, however, if the talk is to another person, for as Piaget has said, it is only then that we encounter cognitive conflict. Hence, a good classroom will have many different types of organization for different purposes.

When children need to share a finished piece of writing, or talk with each other about a piece of writing in progress, space must be provided in the classroom. When children are having shared reading time, working in pairs, they will use various spaces around the room where they can read to each other. Science groups will cluster around the tables where the activities are taking place, and discussion will accompany that activity. Talk for learning includes questioning, focusing attention, problem solving, brainstorming, and making understanding more precise and more retrievable. These purposes apply to all areas of the curriculum and to all learning tasks. There are very few occasions where children need to be alone and working independently. Such occasions might include time for composition, time for personal reading, and time for personal study. It is important that children have quiet time for their own work, but in our schools in the past, that was not a problem. Creating time and space for group work and the attendant speaking and listening has, however, been problematic, and has not been given the time and attention it needs.

One of the greatest concerns expressed by beginning teachers is loss of control in the classroom. Often, when children are talking together it looks as though the teacher may have lost control. However, if children and their ideas are respected, and if talk is valued, then some control has to be given up to the students. Children can be trusted to talk, and they can be trusted to ask interesting and challenging questions. In sum, children can be trusted to learn. It may take longer to cover the content if children talk about what they are learning, but children will more likely remember what they have learned, and understand it more thoroughly if they have had the opportunity to ask their own questions, offer their own opinions, and listen to the ideas of others. This process rejects the idea that there is always one right answer to a question and that the teacher has that answer. Children discover answers for themselves and come to realize that there are frequently many right answers to a question, depending upon their context, point of view, and experience. Children can develop confidence in their abilities as learners and thinkers when they are given the opportunity to express their thoughts and explain or justify their understandings. Talking together is a major way in which human beings share understandings and develop new perspectives on the way the world works.

Writing for Learning

Fulwiler (1987) outlined five basic assumptions about language and learning, three of them particularly important with regard to writing for learning. Firstly, when people articulate connections between new information and what they already know, they learn and understand that new information better (Bruner, 1966). Secondly, when people write about new information and ideas—in addition to reading, talking, and listening—they learn and understand them better (Britton, Burgess, Martin, McLeod, and Rosen, 1975). Thirdly, when people care about what they write, and see connections to their own lives, they both learn and write better (Moffett, 1968).

Barnes (1975, 76) says that writing is a way for writers to take an active part in their own learning: "as pupils write they can—under certain circumstances—reshape their view of the world, and extend their ability to think rationally about it." Writing for understanding should give learners the opportunity to examine ideas until they have clarified them, and they can then present those ideas in a form that others may have access to, if desired. James Britton (1982, 139) refers to this same process as "shaping at the point of utterance." The advantage of writing about ideas as they are being processed is that the learner is forced to focus on them to a far greater degree than when simply talking about them. Talked-over ideas are easily lost; we may be easily distracted and lose the thread of our thoughts. Writing provides a record of where we have been in our thinking. We can go back and re-examine writing and get an overall picture of the development of our ideas and where we need to focus next. As D'Arcy (1989, 2) says, we can "retain, re-collect, re-construct, re-create, and re-present." We engage in what James Moffett has termed "the revision of inner speech" (1979, 278). This process appears to be basic to learning, and particularly important in the kind of writing seen in learning logs, think books, and dialectic journals across the curriculum. Chapter 9 in this book discusses these formats in depth.

Reading for Learning

Reading instruction has traditionally been viewed as a two-stage process, with children initially learning to read, followed by a stage when they are reading to learn. This dichotomy was reflected in a focus on basic reading skills for younger children and on reading in the content areas for older children. Authors and publishers of instructional materials designed for the learning-to-read stage were generally more concerned with vocabulary control and systematic introduction of skills than with the content of what children were reading. They included almost exclusively story material, providing the children with few opportunities to read informational texts. Those who designed instructional materials for older children frequently included a separate section or workbook devoted to reading in the content areas. They examined each content area—social studies, science, and literature—and developed a list of reading skills specific to the areas and designed tasks to develop each of the skills. More generic skills such as using a table of contents and locating information were also included.

We now realize that the two stages of learning to read and reading to learn are neither separate nor sequential. Children learn to read and to use reading at the same time. As adults we continue to learn to read throughout our lives, extending our reading strategies every time we encounter a new task such as reading a manual for a word processing program or using the computer catalogue in the library.

The recognition that learning to read and reading to learn are simultaneous processes has led to a change in the type of reading material provided for young children in language arts classrooms. Today, most **basal reading series** include poetry and stories selected for their literary quality and at least some informational material. Most language arts teachers expose young children to a wide range of children's literature including both fiction and factual material as well as magazines, children's newspapers, computer programs, posters, and so on.

There has also been a change in the way reading to learn is taught. We now know that the most effective reading teaching and learning happens when children are reading "real" books and other print sources, rather than completing decontextualized reading tasks. We also know that children need to learn how informational materials differ from story material and the implications these differences have for how we read.

Integrating Language Arts

There are at least three different levels of **integration** that can be considered in elementary classrooms. One is the simple integration of all language arts—reading, writing, speaking, and listening—into one set of activities. A further level of integration involves different subject areas across the curriculum. A third level can occur when children integrate their own knowledge and experience of the world with their school learning, which, of course, includes all the language arts.

In one Grade 4 classroom in Nova Scotia, as the children learn about **expository writing,** they put together a book on the history of one small community in their area. The teacher completes this oral history project every year, and knows that with careful planning and organization, and the interest and enthusiasm of the children, it will be successful. The books are printed in paperback by a local publisher and sold in the community (see Petite Rivière, 1993a). The work involves both social studies and language learning, and the teacher combines the available time from both subject areas in order to maximize the time for the project. During the process, the children collect information from community members, learn how to search for material for the book, and make decisions about what to include and what to leave out, how to lay out pages, and how to select illustrations. They discuss what they have read and heard, including the meanings of words used in the past but no longer in common usage today. They write, read, conference, draft, edit, and generally engage in a truly integrated learning activity that connects their own lives and experiences with life in the classroom. Another example of this kind of integration occurred when a teacher developed a social studies project in her classroom on advertising. Both projects are described in detail in Chapter 9 in a classroom vignette.

Teachers and Students in the Classroom

A number of prominent psychologists and educators have pointed out the importance of interaction in learning. Jean Piaget (1973) and Margaret Donaldson (1978) maintain that learning is a continuous process of making hypotheses, encountering conflicts, and resolving them by forming new hypotheses. They maintain that interaction with others is a major source of cognitive conflict. It is only when we encounter and talk with others (or read their ideas) that our own experiences and ideas are challenged. This can be an uncomfortable process—one that challenges us to be open and ready for growth. Vygotsky (1962; 1978) stresses the role of collaboration, cooperation, and collective activity in learning. He hypothesized a "zone of proximal development" that is the "area of difficulty just beyond the point at which the child can solve problems independently; it is the area in which the child can solve problems in collaboration with others, especially with an adult or more competent peer" (Lindfors, 1987, 273). Vygotsky also reminded us that what children can do with help today they can do alone tomorrow. Children do indeed support each other's learning and we see this as we watch them in group or partner work. They compliment, encourage, support, and challenge each other.

Classroom Discourse

While the potential for classroom interaction to facilitate language learning is great, observations of children and teachers reveal that ideal classroom interactions are not easy to achieve. One of the reasons this is so difficult is that power relationships pervade all aspects of language interactions in classrooms. According to Edwards (1980), a major source of difficulty is the sharp distinction in the classroom between the teacher ("the one who knows") and the students ("the many who do not"). Because of this distinction, the major role of students is to listen and the major role of teachers is to tell. In addition, it is the teacher who decides what counts as knowledge and who "owns" instructional talk. The teacher determines who speaks, what they talk about, how long they talk, and how well they talked. Consequently, the teacher does most of the talking, and when he or she does ask questions, they nearly all require students to provide information that the teacher already knows.

Cazden (1988) notes that the most common **discourse** pattern in classrooms is a three-part sequence of "teacher-initiation, student-response, teacher-evaluation" (IRE pattern). When children come to school, they must learn to speak within this structure but children from some homes are more familiar than others with the structure. The children from Trackton in Heath's study described earlier, for example, were far less familiar with this type of interaction than those from Maintown. While the IRE pattern is appropriate for some purposes (e.g., having children learn number facts), it is far less appropriate for others, such as exploring gender bias. Although it is easy to imagine talk in which ideas are explored, it is much harder to do it, largely because it means more than a change in who talks when. As Cazden notes, it involves a different conception of knowledge and teaching.

The Role of Teachers

This chapter has outlined a view of language learning that puts responsibility on children and actively involves them in their own learning. This implies that the teacher has a role different from the traditional one of the teacher as the dispenser of information and the authority on all things to be taught and learned in the classroom. What might that role be in a more democratic classroom? The role would clearly be multifaceted with one aspect involving the teacher as a *provider* of resources, and an organizer of space and time so that children have the opportunities and materials they need for learning (Lindfors, 1987).

The teacher is also a *demonstrator* (Smith, 1983) who shows how something is done. This doesn't simply mean demonstrating science experiments or basic literacy skills, but it means actively engaging in the behaviours and skills we want children to learn. Teachers must be seen to be readers and writers and thinkers. A further role that teachers have is that of *learner*. Learning is a lifelong activity, and it's important for children to see teachers' own enthusiasm, questioning, and learning processes. They may never see them in operation anywhere else. Teachers have much to learn with and from children.

Booth stresses the importance of teachers being lifelong learners. In addition to further education and professional reading, he highlights networking as a means of professional development. In Queenston School where he works, these networks involve teachers working together in grade groups, team-teaching in multigrade family groupings, and collaborating on projects. In addition, several teachers are involved as researchers in their own classrooms. Booth (1994, 351) writes: "As they examine their own classrooms and tell their stories about their children, teachers begin to gain an understanding of how children develop and how social needs determine language."

Another crucial role for the teacher is that of *responder*. When we are learning something new it is helpful to have someone respond to our questions, question us further, support our learning, and let us know how we are doing. That is not the same as judging our performance. Response is genuine and productive, and occurs as teachers actively understand what children are trying to do and attempt to further that learning. It is one way children can be encouraged to stay focused and engaged with the learning event. Connected to this is the role of teacher as *observer*. Through observing children, teachers can get ideas for future activities, gain insight about children's learning processes, and understand what individual children know and can do. This is critical for children to be working within their "**zone of proximal development**" (Vygotsky, 1962; 1978) in the classroom.

Through observing and responding a teacher can provide the support children need to be successful in the language learning classroom. This support is frequently referred to as "scaffolding," a term used by Bruner (1975, 12) to refer to interaction between young children and their mothers in which the mother supports "the child in achieving an intended outcome." The child decides to do something and the mother provides a scaffold that allows the child to move from what the child can do to what he or she wants to do. Many people use this term to refer to what teachers do in classrooms as they work with children. Searle, however, questions using the term to describe what happens in schools because, in contrast to the home environment, the child at school rarely remains in control of the language and the experience. In relation to the scaffolding metaphor Searle asks: "Who's building whose building?" (1984, 480). He believes that too often in schools it is the teacher who sets the agenda and then helps the child to accomplish that agenda. Children need to adapt their own language resources to achieve purposes they set for themselves.

Children in the Language Classroom

As indicated by Searle (1984), it is important that children take charge of their own language learning. They need to have a sense of ownership over both their knowledge and their language. They need to feel that their talk, reading, and writing belongs to them, not to the teacher. They will not develop this sense of ownership if the teacher always tells them what to read, write, and talk about or is always the authority on how well they read, write, and talk. By making choices about their language learning, children begin to feel like readers and writers. They feel as if they belong in the "magical circle of the literate."

Inside **the Classroom**

Linda Graves recalls an experience with a young student writer in her Saskatoon classroom.

I remember a time when I was working with Desira in our Writer's Workshop. Desira had written a wonderful story about Fluffy, her cat. The minilesson I had introduced to the students that morning was on leads. We looked at lots of books and discussed how the authors began their stories. Students were eager to share their favourite books and why they thought each lead was used to introduce each story. We also looked at our own writing and shared our leads. I read to the students my writing about our class cat, Kizmit. The children had lots of helpful suggestions on how I could "hook" the reader. I asked the students to think of two or three different ways they could write a lead on the story they were presently working on. Off they went to their special places in the classroom and hallway to weave more ideas on leads.

Desira was sitting quietly in a corner of the classroom hard at work. She had written three leads and was trying to decide which one she would like to use. I poured over her work with her, asking her to read me the leads.

1. Once there was a cat who's name was Fluffy. he is potty trained. and he tears all the walls up. Sometimes he bites and scratches me and my sister but he thinks he's playing.
2. there was a cat his name is Fluffy. he always crys for food. When we say no to him. he jumps in the Garbage can.
3. Meaww Meaww Where's my Dinner cried Fluffy no food said Desira.

I loved them all but my favourite was "Meaww Meaww." That is the one I wanted Desira to choose. With my teacher control finger poised on the start button, I almost said to her, "Desira, this is the best one. Why don't you lead your story with that?" But I stopped and told myself, "If you want these children to be the masters of their own writing, then you must allow them to make the choices they want." A rather tough thing for me to do. Regaining my composure, I then asked Desira what lead she was going to choose. She did not choose my preferred lead, but rather chose one that perhaps was more conventional and more like the leads she had read in other books. Desira was either not willing or not ready to take a risk that day and I had to support her decision hoping a day would come when she would.

continued

Desira learned something about leads that day but perhaps it was I who learned the most. We must allow students to make choices for themselves if we truly want to empower them, to help them become masters of their own destinies. Desira went on from this day with the feeling that she had control over her writing, and that is exactly where the control should be. We must guide student writing, not take ownership for it. Thanks, Desira—you were my teacher today!

Linda Graves played all of the roles described above—provider of resources, demonstrator when she read her own writing, observer as she examined the leads Desira had written, and responder when she encouraged Desira to make her own choice. Most of all, however, she was a learner as her interaction with Desira helped her to more fully understand the importance of helping children gain control over their own writing.

Children also need to have a safe, secure learning environment where they can take risks. There is a marked contrast between the way children learn to talk at home and the way they are generally taught to read and write at school. Parents try to understand their children even when their oral language is far from the adult form. They reinforce children's efforts to communicate by responding in a meaningful way. At school, we are far less likely to respond positively to children's early reading and writing efforts when they are approximations rather than accurate responses (Holdaway, 1979). No one expects a young child to speak in completely grammatical sentences with perfect pronunciation the first time he or she talks; in reading and writing, however, accuracy is frequently required from the beginning.

Children are not likely to take risks or develop ownership unless they view themselves as effective, successful language learners. Teachers can help to ensure success by adapting their expectations as well as the difficulty levels of tasks for different children. For example, in a kindergarten class, the teacher might have very different expectations for what young children will be able to do with a predictable book such as *Brown Bear, Brown Bear, What do you see?* after it is read to them. Some children will be able to identify words in the book as they reread it. Other children may point to the words, as another child reads, in order to develop their understanding of the one-to-one relationship between words in oral and written language. Still others may listen and chime in as they "talk like a book" (Clay, 1972) to learn what written language sounds like. In other words, different children do different things with the same book in order to achieve different objectives.

There are other times, however, when children read different books to achieve similar learning goals. An important goal for all children in primary grades is to develop sight vocabulary that they can identify quickly in order to become fluent, automatic readers. It is estimated that children need to read a minimum of three and one-half hours per week in order to achieve **automaticity** in their reading (Rossman, 1987) and they need to be reading books at a fairly easy level. Since children in any classroom read at a range of different reading levels, they will need to read books at different levels to develop the required automaticity.

Statement of Beliefs

Most chapters in this book end with a traditional summary of the major points in the chapter. Rather than a traditional summary for this chapter, however, we decided to conclude by presenting a list of our beliefs about language learning. These beliefs are based on solid research findings and serve as a conceptual framework for the following chapters.

We believe that:

- we learn language by using it in purposeful situations where we interact with other people.
- we learn language by using it; we learn to read by engaging in reading activities that are meaningful; and we learn to write in the same way.
- language is central to learning in that we use language to process much of our thinking.
- knowledge and meaning are socially constructed.
- people from different areas, cultures, and social situations use language differently, and one is not better than the other: they are simply different.
- language and literacy are not politically neutral: the success of children in school is related at least partly to the match between their knowledge and language patterns and those of their teachers.
- language learning classrooms must be based on inclusive practices that ensure success and ownership of language by all children.
- the teaching and learning of talking, listening, reading, and writing must be holistic, integrated, and always purposeful.

Children's Books Noted in Chapter 1

Babbit, N. (1975). *Tuck Everlasting*. New York: Farrar, Strauss, Giroux.

CHAPTER 2

Planning the Language Arts Program

Arranging children's desks in groups encourages cooperative learning.

OBJECTIVES

- to be aware of basic principles for organizing language learning classrooms
- to understand the nature of basal series and whole language
- to critically examine materials and to base selections on curricular goals
- to know how to organize time, space, and children in order to arrange whole class, small group, and individual work
- to be aware of the range of children in language learning classrooms

Introduction

Each day when the children enter David Paul's Grade 2 classroom, they are greeted with a letter to them on the chalkboard. In the letter, David tells about unusual class activities they will do that day or comments on class events from the day before. Today, the children read the letter, and David helped them use strategies to identify unfamiliar words. He then drew the children together on the floor in a group and read them a poem about a dragon to set the theme for the group composition they would write later. As he read, he stopped at the end of some lines to give the children an opportunity to predict meaningful words.

David then told the children that they were going to write a composition together about an imaginary pet dragon. He planned this instructional activity because he had noticed that many children in the class were having difficulty generating and organizing ideas in their compositions. As the children in the class brainstormed ideas, David wrote them on the whiteboard. Then with the assistance of the teacher's questions, the children organized the ideas into groups. As they did so, David used coloured markers to circle ideas in each group, e.g., how the pet dragon looks, what it does, what it eats. The children discussed what they wanted to write and then dictated ideas while David recorded their ideas on chart paper. The completed composition was then read as a whole and some suggestions were made for revisions. The revised composition, carets and all, was placed in the writing centre.

While the group was still intact, David and the children discussed how they would use their remaining time. He provided them with a sign-up chart to control the number of children who selected each group activity as well as to keep a record of what activities each child completed during the week. Some children indicated that they were going to continue writing a composition from their writing files. Others decided to read independently or write a response in their journal to a book they were reading. One group of children chose to play a dragon game David had developed to reinforce a problematic spelling pattern (final e). Another group was working on a puppet play based on a story they had read in class.

While the children were working independently or in small groups, David asked six children to join him at a small table in the corner of the room where he conducted a directed reading–thinking activity (see Chapter 7) with a level one text. He had noticed that these children were making limited use of their own knowledge when they read. Their responses to what they were reading tended to focus on story details rather than linking story events or characters to their own lives.

With five minutes left before recess, David asked the class to come back together to share what they had learned that morning. One child talked about a book she was reading and another shared a piece of writing he was working on. The group working on the puppet play said they had completed their puppets and would be ready to share their play with the class the next day.

The children in this classroom were involved in a variety of listening, talking, reading, and writing activities during a ninety-minute period as well as during other parts of the school day. They worked with the teacher, with other children, and by themselves. They completed some assigned activities and were able to select others based on their interests and skills. The children moved from one activity to another with very little waiting or off-task behaviour. This did not happen by accident, but rather reflected careful planning and organization of the program. Careful planning leads to meaningful learning for children, which, in turn, motivates them and reduces behaviour problems. Planning and organization are key to effective classroom management.

Principles for Planning and Organization

Different classrooms reflect different views of language learning. When desks are arranged in rows and children face the front, the focus is generally on teacher talk, with the teacher making nearly all of the decisions about what children do and when they do it. In other classrooms, children's desks are arranged in groups with the children facing one another. This encourages student talk and cooperative learning. While no single organizational structure is appropriate for all classrooms, the following general principles, based on ideas presented in Chapter 1, are recommended as a basis for program planning and organization. The key word in most of these principles is *balance*.

Balance among the Language Arts

Until the past two decades, most language arts time was allocated to reading instruction and restricted largely to use of one **basal reading series**. More recently, the work of educators such as Graves (1983) and Calkins (1994) has lead to a sharp increase in time spent writing in elementary schools. Indeed, in some classrooms the majority of language arts time is devoted to writing, and teachers appear to assume that children will learn to read by reading their own writing. What we need to strive for in language learning classrooms is balance between not only reading and writing, but across all areas of language learning.

This does not mean that the same amount of time will be devoted to speaking, listening, reading, and writing every day. When a new theme is introduced, children may initially spend more time listening and reading. Later on, they may spend more time writing or working together in groups. However, children need to spend at least some time speaking, listening, reading, and writing every day. In any language arts unit, it is important to ensure that there is a balance in the time allocated to these different areas.

Integration

Balancing the amount of time children spend on each area of language arts does not mean that each area should be taught separately. Knowledge about how stories are organized helps children to construct meaning when they're both reading and writing. Knowledge about the relationship between letters and sounds helps children to both spell and identify words. Teaching reading and writing in an integrated way throughout the school day helps children transfer strategies and knowledge developed in one context to other areas of the curriculum.

When language areas are taught separately, children may view them in isolation and approach them very differently. This is illustrated in the reading and writing of one fourth-grade girl who was receiving reading instruction from one teacher and writing instruction from another. She approached reading as a word-by-word sounding-out activity; the words she said tended to look like those in the story she was reading, but they did not make sense or sound right. Her writing, however, was markedly different. Here she showed far less concern with print (spelling many words incorrectly) but generated a well-formed story with elaborate ideas. However, both she and other people had difficulty reading what she had written. She needed to integrate the effective meaning-making strategies she used when writing with her use of print when reading. In addition, she needed to integrate her knowledge of letter sounds used when reading to produce more readable spellings in her writing. A more integrated program would have helped her to make these links.

Balance between Teaching and Practice

In order to become good at doing anything, whether it's riding a bike, swimming, or writing, we need to spend time doing it. Many children spend relatively little time at school actually reading. Anderson, Hiebert, Scott, and Wilkerson (1985) reported that the average daily time spent reading in the primary grades was only seven minutes. They found that most time allocated for reading consisted of the teacher talking about reading or the children completing worksheets. While there is little doubt that children need to spend time reading at home as well as in school, Stanovich (1986) has shown that this happens much more frequently with good than with poor readers. For many poor readers, their *only* reading is done at school.

While children certainly do need time at school to practice reading, some class time also needs to be devoted to teaching reading. Some educators (such as Pressley & Rankin, 1994) have expressed concern that in many North American schools, not enough reading instruction is provided, particularly for at-risk children. It *is* important that children have opportunities to figure out how written language works, but it is not necessary that they invent *everything* on their own. When teachers carefully observe children's needs, they can greatly facilitate language development through carefully planned, explicit lessons. Again the answer is balance, so that children receive guidance when they need it but also have lots of opportunities to use language.

Security and Challenge

As indicated in Chapter 1, children need to be in a secure learning environment in which they can take risks. They need to experience success with most of the activities they complete. When activities are too difficult day after day, children often become discouraged and lose confidence in themselves as learners. Practice with relatively easy reading and writing activities is also necessary in order for children to develop mastery and fluency.

If all activities are too easy, however, children will not be challenged to learn to their potential. At least some of the time, they need to be working in their **zone of proximal development** (Vygotsky, 1978). At this level, work is too difficult for them to complete independently, but they can achieve success with the help of their teacher or other students. To maximize language learning, there needs to be a balance between language learning experiences that are easy and those that are more challenging.

In order to plan instruction so that all children experience both the security and challenge needed to facilitate their learning, a great deal of information is needed about their skills and interests. Assessment is essential to the planning of effective language arts programs. Several techniques for assessing children's talking, listening, reading, and writing are described in Chapter 11.

Balance in Power Relationships

Empowerment is a current buzzword in education (Clarke, 1990). In some language arts programs, it has become a major goal. This does not mean that teachers relinquish all power in the classroom and that children make all the decisions. However, it does mean that teachers do not make decisions about everything that will be taught and learned in the classroom. As children begin to take responsibility for their own language learning, the relationship between teachers and children becomes more collaborative and less hierarchical (Vygotsky, 1962; 1978).

By working collaboratively in classrooms, children develop a sense of ownership of both their knowledge and language. They feel that their talk, reading, and writing belongs to them, not to the teacher. But they will not develop this sense of ownership if the teacher always tells them what to read, write, and talk about, or is always the authority on how well they read, wrote, and talked. By making choices about their language learning, children begin to feel like readers and writers—they belong to the literacy club.

Selecting Materials and Programs

Basal Series

Basal reading series have dominated the teaching of reading in North America since the early part of this century. These series consist of a teacher's guide, a student's anthology, and a workbook plus other materials such as tests, worksheets, audiotapes, and computer software. Goodman, Shannon, Freeman, and Murphy indicate that basal readers were developed in the first two decades of the twentieth century to reflect the learning theories and research of that time and the "expectations of a public and profession enthralled with business, science, and psychology" (1988, 19). There was concern about the quality of reading instruction, and the explicit instructions in teacher's guides were presented as a solution to inadequate supervision of reading instruction and a poorly educated teaching staff. This guidance both to students and teachers through structured skill development was the fundamental characteristic of basal reading programs. The promoters of basal series believed that all teachers needed to do was follow the instructions in the guides and all children would learn to read. Although this promise of basal readers has never been realized, these series have dominated reading instruction throughout most of this century and their format has changed very little. Those older than twenty-five may recall the characters Dick and Jane or Tom and Betty from our elementary school readers. Goodman, Shannon, Freeman, and Murphy (1988) reported that more than ninety percent of elementary school teachers in the United States were still using basal reading series in the 1980s. A recent examination of provincial department of education guidelines in Canada revealed that all provinces still include lists of basal materials, although the trend is toward recommending rather than mandating their use (Gordon, 1991).

Initially, Canadian basal reading programs were essentially Canadianized versions of programs from the United States (Murphy, 1991). That was true of the Tom and Betty and Dick and Jane materials. However, over the past twenty years, Canadian programs have begun to be developed in Canada and these programs are quite different from the basal series produced in the United States. One major difference is the attempt by Canadian publishers to produce integrated language arts series rather than focusing exclusively on reading.

Another major difference is an attempt to include more children's literature. Basal reading series in the United States have been criticized because they include so much material that has been written specifically to teach reading. Even when children's literature is included, it is often adapted to such an extent that it is almost unrecognizable (Goodman, Shannon, Freeman, and Murphy, 1988). In contrast, many Canadian basal series claim to offer quality children's literature. Murphy (1991) analyzed five basal series that were authorized widely across the country to determine how much children's literature was actually incorporated into the series. Beyond the Grade 1 level, she found that Canadian series do contain a high proportion of reprinted children's literature. However, at the Grade 1 level, a considerable amount of material is written specifically for the series. Rather than the controlled vocabulary of the basal series of the 1950s and 1960s, the newer basals use predictable or repetitive patterns. Again, the result is that young children are exposed to limited, controlled material rather than to authentic literature in the initial stages of learning to read.

The impetus for including more literature in Canadian basal series is, in part, a reflection of the influence of **whole language** on language arts instruction in this country. Two provinces, Nova Scotia and Quebec, have adopted a whole language curriculum, and in other provinces, the use of holistic approaches and children's literature are recommended (Gordon, 1991). Not everyone feels that the movement toward whole language is desirable (e.g., Simner, 1993 in Canada, Pressley and Rankin, 1994 in the United States, and Moller, 1991 in England). Part of the controversy may reflect confusion about the nature of whole language. The next section will try to clarify what whole language is—and what it is not.

Whole Language

Most writers indicate that whole language is a philosophy or set of beliefs rather than an approach or technique. McKay (1993), for example, argues that whole language is a philosophy about learning, language, and the nature of relationships between children and adults. At the core of whole language is a focus on meaning as the essence of language learning, and on children learning language through using it.

Language is also seen as indivisible, with the whole always being greater than the sum of the parts (McKay, 1993; Goodman, 1986). In other words, the meaning a child constructs for a story is always more than the sum of the pronunciations and meanings of the individual words in the story. Hence, whole language advocates question activities in which children focus on individual skills in isolation from reading and writing. For example, rather than teaching spelling or **phonics** as isolated skills, whole language teachers help children learn how to use letter sound cues within the context of reading and writing connected texts. Teaching proceeds from the whole to parts rather than from parts to the whole.

Language is viewed as personal, social, and cultural. "It is driven from the inside by the need to communicate and shaped from the outside towards the norms of the society" (Goodman, 1986, 26). What happens at school is based on what children already know and can do, and what the children learn is used in their interactions in the home and community. The language arts program is connected with the rest of their school programs and their lives.

The political nature of language learning is also recognized. Goodman (1986) writes about the empowerment of children as they make decisions about their own language use. McKay (1993) and Shannon (1989) write about children and teachers controlling the teaching and learning process.

While whole language has less to do with methods and practices than with philosophy and beliefs, some practices have been identified that are consistent with whole language (Altwerger, Edelsky, and Flores, 1987). In whole language classrooms, children engage in "real" reading and writing rather than exercises in reading and writing. They read more quality children's literature rather than working with material written to teach children how to read. They write regularly and for a variety of purposes. Assessment is based on observation of children as they talk, read, and write rather than on **standardized tests**. Froese (1990, 2) defines whole language as "a child-centred, literature-based approach to language teaching that immerses students in real communication situations whenever possible."

Much of the misunderstanding surrounding whole language appears to involve statements regarding what it is not rather than what it is (Newman and Church, 1994). Some parents and teachers, for example, believe that there is no place for phonics or spelling instruction in whole language programs, because skills tend to be taught in the context of the reading and writing process rather than as separate skills or in a separate time slot in the school day. Skills also tend to be taught incidentally in minilessons, when a teacher notes a particular need, rather than in a systematic set of planned lessons. A major question about the effectiveness of whole language relates to the effectiveness of this incidental teaching of skills (Harker, 1991). Some children appear to require that skills be taught in a more sequential manner to become fluent readers and writers (Pressley and Rankin, 1994). While there is nothing in whole language philosophy to preclude the systematic teaching of skills to children who need to learn them, this teaching happens in the context of reading and writing, making it much less visible to parents and educators.

The Canadian Compromise

The compromise of Canadian publishing companies in the basal series–whole language controversy has been the **basalization** of whole language. As noted earlier, most provincial departments of education still recommend basal series, and most of the series currently recommended claim to be consistent with at least some whole language beliefs (Simner, 1993). Hence, this type of material is available in most elementary schools in Canada, and some jurisdictions require teachers to use it as the core of language arts programs. This new generation of basal materials has many positive features. The quality of the literature beyond the Grade 1 level is much better than it was in the series popular until the 1980s. The teachers' guides focus on meaning and do make suggestions for integrating language arts.

However, several educators have questioned whether it is possible to basalize whole language. Cameron and Mickelson (1989) question whether separate workbooks, flash cards, computer programs, and other components that fragment reading and writing are consistent with whole language beliefs. In addition, there appears to be a contradiction between the belief that power and control should be in the hands of teachers and children and the purpose of basal readers, which determine not only what children should read but also what teachers should do with these materials. Rather than empowering students and teachers, Shannon (1989) maintains that the basalization of whole language in Canada has tended, instead, to place control and power in the hands of publishers and editors.

When basal materials are used in language arts programs, the major challenge is for teachers and children to remain in charge of the programs, selecting from and adapting the materials provided rather than using them in a rigid, inflexible manner. This is not always easy to do. The series are intimidating, partly because they were developed by experts in language arts and cost a great deal to produce. However, it is important to keep in mind that the experts who developed the materials do not know the children in any one classroom. It is teachers who are the experts about the interests and needs of the children in their classrooms, and hence, it is teachers who need to critically examine the materials in basal series to determine if, when, and how they should be used.

While basal series are still widely recommended and used in Canada, most teachers who use these materials supplement them with **trade books** (books written for children and sold in book stores). This is what David Paul does in his classroom, exposing the children to a wide range of materials beyond *Impressions*, a Canadian whole language series. A few teachers reject basal materials altogether and base their language arts program on children's literature. The use of children's books either as the core of language arts programs or in addition to basal series has become so widespread that an entire chapter of this textbook is devoted to a description of children's literature. However, it is important to note that including children's literature in the classroom may not necessarily lead to a significant change in the nature of language arts instruction.

Jobe and Hart (1991, 147) have expressed concern about what they call "the basalization of children's literature." In other words, even when basal series are not being used, they may still influence what happens in classrooms. Jobe and Hart note that what many teachers are doing with children's books is very similar to what they did with stories in traditional basal reading materials. In novel studies, for example, many teachers still assign a chapter to be read and ten questions to be answered, many still develop fill-in-the-blank workbook exercises about the stories, and many still ask children to define words on a list from the story and use them in a sentence. Jobe and Hart suggest that there is still a "dominant feeling that teachers have the answers and the kids must guess what they think." (1991, 147).

Selecting a Range of Topics and Materials

Regardless of whether teachers use a basal series as part of the language arts program, there is a need for a wide range of printed materials in the classroom. By including materials that cover a range of reading levels, all children will have the opportunity to read both challenging and easy material every day. Having material on a range of topics and cultures provides at least some material related to each child's interests. From the available materials, children need to be allowed to choose at least some of the books they read. When materials are selected by someone else (the publisher or teacher), children do not gain a sense of ownership or control over their own reading. They often feel that they are reading for someone else rather than for themselves. David Paul gave children in his classroom control over what they read by allocating 15 minutes every day to drop everything and read (DEAR) right after lunch. This was a time when all the students read books of their own choice.

Similarly, children need opportunities to write on topics of their own choice. Not only does this take advantage of the unique knowledge and experience each child brings to the classroom but it also helps children to feel like writers. If children learn to rely on story starters to serve as a beginning point for their writing, they may not develop a sense that their writing belongs to them. This does not mean that teachers will never assign specific books or topics, but that at least some of the time, children should select what they read and write. On the day described at the beginning of this chapter, David Paul assigned a writing topic to help children learn how to brainstorm and organize ideas before writing. When writing independently, the children wrote on topics of their own choice.

But what range of topics and materials are appropriate? Should children be allowed or encouraged to write about any topic they want to or read anything in the classroom? How do teachers feel about comic books or Stephen King novels in the classroom? Mitchell and Cheverie (1989) write about taste and sensibility in what children read and write. While provincial departments of education examine textbooks in relation to sexist, ageist, and racist guidelines, Mitchell and Cheverie suggest that teachers are on their own when it comes to issues of ethics, aesthetics, taste, and sensibility in the content of children's writing. What should teachers do when children write "stories that contain excessive violence, a senseless slaughter of a kangaroo, the torture and torment of an alley cat, a play-by-play description of a violent television show or rock video" (Mitchell and Cheverie, 1989, 184)? What should teachers do when children write about problems at home such as divorce and abuse? While there are legal guidelines about abuse, teachers are caught in the dilemma of the child's "right to write" and their role in socialization and moral development. Mitchell and Cheverie suggest that rather than censoring children's writing, teachers should use it as a basis for discussing issues of ethics, aesthetics, taste, and sensibility.

Thematic Organization

The most common way language arts materials are organized is according to themes. This organization is evident in most of the basal series developed in Canada, with suggestions for children to talk, read, and write about each theme. These themes often transcend the language arts period and are integrated into many of the subjects discussed during the day.

Clearly, one advantage of **thematic organization** involves transfer of knowledge and skills from one context to another. Another advantage is the opportunity for children to examine a topic in depth, to go beyond the superficial. In addition, by selecting books on a common topic at a variety of reading levels, the needs of learners at varying levels of reading proficiency can be met. Thematic organization also leads to opportunities for children to work cooperatively on a common topic or problem. However, themes are not the only way to organize language arts programs. In the *Waves* series (Houghton Mifflin Canada), for example, material is organized by **genre**. For each level, there is one book devoted to science material, another to poetry, and still others to folk tales and novels.

One potential disadvantage of thematic organization is that even when the teacher selects the theme in consultation with the children in the classroom, some children will be more interested in it and have a greater sense of ownership than others. Choosing broad rather than narrow themes (e.g., not dinosaurs but rather things larger than life) is one way to get around this problem. Another potential problem is that the theme might take precedence over curriculum concerns, with the result that goals in a specific subject area become secondary in importance. The most sensible approach is to make links when appropriate, but not to force links that distort curriculum goals or fail to serve children's learning needs. There are many advantages to themes, but children's learning rather than themes needs to drive the language arts program. As always, planning a thematic program needs to begin with an assessment of the needs and interests of the children in the class.

Inside the Classroom

When Theresa Pond was a first grade teacher, she organized most of her program thematically. One day we visited her classroom at Holy Family School in Edmonton to learn about how she planned and implemented it.

On the day of our visit, the children were working on the theme "myself and my friends," and focusing on their body parts related to the "The Physical Me" aspect of the unit. Theresa planned activities related to this theme in all areas of the curriculum.

When the children arrived at school in the morning, they put their coats beside life-sized pictures of themselves that they had previously drawn and painted and that were hung next to their coat hooks. The children then worked in a circle group to discuss and group parts of the body. Theresa then printed them on the chalk board, and the children read them. In mathematics, the children counted fingers and toes, and added and subtracted them. They then drew their friend's head and put a name on it. Thematic work was discontinued at that point in the school day and the children read individually from books in the classroom library. Everyone in the classroom read, including the teacher. Theresa then drew the children back together to reflect on what they had accomplished during the morning. At that point the school principal arrived. She lay down on a large piece of paper and the children traced her outline. While they were doing this, the teacher asked them to think about body parts and what each part could do. When the outline was complete, the children discussed what each body part does. Hands, for example, are used for touching, slapping, writing, dropping, and even hand-stands! Each body part was labelled and each action put on a card. These cards were then used in a learning game, where children put each part into action. Following

continued

this, Theresa read the children a book called *Eyes Can*. As the final activity before lunch, each child drew an eye and they discussed what the eye can do. This was followed by the children tidying up the classroom, a job made easier by mailboxes on chair-backs and trays on each table for pencils and glue.

What we saw that day in Theresa's classroom was just the tip of the iceberg. What we did not see was the extensive and careful planning that went into each of the thematic units in her program. She began by selecting materials about the theme, choosing core books, and developing objectives related both to the materials she had selected as well as the needs and interests of the children. She extracted main concepts and key vocabulary to develop tasks and activities across the curriculum.

At the time of our visit, Theresa was using semantic maps to organize both the overall unit and daily lessons related to each aspect of the theme. On these semantic maps, she included what curriculum areas were involved as well as the objectives she hoped to achieve in each area. When she completed graduate work on learning styles, she began to integrate this knowledge into the design of learning activities. Students were provided with opportunities to work on tasks consistent with their preferred learning style, as well as try different ways of learning and thinking. Evaluation was based on an analysis of process and product using observation and questioning of the children. In this way, Theresa was able to assess the learning of each child to serve as the basis for planning the next thematic unit in her program.

Theresa Pond planned her program to provide her students with a continuous, integrated learning experience. She used a wide variety of materials and activities to meet the range of interests, learning styles, and learning needs she had identified through informally assessing the children. However, not all of her program was related to themes; she moved away from them at times to achieve specific learning goals and to meet the needs of individual children.

The vignette also illustrates professional development in action. Theresa Pond has continued to grow and is currently teaching music at Holy Family school.

Nonbook Resources

Sometimes we imply to children through what we do and say that books are the only legitimate source of reading materials. Yet when we think about all the different items we read each day, books are only one of many reading sources. Newspapers, magazines, TV guides, brochures, advertisements, signs, and labels are only some of the items we read in a normal day. If we want children to become literate and read widely for both information and pleasure, we need to ensure that they read a wide variety of materials in school.

Most young children are aware of print in their environment before they go to school. They know the sign for McDonalds, and they can identify their favourite cereal by looking on the box. When they begin school, they encounter print in their classrooms: their names, the names of their classmates, the days of the week and months of the year on the calendar, and words on tape recorders and computers in the classroom. By making this print the focus of instruction, teachers build on children's experiences with printed language and help children make use of it. Chapter 5 includes suggestions for how **environmental print** in the classroom can be used to foster children's **literacy** learning.

For older children, pamphlets and brochures from a variety of sources (e.g., travel agencies, tourism bureaus, flyers, and advertisements) can be selected for instructional activities. Because we are so inundated with advertisements trying to convince us to buy products, children need opportunities to learn to critically read these materials. For example, a Grade 6 class might discuss advertisements for jeans, discussing why the models are always young and attractive. A section on **critical literacy** is included in Chapter 6.

Newspapers are another source of print that most of us read nearly every day. We read newspapers for both entertainment and information about current news and events in our area. We read them to decide where to shop for groceries and which movies to go to. Many local newspapers employ education specialists and provide newspapers and suggestions for their use to classroom teachers upon request.

There are also newspapers and magazines designed specifically for children. Materials are available at a range of reading levels and focus on a variety of areas including outdoor life, science, and popular culture. Some of those available are listed in Exhibit 2.1. These materials can be used for several instructional activities, particularly in relation to content area reading. They provide up-to-date information on a range of topics related both to curriculum and children's interests. Techniques for helping children construct meaning from informational material are presented in Chapter 7.

Technology in the Language Arts Program

As a society, we have a strong belief in technology to solve our problems and help us achieve the "good life." In language arts education, this has lead publishers to produce audiotaped stories, videotapes, picture sets, overhead transparencies, puppets, and, more recently, a wide range of computer programs.

EXHIBIT 2.1

Children's Periodicals

Scholastic Classroom Magazines

Let's Find Out (Kindergarten): Mini-books, news stories, classroom photo stories, activity pages.
Storyworks (Grades 4 to 6): Fiction, nonfiction, poetry and classroom plays, interviews with authors, hands-on activities, student-written book reviews.

Scholastic Canada Limited
123 Newkirk Road
Richmond Hill, ON L4C 3G5

Ranger Rick

Grades 4 to 6: Nonfiction, fiction, photo stories, activities, environmental tips about wildlife around the world.

National Wildlife Federation
1400–16 St. N.W.
Washington, D.C. 20036-2266

National Geographic World

Grades 4 to 6: Nonfiction, photo stories, activities for junior members of the National Geographic Society.

National Geographic Society
P.O. Box 2330
Washington, D.C. 20013-2330

Ladybug and *Cricket*

Ladybug (Kindergarten to Grade 3): Stories, poems, activities, songs, some nonfiction.
Cricket (Grades 4 to 6): Stories, poems, activities, nonfiction.

Box 300
Peru, Illinois 61354-9974

Weekly Readers

Several children's newspapers are available at a variety of age/grade levels.

Xerox Educational Publications
1250 Fairwood Ave.
P.O. Box 444
Columbus, OH 43216

Chickadee and *Owl*

Chickadee (Ages 6 to 9): Stories, nonfiction, activities, posters.
Owl (Ages 9 to 12): Nonfiction, activities, posters, comics.

179 John St., Suite 500
Toronto, ON M5T 3G5

Sesame Street and *Kid City Magazines*

Sesame Street Magazine (Ages 2 to 6): Stories, poems, activities, posters, children's drawing and writing.
Kid City Magazine (Ages 6 to 9): Stories, puzzles, word games, projects.

P.O. Box 52000
Boulder, Colorado 80322-2000

Audiovisual Aids in the Classroom

Many basic audiovisual aids commonly used in classrooms require very little specialized knowledge. These include picture sets and displays on flannel boards, chalkboards, magnetic boards, and bulletin boards. Often these displays involve children's written work, but flannel and magnetic boards are also used to help children understand and retell stories with the use of characters and settings.

Transparencies, filmstrips, and slides are also widely used by teachers to stimulate oral and written language. Providing visual along with auditory cues helps children who learn more easily when they see than hear something. As well, it helps those who are learning English as a second language to understand and develop new concepts.

Films, television, audiotapes, and videotapes are also used in language arts programs. Audiotapes of books at listening centres provide children with opportunities to hear stories and increase their listening skills. Films, television, and videotapes provide them with both visual and auditory input to stimulate oral and written language. Children need to learn to analyze and evaluate what they are exposed to through these technologies. Teachers can accomplish this by providing opportunities for students to discuss, analyze, and critique what they see and hear. In particular, children need to learn how to critique advertising on television so that they become more sophisticated consumers. In addition to being a receptive medium, video, in particular, has considerable potential as an expressive medium for children to create their own productions.

The major question about using audiovisual media in the classroom is the extent to which these media are integrated into the curriculum and help children meet learning objectives. Careful selection and planning are required to ensure that audiovisual media are used not for their own sake but rather to further learning objectives.

Computer Technology in the Classroom

Many people view computers as having far greater potential for education than other forms of technology. They believe computers will revolutionize the way we learn and teach, and that we need to get on board with the computer revolution or be left behind. However, others such as Olson and Sullivan (1993) urge caution: "It is plain that a new day is upon us. But where we are going is in question." Before looking at possible uses of computer technology in the language arts classroom, some issues related to their use will be discussed.

At the classroom level, computers appear on the surface to place more control into the hands of children, since children operate them individually. The extent of the child's actual power is, of course, determined by the way computers are used in the classroom and the types of software available. Some skill-and-drill programs do not empower children any more than do workbooks and worksheets. Whether computers will lead to individual autonomy or to dependence depends on how they are used.

Questions about technology and the distribution of power go beyond the classroom door as well. Olson and Sullivan (1993) note that computers appear to be classless and genderless, but even from the standpoint of availability, children in middle-class neighbourhoods have greater access to computers than do children in working-class neighbourhoods. This is true both at home and at school, and the differences do not stop there. The type of training received with computers varies depending on whether it is being offered in the academic or business stream. In the business stream, the emphasis is on "mechanical and routinized tasks to service the machine"; in the academic stream, the emphasis is on "general and symbolic processes that lead to long-term control" (Olson and Sullivan, 1993, 429). Because of the uneven distribution of boys and girls in these two streams, many girls develop mechanical skills that do not lead to high-level careers. There is also a tendency for richer schools to teach programming skills whereas poorer schools use computer-assisted instruction. Olson and Sullivan argue that the use of computers in the schools appears to be doing little to equalize opportunities across class or gender and, indeed, may lead to greater inequalities.

Another issue is the degree of emphasis that has been placed on buying computer hardware and software as compared with training teachers and planning curriculum. Because nearly all the focus has been on acquisition, and little on integrating computers with the curriculum, computers are often under-used even when they're available (Rennie, 1990).

Using Computers in Teaching Language Arts

Three major functions of classroom computers have been identified—as tool, tutor, and tutee (Strickland, Feeley, and Wepner, 1987). As tutors, computers are used to monitor student learning and provide practice. As tutee, they give children opportunities to teach the computer how to solve problems through programming. As tools, computers help organize and process information.

Computer as Tool

Word processing is by far the most common way computers serve as tools in elementary language arts classrooms. There are hundreds of word processing programs for writing, editing, storing, and printing texts. Many of them allow children to insert graphics and illustrations into text as well. Language arts teachers sometimes type children's language experience stories directly into the computer rather than writing them on charts. This speeds up the process and the stories can be printed for the children to take them away and practise reading on their own. Language experience stories are an effective means of fostering children's **emergent literacy** development and will be described in Chapter 5.

A far more common way that children use word processing is for composing, revising, editing, and printing their written compositions. However, there are questions both about whether using word processors improves children's writing and also about when to introduce this tool. In relation to the first question, "There is some, albeit mixed, evidence that in making it easier to compose and revise, to see problems in text, and to share texts, children learn to be better writers and readers" (Bruce, 1991, 537). In addition, computers are motivating and associated with more positive attitudes about writing.

Children are most commonly introduced to word processing around Grade 4 (Strickland, Feeley, and Wepner, 1987), although word-processing programs are also available for younger children. Some of the newer programs such as *Kidworks 2* (Davison, 1992), designed for children in kindergarten through to age ten, are able to read the children what they have written in order to aid in revision and editing.

Another question about word processing involves teaching keyboarding skills. Children who have not developed these skills waste a great deal of time using a two-finger hunt-and-peck method, time that could be better spent on composing. Most educators agree that children need to be taught keyboarding, either using computer programs designed for this purpose or by more traditional teaching techniques, and that they need time to practise these skills (Strickland, Feeley, and Wepner, 1987; Rennie, 1990). But in order to accomplish these goals, children need regular and frequent access to computers.

Word processing programs are used for creative writing, for writing reports in other subject areas, for making journal entries, for writing letters to authors, for producing class or school newspapers, and so on. In a sixth grade class recently visited, tables were organized into pods of four and each child had his or her own computer. These children had already acquired considerable keyboarding skill and they used their computers for most of their writing, both in language arts and other subject areas. There were several printers available in the room to enable children to produce hard copies of their writing easily and quickly. The school is not in an affluent area and the children were using older Apple IIE computers. However, every student had access to the computer for writing whenever needed. This classroom is the exception rather than the rule. Although most people recognize the advantages of using word processors in the writing program, this is still not a widespread practice. Rennie noted in 1990 that more than 75 percent of students in Alberta schools were not regularly using a computer for writing.

The other major way computers are used as a classroom tool is to organize information. Database programs provide teachers and children with a computerized filing system to store and retrieve information. Teachers often keep student records on database, recording test scores, books read, assignments completed, language strengths, language needs, and so on. Students make less use of database programs, but in some classrooms they record information about the books they've read for other children to use as a resource when selecting books or researching.

Computer as Tutor

Much of the early software to develop reading and writing skills had the appearance of worksheets on computer. However, there were some exceptions. *The Puzzler* (Sunburst), developed by a team at Queen's University, for example, involved children in making predictions as they read a text prompting them to evaluate and modify their predictions throughout. Rather than telling the children the "right" answer at the end of each story, the authors provided them with a selection of answers given by other children. This program clearly portrayed reading as a meaning–making process.

Recently, with the advent of CD-ROM, an increasing number of interactive software programs are becoming available. *Discis* books, for example, present popular children's books on the screen; as the children read, they can request both word pronunciations and oral explanations of word meanings.

An even newer program, *Wiggleworks* by Scholastic, is being marketed as a total language arts program. Developed for kindergarten to Grade 2 children, *Wiggleworks* includes books on CD-ROM, children's books, teacher's guides, audiotapes, an assessment package, and other support materials. For each CD-ROM book, children can do four types of activities: 1) The book is read to them. 2) They read and request help with words they do not know. 3) They modify the pictures and print in the books, and print a copy of their modified book. 4) They write their own stories. In addition, a magnetic board is available on computer for word building, and children can develop a personal list of words to serve as a resource when they are writing. In addition to the tutorial component of *Wiggleworks*, a built-in management system allows the teacher to select which activities will be available to each child and keeps a record of what each child does on the computer daily.

Software for computers still tends to be variable in quality and reflects a range of views on language learning. The major question teachers need to ask when evaluating software is whether language is presented in a meaningful, functional context as compared with rote skill practice. It is also important to ask whether the software will help children meet the objectives of the language arts program. As with other audiovisual aids, computers are most effective when integrated into the curriculum.

Computer as Tutee

Creative software packages or simple programming languages such as BASIC or LOGO provide children with the opportunity to tell computers what to do. This engages children in problem solving and, hence, involves similar thinking skills to those involved in reading comprehension. However, the link between programming and language arts is indirect, and programming is generally not included in language arts programs.

A volunteer helps a kindergarten child read a story on the computer.

Future Directions

Computer technology is developing at a very rapid pace with new hardware and software becoming available almost daily. Hypermedia software programs, for example, are beginning to make their way into schools. These systems enable teachers to link pages of graphics and print into a lesson or presentation. Computer networks are also becoming available to children in schools. Most are school or classroom-based with computers networked so that children can share software packages and write back and forth to one another and to their teacher. Some children are connected to the Internet, accessing and sharing information with people outside of school. This provides opportunities for children to critique what they are reading as well as to develop a strong sense of audience.

With these new developments, it is not surprising that some people are convinced that computers will revolutionize education. However, "if we are to use computers as tools, tutors and machines to serve our students, we must examine the full range of their actual use and, in conducting our examination, be resolved to keep control and have this new cultural invention serve democratic ends" (Olson and Sullivan, 1993, 439).

Time in the Language Arts Classroom

Long and Short Time Blocks

In allocating time, teachers must decide whether to divide language arts into a series of separate time periods devoted to different aspects of language arts, or to designate large time blocks for language arts and organize a range of activities within this block. A major advantage of the first method is accountability: it is relatively easy to account for how much time has been spent on each aspect of the language arts curriculum. For example, if parents are concerned about spelling, you can assure them that a certain number of minutes are devoted exclusively to spelling instruction every week. This way of allocating time also provides a great deal of predictability for the children. They know what they will be doing at each point during the school day. However, there are several disadvantages to this method.

First, this way of allocating time does little to foster links between talking, reading, and writing. For example, when phonics is taught in a separate ten-minute block each day, some children will not see its relevance for writing or reading. Second, separate time blocks make it difficult to pursue children's needs and interests as they arise in the classroom. Instead of teaching children a strategy when they need it, the teaching is put on hold until the appropriate time in the school day. In addition, just when children get really interested in a topic they are discussing, it is often time to switch to another subject area. Third, short time blocks necessitate many changes in activity during the day and a considerable amount of time is lost during transitions between activities. Children may spend up to 20 percent of the time allocated to language arts in transition between activities (Benterud, 1983).

The alternative is to organize one or two larger daily time blocks for language arts and to include language learning opportunities in other subject areas as well. The major disadvantage of this type of organization is the difficulty of balancing time spent on each area of the language arts. Careful planning and record keeping are necessary to ensure that each child receives a balanced language arts program. However, the advantages far outweigh the disadvantages. There is more flexibility to pursue children's interests and learning needs. Activities are not cut off while children are still engaged in meaningful learning. Nor are activities prolonged to fill a predetermined time slot when children are no longer interested or learning.

Time for Group and Individual Work

In the 1960s and 1970s, children spent most of the time allocated to reading instruction working in achievement groups or completing seat work. Today, many teachers devote at least some time to large group instruction. Wiseman (1992) recommends two types of activities for use with the whole class—instructional or focus time and sharing time.

At the beginning of each day, many teachers bring children together to explain what they will do for the day. This gives children an opportunity to be involved in planning and helps them to set goals for their own learning. The teacher might also teach a strategy or introduce a new genre to the whole class. In the example at the beginning of this chapter, David Paul used a minimal-cues message to teach strategies for identifying words to all the children in his class. He also read a poem to the class and had the children brainstorm ideas for a writing project. The amount of time spent on large group instruction varies with the day and needs of the children.

Sharing time near the end of the language arts time block provides children with an opportunity to talk about what they have accomplished and evaluate their learning. They may discuss books they have read, read aloud what they have written, or talk about what they have learned. This provides both the children and the teacher with an opportunity to evaluate the effectiveness of instruction and serves as the basis for planning the next day's objectives and activities.

As indicated earlier in this chapter, children need to read and write independently every day, and during at least some of this time, they need to be in control of what they read and write. In David Paul's classroom, time was set aside every day to drop everything and read. During this time, children selected books of their own choice and read to themselves. Some sat at their desks, while others sat on comfortable pillows at the back of the room. The teacher also read because he knows that he is a significant model for his students. He demonstrated his commitment to independent reading both by allocating time in a busy school day for it and by reading himself during this time.

Time Guidelines

Each teacher's actual daily timetable will depend on many factors, including requirements of the school system or provincial department of education, the philosophy of the school, and times allocated for recess, lunch break, gym, library, and so on. Some general guidelines for daily schedules are provided in Exhibit 2.2, adapted from Wiseman (1992).

However, it is important to keep in mind when using these guidelines that the times recommended will extend across subject boundaries since language learning is involved in all areas of the curriculum. This is particularly true at the upper elementary level where a considerable amount of the independent reading and writing children do will relate to social studies and science units.

EXHIBIT 2.2

Time Guidelines for Language Arts Activities

Activities	Grade 1–2	Grades 3–4	Grades 5–6
Reading to children	daily 10–20 mins.	daily 15–20 mins.	daily 15–20 mins.
Independent reading (some self-selected)	daily 10–20 mins.	daily 15–30 mins.	daily 20–30 mins.
Independent writing	daily 15–30 mins.	daily 20–30 mins.	daily 30–40 mins.
Small group instruction and language activities	daily 15–20 mins.	daily 15–30 mins.	daily 15–30 mins.
Whole class instruction and sharing	daily 15–30 mins.	daily 15–30 mins.	daily 15–30 mins.

Organizing Space

The physical arrangement of the classroom reflects the goals and philosophy of the language arts program. A classroom in which children's desks face one another invites children to talk together and engage in cooperative learning. Teachers do not have much control over the amount of space or type of equipment or furniture in their classrooms, but they do have control over how that space and furniture are arranged. As indicated above, classroom space needs to be organized to facilitate children working together as a whole class, children working together in groups, and children working independently. Reading and writing materials also need to be easily accessible.

The children's desks in David Paul's classroom were organized in rows. He used this physical arrangement at the beginning of the day for large group instruction by having children discuss the minimal cues message on the chalkboard. He then asked the children to push aside the desks in the middle of the room to create a space for them to sit on the floor while he read them the poem. He preferred this arrangement so the children would be closer both to the book and to one another. In some classrooms, a rug in one corner provides a place for children to come together for whole class discussions, to listen to their teacher read, and to share what they have accomplished. Children can also be organized for whole class activities by placing their desks together in groups, as shown in Exhibit 2.3, so that all children can view the board and screen. Tables can easily replace groups of desks in this arrangement.

In David Paul's classroom, children worked together in groups in many different locations. They played learning games at a table placed at the perimeter of the room; they sat together in pairs on the floor or in adjacent desks to read books to each other; a small group joined the teacher at a small table for a minilesson using the directed reading–thinking activity. Group work encourages children to work cooperatively and provides opportunities for oral language development. The classroom organization depicted in Exhibit 2.3 places a high value on children working together. In addition to placing desks in groups, a table on one side provides a place for children to come together to work with the teacher on a minilesson or to work with each other on projects.

EXHIBIT 2.3 **Physical Arrangement of the Classroom**

1. Chalkboard with pull-down overhead screen
2. Storage
3. Teacher's desk
4. Students' desks in groups
5. Storage
6. Centre
7. Small group meeting area
8. Writing centre
9. Display
10. Computer station
11. Listening centre
12. Reading centre

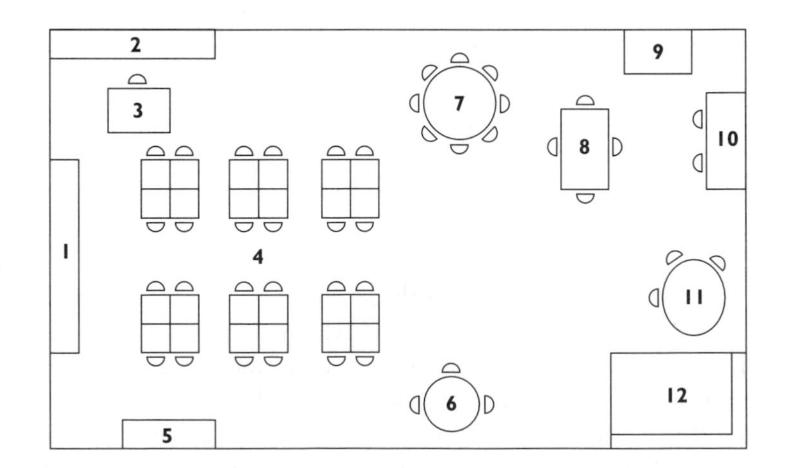

Learning centres are another way to provide opportunities for children to work together in groups. Some centres, such as reading or writing centres, are permanent. Reading centres generally include a classroom library, comfortable rugs, chairs or cushions, and often a listening centre with taped stories. Morrow (1989) indicates that well-designed classroom libraries significantly increase the number of children who choose to participate in literacy activities. She recommends that materials selected for reading centres appeal to a variety of interests and be at a range of reading levels to meet individual needs. She also recommends that materials include all the types of children's literature described in Chapter 3 as well as newpapers and magazines. New books and materials need to be introduced to the centre regularly to ensure continued interest. Children can be involved in planning and managing the reading centre, developing rules for its use, naming it, and keeping it neat.

Writing centres often include a display area for children's writing, materials for writing, and at least one computer and printer. Morrow (1989) also recommends including materials for making books and placing books made by children in the reading centre to share with other children. Other centres are less permanent, often being set up on a thematic basis related to topics in social studies, science, and other subject areas. While learning centres can be very useful in facilitating children's language development and cooperative learning, one caution is in order. Sometimes centres seem to be valued for their own sake rather than for how they contribute to learning and curricular goals. As with computers and other instructional tools, learning centres need to be integrated into the curriculum to maximize their usefulness.

In David Paul's classroom, most independent work was completed by children at their desks. Having desks arranged in rows facilitates independent work although children are still able to consult with their neighbour if they need help. The children in David's classroom also often found a quiet space on the floor when they were working independently. While the classroom depicted in Exhibit 2.3 is more conducive to small group than individual work, children do have individual desks and there are many spaces around the perimeter of the room where children can go to work alone. The reading centre, in particular, is appropriate for both group and individual reading.

Organizing Children

Children in most schools are organized by grades on the basis of their age, although some progress through the grades more quickly and others more slowly as a result of grade repetition. Sometimes class placements are based upon grouping by special needs, e.g., visually impaired, mentally handicapped. This does not mean that most classrooms contain a heterogeneous group of children. Indeed, in schools and classrooms, children are organized in various ways in an attempt to create more homogeneous groups. In a review of literature on grouping practices, Barr and Dreeben (1991) note that in the primary grades, most reading instruction is provided in ability groups while in the intermediate grades, total class instruction is dominant. Exclusive use of either of these grouping practices won't likely meet the individual needs and interests of children in any classroom. Instead, children need to be organized in different ways throughout the school day.

Whole Class Instruction

Talking and working together as a whole class helps to develop a community of learners, a community in which children help and respect one another. Children learn a great deal from one another. This learning is enhanced by providing the opportunity to interact with children of differing abilities rather than only with those at a similar level of language achievement. Whole class instruction is also an efficient use of teacher time. When introducing children to a new theme or strategy, it is more efficient to work with all of them at the same time than to teach the same thing to each child individually. Because of individual differences in language development and needs, however, whole class instruction needs to be supplemented with other ways of organizing children.

A student teacher interacts with a small group of children.

Grouping Children for Instruction

The most common basis for organizing children into groups for reading instruction has been reading ability (Barr and Dreeben, 1991). Within schools, this involves assigning children to classes on the basis of their achievement scores, cross-class grouping, or tracking. Within classrooms, children are placed in ability groups for reading instruction, and sometimes these groupings are maintained in other areas of the language arts as well. Whether at the school or classroom level, the major purpose of this type of grouping is to produce a more homogeneous group in terms of reading needs, making it easier for the teacher to plan and give appropriate instruction.

Despite the long history of ability grouping, recent reviews of research about it have produced few conclusive findings to either support or refute its impact on reading achievement. As a result, many educators are now questioning the value of this type of grouping practice (Indrisano and Paratore, 1991; Barr and Dreeben, 1991). Ability grouping may offer some advantage to academically gifted students, but results are far from clear even for this group, and questionable for average and low-ability groups.

Researchers have also investigated whether children are taught reading differently in high-ability as compared with low-ability groups. Again the findings are inconsistent, although some studies indicate a stronger focus on decoding for low-ability students, more emphasis on critical thinking for high-ability students, and a lower rate of engaged time for low-ability students (Indrisano and Paratore, 1991). In light of these findings and current interest in more holistic language instruction, ability grouping is coming under increasing criticism. Some teachers have abandoned the practice, moving to whole class instruction instead. However, in an effort to meet a wide range of reading interests and needs, other teachers are moving to different ways of organizing children into groups.

In the classroom described at the beginning of this chapter, David Paul organized children into interest groups, special needs groups, research groups, and pairs. All these groupings are far less permanent than ability groups. Interest groups in his classroom were sometimes set up for one day, for example, when children came together to play a game. Other groups, such as the one working on the puppet play, stayed together for several days. Interest groups are generally made up of children at different ability levels, and they tend to exist for a relatively short time, being disbanded when their purpose has been achieved.

Research groups are similar to interest groups in that they are temporary, although teachers are generally instrumental in their formation. In addition, their focus is on a topic that the children research rather than on completion of an activity or pursuing an interest. The teacher and students together often set specific goals and a written or oral presentation is often produced at the end. Like interest groups, these groups are often composed of children of varying ability levels.

The basis for forming special needs groups is different from that for interest or research groups. Through careful classroom observation, teachers identify an aspect of reading, writing, listening, or talking where several children need help. David Paul identified several children who needed to make greater use of their own knowledge as they read. He brought these children together into a small group for a few days to help them understand the importance of their knowledge and develop strategies for using it as they read. Once the objectives for special needs instruction have been met, these groups are disbanded.

David Paul organized the children in his classroom into pairs for part of the language arts time. Each pair found a space and shared books. While one child read, the other listened, providing each child with much more reading practice than is the case when children read orally in groups or the whole class. Because the children chose the books themselves, the books interested them and were also at an appropriate level. The pairs David set up were collaborative, with the children working together on a common activity and helping each other at points of difficulty. Collaborative pairs are also appropriate for other types of activities such as problem solving and writing (Indrisano and Paratore, 1991).

A more common way of organizing children into pairs involves peer tutoring, either with same-age or cross-age dyads. Generally, a more proficient reader or writer is paired with a child who is less proficient, and they complete a specific activity designed to facilitate skill development. One type of activity that is appropriate for peer tutoring is paired reading. As with most types of grouping, research has yielded conflicting results on peer tutoring, although it works best when programs are structured, short in duration, and focused on specific skills (Indrisano and Paratore, 1991). According to Topping (1989), both the child being tutored as well as the one doing the tutoring benefit from the experience.

Many of the groupings described above lend themselves well to cooperative learning. Slavin (1980, 315) defines cooperative learning as a technique in which "students work on learning activities in small groups and receive rewards or recognition based on their group's performance." Golub (1994) provides several examples of cooperative groups in the language arts classroom. In one scenario, two students work together to complete a writing task, discussing what they will say and how they will say it. When they finish writing, they hand in one paper with both names on it. In another scenario, a group of students attempting to make sense of a poem first jot down questions they have about the poem and then discuss and share different interpretations. The understanding they come to as a group is different and often deeper than most children could have constructed individually. Still another example involves students working on a project where different children complete different parts, meeting regularly to discuss what they are doing. Again one paper is handed in as a result of this work.

Cooperative learning changes the traditional authority structure of classrooms by placing more control in the hands of children. Another major difference is that, instead of each child being evaluated individually, children work together for a group reward. This encourages children to work cooperatively rather than competitively. When we organize children into groups but still base rewards on individual achievement, we foster competition rather than cooperation in the groups. Some of the benefits claimed for cooperative learning groups include increased exchange of ideas, development of social skills, wider acceptance and respect for other children, and increased learning (Mayfield, 1992).

Individual Reading and Writing

There is little doubt that children need classroom time to read and write in order to become good readers and writers. It is not enough to allow children to select a book to read or to write something of their own choice after they complete their other work, or to suggest that they do these types of activities at home. Independent reading and writing need to be scheduled into each school day.

Inside the Classroom

Joyce Bodell, a teacher at Mountain View Elementary School in Coquitlam, B.C., spent seven years teaching at the primary level. Here she describes how she and another teacher organized a parent shared reading program in their classrooms.

During the three years that I taught in a primary open-area classroom of approximately fifty children in Grades 1, 2, and 3 with my teaching partner, Cindi Seddon, we began each day with a twenty-five minute period that we called Morning Reading Time. We sent out an invitation for parents and other care-givers to join us and included frequent reminders in the monthly newsletters we sent home. Every day at least six and sometimes up to fifteen care-givers joined us during this time. We included grandparents, nannies, aunts, and uncles in our invitation. We also encouraged the principal and learning assistance teachers to join us. Occasionally, older siblings from the high schools would bring their younger brother or sister to school and stay for reading. My own mother even showed up from time to time!

The main agenda for Morning Reading Time was quite simply reading. We generally left it up to children and parents to choose the books or other reading material and whom to read with. Not all of the children were engaged with adults during this time, nor did we require them to do so.

Children had regular access to a wide variety of reading materials that accommodated their many reading abilities and interests. Big books, pattern books, trade books, picture books, poetry, novels, nonfiction books, pocket chart nursery rhymes, cassettes with books to read along with at the listening centre, their own stories, poems, and research reports that they had written, posters, magazines, letters they had received, felt-board characters for oral storytelling, packets of word cards that they had made of words that they wanted to know how to read—the list was almost endless.

Parents read aloud to their children or listened to their children reading to them. Usually other children would join in to listen or take turns reading aloud. It was not

continued

uncommon to see a mother, father, or grandparent seated on the floor, holding a child on his or her lap, and surrounded by a group of children listening intently to a story. Some children preferred to go off by themselves to read together in a small group or independently. Most days, a group of children elected to go to the listening centre, where they donned headphones and opened books to read along with the cassette. Often, some children at the pocket chart, pointer in hand, led themselves through a nursery rhyme, or went through the morning calendar, reading the days of the week or months of the year, or reread yesterday's Morning Message from the chart stand or blackboard. There was usually a "novel corner" for children who had expressed an interest in chapter books; here a parent read a part of the novel each day. Many parents and children chose to bring special books from home to read together during this time, an act that conveyed the understanding that books can be treasures.

The two teachers circulated throughout the room until everyone was engaged. Then we took the opportunity to listen in, to sit with individual children and listen to them read, or to read aloud to a group of children who had a book but no available parent to read to them.

Children brought blank cassettes to record their reading. About once every four weeks or so, each child read aloud for about five minutes to one of us while we listened and tape-recorded. This provided us with an audio record of their reading, which we used when doing assessment and evaluation. A popular activity for many of the children was listening to their own cassettes of themselves reading. A concrete record of their progress, these cassettes could be sent home for parents to listen to.

Once the program was well under way, usually in January, we implemented accountability. Children began to maintain a written record of what they had been reading. This enabled us to keep track of their choices in terms of both complexity and diversity. Many parents chose to help their children document their daily reading in these logs. This provided parents with another opportunity to observe and engage with their children in a purposeful writing activity. We also introduced Reading Response journals, first modelling with the whole class after reading a story together, and then requiring them, particularly the older children, perhaps once a week, to do their own reader's response based on what they were reading.

Inviting care-givers to share reading accomplishes a number of goals that are central to early literacy and social development. Children are offered the chance to read with their parents and friends; to make selective choices about what they read; to

continued

make collaborative decisions with their parents and partners about what they will read together; to revisit familiar stories or to challenge themselves with more difficult or unfamiliar material in the midst of comfortable and supportive relationships. Parent shared reading also endorses the importance of reading as a social endeavour by affording collaborative participation in a positive and purposeful context.

Parent shared reading enables parents to participate meaningfully in their child's classroom. They are not just sitting at the back of the class doing cut-and-paste for the teacher. They are actively engaged in helping their children learn to read. Secondly, parents provide invaluable role models of adults who love to read, thereby reinforcing the highly important message that teachers want to convey—that reading is not just an assignment. It is a well-loved activity that enables us to travel to worlds that we might otherwise never know and to gather knowledge that we might otherwise never attain.

There are also many tangible benefits of parent shared reading for teachers. The fact that many children are engaged with other significant adults gives the teachers the opportunity to observe the choices children are making about what they read and whom they read with. Further, it enables the teacher to spend time with individual students, listening to them read, reading aloud and discussing the text with them, connecting with them on a personal level. Teachers can also observe individual students and make notes, or observe the group at large, taking time to note the dynamics between particular individuals.

Inviting parents into the primary classroom to read with their children is a genuine literacy experience that enriches all the participants. Children gain the opportunity to read and learn alongside their parents in the classroom. Parents are given a meaningful opportunity to be actively involved with their children in what is probably the most important achievement that children accomplish in their primary years—learning to read!

The type of program described in this vignette clearly takes considerable time and effort to plan. There are more people to organize than when the classroom door is kept firmly closed. The teacher needs to organize a wide range of reading materials that are an integral part of the reading program and keep records on what children are reading. With additional people in the classroom, organization of space becomes more of a challenge. However, as Joyce Bodell points out, bringing the community into the language arts classroom offers many benefits to both parents and children.

There is no one magic way to organize children so that all their needs are met all the time. However, by providing daily opportunities for them to work together in the whole class, in groups, and individually, most of the children's needs are being met most of the time. The key to effective classroom organization is flexibility in the types of groups formed, the length of time they exist, and the range of children in groups. The challenge of organizing an effective language arts program becomes even more daunting when the learning needs of all children are taken into account. The remainder of this chapter will focus on the wide range of children in today's classrooms.

Meeting the Needs of All Children

Children come to school with very different language and literacy backgrounds. Some come from a cultural background different from that of mainstream society and others live in poverty. Many of these children begin school with oral language and literacy backgrounds that are very different from those of other children, or with very limited experience with written language. An increasing number of children begin school in Canada with no or limited proficiency in the English language. Other children may live in print-rich homes but, because of a wide variety of learning problems, have difficulty learning to read and write.

In the past two decades there have been marked changes in how students with disabilities are viewed and educated in North America. For many years, segregated classes and schools were the most prevalent and preferred system for educating these students. Children were labelled according to conditions, e.g., mental, physical, emotional, and learning deficits, and placement was based on this categorization. Some children with severe disabilities were denied education in publicly funded schools. However, in the mid-1970s, legislation was passed in the United States protecting the rights of individuals with disabilities and there has been considerable movement away from segregated classes toward educating children in the "least restrictive environment" (Wilson and Cleland, 1985, 331).

The impact of this legislation has been felt in Canada, resulting in several provinces passing laws that require school boards to provide education for all students (Bachor and Crealock, 1986). There has also been a strong trend in Canadian classrooms away from segregation to **mainstreaming** of special needs children. Mainstreaming means integrating students with special needs into regular classrooms. For students with mild disabilities this generally involves integration into the regular class. Students with more severe disabilities are integrated into regular classes whenever possible, but many still receive at least part of their education in segregated classes, and specialists are often involved in helping to plan and implement their programs.

Many benefits of mainstreaming have been proposed for special needs children including increased independence, acceptance from others, and more positive self-concept. The other children also benefit by increasing their awareness of individual differences, developing positive attitudes to people with handicaps and coming to respect what they can learn from these students. However, as Bachor and Crealock (1986) indicate, these benefits will not be attained if special needs children are simply dumped into regular classrooms with no support for either the teacher or students. Unless there is sufficient preparation for integration of special needs children, both teachers and students may develop negative rather than positive attitudes. Support services and resources are needed to help teachers handle the increased workload involved in teaching a wider range of children.

The majority of special needs students in schools are those with mild disabilities, those from different cultural backgrounds, and those learning English as a second language. Children with visual impairments, hearing impairments, and severe mental disabilities make up the minority of special needs students. When they are placed in regular classrooms, it is recommended that teachers collaborate with specialists in order to develop appropriate language learning programs.

Although putting special needs children in separate classrooms is highly questionable, this approach is still used across the country for children with severe disabilities for both administrative and program purposes. Hence, this section will focus on students with less severe disabilities, while recognizing that definitions are unclear and groups overlap and labels tell us little about how to teach children.

Cultural Differences

As indicated in Chapter 1, there is considerable evidence that literacy is related to sociocultural variables. Literacy levels are lower among the poor than rich, among rural than urban populations, and among minorities.

Jacobs and Jordan (1993) outline several explanations that account for the relative lack of success of these children in our schools. Most of these explanations place the responsibility for low school achievement on the cultural groups themselves. Now widely discredited, one of these explanations states that social class and IQ are largely the result of genetic differences.

The most widely held view sees environment rather than genetics as the cause. The child's home and community don't provide the experiences, attitudes, and values needed to succeed in school. As a result, it is believed that children arrive at school with deficient language and cognitive development. A major criticism of this view is the inappropriateness of evaluating poor people from a middle-class perspective, rather than attempting to understand them from their own perspective. This view also ignores the heterogeneity that exists among poor people in race, language, and culture.

Another explanation shifts the focus of responsibility from minority groups to schools and society. Schools are seen as reproducing hierarchical social relations in the economy and streaming groups into different economic slots. In this theory, schools contribute to inequality by valuing the cultural capital (ways of talking, acting, socializing) of the mainstream while devaluing that of other children. A variation of this view is that, as non-mainstream children grow older, they recognize inequalities within the school and society and start to rebel against them.

Along with Heath (1983), we believe that differences between minority and majority cultures in interactions, language, and cognitive styles lead to conflicts between the school and minority children. The cultures of minority groups are not deficient; rather they are different, and we need to take these differences into account when adapting language arts instruction for these children.

Children from different cultural groups may experience discontinuity when they enter school because of differences in how literacy is viewed and used in their communities, compared with how it is treated at school. It is crucial that we acknowledge and respect the literacy and language background these children bring to school. In order to do this, we need to become familiar with the cultural backgrounds of the children in our classrooms and incorporate this into language learning activities whenever possible.

Cultural groups often differ in patterns of verbal interactions. Both their stories and questions are different. Students from a cultural minority might tell or write different stories from those of the rest of the children. Similarly, these children may not respond to labelling types of questions during story reading time but are more successful when teachers adapt their questions to more accurately reflect the questions the children have experienced in their homes. As Heath (1983) found in her study, when teachers made these adjustments, children not only began to participate more in the classroom but they learned to respond to other types of questions as well. It is also important that literature brought into the classroom reflects the range of cultural backgrounds there.

As with all children, teachers need to expect those from diverse cultural backgrounds to be successful in the classroom. By focusing on the special attributes and talents of each individual, differences can be seen in a positive rather than negative light.

Limited English-Language Facility

Canada's immigration policy is currently producing a steady flow of non–English-speaking immigrants into the country, increasing the likelihood that at some time most teachers will have children with limited English language proficiency in their classrooms. For all ESL children, the goal of instruction is twofold: to help them learn English and to help them move ahead cognitively (Allen, 1991). Our task as teachers is to create a learning environment to achieve these two goals.

Perhaps most crucial is that children be immersed in meaningful language experiences rather than rote drill exercises. The reading materials used in the classroom should be written with natural language patterns rather than being contrived and having limited vocabulary. It is particularly important that teachers ensure that children with limited English proficiency receive language arts instruction they can understand. This can be facilitated by using visual aids such as pictures and filmstrips, as well as gestures and facial expressions to clarify meaning. It is unclear whether speaking more slowly or pausing between sentences, clauses, and phrases assists low-proficiency English speakers (Derwing, 1990). However, it does seem that building in comprehension checks and responding to requests for clarification aids comprehension (Pica, Young, and Doughty, 1987). In addition, providing language instruction in a meaningful context, e.g., a learning centre set up as a store, can provide strong support for meaningful learning by both children with limited English proficiency and others.

Children with limited English proficiency need lots of opportunities to work together in pairs and small groups with their English-speaking peers on meaningful tasks that involve purposeful talk. Listening and talking in authentic communication aids comprehension.

Shared reading provides a rich context for the literacy learning of children with limited English proficiency. Big books are ideal to use with these children because of the support given by pictures. It is important to point to pictures during discussion of the story to help children link meaning to words being used in the story. Picture story books, listed in Chapter 3, also provide a rich resource for helping children develop both language and literacy knowledge. By watching the teacher run his or her finger under the printed words during reading, children who have been exposed to quite different writing systems, e.g., Mandarin, Hebrew, develop an understanding about the directional characteristics of the English language.

Learning Disabilities

It's important to realize that the notion of learning disabilities is socially constructed. We determine what is normal and hence, abnormal; we define the child as the problem. This is a crucial point because many people believe that these labels somehow define objective reality. Perhaps one of the reasons this view is so widespread is because it has been around for such a long time.

In the late 1800s, James Hinshelwood began to study and write about congenital word-blindness. He hypothesized that the source of the problem lay in children's brains, and this view persists to this day, in spite of evidence to the contrary (Coles, 1987). In the 1920s Orton replaced the term congenital word-blindness with strephosymbolia (mixed symbols) and this term was, in turn, replaced by dyslexia. In the 1960s the term "learning disabilities" began to be used widely and this continues to be the term educators use today. The term "dyslexia" is used primarily by medical practitioners. Both terms, however, reflect the medical model; a problem is labelled to indicate what is wrong with the individual and then appropriate treatment can be prescribed. Indeed, in medicine, treatment follows logically once the doctor makes a diagnosis. If individuals have a bacterial infection, a doctor prescribes antibiotics and they get better. This is not the case for children who have difficulty learning to read. Knowing that a child has dyslexia does not lead directly to treatment, but it does have some other results.

For the child and the child's parents, using the terms dyslexia and learning disability is both a help and a hindrance. On the one hand, it helps parents feel that they did not do anything wrong in raising their children and gives them a sense that they finally have an answer to the frustrating question of why their child is having difficulty learning to read. It also removes other more derogatory labels such as dumb, lazy, or bad. On the other hand, there are some negative consequences of labelling children as having dyslexia or learning disabilities, because these conditions are viewed as relatively permanent. People have to live with these labels for the rest of their lives, viewing themselves as defective learners in new situations. Hence, in the short term, the label may bring some relief, but in the long term it can be devastating for an individual.

Another problem involves the responsibility for the problem. The term dyslexia or learning disabilitiy implies that the problem is in the child, and hence, there is little need to even consider the effectiveness of the school program the child has been getting or the home context the child lives in. Since the problem is in the child's head, it is the child's head we need to change.

Instead of this relatively simplistic explanation, it appears that reading difficulties have multiple causes, including factors both within and outside of children. The combination of factors is somewhat different for each child who has difficulty learning to read. The effects of these factors also vary, from children who are word-callers (pronouncing words correctly but not constructing meaning) to children who have so much difficulty processing print that the meaning they construct reflects very little of the author's message. Other children have developed strategies for dealing with print but read so little that they have to direct most of their attention to word identification and hence, have little left for making meaning. The variations go on and on. Regardless of the nature of the child's problem, however, there is often a mismatch between the child's needs and the instructional program in the classroom. Most of these children are asked to read material that is far too difficult, whether because of inadequate strategies for processing cues in words or insufficient background knowledge of the concepts involved.

When diagnosing reading difficulties, Lipson and Wixson (1991) include an analysis of the teaching techniques and materials, and an examination of the match between them and the needs of the child. This is relatively unique in textbooks on reading difficulties; most focus exclusively on the child during the diagnostic phase and do not consider reading instruction as a possible source of the problem. This is not a finger-pointing or blaming exercise but rather a recognition that both the source and solution of the child's difficulties lie in the interaction between the child and the instructional context. What we need to strive for as teachers is a maximal match between the child's needs and our teaching.

Mild Mental Handicaps

It is estimated that approximately 2 to 5 percent of the population have a mild mental handicap (Bachor and Crealock, 1986). As with learning disabilities, mental handicap (formerly called mental retardation) is generally considered to reside in the individual. However, again, mental handicaps are affected by social factors. For example, the ranges on IQ tests constructed for this purpose vary: some say an IQ between 55 and 80 means a mental handicap, while others choose between 52 and 67. Other evidence of the social nature of mental handicaps is the fact that minority groups, children with behaviour problems, and males are overrepresented in this group. In addition, for most children with mild mental handicaps, no biological cause can be determined (Gillespie-Silver, 1979).

The major distinguishing feature of these learners is that they progress through the same stages of cognitive development as people of average intelligence, but at a slower rate (Gillespie-Silver, 1979; Bond, Tinker, Wasson, and Wasson, 1994). Similarly, language development in this group is slowed down but not qualitatively different. Hence, most of the teaching techniques suggested in later chapters of this book are just as appropriate for children with mild mental handicaps as for other children. The major difference is the rate at which instruction proceeds, with numerous opportunities for repetition and practice. However, as with all children, the goal is to determine each individual child's needs and to match instruction as closely as possible to these needs.

Chapter Summary

While no organizational structure is best for all language arts classrooms, several general principles provide a basis for program planning and organization. First, it is important that there be a balance in the amount of time and attention devoted to each area of language arts. Second, the organizational structure also needs to facilitate integrated learning across the curriculum. Third, children require both instruction to develop effective language strategies and practice to ensure that they incorporate the strategies into their language use. Fourth, it is important to provide children with a secure learning environment, where they are challenged but experience success. Finally, we need to organize classrooms so that children take control of their own learning, so that we work collaboratively with them rather than assuming authority over their language use.

There are four major variables teachers can control as they plan and organize language arts programs: materials, time, space, and children. Traditionally, basal reading series have provided the material for language arts programs throughout both the United States and Canada. More recently, there has been a movement to whole language programs. While whole language is a philosophy rather than a teaching approach or technique, programs based on it focus heavily on meaning, on children using language rather than learning about it, and on using children's literature rather than basal series. Publishing companies in Canada have attempted to retain their share of the market by producing basal series that reflect whole language principles. While some educators question whether it is possible to do this, these series are recommended by provincial departments of education across the country.

Whether or not teachers choose to use a basal series, it is important to make a wide range of materials available. These materials need to reflect both the range of interests and reading levels of the children. Many teachers select and organize materials according to themes, but the most important criterion to use when selecting any material, whether a book, magazine, videotape, or computer program, is the extent to which it is consistent with the philosophy of the language arts program and will contribute to children's language learning. Many people believe that computers will revolutionize the way we teach language arts. Computers are currently being used as tools, tutors, and tutees in classrooms. However, we need to ensure that use of computers does not widen the disparity between high-and-low income children or between females and males, and that computers contribute to democratic goals.

When making decisions about the organization of time, space, and children, teachers need to provide for whole class instruction, small group work, and independent practice. Whole class instruction is effective for helping children to set learning objectives, for teaching new strategies to all the children, for reading to the children, and for evaluating accomplishments. Allocating time for one or two large daily time blocks for language arts provides flexibility and facilitates integration.

Ability groups have traditionally dominated language arts classrooms, but more recently children work in interest, research, special needs, and paired groupings. Cooperative learning rather than individual competition is becoming increasingly common in elementary language arts classrooms. Learning centres are one way to encourage children to work in groups. It is also important that children have opportunities to read and write independently each day and that at least some of the time, they choose what they read and write about.

One of the biggest challenges we face as language arts teachers is to meet the needs of all of the children in our classrooms. Cultural, linguistic, social class, and learning differences among students need to be taken into account when planning and organizing language arts programs. The cultures of minority groups are viewed as different, not deficient. There are increasing numbers of children entering schools with English as their second language. It is important that these children understand what they see and hear, and that they be immersed in meaningful learning experiences. The labels "learning disabilities" and "mental handicaps" are both social constructions, and for both groups the teacher's main goal is to maximize the match between the child's needs and the classroom teaching.

Selected Professional Resources

Pike, K., Compain, R., and Mumper, J. (1994). *New Connections: An Integrated Approach to Literacy*. New York: HarperCollins Publishers.
This book provides theoretical information and practical applications for an integrated literacy program. Included are chapters on approaches to literacy instruction, organization, classroom management, thematic instruction, use of computers, and meeting the needs of all children.

Froese, V. (1990). *Whole Language: Practice and Theory*. Toronto: Prentice-Hall Canada.
Written from a Canadian perspective, this book provides information on how to structure, plan, and teach a whole language program.

Booth, D. (1994). *Classroom Voices: Language-based Learning in the Elementary School*. Toronto: Harcourt Brace & Company Canada.
The focus of this book is the language-based learning program in one Ontario school. The first two chapters are on planning and organizing programs. A special feature is the inclusion of numerous teachers' and children's stories throughout.

Children's Materials Noted in Chapter 2

Discis: Helping children read and learn. (1994). Buffalo, NY: Discis Knowledge Research Inc.
Kidworks 2. (1992). Torrance, CA: Davidson & Associates.
Impressions. (1984). Toronto: Holt, Rinehart & Winston of Canada.
The Puzzler. (1984). Pleasantville, NY: Sunburst Communications, Inc.
Wiggleworks: Scholastic beginning literacy system. (1994). New York: Scholastic Inc.
Waves. (1992). Toronto: Houghton Mifflin Canada Ltd.

CHAPTER 3

Children's Literature

A teacher librarian conducts a book talk with Grade 2 students.

OBJECTIVES

- to be able to locate appropriate materials for teaching in the elementary school
- to be aware of Canadian books, authors, and illustrators
- to note books for children produced by aboriginal Canadian authors and illustrators
- to understand the value of children's trade books in developing enthusiastic readers who turn to reading for pleasure

Reading and Children's Literature

Most people are exposed to books and oral storytelling from a very early age. It is one of the fundamental ways in which we learn about our culture, and become part of it. A great deal of what we learn comes from books, even before we are able to read. In *Each Peach Pear Plum*, by Janet and Allan Ahlberg (1978), the charming, gentle illustrations are rich in the nursery rhymes, folklore, legends, and fairy tales of western European culture. We see Cinderella, Mother Hubbard, and the Three Bears living together in "storyland," helping and taking care of each other.

In addition to what children learn about values, culture, and life, they also learn about handling and reading books, much of what Holdaway (1979) refers to as "literacy set." Children learn directionality—which way is the right way up for a book and which way the story moves. They learn that books are a pathway into pleasurable experiences. Books such as *Each Peach Pear Plum* show children that reading can be active.

Children also learn what reading *is* from **picture books**, and they learn how to read different kinds of books in different ways. Much of what children learn in these early experiences with books will help them in reading more complex books when they're older. It is a long journey from *Each Peach Pear Plum* to *The English Patient*, but the two books are related in many different ways, in terms of the role the reader must play. One of the features these books have in common is that good readers recognize, after reading only a page or two, that the books are worth interacting with, and persisting with. In *The English Patient* the nurse reads each night: "She entered the story knowing she would emerge from it feeling she had been immersed in the lives of others, in plots that stretched back twenty years, her body full of sentences and moments, as if awaking from sleep with a heaviness caused by unremembered dreams" (Ondaatje, 1992, 12). Most successful readers have a similar experience when they enter a good book, and it is this experience that can be developed and nurtured by early interaction with books both in and out of school.

In order to create meaning from *The English Patient*, the reader must piece together a number of different **narratives** embedded in the novel. Readers must fill in the gaps between these narratives, reading between the lines. Who is the English patient? What has happened to him? Who is the nurse? Why is she in an abandoned villa in Italy at the end of the Second World War? The reader must be aware of the clues that enable several coherent stories to emerge from Ondaatje's text (for there is surely more than one). In *Each Peach Pear Plum*, the reader similarly learns to watch for clues so that meaning can be created. The pictures have to be examined carefully, and the reader must watch for the links that enable a story to unfold.

Children's early experiences with books such as *Each Peach Pear Plum*, and the experiences they have reading in the upper elementary grades affect how they perceive themselves as readers, and whether or not they think reading is relevant, pleasurable, and worth the time and effort needed. When children learn from their teachers, and from reading good books in elementary school, that books *are* worth the time and effort required of a reader, they are more likely to become readers as adults. This requires that teachers also enjoy reading and invite children into the world of books with enthusiasm and excitement. The following quotation from Sarah Louise Arnold's book *Reading: How to Teach It* first appeared in 1889, long before awareness of sexist language developed, but it's still a powerful piece of prose.

> *Learning to read is an important part of the child's training, but learning* what *to read is quite as important. A child's mastery of the printed page may leave him with the key to that which is base and ignoble in literature, or it may open to him that which is noble and inspiring. His newly gotten power may unlock for him the dime novel or the* Iliad. *Whether he turns to the one or the other depends largely upon his early associations. It is determined especially by his early teaching. (cited in Smith, 1965, 117)*

Children who learn to appreciate good books are at an advantage in life, not only because literate and knowledgeable people acquire status and good jobs, but because they can relate to the culture they are part of, and they can appreciate their history and the place they hold in the scheme of things. Reading good books connects us with the rest of humanity, and lets us know that our feelings and experiences are not unique, but part of what makes us human.

Bringing Children and Books Together

Picture Storybooks for K to Grade 6

There is an important distinction to be made between teaching children how to read and teaching them to become readers. It is not a matter of teaching one *or* the other, but how

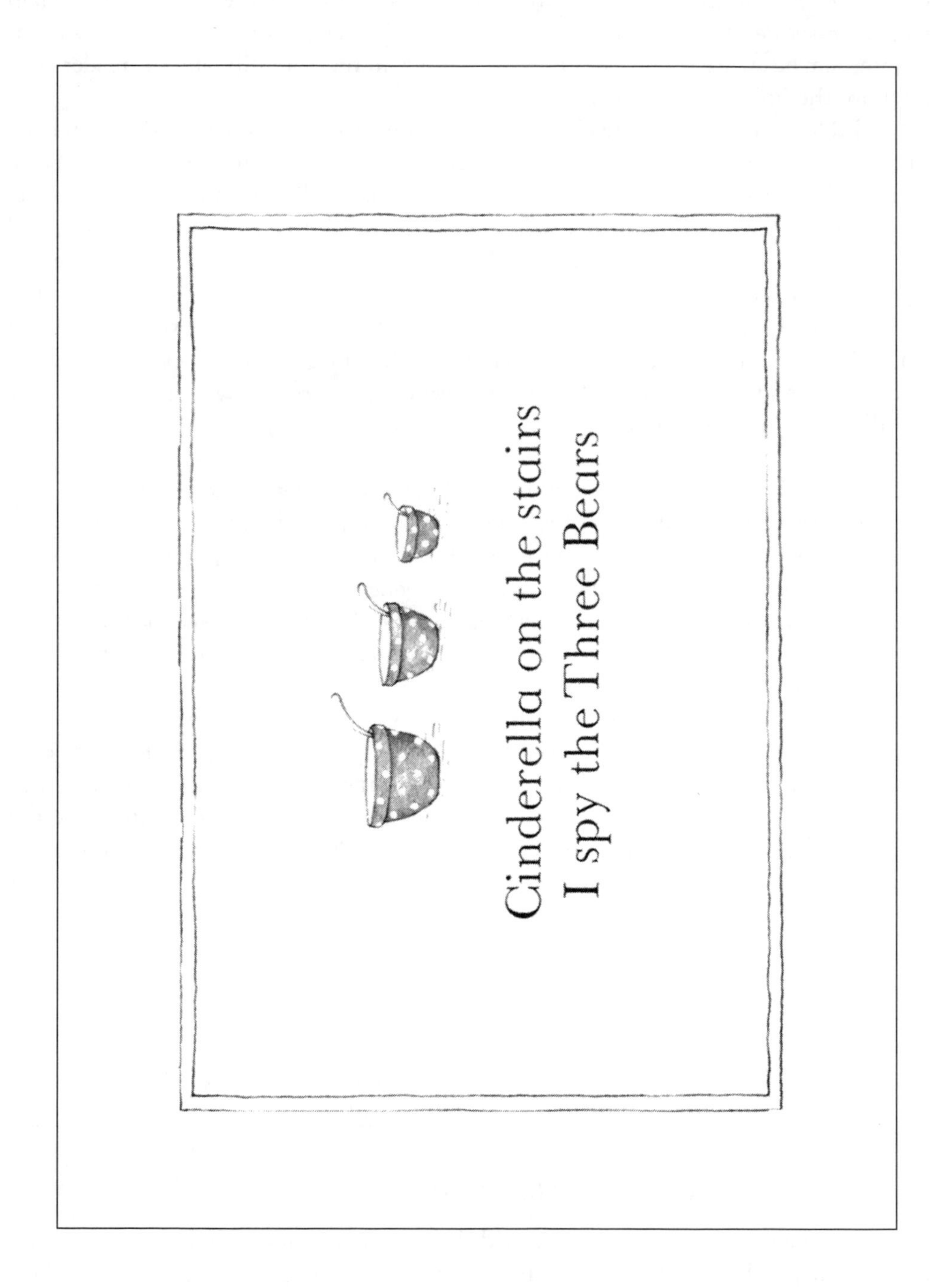
Cinderella on the stairs
I spy the Three Bears

From Each Peach Pear Plum *by Janet and Allan Ahlberg (1978).*

to effectively teach both at the same time. In the olden days, teaching reading was considered a skill-and-drill affair, with lots of worksheets and activities about reading (what James Britton referred to as "dummy runs"). There was much measurement of reading ability and concern about whether a child was reading at grade level. There was a certain emphasis on whether children could perform certain reading skills in isolation from real text.

Today, it is more difficult to determine the grade level of a specific text, since we more fully understand the complexity of texts, and how readers respond to them. We know that reading should be taught using real texts. However, it is not until we look in detail at books such as *Each Peach Pear Plum*, *Rosie's Walk* (Hutchins, 1969), and *Come Away from the Water, Shirley* (Burningham, 1977), that we fully understand the reading lessons children are receiving from these books. Meek (1988) refers to these as "private lessons"—the lessons good readers learn about reading without formal instruction. They are lessons young children frequently learn faster than their more blinkered adult companions, who have often become constrained by print and driven by plot. *Come Away from the Water, Shirley* tells one version of the story through the pictures (and Shirley's eyes) and another version through the text (and the parents' eyes).

When reading picture books initially, adults usually miss two major elements that young children will almost always attend to; adults do not look closely at the pictures, and they do not perceive that more than one story can happen in a book at the same time. Children are sophisticated readers of picture books mostly because they have not become constrained by print. A good picture book tells its story through pictures as well as text. *Rosie's Walk* contains one sentence, thirty-two words, and twenty-seven pages of pictures, but it is a story that, if told in words alone, would take many paragraphs, and lose much of its allure. *Rosie's Walk* contains at least two tales; Rosie's and that of the fox, who is not even mentioned in the text. The lesson, which applies to *The English Patient* and many other adult books, is an important one; there is more than one story in any book, there is more in any book than is written on the page. One fifteen-year-old, when reading *Rosie's Walk*, got to the page depicting the flour mill before she realized there was a fox in the story! She had paid attention *only* to the text. An eighteen-year-old stopped reading the book on the fourth page and said out loud, "Oh, I get it now!" Young readers "get it" because they look for multiple cues, not only text.

These young readers are engaging in completely different reading experiences than previous generations of children because they have more challenging, interactional, and better-written texts. These children are more likely to grow up with different expectations of reading than children in the past, and they are also likely to have different reading skills. Hopefully, more of these children will be able to enjoy such novels as *The English Patient* when they grow up, and will continue to read for pleasure as well as information.

Picture books are not just for pre-readers and beginning readers, just as wordless books like *Sunshine* (1981) and *Moonlight* (1982) by Jan Ormerod are not only for children who cannot yet read. *The Tunnel* (Browne, 1989) is a book written and illustrated for children in the upper elementary grades. Like *Each Peach Pear Plum* in its **intertextual** references to *Red Riding Hood* and many other fairy tales, it requires many readings to unravel its **polysemic** text and illustrations. The reader has to fill in many gaps between text and picture. These gaps are the parts that actively engage readers and call on all of their interpretive and inferential skills (which Eco refers to as "inferential walks" [1978]). But this type of reading distinguishes the good reader from the merely competent. Many adults struggle when reading *The Tunnel* because Browne alludes to the more disturbing aspects of growing up, and readers plug in their own experiences and respond at deeply personal levels. Other readers encounter difficulty in following the story and feel that Browne omits too much, leaves too many gaps. These readers want the story laid out for them more explicitly, so that they receive a more direct message from the author, and have to do less work themselves.

This highly inferential and personal aspect of reading is one that many publishers, and some writers, still do not fully understand. Take, for example, the rewritten version of *Peter Rabbit,* published by Ladybird Books in 1987. This is the original Beatrix Potter (1902, 9–10) opening to the story:

> *Once upon a time there were four little Rabbits, and their names were*
> *Flopsy,*
> *Mopsy,*
> *Cotton-tail*
> *and Peter.*
> *They lived with their mother in a sand-bank, underneath the root of a very big fir-tree.*
>
> *"Now, my dears," said Old Mrs Rabbit one morning, "you may go into the fields or down the lane, but don't go into Mr. McGregor's garden: your father had an accident there; he was put in a pie by Mrs McGregor."*

Here is the revised version:

> *Once upon a time there were four little rabbits. Their names were Flopsy, Mopsy, Cotton-tail and Peter. They lived in a burrow under the root of a big tree. One day they were allowed to play outside. "Stay near home," said their mother. "Please don't go to Mr McGregor's garden."*
>
> *"Why not?" asked Peter.*
>
> *"Because he doesn't like rabbits," answered Mrs Rabbit. "He will try to catch you."*

As can immediately be seen, the poetry is gone and the introduction has lost much of its appeal. It is, perhaps, no longer a book that experienced readers would bother to read. Readers do not need to have everything spelled out for them just because they are young. Adult readers, who share these books with children, enjoy the black humour in the death joke (and it makes sense to children since that *can* happen to rabbits). Mother Rabbit (now no longer old) tells the young rabbits they may play outside. Where else would young rabbits play? The explicit message in the original text about the fate of adventurous rabbits is replaced with the veiled threat that today's children are all too familiar with (don't talk to strangers).

Ladybird Books felt that the story needed updating to be relevant to the lives of children in the 1990s, and that the language of the original was inappropriate for current readers. However, neither the teachers nor parents we know have encountered any difficulty with the original language or story. They do, however, seem to have little interest in the rather didactic revised version.

Picture books teach important concepts about reading that can only come from working with real texts, and they are important in forming the attitudes of young children toward books in general. A wealth of excellent picture books is available for children in the elementary grades today—books containing artistry, excellent writing, and vivid imagery. It is no accident that many of them were orginally published in Great Britain or Australia before being published in North America. In those countries, children's literature and writing for child audiences have long been respected and encouraged. Those countries nurture a tradition of treasuring books for children and their writers pay enormous respect to the abilities of young readers. Publishing houses there have been leaders in publishing children's books that present new challenges to their readers and respect them.

Exhibit 3.1 lists some picture books appropriate for children in the elementary grades, and Exhibit 3.2 lists picture books that are specifically Canadian. Exhibit 3.3 lists wordless books appropriate for children from preschool to Grade 3. A list of picture books suitable for older readers is in Exhibit 3.4. Children in preschool and kindergarten will enjoy sitting alone or in small groups looking at many of these books. In kindergarten and Grades 1 and 2, it is appropriate for a teacher to share these books with the class, especially if a big-book version is available, providing that all the children can see the pictures. It is also important for teachers to take a close look at the pictures beforehand (part of the preparation required), for children will often focus on the pictures and ask many questions about them. The observations children make and the questions they ask must be acknowledged as part of their response to the book and a teacher must be ready to discuss them. Some older readers may at first feel offended that they are being asked to read a picture book, but our evidence indicates that once older children have read the first few pages, they will be hooked into the story.

EXHIBIT 3.1

Picture Books

Ahlberg, J. and A. (1986). *The Jolly Postman*. London: Heinemann. (U.K.)
Briggs, R. (1975). *Father Christmas Goes on Holiday*. Harmondsworth, U.K.: Puffin Books. (U.K.)
Brown, R. (1985). *The Big Sneeze*. London: Beaver Books. (U.K.)
Browne, A. (1983). *Gorilla*. London: Julia MacRae Books. (U.K.)
Burningham, J. (1977). *Come Away From the Water, Shirley*. New York: Harper. (U.K.)
Carle, E. (1974). *The Very Hungry Caterpillar*. Harmondsworth, U.K.: Puffin Books. (U.S.A.)
de Paola, T. (1978). *Nana Upstairs, Nana Downstairs*. New York: Penguin. (U.S.A.)
Emberley, B. & E. (1967). *Drummer Hoff*. New York: Simon and Schuster Inc. (U.S.A.)
Fox, M. (1983). *Possum Magic*. New York: Harcourt Brace Jovanovich. (Australia)
Graham, B. (1992). *Rose Meets Mr. Wintergarten*. London: Walker Books. (Australia)
Keats, E. J. (1969). *Goggles*. New York: Macmillan. (U.S.A.)
Kent, J. (1971). *The Fat Cat*. Harmondsworth, U.K.: Puffin Books. (U.K.)
Mayne, W. (1981). *The Patchwork Cat*. London: Jonathan Cape. (U.K.)
McKee, D. (1980). *Not Now, Bernard*. London: Anderson Press. (U.K.)
Ross, T. (1993). *The Three Pigs*. London: Arrow Books. (U.K.)
Van Allsburg, C. (1985). *The Polar Express*. New York: Houghton Mifflin. (U.S.A.)
Vaughan, M., and P. Lofts. (1984). *Wombat Stew*. Sydney: Ashton Scholastic Pty. Ltd. (Australia)
Wagner, J. (1978). *John Brown, Rose and the Midnight Cat*. New York: Bradbury. (Australia)
Yolen, J. (1987). *Owl Moon*. New York: Philomel Books. (U.S.A.)

EXHIBIT 3.2

Canadian Picture Books

Bourgeois, P. (1986). *Franklin in the Dark*. Toronto: Kids Can Press.
Chase, E. (1984). *The New Baby Calf*. Richmond Hill:, Ont.: North Winds Press.
Cumming, P. (1993). *Out on the Ice in the Middle of the Bay*. Toronto: Annick Press.
Gilman, P. (1985). *Jillian Jiggs*. Richmond Hill, Ont.: North Winds Press.
Gilman, P. (1992). *Something from Nothing*. Richmond Hill, Ont.: North Winds Press.
Lawson. J. (1992). *The Dragon's Pearl*. Toronto: Oxford University Press.
Little, J., and M. De Vries. (1991). *Once Upon a Golden Apple*. Markham, Ont.: Viking.
Lunn, J. (1988). *Amos's Sweater*. Toronto: Groundwood Books.
McFarlane, S. (1991). *Waiting for the Whales*. Victoria, B.C.: Orca Book Publishers.

Mollel, T. (1991). *Rhinos for Lunch and Elephants for Supper*. Toronto: Oxford University Press.
Muir, S. & M. (1987). *Albert's Old Shoes*. Richmond Hill, Ont.: North Winds Press.
Munsch, R. (1980). *The Paperbag Princess*. Toronto: Annick Press
Munsch, R. (1985). *Thomas's Snowsuit*. Toronto: Annick Press.
Munsch, R. (1985). *Mortimer*. Toronto: Annick Press.
Ryan-Lush, G. (1994). *Hairs on Bears*. Toronto: Annick Press.
Vaage, C. (1995). *Bibi and the Bull*. Edmonton: Dragon Hill.
Wallace, I. (1984). *Chin Chiang and the Dragon's Dance*. Toronto: Groundwood Books.
Wynne-Jones, T., and K. Nutt. (1985). *Zoom Away*. Toronto: Groundwood Books.
Wynne-Jones, T. (1993). *Mouse in the Manger*. Toronto: Viking.

EXHIBIT 3.3

Wordless Books

Anno, M. (1970). *Topsy-Turvies*. New York: Walker/Weatherhill. (U.S.A.)
Aruego, J. (1971). *Look What I Can Do*. New York: Scribner. (U.S.A.)
de Paola, T. (1978). *Pancakes for Breakfast*. New York: Harcourt Brace Jovanovich (U.S.A.)
Goodall, J. (1988). *Little Red Riding Hood*. New York: M.K. McElderry Books. (U.S.A.)
Hutchins, P. (1971). *Changes, Changes*. New York: Macmillan. (U.K.)
Keats, E. J. (1974). *Kitten for a Day*. New York: Four Winds Press. (U.S.A.)
Mayer, M. (1974). *Frog Goes to Dinner*. New York: Dial Press. (U.S.A.)
Mayer, M. (1976). *Hiccup*. New York: Dial Press. (U.S.A.)
McCully, E. (1984). *Picnic*. New York: Harper & Row. (U.S.A.)
McCully, E. (1987). *School*. New York: Harper & Row. (U.S.A.)
Ormerod, J. (1981). *Sunshine*. Harmondsworth, U.K.: Puffin Books. (Australia)
Ormerod, J. (1982). *Moonlight*. Harmondsworth, U.K.: Puffin Books. (Australia)

Grade 6 children respond very powerfully to books such as *The Tunnel* (Browne, 1989) and *Gorilla* (Browne, 1983). One Grade 6 class we know spent most of a noon-hour looking at the pictures in *The Tunnel*, picking out the hidden characters and references to fairy tales. More on children's responses to *Gorilla* will be found in Chapter 10.

Beginning Novels for the Middle Grades

As children become more familiar with books and story structure, and as their reading abilities become more sophisticated, they move from using pictures as a primary means of creating meaning to an increased emphasis on text. Many excellent novels are available for young readers, books that children in Grades 2 and 3 often call chapter books.

EXHIBIT 3.4

Picture Books for Grades 4 to 8

Abells, C. (1986). *The Children We Remember*. New York: Greenwillow. (U.S.A.)
Anno, M. (1980). *Anno's Medieval World*. New York: Philomel. (U.S.A.)
Barbalet, M., and J. Tanner. (1992). *The Wolf*. Toronto: Doubleday. (Canada)
Baylor, B. (1986). *I'm in Charge of Celebrations*. New York: Charles Scribner's Sons. (U.S.A.)
Blake, W. (1993). *The Tyger*. New York: Harcourt Brace Jovanovich. (U.S.A.)
Bouchard, D., and R.H. Vickers. (1990). *The Elders Are Watching*. Tofino, B.C.: Eagle Dancer Enterprises Ltd. (Canada)
Briggs, R. (1982). *When the Wind Blows*. New York: Schoken. (U.K.)
Browne, A. (1984). *Willy the Wimp*. New York: Knopf. (U.K.)
Browne, A. (1989). *The Tunnel*. London: Julia MacRae Books. (U.K.)
Davidge, B., and I. Wallace. (1993). *The Mummer's Song*. Toronto: Groundwood Books. (Canada)
Goble, P. (1984). *Buffalo Woman*. New York: Aladdin, Macmillan. (U.S.A.)
Hall, D. (1984). *The Man Who Lived Alone*. Boston: David Godine. (U.S.A.)
Hutchins, P. (1980). *The Tale of Thomas Mead*. London: Macmillan. (U.K.)
Innocenti, R. (1985). *Rose Blanche*. Mankato, MN: Creative Education. (U.S.A.)
Macauley, D. (1979). *Motel of the Mysteries*. Boston: Houghton Mifflin. (U.S.A.)
Macauley, D. (1985). *Baaa*. Boston: Houghton Mifflin. (U.S.A.)
Noble, T. (1987). *Meanwhile Back at the Ranch*. New York: Dial. (U.S.A.)
Noyes, A. (1981). *The Highwayman*. London: Oxford University Press.
Oberman, S. (1994). *The Always Prayer Shawl*. Honesdale, PA.: Boyds Mills Press. (U.S.A.).
Rylant, C. (1986). *Night in the Country*. New York: Bradbury Press. (U.S.A.).
Sendak, M. (1981). *Outside Over There*. Harmondsworth, U.K.: Puffin Books. (U.S.A.).
Thomas, D., and T.S. Hyman (illus.). (1985). *A Child's Christmas in Wales*. New York: Holiday House. (U.K.)
Turner, A. (1985). *Dakota Dugout*. New York: Macmillan. (U.S.A.)
Van Allsburg, C. (1984). *The Mysteries of Harris Burdick*. Boston: Houghton Mifflin. (U.S.A.)
Yee, P. (1991). *Roses Sing on New Snow*. Toronto: Groundwood Books. (Canada)
Yorinks, A. (1986). *Hey, Al!* New York: Farrar. (U.S.A.)
Zhang, S. N. (1993). *A Little Tiger in the Chinese Night*. Montreal: Tundra Books. (Canada)

They fall into all the major **genres** or types of fiction. Picture books are a genre of literature, and include subclasses of counting books, ABC books, concept books, storybooks, and others. **Traditional stories** are yet another genre of literature, with subclasses of fairy tales, folk tales, legends, myths, and fables. They are mostly short stories, many of them picture books. Traditional literature was originally passed from generation to generation orally, and it was not until the seventeenth century that much of it was finally written down. Even now these stories continue to change as authors develop sensitivity to their audience, and to current notions of what is appropriate content for children. Many stories have been recently rewritten and illustrated by such author-illustrators as Jan Brett (see *Goldilocks and The Three Bears*, 1987).

Novels for children in the upper elementary grades fall into the genres of contemporary **realistic fiction**, mystery stories, **historical fiction**, **time-slip fantasy**, **high fantasy**, and **science fiction**. Many books are a combination of genres. For example, *Goldilocks and The Three Bears* (Brett, 1987) is both picture book and fairy tale, while *Tuck Everlasting* (Babbitt, 1975) combines fantasy and folk tale. These combinations of genres seem to constitute many of the early novels read by children in Grades 2 to 4. *Jacob Two-Two Meets the Hooded Fang* (Richler, 1975) is a combination of fantasy and realistic writing, and is frequently one of the first chapter books children encounter, other than novels such as *Charlotte's Web* (White, 1952), which is usually read to children. A selection of novels suitable for middle grade readers is in Exhibit 3.5.

Once children have begun the move from picture book to novel, their selection of books will be determined largely by the encouragement of the teacher, their peers, and their own interests. One of the teacher's roles is to make good book suggestions to children, based on their interests and reading ability. This is important because a novel requires a greater investment of time and effort than a picture storybook, and children need to know that a book they select has the potential to engage them as well as be readable. Readability is not dependent upon the complexity of language alone, but has much to do with the structure of the book, and what experience the reader is required to bring to it. Research shows that strong interest can transcend a reader's abilities (Hunt, 1970). Research also shows that it is vitally important that teachers read the books their students are reading, so they can discuss the books with them (Pantaleo, 1994). Such teachers will likely do a better job of encouraging children both to select, read, and enjoy books.

A Grade 3 student selects a library book.

The Importance of Canadian Literature for Children

Over the years, Canadians have become accustomed to receiving media largely from the U.S.A. and Britain. Children's print materials are no exception. In the 1980s this trend shifted as Canadian publishing companies produced Canadian basal reading series and increased their publication of trade books for children and young adults. It has been difficult for many Canadian authors to break into the market, but many have been successful, resulting in many excellent

EXHIBIT 3.5

Selected Canadian Literature for Grades 4 to 7

Bedard, M. (1990). *Redwork*. Toronto: Lester & Orpen Denys.
Bedard, M. (1994). *Painted Devil*. Toronto: Lester Publishing.
Bly, D. (1993). *The McIntyre Liar*. Edmonton: Tree Frog Press.
Brouwer, S. (1993). *The Accidental Detectives: Shortcuts*. Wheaton, IL: Victor Books.
Buffie, M. (1987). *Who is Frances Rain?* Toronto: Kids Can Press Ltd.
Burnford, S. (1963). *The Incredible Journey*. Toronto: Little, Brown and Co.
Calvert, P. (1993). *Picking up the Pieces*. Toronto: Maxwell Macmillan Canada.
Doyle, B. (1982). *Up to Low*. Toronto: Groundwood Books.
Eyvindson, P. (1987). *The Wish Wind*. Winnipeg: Pemmican Publications.
Godfrey, M. (1987). *It Seemed Like a Good Idea at the Time*. Edmonton, Alta.: Tree Frog Press.
Godfrey, M. (1988). *Send in Miss Teeny Wonderful*. Richmond Hill, Ont.: Scholastic TAB Publications.
Houston, J. (1979). *River Runners*. Toronto: McClelland and Stewart.
Hudson, J. (1984). *Sweetgrass*. Edmonton: Tree Frog Press.
Hughes, M. (1982). *Hunter in the Dark*. Toronto: Clarke, Irwin.
Little, J. (1984). *Mama's Going to Buy You a Mockingbird*. Toronto: Penguin Books.
MacKay, C. (1979). *Exit Barney McGee*. Richmond Hill, Ont.: Scholastic.
Mowat, F. (1956). *Lost in the Barrens*. Toronto: Little, Brown and Co.
Pearson, K. (1987). *A Handful of Time*. Markham: Viking Kestrel.
Reynolds, S. (1991). *Strandia*. Toronto: HarperCollins.
Smucker, B. (1979). *Days of Terror*. Toronto: Clarke, Irwin.
Smucker, B. (1989). *Jacob's Little Giant*. Toronto: Puffin Books.
Taylor, C. (1985). *Julie*. Saskatoon: Western Producer Prairie Books.
Truss, J. (1982). *Jasmin*. Toronto: Groundwood Books.
Weiler, D. (1993). *RanVan the Defender*. Toronto: Groundwood Books.
Wynne-Jones, T. (1993). *Some of the Kinder Planets*. Toronto: Groundwood Books.

Canadian books for children. The Canadian Children's Book Centre in Toronto publishes lists of books, information about authors, and a newsletter called *Children's Book News*. Exhibit 3.6 is a list of Canadian fiction for children in Grades 4 to 7.

Why is it important to have Canadian materials in Canadian schools? If children are to know themselves and the country in which they live, they must be able to read about it, in fiction as well as nonfiction. Through reading stories that take place in other regions of the country, children become familiar with that part of the country and can identify with it. Likewise, through reading stories that take place in foreign countries,

EXHIBIT 3.6

Beginning Novels Gr4-7

Catling, P. S. (1952). *The Chocolate Touch*. New York: Morrow. (U.S.A.)
Dahl, R. (1970). *Fantastic Mr. Fox*. New York: Knopf. (U.K.)
Fleischman, S. (1986). *The Whipping Boy*. New York: Greenwillow. (U.S.A.)
Little, J. (1985). *Lost and Found*. Markham: Viking Kestrel. (Canada)
MacLachlan, P. (1985). *Sarah Plain and Tall*. New York: Harper and Row. (U.S.A.)
Gardiner, J. R. (1980). *The Stone Fox*. New York: Crowell. (U.S.A.)
Roy, R. (1982). *Where's Buddy?* New York: Clarion Books. (U.S.A.)
Richler, M. (1975). *Jacob Two-Two Meets the Hooded Fang*. New York: Bantam Books. (Canada)
Roberts, K. (1988). *Hiccup Champion of the World*. Vancouver: Douglas and McIntyre. (Canada)
Smith, D. (1973). *A Taste of Blackberries*. New York: Crowell. (U.S.A.)
Steele, M. (1993). *Featherbys*. Victoria: Hyland House Publishing Pty. Ltd. (Australia)

those countries become less foreign to the reader. *Playing Beatie Bow* (Park, 1980) is a novel that takes the reader into the Australia of the past as well as the present.

Canadian children have, in the past, had little they could identify with. It is sometimes difficult for them to make sense of the cultural and language differences in books written in Britain, for example. Small differences in vocabulary can distract a developing reader from the meaning of the text.

On the other hand, children feel good reading a story written in language familiar to them and one that takes place in Edmonton, Toronto, Halifax, Saskatoon, or Vancouver. These are places Canadian children have heard of and possibly visited. Children can imagine the prairie, mountains, or seacoast, and they learn that stories can take place anywhere, not only in exotic settings. They also learn that Canadian people can become writers, and that these authors live in places the students might live in or visit. Authors become "real" and writing becomes a possible profession. Well-known authors are able to visit schools, and demonstrate some of their hard work and the craft of writing as they speak and read their published work. There are organizations across Canada, such as the Young Alberta Book Society, that exist for the sole purpose of enhancing literacy development and introducing Canadian authors and illustrators to children in schools.

In addition to fiction, it is also helpful to have good nonfiction books about Canada written and published by Canadians. *Buried in Ice* (Beatty and Geiger, 1992), for example, is a book about the Franklin expedition that most children find intriguing, for it tells a fascinating story, explores Canadian history, and displays what our scientists and journalists do at their work. This story received international attention and it allowed Canadians to take pride in their accomplishments and identify with their heritage.

It is important to note the many excellent aboriginal Canadian authors and illustrators creating material for children. The work of C.J. Taylor, a Montreal writer, has become particularly popular, along with the work of Michael Arvaarluk Kusugak, Thomas King, and Jordan Wheeler. A selection of books by aboriginal Canadian authors and illustrators is included in Exhibit 3.7.

Throughout this chapter Canadian materials have been cited, wherever possible, and specific lists of Canadian materials have been prepared. These lists should be helpful to beginning teachers as they develop their own collections of Canadian literature.

Novels in the Upper Elementary Grades

Many children begin reading novels with contemporary realistic fiction, perhaps because it is one of the ways they can come to know the world, and explore issues they have little personal experience about. This genre continues to be the most widely read in the upper elementary grades. Books such as Betsy Byars's *Summer of the Swans* (1970), and Katherine Paterson's *The Great Gilly Hopkins* (1978) are excellent examples of this genre. *Hatchet* by Gary Paulsen (1987), *Pilot Down, Presumed Dead* by Marjorie Phleger (1963), *Night of the Twisters* by Ivy Ruckman (1984), *Hey, Chicken Man!* by Susan Brown

EXHIBIT 3.7

Children's Material by Aboriginal Canadians

Bouchard, D., and R.H. Vickers. (1990). *The Elders Are Watching*. Tofino, B.C.: Eagle Dancer Enterprises Ltd.

Clutesi, G. (1990). *Stand Tall, My Son*. Victoria, B.C.: Newport Bay Publications.

Kusugak, M. (1993). *Northern Lights: The Soccer Trails*. Toronto: Annick Press.

Kusugak, M. (1990). *Baseball Bats for Christmas*. Toronto: Annick Press.

Loewen, I. (1993). *My Kookum Called Today*. Winnipeg: Pemmican.

Loewen, I. (1986). *My Mom is So Unusual*. Winnipeg: Pemmican.

Oliviero, J., and B. Morrisseau. (1993). *The Fish Skin*. Winnipeg: Hyperion Press.

Pachano, J. (1985). *The Changing Times: Baby William*. (one of a series of four books) Chisabi, Quebec: James Bay Cree Cultural Education Centre.

Paul-Dene, S. (1992). *I Am the Eagle Free (Sky Song)*. Penticton: Theytus Books.

Weber-Pillwax, C. (1989). *Billy's World*. Edmonton: Reidmore.

Slipperjack, R. (1987). *Honour the Sun*. Winnipeg: Pemmican Publications.

Taylor, C.J. (1994). *Bones in the Basket*. Montreal: Tundra Books.

(1978), *On My Honor* by Marion Dane Bauer (1986), and *Leaving It to You* by Wendy Orr (1992) are also superb examples. The nine books in the *Walt Morey Adventure Library* (as well as Morey's *Gentle Ben* and *Canyon Winter*) provide thoroughly engaging reading: they contain believable characters, realistic situations, and fascinating adventures.

Mystery stories are another genre much enjoyed by children in the upper elementary grades. Children are excited by the stories and intrigued by their problem-solving nature. They enjoy putting the pieces of the puzzle together, hypothesizing, and making inferences while they act as detectives. Children become very active in their responses to mystery books. Good mystery stories are, however, difficult to find, so when children discover, for example, the Hardy Boys books, the Nancy Drew series, or *Encyclopedia Brown*, they frequently read all the books in the series. Series books have a definite pattern or formula to them, and as readers become familiar with the pattern, they become increasingly better at predicting solutions and fitting clues together. This activity seems to be a requirement for moving along the path to becoming a more mature reader. Once children become tired of these rather predictable plots, they are ready for something more demanding and more sophisticated. The following list includes some excellent titles in the mystery genre.

- Avi. (1981). *Who Stole the Wizard of Oz?* New York: Knopf. (U.S.A.)
- Bellairs, J. (1978). *The Treasure of Alpheus Winterborn.* New York: Harcourt Brace Jovanovich. (U.S.A.)
- Buchan, B. (1975). *The Dragon Children.* Richmond Hill, Ont.: Scholastic TAB Publications Ltd. (Canada)
- Bunting, E. (1988). *Is Anybody There?* New York: J.B. Lippincott (U.S.A.)
- Roberts, W.D. (1988). *Megan's Island.* New York: Atheneum (U.S.A.)
- Shura, M.F. (1989). *The Mystery at Wolf River.* New York: Scholastic (U.S.A.)
- York, C.B. (1984). *Secrets in the Attic.* New York: Scholastic. (U.S.A.)

Historical fiction is a genre many children find difficult to read, because it often requires some knowledge of the story's time period. British author Rosemary Sutcliff's many books of historical fiction for children are superbly crafted, well researched, and extremely well written. However, even teachers can have some difficulty reading these books. *Warrior Scarlet* (1958), for example, is set in the Bronze Age in Great Britain—a period that has no written record and is unconnected with the real lives of most Canadian children. It takes a good reader to savour her descriptive passages, but once into the story, a reader is hooked, for the book addresses issues that are as relevant today as they probably were hundreds of years ago. Historical fiction may not be for every reader, but it helps to create a context and a deeper understanding of many social studies topics, and can create themes for work across the curriculm.

Canadian historical fiction has become more plentiful during the past few years, and there is now a wonderful range by Canadian authors. *Underground to Canada* by

Barbara Smucker (1977) dealing with slavery, *A Very Small Rebellion* by Jan Truss (1977) telling of the Riel rebellion, and *The Sky is Falling* by Kit Pearson (1989) about the Second World War are excellent Canadian examples. Exhibit 3.8 lists more. Other high-quality books of historical fiction (though not Canadian) include *The Slave Dancer* by Paula Fox (1973), *Snow Treasure* by Marie McSwigan (1942), *Number the Stars* by Lois Lowry (1989), *The Summer of My German Soldier* by Bette Greene (1973), and *The Sign of the Beaver* by Elizabeth George Speare (1983).

Time-slip fantasy is a genre that has developed in recent years, but which has its roots in *Tom's Midnight Garden* (1958) by Philippa Pearce. Time-slip usually begins in the present, and then, with the help of some artifact from the past, the main character is transported into a different time, usually a specific period in history. *The Castle in the Attic* by Elizabeth Winthrop (1985) fits into this genre, and so does Janet Lunn's *The Root Cellar* (1981), which is about the American Civil War. A well-known Australian time-slip fantasy is *Playing Beatie Bow* (1980) by Ruth Park. By coincidence, three Canadian time-slip fantasy books were published in 1987: *The Doll* by Cora Taylor, *Who is Francis Rain?* by Margaret Buffie, and *A Handful of Time* by Kit Pearson. In *Who is Frances Rain?*, a pair of spectacles takes Lizzie back into isolated pioneer life in rural Manitoba in the early twentieth century. Through her experiences in a different time, Lizzie is able to deal with her life more effectively and positively.

EXHIBIT 3.8

Canadian Historical Fiction

Bellingham, B. (1985). *Storm Child*. Toronto: James Lorimer.
Clark, J. (1977). *The Hand of Robin Squires*. Toronto: Clarke, Irwin.
Duncan, F. (1976). *Cariboo Runaway*. Don Mills: Burns & MacEachern.
Greenwood, B. (1984). *A Question of Loyalty*. Richmond Hill, Ont.: Scholastic.
Lottridge, B. (1992). *Ticket to Curlew*. Toronto: Douglas and McIntyre.
Lunn, J. (1986). *Shadow in Hawthorn Bay*. Toronto: Lester & Orpen Dennys Ltd.
Martel, S. (1980). *The King's Daughter*. Vancouver: Douglas and McIntyre.
Pearson, K. (1989). *The Sky is Falling*. Markham, Ontario: Viking Kestrel.
Pearson, K. (1991). *Looking at the Moon*. Toronto: Viking.
Pearson, K. (1993). *The Lights Go On Again*. Markham, Ontario: Viking/Penguin.
Reynolds, M. (1993). *Belle's Journey*. Victoria, B.C.: Orca Books.
Smucker, B. (1977). *Underground to Canada*. Toronto: Irwin.
Truss, J. (1977). *A Very Small Rebellion*. Edmonton, Alta.: J. M. LeBel Enterprises.
Paul Yee. (1989). *Tales from Gold Mountain*. Toronto: Groundwood Books.

Fantasy literature is usually popular with children in Grades 5 and 6, but it is sometimes a difficult genre to read because of the complexity and sophistication of its ideas. Fantasy authors include Susan Cooper, C.S. Lewis, J.R.R. Tolkien, Ursula LeGuin, and Madeleine L'Engle. Their books of **high fantasy** (usually a quest story) are well known and have become classics. Many of these stories have their roots in ancient myths and legends, particularly the *Tales of the Mabinogian*, which is a collection of centuries-old Welsh myths. A modern children's version by Gwynn Thomas and Kevin Crossley-Holland (1985) is a wonderful addition to any classroom library.

A recent Australian fantasy novel, *Rowan of Rin* by Emily Rodda, won the Book of the Year Award for Young Readers in Australia in 1994. Other types include the animal fantasy of *Charlotte's Web* (White, 1952) and *The Wind in the Willows* (Graham, 1908), and the toy fantasies *The Borrowers* (Norton, 1952), *The Velveteen Rabbit* (Williams, 1922), *The Indian in the Cupboard* (Banks, 1981), and *Winnie the Pooh* (Milne, 1926). A subclass of fantasy is **science fiction**, which is especially popular among Grades 5 and 6 students. One Canadian author who has had a great deal of success in this genre is Monica Hughes. Her books include *Keeper of the Isis Light* (1981) and *The Golden Aquarians* (1994). Other titles to watch for are *The Mad Queen of Mordra* by Elwyn Yost (1982), and the 1993 **Newbery medal** winner, *The Giver* by Lois Lowry (1993). *A Wrinkle in Time* (1962) and *A Swiftly Tilting Planet* (1978) by Madeleine L'Engle also fit this genre.

Poetry for Children

Huck, Hepler, and Hickman (1993, 452) write:

> *Poetry may both broaden and intensify experience, or it may present a range of experiences beyond the realm of personal possibility for the individual listener. It may also illuminate, clarify, and deepen an everyday occurence in a way the reader never considered, making the reader see more and feel more than ever before. For poetry does more than mirror life; it reveals life in new dimensions.*

Poetry communicates experience by appealing to the reader's thoughts and feelings, and poetry for children is no exception. Each word is carefully chosen for the nuances and emotive meanings it conveys. When working with poetry in the classroom, it is important to remember children's interests and experiences and thus introduce poems that appeal to children today rather than to our sometimes-nostalgic memories of childhood (though good poems will usually appeal to all of us). Experience tells us that children are not interested in static poems that describe the seasons, the weather, or events in nature. Rather, they are interested in poems that invite them to participate, and that relate to their experiences today. Poems of action, rhythm, rhyme, and energy are ones that invite children in. Children usually need to experience poetry as pleasurable and amusing before they can experience the more abstract and sophisticated aspects of many poems. Poetry should be as much a part of the literary world of children as contemporary realistic fiction or picture books. Huck, Hepler, and Hickman (1993) list children's poetry preferences in their book, *Children's Literature in the Elementary School*, which is a good source of information on all genres of children's literature.

Youngsters often enjoy the contemporary poems of Dennis Lee, Jack Prelutsky, and Shel Silverstein. Older children enjoy poems such as *Jabberwocky* by Lewis Carroll and *The Wendigo* by Ogden Nash. Carefully chosen older poems such as those just mentioned, along with the work of Edward Lear and others, do not seem to lose their appeal. These poems call on the reader's imagination as well as sense of humour. Jan Brett (1991) has illustrated a picture book version of *The Owl and the Pussy Cat*, and there are many similar books devoted to single poems. *My Shadow* by Robert Louis Stevenson has been illustrated by Ted Rand (1990), *The Highwayman* by Alfred Noyes was illustrated by Charles Keeping (1981), and William Blake's poem *The Tyger* was illustrated by Neil Waldman (1993). The books of poetry listed in Exhibit 3.9 represent the many that are available.

Nonfiction Books

Nonfiction material plays a major role in every elementary classroom, for it is this genre that provides the resource material for most teaching. Nonfiction books have been improving in quality and presentation for some time, some winning honours such as the Newbery medal. Nonfiction or information books include biographies, one of which—*Lincoln: A Photobiography* by Russell Freedman (1987)—won the Newbery medal in 1988. Many awards have been created specifically for nonfiction books. These include the Orbus Pictus Award for Outstanding Nonfiction for Children established by the National Council of Teachers of English, and the Boston Globe-Horn Book Award, established jointly by the *Boston Globe* and *The Horn Book*. The fact that these awards have been established is a mark of the rising importance and quality of these books.

The information available in any subject area is growing rapidly over time. Keeping a nonfiction collection up-to-date is a major challenge and expense. Books published on a topic ten or fifteen years ago are likely to be out-of-date and inaccurate today. It is therefore important that nonfiction books be purchased for the school or classroom library with discrimination and with the aid of the library selection tools available (such as *The Horn Book Magazine* [The Horn Book Inc.], *School Library Journal* [Bowker], or *Booklist* [American Library Association]). It is also important that the books made available to children are current, and have not sat on the shelves for years without being reviewed. A list of evaluation criteria for nonfiction books (adapted from Freeman and Person, 1992) is presented in Exhibit 3.10.

EXHIBIT 3.9

Poetry

Balaam, J., and B. Merrick. (1989). *Exploring Poetry: 5–8*. Sheffield, U.K.: National Association for the Teaching of English. (U.K.)
Blishen, E. (comp.) (1963). *The Oxford Book of Poetry for Children*. London: Oxford University Press. (U.K.)
Bouchard, D. (1993). *If You're Not from the Prairie*. Vancouver: Raincoast Books. (Canada)
de Paola, T. (ed.). (1988). *Tomie de Paola's Book of Poems*. New York: Putnam's. (U.S.A.)
Downie, D., and R. Robertson. (comp.) (1987). *The New Wind Has Wings*. New York: Oxford. (U.S.A.)
Fleischman, P. (1985). *I Am Phoenix: Poems for Two Voices*. New York: Harper and Row. (U.S.A.)
Fleischman, P. (1988). *Joyful Noise: Poems for Two Voices*. New York: Harper and Row. (U.S.A.)
Goldstein, B. (ed.) (1993). *Birthday Rhymes, Special Times*. New York: Delacorte. (U.S.A.)
Larrick, N. (ed.) (1991). *To the Moon and Back*. New York: Delacorte. (U.S.A.)
Lee, D. (1974). *Alligator Pie*. Toronto: Macmillan Canada. (Canada)
Lee, D. (1977). *Garbage Delight*. Toronto: Macmillan Canada. (Canada)
Merrick, B. (1991). *Exploring Poetry: 8–13*. Sheffield, U.K.: National Association for the Teaching of English. (U.K.)
Prelutsky, J. (1983). *The Random House Book of Poetry*. New York: Random House. (U.S.A.)
Prelutsky, J. (1993). *The Dragons Are Singing Tonight*. New York: Greenwillow Press. (U.S.A.)
Silverstein, S. (1974). *Where the Sidewalk Ends: Poems and Drawings*. New York: Harper. (U.S.A.)
Steig, J. (1988). *Consider the Lemming*. New York: Farrar, Straus, and Giroux. (U.S.A.)
Willard, N. (1981). *A Visit to William Blake's Inn*. San Diego: Harcourt Brace Jovanovich. (U.S.A.)
Wood, N. (1993). *Spirit Walker*. New York: Doubleday. (U.S.A.)

Examples of excellent nonfiction books are: *A Medieval Feast* by Aliki (1983), *The Arctic Fox* by LaBonte (1989), *How is a Crayon Made?* by Oz (1988), *Volcano: The Eruption and Healing of Mount St. Helens* by Lauber (1986), *To the Top of the World: Adventures with Arctic Wolves* by Brandenburg, *Lives of the Musicians* by Krull, *Talking with Artists* by Cummings, and *Buried in Ice: Unlocking the Secrets of a Doomed Arctic Voyage* by Beatty and Geiger (1992). A list of recent Canadian nonfiction books is presented in Exhibit 3.11.

EXHIBIT 3.10

Criteria for Evaluating Nonfiction Books

Format

- Is the book well made so that it will stand up to wear?
- Is the page design uncluttered?
- Is the book visually appealing? Does it invite the reader to browse through it? Does it pique the reader's interest?
- Are there enough visuals and enough colour to make the book appealing?

Organization and Style

- Is the material presented in a clear and unambiguous way?
- Does the book create a feeling of reader involvement and convey a positive tone?
- Does the author use vivid and interesting language?
- Is the content structured clearly and logically with appropriate subheadings?
- Are there reference aids such as a table of contents, index, bibliography, glossary, and appendix?

Content

- Is the content presented in a manner that allows children to connect it with their own experiences?
- Where content has been simplified, does it retain accuracy?
- Does the book include the author's sources as well as additional information for keen readers who want to learn more?
- Is the book current and does it reflect (and mention) current research activity in the field?
- Are the qualifications and experiences of the authors presented?
- Does the book avoid stereotypes and present differing viewpoints?
- Is a distinction made between fact, theory, and opinion?
- Does the book foster a scientific method of enquiry?

Graphics and Illustration

- Are there appropriate and sufficient maps, charts, and diagrams to add to the reader's understanding of the text?
- Are the graphics and illustrations an appropriate size?
- Are the graphics and illustrations clearly understandable and well labelled?
- Do the maps, charts, and diagrams contain appropriate detail?

EXHIBIT 3.11

Canadian Nonfiction

Beatty, O., and J. Gieger. (1992). *Buried in Ice: Unlocking the Secrets of a Doomed Arctic Voyage.* Misissauga, Ont.: Random House.
Bondar, B. (1993). *On the Shuttle: Eight Days in Space.* Toronto: Greey do Pencier.
Chase, E.N. (1984). *The New Baby Calf.* Richmond Hill, Ont.: North Winds Press.
Chase, E.N. (1993). *Waters.* Richmond Hill, Ont.: North Winds Press.
Crelinsten, J. (1992). *To the Limit: The Marvel of Human Performance.* Toronto: Somerville House.
Granfield, L. (1993). *Cowboy: A Kid's Album.* Toronto: Groundwood Books.
Hill, L. (1993). *Trials and Triumphs: The Story of African-Canadians.* Toronto: Umbrella Press.
London, J. (1993). *The Eyes of Grey Wolf.* San Francisco: Chronicle Books.
Reevers, N., and N. Froman. (1992). *Into the Mummy's Tomb: The Real Life Discovery of Tutankhamen's Treasures.* Richmond Hill, Ont.: Scholastic TAB Publications Ltd.
Shemie, B. (1991). *House of Hide and Earth.* Montreal: Tundra Books.
Takashima, S. (1972). *A Child in Prison Camp.* Montreal: Tundra Books.
Thornhill, J. (1991). *A Tree in a Forest.* Toronto: Greey de Pencier Books.

Guidelines for Appropriate Selection of Children's Literature

When selecting books and encouraging children to read them, teachers and librarians have to be aware of some of the more controversial aspects of children's literature. There will always be books that parents, teachers, librarians, and the general public will object to on some grounds. Pressure from any one individual or group can quickly become a subtle or not-so-subtle form of censorship. Even as we select books for the classroom, we might be engaging in self-censorship. The line between censorship and selection is a fine one. Censorship comes from two directions—right wing, objections are raised to explicit sexuality, obcenity, violence, profanity, witchcraft, the occult, New Age thought, fantasy, mythology, and secular humanism (broadly meaning independent thought as opposed to God-given thought). On the left wing, objections are raised on account of racism, ageism, gender bias, treatment of the environment, threats to multiculturalism, human rights, disability issues, and same-sex relationships. All these themes can be found in literature written for children. Recent picture books depicting same-sex relationships, such as *Daddy's Roommate* by Michael Willhoite (1990), have caused controversy, just as older books that are explicitly racist in their treatment of aboriginal North Americans or people of colour have caused controversy.

The first edition of *The Bobbsey Twins* (1904), for example, included a passage (p. 57) about what a good "mother" Flossie was to her dolls, because she protected them from a black doll given to her by one of the servants. Flossie told her friends that the doll didn't really belong in the family. However, since Flossie's mother explained that there were "no asylums for black orphans," the doll was allowed to stay with the others—separated from them by a piece of cardboard. Given the nature of American society at that time, it is hardly surprising to see such blatant racial discrimination in a book for children. What is surprising is that the section was not removed from the book until the 1950s.

Trouble River by Betsy Byars (1980 [orig. 1969]) is a book of historical fiction told from the perspective of pioneer settlers. Unfortunately, the book presents aboriginal Americans as killers, and many teachers have chosen not to work with it because children tend to generalize from the book to the present world. The perspective of the aboriginals, whose land was being confiscated, is not presented. The book creates a negative stereotypical image of native Americans and could be called racist in this regard. If books such as *Trouble River* are used in classrooms, the context of the story must be very carefully explained. When children in a Canadian classroom wrote pen-pal letters to children in a Northern community, where most of the people are aboriginals, they asked questions such as "Do you hunt buffalo?" and "Do you live in a tepee?" Their teacher was surprised at the children's lack of knowledge until she realized that the children had developed these misunderstandings from social studies work in previous grades, and from the general media, including storybooks.

Teachers need to be especially careful in their choice of materials, being attentive to the feelings of parents, other teachers, and students. Many of these issues can be dealt with by talking about a possibly controversial book before introducing it, and by letting parents know about the literature being used in the classroom. A recent publication by the International Reading Association (Simmons, 1994) on the issue of censorship is a valuable reference for those making book selections for children. In addition, the National Council of Teachers of English (NCTE) in Urbana, Illinois, has published a document called *The Student's Right to Read*, which outlines a plan of action for dealing with censorship and a process for dealing with **challenged books**. The NCTE recommends that every school should have a written policy on dealing with challenges to books, and a committee in place to deal with challenges as they arise. A form is available from the NCTE that challengers are asked to complete. The form requires an explanation of why the book is being challenged and whether or not the challenger has read the book. The committee can then consider the challenge and make a decision about the book. Books that have recently been challenged in Canadian schools include, surprisingly, such innocuous ones as *Lizzie's Lion* by Dennis Lee, *Chin Chiang and the Dragon's Dance* by Ian Wallace, *Thomas's Snowsuit* by Robert Munsch, *Father Christmas* by Raymond Briggs, *There's a Cow in My Swimming Pool* by Martyn Godfrey, *Who is Frances Rain?* by Margaret Buffie, and *Where the Wild Things Are* by Maurice Sendak.

Literature portrays all aspects of human nature, and children's literature is no exception. Through the collection of books we make available to children we can help them to appreciate the human condition, and to discriminate good from bad, fair from unjust. We have a responsibility to put our own feelings aside from time to time, and walk in the shoes of those who are different from us when we select literature for the classroom.

Chapter Summary

Children who learn to appreciate good books will likely read for pleasure when they are adults. These children are also more likely to relate to the culture they live in, and to appreciate their history. In recent years there has been an enormous increase in the number and quality of Canadian books published for children. These books give Canadian children a sense of pride and an awareness of the diversity of their heritage.

The quality and range of picture books available for children in elementary grades is amazing. The picture book genre may be the most rapidly growing in terms of scope and quality. Many picture books are now produced for students in upper elementary and junior high schools. Likewise, most novels for children are now available in paperback and there are many genres. Modern classics are part of the cultural heritage of youngsters; books such as *Charlotte's Web* (1952) and *Bridge to Terabithia* (1977). Fantasy novels continue to challenge readers to expand their imagination and their ability. Good books of all genres continue to create intertextual connections that improve reading ability and increase enjoyment.

Nonfiction books have also increased markedly in quality over the last fifteen years. Technology helps create more interesting and understandable diagrams, charts, and maps. Graphics have become more appealing and photographs can be reproduced more clearly. Authors of nonfiction material for children write intelligently for an audience that has access to a great deal of information via television, movies, and computers. Many nonfiction books written for children are equally appealing to adults.

Book selection issues remain as volatile as ever, and it is important that teachers choose books for their classes that reflect a sensitivity to the needs and feelings of the community. Yet, it is also necessary to choose books that will challenge existing assumptions and present points of view that a comunity may not be familiar with.

Grade one students browsing in the library with the teacher-librarian.

As language arts programs move away from basal readers and use trade books as instructional resources, it is imperative that teachers be knowledgeable about books, authors, and illustrators, and be able to talk with children about the books they are reading. Teachers must be able to make recommendations of good books to children. This means that teachers must read books written for children and must become familiar with them and with the interests of their students. If teachers enjoy books, and welcome children into the world of the imagination, it is highly likely that their students will also enjoy books and become lifelong readers.

Selected Professional Resources

Canadian Children's Book Centre. *Children's Book News*. Toronto.
CCBC produces a quarterly newsletter of book reviews and information about authors, illustrators, book awards and current winners, and author and illustrator visits to schools and libraries across Canada during Canadian Children's Book Week. The newsletter is available from them at 35 Spadina Road, Toronto, Ont. M5R 2S9.

Commaire, A. (ed.). *Something About the Author*. Detroit: Gale Research.
This series of books about most published authors in North America and Britain is invaluable when pursuing novel or author studies. The information is easily accessible and entries include reviews of the author's work.

Egoff, S., and J. Saltman. (1990). *The New Republic of Childhood*. Don Mills, Ont.: Oxford University Press.
This book is an excellent resource for Canadian children's materials, with information on Canadian authors and illustrators.

Huck, J., S. Hepler, and J. Hickman. (1993). *Children's Literature in the Elementary School* (5th edition). New York: Harcourt Brace Jovanovich College Publishers.
This text remains one of the most encompassing resources on children's literature. It is an excellent source of information on the different genres of literature, and on planning for instruction in the elementary school. The book provides a wealth of background information and a history of children's literature.

Children's Books Noted in Chapter 3

Ahlberg, J. and A. (1978). *Each Peach Pear Plum*. London: Kestrel Books.
Aliki. (1983). *A Medieval Feast*. New York: Thomas Y. Crowell.
Avi. (1981). *Who Stole the Wizard of Oz?* New York: Knopf.
Babbit, N. (1975). *Tuck Everlasting*. New York: Farrar, Strauss, Giroux.
Banks, L.R. (1981). *The Indian in the Cupboard*. London: Doubleday.
Bauer, M. (1986). *On My Honor*. New York: Clarion.
Beatty, O., and J. Geiger. (1992). *Buried in Ice: Unlocking the Secrets of a Doomed Arctic Voyage*. Mississauga, Ont.: Random House.
Bellairs, J. (1978). *The Treasure of Alpheus Winterborn*. New York: Harcourt Brace Jovanovich.
Blake, W. (1993). *The Tyger*. (illus. by Neil Waldman) New York: Harcourt Brace Jovanovich.
Blue Heron Publishing. *Walt Morey Adventure Library*. Hillsboro, Oregon: Blue Heron.
Brandenburg, J. (1993). *To the Top of the World: Adventures with Arctic Wolves*. New York: Walker and Company.
Brett, J. (1987). *Goldilocks and The Three Bears*. New York: Dodd, Mead and Co.
Briggs, R. (1973). *Father Christmas*. New York: Crow and McCann & Georghegan.
Brown, S. (1978). *Hey, Chicken Man!* Richmond Hill, Ont.: Scholastic TAB Publications Ltd.
Browne, A. (1983). *Gorilla*. New York: Alfred A. Knopf, Inc.
Browne, A. (1989). *The Tunnel*. London: Julia MacRae Books.
Buchan, B. (1975). *The Dragon Children*. Richmond Hill, Ont.: Scholastic TAB Publications Ltd.
Buffie, M. (1987). *Who is Frances Rain?* Toronto: Kids Can Press Ltd.
Bunting, E. (1988). *Is Anybody There?* New York: HarperCollins.
Burningham, J. (1977). *Come Away from the Water, Shirley*. London: Cape.
Byars, B. (1970). *The Summer of the Swans*. New York: Viking.
Byars, B. (1980). *Trouble River*. New York: Viking Penguin, Inc.
Cummings, P. (1992). *Talking With Artists*. New York: Bradbury Press.
Freedman, R. (1987). *Lincoln: A Photobiography*. New York: Clarion Books.
Fox, P. (1982). *The Slave Dancer*. New York: Bradbury.
Godfrey, M., and F. O'Keefe. (1991). *There's a Cow in My Swimming Pool*. Richmond Hill, Ont.: Scholastic TAB Publications Inc.
Graham, K. (1908). *The Wind in the Willows*. New York: Scribners.
Greene, B. (1973). *The Summer of My German Soldier*. New York: Bantam.
Hately, D. (adaptor). (1987). *The Tale of Peter Rabbit*. Loughborough: Ladybird Books.
Hope, L.L. (1904). *The Bobbsey Twins*. New York: Grosset & Dunlap.
Hughes, M. (1980). *Keeper of the Isis Light*. London: Mammoth.
Hughes, M. (1994). *The Golden Aquarians*. Toronto: HarperCollins.
Hutchins, P. (1969). *Rosie's Walk*. London: Bodley Head Press.
Krull, K. (1993). *Lives of the Musicians: Good Times, Bad Times (and What the Neighbors Thought)*. New York: Harcourt Brace Jovanovich.
LaBonte, G. (1989). *The Arctic Fox*. Minneapolis: Dillon Press.
Lauber, P. (1986). *Volcano: The Eruption and Healing of Mount St. Helens*. New York: Bradbury Press.

Lear, E. (1991). *The Owl and the Pussy Cat.* (illus. by Jan Brett). New York: Putnam's.
Lee, D. (1984). *Lizzie's Lion.* Toronto: Stoddart.
L'Engle, M. (1962). *A Wrinkle in Time.* New York: Farrar, Strauss and Giroux.
L'Engle, M. (1978). *A Swiftly Tilting Planet.* New York: Farrar, Strauss and Giroux.
Lowry, L. (1993). *The Giver.* Boston: Houghton.
Lowry, L. (1989). *Number the Stars.* Boston: Houghton.
Lunn, J. (1981). *The Root Cellar.* New York: Scribners.
Milne, A.A. (1926). *Winnie the Pooh.* New York: Dutton.
McSwigan, M. (1942). *Snow Treasure.* New York: E. P. Dutton.
Moray,W. (1972). *Canyon Winter.* New York: E. P. Dutton.
Moray, W. (1965). *Gentle Ben.* New York: E.P. Dutton.
Moray, W. (1970). *Gloomy Gus.* Hillsboro, OR: Blue Heron Publishing.
Munsch, R. (1985). *Thomas's Snowsuit.* Toronto: Annick Press.
Norton, M. (1953). *The Borrowers.* San Diego: Harcourt.
Noyes, A. (1981). *The Highwayman.* (illus. by Charles Keeping). London: Oxford.
Ormerod, J. (1981). *Sunshine.* Harmondsworth, U.K.: Puffin Books.
Ormerod, J. (1982). *Moonlight.* Harmondsworth, U.K.: Puffin Books.
Orr, W. (1992). *Leaving It to You.* Melbourne, Australia: Angus and Robertson.
Oz, C. (1988). *How Is a Crayon Made?* New York: Simon and Schuster.
Park, R. (1980). *Playing Beatie Bow.* Sydney: Thomas Nelson Australia.
Paterson, K. (1977). *Bridge to Terabithia.* New York: HarperCollins.
Paterson, K. (1978). *The Great Gilly Hopkins.* New York: Thomas Y. Crowell.
Paulsen, G. (1987). *Hatchet.* New York: Bradbury Press.
Pearson, K. (1987). *A Handful of Time.* Markham, Ont.: Viking Kestrel.
Pearce, P. (1958). *Tom's Midnight Garden.* London: Oxford University Press.
Phleger, M. (1963). *Pilot Down, Presumed Dead.* New York: Harper and Row.
Potter, B. (1902). *The Tale of Peter Rabbit.* London: Frederick Warne & Co.
Richler, M. (1975). *Jacob Two-Two Meets the Hooded Fang.* New York: McClelland & Stewart.
Roberts, W.D. (1988). *Megan's Island.* New York: Atheneum.
Rodda, E. (1993). *Rowan of Rin.* Norwood, S.A.: Omnibus Books.
Ruckman, I. (1984). *Night of the Twisters.* New York: Crowell.
Sendak, M. (1963). *Where the Wild Things Are.* New York: Harper.
Shura, M.F. (1989). *The Mystery at Wolf River.* New York: Scholastic.
Smucker, B. (1977). *Underground to Canada.* Toronto: Clarke, Irwin.
Sobol, D. (1963–94). *Encyclopedia Brown Series.* New York: Lode Star Books.
Speare, E.G. (1983). *The Sign of the Beaver.* Boston: Houghton.
Stevenson, R.L. (1990). *My Shadow,* (illus. by Ted Rand). New York: Putnam.
Sutcliff, R. (1958). *Warrior Scarlet.* Harmondsworth, U.K.: Puffin Books.
Taylor, C. (1987). *The Doll.* Toronto: Douglas and McIntyre.
Thomas, G., and K. Crossley-Holland. (1985). *Tales from the Mabinogian.* New York: Overlook Press.
Truss, J. (1977). *A Very Small Rebellion.* Edmonton: J.M. Lebel Enterprises.

Wallace, I. (1984). *Chin Chiang and the Dragon's Dance*. Toronto: Groundwood Books.
White, E.B. (1952). *Charlotte's Web*. Harper and Row.
Willhoite, M. (1990). *Daddy's Roommate*. Boston: Alyson Wonderland Publications.
Winthrop, E. (1985). *The Castle in the Attic*. New York: Holiday.
York, C. (1984). *Secrets in the Attic*. New York: Scholastic.
Yost, E. (1982). *The Mad Queen of Mordra*. Richmond Hill, Ont.: Scholastic TAB Publications Ltd.

CHAPTER 4

Language Development and Oracy

Grade 4 students engaged in small group science discussion.

OBJECTIVES

- to understand and be able to discuss the components of language
- to be aware that research in language acquisition is relatively new, and that perspectives develop and change
- to understand that language competencies continue to develop throughout life
- to know that language and social context are intertwined
- to know that language and learning cannot be separated
- to learn instructional strategies for enhancing listening and talking in classrooms

Language Development and Oracy

Children know what language is because they know what language does (Halliday, 1969). Infants vocalize in order to express pain, gain comfort, and interact with their caregivers. As they begin to make meaningful sounds, they learn that language is an effective vehicle for letting other people know what they want and what they mean. In fact, Halliday maintains that through speaking children learn how to mean (1975b). In other words, children learn language because they quickly see that it enables them to make sense of and, to some extent, control their world. Through language, children can have their needs met, have other people do things on their behalf, live in the world of the imagination, inquire, tell about who they are, tell what they know, and develop friendships. As we watch children in classrooms, playgrounds, stores, and other public places, we see and hear them using language with amazing proficiency. When children enter our kindergarten classrooms, they already know many of the rules of grammar and usage. In five years or so they have mastered the complex system we know as language, and they can use it to do a multiplicity of jobs. Most of this language is learned in two years, between the ages of two and four. At this age, children have often been called linguistic geniuses. The language they learn is complex. They learn things that as adults we take completely for granted, and often we are not even aware that these features of our language exist.

This chapter explores language development both before children enter school, and while they are in elementary school. If language is to be taught as part of the elementary school curriculum, it is important that educators understand language development. It is not enough that teachers and language consultants are able to use language appropriately. They also need to understand important concepts and principles that have implications for the ways teachers can work with children in school. Many of these concepts and principles can be identified in the language of very young children. It is these guiding principles and concepts upon which this chapter is based. Understanding the nature of language development also facilitates understanding the role of language in learning. In school, children must do two things in language arts: they must continue to refine their language abilities, and they must also use language in order to learn.

Language Structures

As adults, we take a great deal of our language abilities for granted. We are not usually aware of exactly what facets of language we once learned. Linguists describe language in terms of **semantics**, **morphology**, **syntax**, **phonology**, and **pragmatics**. These elements of language are important concepts for educators to understand as well, for they form the basis of the language arts programs taught in schools. Although each of these areas of language is interrelated, for the sake of convenience, they will be discussed independently in this chapter.

The ability to manipulate these features of language with relative ease and fluency is called **native speaker ability**. It is part of what we know when we understand the difference between "That mom is awesome" and "That, mom, is awesome". It's what helps to create the humour in children's books such as *Amelia Bedelia* (Parish, 1963), when Amelia "checks the laundry," "dresses a chicken," and "draws the drapes." A whole array of cultural, social, and contextual factors influence native speaker ability.

Semantics

Semantics refers to the meaning component of language. More than simply the words we learn and use, semantics includes the highly cultural nature of language—how our language performs the job the culture requires it to do. Every culture has its own world view, which is encompassed in its language. All members of a culture tacitly agree on the meanings of words and phrases. In English we have a verb tense system that marks when an event occurs. Some languages, however, do not mark verb tenses in the same way as English: for example, in order to indicate that something happened in the past, they might say "before now." The way in which a culture chooses to classify the world is arbitrary. The English language has many words for colour, whereas some languages make only a binary distinction (roughly equivalent to light and dark), although the physical perception skills of all people are the same. Similarly, Inuktitut has many words for snow, depending on its type and location, how it can be travelled over, and what it is used for. In English we have a range of words for snow only if we ski or live in the North and need to describe road and ice conditions. Many of the English words used in these instances, however, are adjectives, describing the snow, not substitutes for the word snow itself. Another example of language differences is that Russian makes an explicit distinction between alienable and inalienable possessions; for example, my pen and my arm. The English language does not make this difference overtly.

Idioms and compound words are also part of the system of semantics. These are phrases whose meaning is not related to the meanings of the individual words in the phrase. For example, "to kick the bucket" has nothing to do with either kicking or a pail: it means "to die." The meanings of idioms have to be learned in the same way as individual vocabulary items; they are unique and have to be understood in context.

In the same way, native speakers learn compound words—two separate words that together create a new, single meaning. We understand what a houseboat and a housefly are, and know the difference between them. We know that a houseboat is "a house that is also a boat," but that a housefly is *not* "a house that is also a fly" but a fly that lives in houses. We know we can say that a plate broke, or a briefcase handle broke, but we would not say that a sweater broke, or a newspaper broke. These are examples of the colloquial restrictions that native speakers learn. All of this is part of our semantic knowledge.

Morphology

Morphemes, the building blocks of meaning, are the smallest meaning units of language. Helping to create meaning within words and sentences, they consist of root words such as ball, girl, play, and fast. They also include such elements as the *ed* suffix, which denotes past tense, the *s* suffix, which denotes plural, and the *er* suffix denoting "one who does" (e.g., a singer is one who sings). Prefixes are also examples of morphemes, e.g., *anti* as in antihistamine or antiseptic. Since morphology is a complex area of language, it has been dealt with only superficially here.

Syntax

The basic unit in syntax is the sentence. Syntax is the way words are strung together to create meaning. Syntax in English consists mainly of word order. A change in the word order of a sentence can either drastically, or minimally, change meaning. Rarely do changes in syntax have *no* effect on meaning. To illustrate syntax, take the sentence "I saw the kitten in the garden," and insert the word "only" at various points throughout to see the major shifts in meaning. For example, "Only I saw the kitten in the garden" is quite different in meaning from "I saw only the kitten in the garden," and from "I saw the only kitten in the garden."

As children get older, they have growing capacity to embed more and more meaning into each sentence by using clauses and phrases, making the sentence more compact and yet richer in meaning (Hunt, 1965). A young child may say, in conversation with a partner, "I have a cat. He's called Sam. I like him. He's grey. He's my friend." An older person might combine these basic (or kernel) sentences and say something like, "I have a grey cat called Sam, who I like very much because he's so friendly." The result is a more fluent language style as well as a more economic way of expressing meaning—in short, a more mature form of syntax.

The words "grammar" and "syntax" are frequently used interchangeably. Syntax is a term linguists use to describe how human beings organize their language structures. Grammar is a term teachers use to define a prescriptive set of rules to follow. It is important to note the difference between what is acceptable or appropriate and what is considered correct grammar. The words describing parts of speech such as nouns, adjectives, adverbs, and so on, are helpful in enabling us to talk about language and how we use it. Grammar is rarely studied as a set of rules in elementary school today, although in the past, it was a major part of the curriculum. Today we are more interested in children being able to use these rules in their speech and writing, rather than being able to identify them. The focus is more on appropriateness in various contexts than on correctness. This aspect of language teaching and learning will be dealt with in later chapters, especially Chapter 8.

Phonology

The phonology of a language is its sound system. Every language has a set of sounds that enable its users to communicate meaning. The smallest units of sound in a language are phonemes. The English language has between forty-five and fifty-two different phonemes (depending upon the classification system and dialect). Phonemes are not the same in all languages, and what constitutes a phoneme in one language may not constitute one in another. English has the phonemes *l* and *r*, but these are not meaningful sounds in Japanese, for example. As a result, Japanese people who learn to speak English frequently confuse these sounds because they were not distinguishable in their first language. In the same way, English speakers have difficulty pronouncing many Swahili words beginning with *ng* as in *ngoma*, which means "drum" (Lindfors, 1987, 55). Even though this sound is a separate phoneme in English (note the difference between rim and ring), English speakers do not hear it at the beginning of a word and hence have difficulty pronouncing it when it appears there. The nearest we have to this sound in English occurs in the words *ring* and *think*.

When the phonology of a language is transcribed into symbols, it is referred to as the **graphophonic** system. In English, these sounds are represented by the twenty-six letters of the alphabet. This sound–symbol relationship is a major part of literacy, and a major part of the language learning program in elementary school, particularly in the primary years. It is important to note that the phonological system (the sound system) and the orthographic system (written system) are two quite distinct systems of language, each with their own conventions.

A further element of phonology is **intonation**, which consists of stress, pitch, and juncture. Stress is the emphasis placed on different words, pitch is the level of the voice, and junctures are the pauses that add or emphasize meaning. When we try to add intonation to writing, we do it through punctuation.

The phonology of a language varies from one **dialect** to another. To some Canadians, the words *metal* and *pedal* rhyme, and the *t* in *congratulations* sounds like the *d* in *graduation*. The words *cot* and *caught* are homonyms in Canadian English, but for some American or British speakers, the words have very different vowel sounds. *Calf* and *half* sound like *laugh* to most Canadian speakers, but sound like *scarf* (without the emphasized *r*) to British speakers. These differences in speech patterns can sometimes create difficulties for people in communicating meaning, but on the whole, we manage to communicate in English whether we are from South Africa, Australia, Wales, or Canada.

Pragmatics

Pragmatics examines the way that speakers use language in context. For example, *the phone is ringing* is usually a request for someone else to answer it, not simply a statement of fact. It is the speaker's intent that is of concern. Children do not learn language in isolation. The sounds, meanings, and grammatical principles learned are embedded in the social-interactive framework of the child's world. It is the rules governing how language is used in this social context that make up the pragmatic component of language. In order to be effective communicators, children must learn to take both the speaker's and the listener's roles and perspectives into account at the same time. They must modify such words as *this* and *that*, *here* and *there*. They must be able to initiate a conversation, contribute to the topic, request clarification, create smooth changes in topic, provide both verbal and nonverbal feedback in order to keep the conversation going, monitor timing and pauses in the dialogue, and conclude the interaction appropriately. Perceived social incompetence is often a lack of strong pragmatics abilities. Conversely, strong pragmatics abilities are perceived as social competence and confidence (Mueller, 1983). These skills, together with linguistic competence, form what is known as communicative competence.

Perspectives on Language Acquisition

Until the 1950s researchers believed that children learned language through the feedback they received to their utterances. Children were seen as passive in their language learning—not initiating, but reacting and responding to the language of others. It was a

behaviourist view of learning, which postulated that children learn language as they are reinforced for their responses to a variety of stimuli (Skinner, 1957; Staats, 1971). This reinforcement could be either positive or negative depending on the appropriateness of a given response. For example, if a child says "Ma-ma-ma-ma," the child will likely receive a positive response, just as when a child first waves a hand in a gesture of farewell. Children receive cuddles, smiles (or frowns), soft verbal responses or angry retorts from their caregivers as they explore their environments and experiment with language. The behaviourist view of language acquisition was complex, and it has been presented simplistically above. However, it became apparent that this view could not account for all the things a child learns to *do* with language, nor for the vast amount of language a child learns, nor the unique utterances a child makes.

The behaviourist view of language acquisition gave rise to a plethora of language learning research with chimpanzees, mules, and other animals. Much of the research was carried out by Terrace (1979) who, after working in this field for five years, finally recognized that what the animals were learning was not a language in the sense that humans use language. The animals certainly were responding to their trainers through printed and verbal symbols, but it was not language. Certainly, some of what children learn in their early years is attributable to behaviouristic responses from caregivers, but the majority of language learning is far too complex to occur solely as a result of this effect.

In the 1950s, Noam Chomsky, a linguist at Harvard University, developed a completely new view of language learning that became known as the innatist view. Chomsky (1957) argued strongly that children have a predisposition for learning language; that some built-in device enables them to learn it quickly and easily. This device, which Chomsky labelled a Language Acquisition Device (LAD), has only to be triggered by language input of some kind, and children will learn language. It is as though children have a custom-built software package that allows them to access language and use it after minimal "messing around" and "testing" of the program.

Shortly after the publication of Chomsky's major work (1957), Eric Lenneberg (1964) postulated that language must be learned in stages, such as those in children's physical development. Lenneberg pointed out some parallels between physical development and language development. He also maintained that there is a critical period for language development—from birth until about the age of thirteen, when the brain has matured. Lenneberg's work supported the innatist claim that genetic inheritance does not simply give human beings a mental ability for learning in general, but that it also provides a specific language learning ability. Lenneberg believed that exposure to language in the environment was a necessary and sufficient condition for language learning to occur, whereas Chomsky believed this capacity to be some kind of unconscious knowledge of language universals, built into the brain and activated when young children encounter a stream of meaningful language around them.

In a completely different approach to exploring language development, some researchers (including Donaldson, 1978) suggested that all children possess a general capacity for inference, and it is this capacity that allows them to develop language. A child actively tests hypotheses and makes inferences in order to learn language.

All these approaches focus on the nature of the child's innate ability to learn language. It was not until the early 1980s that a new approach to language learning was put forward. In many ways this new approach has at its base the old nature-versus-nurture controversy, for it involves the role of both the individual and the culture in the development of language.

The **interactionist** view of language development is that there must be a fully functioning human being (i.e., biologically intact; capable of developing language), and a fully functioning social system (i.e., an intact social environment) in place before language development can occur (John-Steiner and Tatter, 1983). In other words, language is contextualized; it happens in real situations for real purposes. If there is not an intact social system in place, or if a child is disabled in some way, then normal language learning may not take place. If there is no interaction between the child and the social system, this will create a lack in language learning. Rather than seeing culture, society, and the child's psychological makeup and cognitive abilities as separate entities, the interactionist views all of them as interdependent, much like a woven tapestry. The child is part of the culture as much as the culture is part of the child. Language learning involves both learning about the culture and about being an individual who is a part of the culture. These facets of human life cannot be separated and examined in isolation; they are each part of the other, interacting and causing the unique development of each individual.

One of the most startling illustrations of the interactionist concept of language learning occurred in 1970, when a thirteen-year-old girl named Genie (a pseudonym) and her nearly blind mother arrived at a social services office in Los Angeles, asking for help (Rymer, 1992). The girl was stooped, could not talk, drooled uncontrollably, and was not toilet trained. She appeared to be about six or seven years old. The child had been kept in one bare room, strapped to a potty chair during the day or tied into a crib with sides at night, and fed only soft food such as oatmeal, boiled eggs, and crushed bananas. As a result, she could not walk properly or chew food. Her father had forbidden the child to have contact with any member of the family and so she was never spoken to. The father took food to her, and when he did so he barked like a dog. Genie was terrified of dogs and cats. Soon after the family came to the social services office, the father committed suicide.

In the years that followed, various researchers worked with Genie, trying to socialize her and teach her language. One of the researchers, who was very fond of Genie, wanted to adopt her. Unfortunately, the case ended up in court, as various individuals and agencies fought over who should be responsible for Genie, where she should live, and who should have custody of her. The debate over the ethics of this case continues today, for Genie provided a new and unusual challenge for social workers and researchers. Since the case was unique, it is not surprising that researchers fought for access to Genie, and did not handle the ethics of the situation as diligently as would be expected today. As a young adult, Genie entered a hospital for the mentally ill, where she still lives. No one agency or person had custody of Genie and as she grew up and lost her cuteness and appeal; various researchers and social services appeared to let go of responsibility for her. Apparently, no other home could be found for her, though evidence of mental illness was never established. A 1993 CBC radio documentary about Genie reported that today she hardly ever talks. She engages in repetitive behaviours such as filling a jug of water and drinking from it.

Over a period of a few years, Genie experienced some success with language learning, first learning the labels for certain objects, and speaking single words, often echoing what the researcher had said. Genie went on to two-word utterances, telegraphic speech, and sentences that were simple, yet meaningful, although she omitted all the little structure words. In other words, Genie learned a vocabulary and a phonological system, but she never learned syntax.

It is difficult to determine whether Genie was mentally handicapped from birth, or whether the lack of social contacts in her first thirteen years prevented her from developing her cognitive abilities. Certainly, Genie never developed fluent language ability, though she was apparently making excellent progress before she was placed in the mental hospital. Her story suggests that there might indeed be a critical period in language development, but since Genie's language education ended while she was still learning, it's not clear. The case of Genie is, fortunately, one of the only demonstrations of what might be the necessary and sufficient conditions for language development. We don't know whether Genie had a mental handicap, although she was certainly abused. Clearly she did not learn language. From the evidence it appears to be a result of the lack of care and social interaction she suffered as a child.

Preschool Language Development

Most caregivers talk to their infants as though they were equal participants in conversation. When a mother changes a baby's diaper she usually talks to the child, smiles, tickles the infant, and converses as though the infant understands the language and will respond. We hear a mother saying:

> *Do you want your diaper changed? Oooh, you're all wet! No wonder you were making a fuss. Let's see what we can do. There, does that feel better? Let's go see what Jennifer's doing.*

This interaction is vitally important to young children, and before long, they begin to make sounds; to babble and coo and explore the sounds they are capable of making. By the time children are nine or ten months old, they can make all the sounds for all the languages in the world, but children with normal hearing suddenly begin to drop some sounds, and make only those they hear around them. They also adopt the intonation pattern and rhythm of the language they hear. By the time children are about a year to eighteen months old, the sounds they make are more and more like words. Children who have hearing problems, however, will drop all the sounds they have been making and will either not develop speech, or be delayed in speech development, depending on the severity of their hearing problem.

The first stage of language development is that of the holophrase, or one-word-utterance. Here a child uses one word to communicate a myriad of meanings. *Puppy* can mean anything from *Look at the puppy* to *I want to hold the puppy* to *That is a puppy*. Children know what they mean, however, and if they don't get an appropriate response, they will let their conversational partners know! When studying this very early stage of language development, Michael Halliday (1969) first identified the functions of language. Children learn to create words and string words together because they have things they want to do. They have needs, ideas, and relationships that are important, and can best be expressed through language. It is the use of language that is the driving force behind its development.

Children speak their first words generally anywhere between the age of ten months and two years. The age when children's first words appear does not seem to influence their language development in any significant way. Children begin to speak at different ages and go through the various stages of language development in vastly different time frames. However, children's first words are usually labels for items in their environment that they act on. First words might include *cookie*, *milk*, *kitty*, *ball*, *sock*, and *daddy*. They aren't likely to include *crib* (unless the child has learned to let down it's side!), *diaper*, *powder*, or any other word used to label something in the child's world, unless the child has control over it, and it is relevant to the child's intentions.

The second phase of development is the two-word utterance, where children string two words together to create more specific and detailed meanings. *Daddy gone*, *More milk*, *Cup fall* are examples of speech at this stage of development. The stage marks a breakthrough in language because children move from simple labelling and the use of one word to a more sophisticated use of language. This stage is followed by telegraphic speech, where children string three or more words together to create meaning, still missing out all the structure words, so their language sounds like a telegram. A child might say *Mummy go store*, or *Nana come now*. From here children move on to creating complete sentences, and by the age of four, their language is likely to sound very much like that of adults. Roger Brown (1973) at Harvard University was one of the key researchers to describe in detail the sequential development of children's speech. Brown studied the development of questioning and sentence combining, while researchers such as Clark and Clark (1977) studied children's early interactions with their caregivers. Research shows that although there are general patterns and trends in language development, children pass though these stages and phases at different rates. The most important influence on their language development is the language and playful interactions that take place between the child and the primary caregiver.

Language Development in Elementary School

When children come to school at the age of five or six, they have mastered the complexities of the language system. They understand syntax and phonology, and they can create a multitude of meanings from what they say and hear around them. They are aware of the printed symbols they see in their environment and can recognize print symbols, such as those on cereal boxes, grocery stores, and fast food restaurants. Most children know how to handle books by this age and take delight in being read to by a caregiver. They take pleasure in playing with language, and are beginning to understand the subtleties of language that create humour.

Early in the 1950s Walter Loban (1963) undertook a longitudinal study of children's language development. He tracked one group of children in the Oakland area of California throughout their years of schooling from kindergarten to Grade 12. The study proved to be a landmark in our understanding of children's language development during the elementary years. Loban showed that children who enter school with low language abilities are likely to remain lower than other children in their language abilities throughout their schooling. Likewise, children who enter school with high language ability retain that advantage throughout their schooling. Not only that, but those children with high language proficiency make the greatest progress and improve their language abilities the most, while children who have low language ability fall further and further behind their peers. This finding was one of the motivating forces that led to the development of Head Start programs in the United States in the 1960s (Early intervention and support services were provided for poor preschool children and their families to try to break the poverty cycle.) Loban also demonstrated that the direct teaching of grammar has little or no impact on the language development of elementary school children. Since this research was published in 1963, curriculum developers have struggled to balance teaching the forms of language with the use of language in schools. A third major finding of Loban's study was that reading and writing abilities are related. Fourthly, boys are both more likely to have problems with language *and* to appear in the group with the highest language ability. Overall, what Loban showed is that children learn language by using it, and that children's progress on this lifelong journey is strongly affected by what happens to them before they enter school.

Throughout the school years, children continue to develop and refine their language abilities in all areas, especially language structure, language use, and **metalinguistic awareness** (the growing ability to use language to talk about language as a formal code) (Lindfors, 1987). This metalinguistic awareness is part of children's thinking in general. Donaldson (1978) posited that young children's thinking is embedded; they make sense of language in the context of their everyday lives and experiences. In other words, children relate what they learn to what they know, and make sense of new experiences only in the context of what is familiar. A six-year-old child, hearing that the family was going to Seattle, said that he didn't want to go to Seattle because "I don't even know who Attle is anyway." Seattle was not a city this boy had heard of, and so he made sense of "going to Seattle" in terms of going to see friends. Donaldson showed that children also make sense of tasks they are asked to do in school in similar ways. If children learning a new concept work with concrete objects in the context of a familiar situation, they are more likely to understand the concept than if they were taught without concrete objects and in an unfamiliar context. As children get older they are able to understand language and thinking without embedding it in their everyday experiences. Donaldson maintains that by the age of eleven children can consider language outside the context of their own experiences. They can reflect on language as an entity separate from themselves, and hence manipulate it and learn about it with a new awareness.

Language Development and Social Context

Throughout the elementary school years, children creatively construct language in social situations. They actively figure out how language creates meaning by observing what it does. Children use forms of language they have never encountered before, which refutes a totally behaviouristic theory of language learning. Children could not possibly invent, in a vacuum, all the ways in which they use language. From birth to age six, children learn an astounding average of twenty-one new words a day (Miller, 1977). Children attend selectively; they use whatever is relevant to them. They speak and take note of how others respond; they notice how other people express meanings; they ask questions, imitate what other people say (and how they say it), and they use some general principles for figuring out how language works.

The primary social context for children's language learning is, of course, the home. Here, children first learn language in interaction with their caregivers. Slowly, the child's world gets larger. Children visit other homes, the daycare centre, stores, the playground, the doctor's office, and so on. When they enter school, they encounter a whole new social context, where language is used differently from at home. Generally, there is far less interaction in school than at home.

Some remarkable studies have explored the language environments of both home and school. Barbara Tizard and Martin Hughes (1984) examined the language at home and at school of four-year-old children in nursery schools in the United Kingdom. Their finding was that children do not encounter a richer language at school than at home (contrary to popular belief) primarily because of the nature of the interactions. Teachers have less time to devote to individual children, and are busy with the organizational aspects of teaching. They are not usually involved in doing things *with* children, which is when most language interactions occur with children at home (whether we are making dinner together or watching television together). Teachers speak *to* children but generally not *with* them.

Shirley Brice Heath (1983) conducted a ten-year study (referred to in Chapter 1) of language interactions in three communities in the United States that shared the same school. She found that language was used very differently in the three communities. When black working-class children went to school with mostly white middle-class teachers, the children from the black community had difficulties understanding and being understood. It was not only how they spoke, but how language was used that was the problem. The teachers had difficulty understanding "how and why the children used their language as they did" (Heath, 1983, 278).

An example of this was in naming practices. The black children often did not respond when the teachers called them by the name listed on the attendance register. When the teachers asked the children for their nicknames they received no response. When the teachers learned the nicknames used in the community from parents and others, they found them unacceptable for use in school (e.g., "Frog" and "Red Girl"). When they tried to develop new nicknames for the children, they received a negative response. In the black community the children were used to being addressed by their nicknames and most of them were not even familiar with their legal first names. In addition, they were taught not to respond to strangers or to white people asking questions about themselves or their families. Anything personal belonged only within the family. Naturally, the black children did not respond to the names the teachers gave them since these names had no authenticity for them. The white children, on the other hand, were taught to be polite, to respond when called upon, and to answer to their given names.

Similarly, how to define and show politeness differed between the two social groups. Black children would chatter freely with their neighbours, and not pay attention when the teacher attempted to have circle time or story time on the rug. Their socialization had taught them to pay attention to their friends and neighbours rather than to an authority figure from outside the community. Once the teachers became aware of, and understood the implications of the social differences in the use of language, they were able to more readily accept the black children and not simply label them as poor language users and slow learners.

Probably the most extensive study of language development completed in the social contexts in which children live is the Bristol Study conducted in England by Gordon Wells (1986). Wells followed thirty-two children from the age of two to nine years, tape-recording a number of fifteen-minute segments of their oral language interactions every day. The children had radio microphones around their necks, so the data were collected at various times and in a variety of contexts. The talk was analyzed for grammatical complexity and for the functions of language used. Wells challenged previous research findings (Tough, 1976) by showing that children from homes of low socioeconomic status did *not* exhibit impoverished language use. At home, those children used language much the same as the children of high socioeconomic status. However, what Wells did show was that the language of all thirty-two children was suppressed at school. Wells states "For no child was the language experience of the classroom richer than that of the home—not even for those believed to be 'linguistically deprived'" (1986, 87). Wells discovered that teachers dominated conversation and that much of the talk children engaged in at school was inauthentic, lacking the purpose and spontaneity of real talk. These findings coincide with Tizard and Hughes's findings regarding the language of four-year-olds. Clearly, there is a problem with oral language in classrooms. These studies demand that we explore the possibilities for expanding children's oracy in school, and determine the causes of the current failure to address this important area of language arts.

In the world of home, playground, street, shopping mall, club, and so on, children continue to expand their language strategies. As they interact with more people, and with people in different social contexts, they continue their efforts to make sense of language and continue to expand their phonological, morphological, syntactic, and semantic knowledge. In this capacity, the classroom could be particularly important, as children need teachers who will support and stretch their efforts in language development. Teachers and children need whole, interactive language contexts that enable them to communicate, learn, and express their own thoughts and feelings. In other words, *children need to use language in school for the same purposes for which they use language out of school.* They need to write real letters to real people for real purposes, share their stories with people who are interested in hearing and responding to them, read real books and magazines for pleasure and information, and generally engage in real-world language events, including listening and speaking.

James Britton (1970) used the phrase dummy runs to describe many of the language experiences children are required to engage in at school (see Chapter 1). He maintained that children must *practise* language in the sense that a doctor practises medicine and a lawyer practises law, and *not* in the sense that a juggler practises a new trick before performing. When doctors practise medicine, they are totally engaged in problem solving with their patients in a professional capacity that calls upon all their knowledge and skills. When jugglers practise tricks, they repeat the same moves over and over as a rehearsal for the time when they will finally perform in front of an audience. Children do not need to rehearse language in school for a time when they will have to use it in the real world. They must use language in problem solving and in interaction with their world, calling into play all of their knowledge and skills. Harste, Woodward, and Burke (1984, 9) suggest that "control of form is not a prerequisite to the language process." Unfortunately, much of school learning has frequently divorced meaning from form (Ferreiro and Teberosky, 1982). Much of the work in school, particularly many fill-in-the-blank exercises, does not teach language, it tests pieces of language. It does not require children to use language; it encourages children to engage in teacher pleasing and rehearsal.

Fortunately, over the past decade new instructional resources have become available for teachers and children. These resources include basal reading materials by reputable authors of children's literature, and often incorporate items from published children's trade books. Activities include various responses to literature rather than right or wrong answers. Teachers are paying more attention to the process of writing and to the role of writing and reading across the curriculum. Overall, there has been a shift toward a more child-centred curriculum, with more cooperative group work and more opportunity for children's language and thought.

Language in Learning

To this point, this chapter has focused on how children learn language. The next part of the chapter focuses on how language helps children to learn, or how language influences cognition. Each one of us has a theory of how the world works, and we develop that theory through our experiences of the world. Language plays a very large role in this process as we replay events to ourselves and others, and in doing so make greater sense of them. We listen or read others' opinions and ideas and gain clarification on our own ideas, thus learning. We relate new experiences to old and continue to make sense of them all. The language we have at our disposal enables us, to a large extent, to perform this learning.

Language allows us to shape our thoughts, to ask questions, to explore, to clarify, and to create meaning. Words allow us to put meanings together, and to create new understandings. Whether we are children or adults, we can see the same process taking place. An undergraduate education student reads a chapter in a textbook in order to prepare for a test. She learns the material well and she answers the questions on the test to the satisfaction of the examiner. How much has really made sense to the student? How much of that material will the student be able to apply? This probably will not be known until the student engages in conversation with the instructor, or with a fellow student, or finds herself in a classroom, or a meeting, where the subject matter of the textbook chapter is being used and discussed. Only then will the understandings really be tested. What did that chapter really mean? What does a specific phrase mean? How does one apply this idea in a classroom context with real children? How does it affect planning for instruction? Why is it necessary to know this? What does it mean to the individual student? The answers to all of these questions will be different for each student in the class, but as these questions are raised and discussed with peers, new understandings emerge and new ways of approaching the material are apparent.

This is what is meant by the role of language in learning. Information is not simply processed in isolation, but is shared, built on with peers, and discussed as it relates to real people and real contexts. This is one of the strongest reasons for having students engage in group projects, where they can study and work together, pooling information and helping each other to clarify and test out specific learnings. The value of group work varies depending on the commitment of individual members to the group, the need to know of the individual group members, and the compatibility of their working styles (which often needs to be worked out as part of the group process). Through group interaction and exploratory talk, students question, make meanings more precise, and reinterpret past experience (which is why a personal story is often told in order to make a point). Interaction becomes crucially important as learners stretch their limits and move into areas that are uncertain, going beyond personal experience and specific situations. It is this concept of the role of language in the learning process that has caused educators to focus on processes such as collaboration, cooperation, group work, and the value of oral language in the classroom.

Sometimes we talk ourselves into understanding, but sometimes we write our way into understanding. Writing can create new worlds for the writer (and reader), but it may be that writing, even more than speech, "not only reflects our knowing ... but ... also causes our knowing" (Dillon, 1985, 9). We write letters, lists, papers, reports, and notes, but we also write for ourselves. Journal writing is one way in which we write for ourselves, as we attempt to recall and understand. Writing and then rereading our thoughts, pondering them, and revisiting them kindles personal and cognitive growth that we often cannot complete with other people. It is a task we have to accomplish alone. Writing causes us to make our ideas separate from ourselves—putting our thoughts out there so we can examine them and hold on to them for future reference and ongoing reflection. This process is part of the decontextualization of thought (what Donaldson calls disembedded thought). We can move into a more detached realm, and see our thoughts as things to be played with and built on; our thoughts are not only part of our self but part of a larger world with more abstract and less personal meaning. We move from the contextualized (embedded) to the decontextualized (disembedded), and we move from the known to the unknown. We begin with our own experiences and our own ideas, and we move beyond them to a wider world, accommodating and assimilating the new.

Communicative Competence

Communicative competence refers to the ability to put together all aspects of language, including nonverbal communication, and use them as a native speaker does. It is not simply linguistic competence, where a speaker knows the language and the rules of that language; it is the ability to make sense of the world through language, to use language in diverse ways and situations to accomplish specific purposes. Linguistic competence is only part of communicative competence.

Communicative competence refers to language in use. A large part of communicative competence includes the pragmatics of knowing the appropriateness of responses and interactions. Most responses and interactions we encounter are comfortable and acceptable. When a response or interaction is not comfortable, or not acceptable, we feel it. Sometimes, we are face-to-face with our interlocutor and we can take note of the nonverbal aspects of the communication; the expression on a person's face, the distance between ourself and our partner. But even if we are not in face-to-face communication, we might have the feeling that something is not appropriate. We might begin to question the interaction and ask, "What is really going on here?"

The following telephone conversation is an example of a lack of communicative competence.

Anne: You know what?
George: *No, I don't know. Tell me.*

Anne: You know what?
George: *No.*

Anne: Are you there?
George: *Yes, I'm here.*

Anne: You know what?
George: *Anne, what do you want to tell me?*

The above excerpt from a telephone conversation came from a call made by a resident of a group home to one of her caregivers. Anne, who initiated the call, appeared to lack social competence. She violated basic rules of conversation, and it was difficult for George to know the purpose of her call. In fact, she did not have the communicative competence necessary to state her purpose and relay her message to George. The dialogue did not proceed as George expected. The one essential element of communication is that it be purposeful. When the purpose of a conversation is not apparent, the whole event becomes meaningless.

Communicative competence includes the pragmatics of knowing how to open a conversation, establish rapport, take turns, get to the point, ask questions, clarify, check for understanding, be relevant, not talk for too long, supply all information necessary, and be truthful, clear, and comprehensible. If any of these elements are missing, a distortion in communication will occur. Usually, the conversational partner will correct the situation by asking relevant questions, focusing the speaker, or stating directly that a problem exists (e.g., "I don't understand what you're talking about"). Naturally, we try to be as tactful as possible, in order to keep the conversation focused and flowing.

Children develop communicative competence as they use language to achieve their own specific purposes. Halliday (1969) noted seven functions of language in young children (described in Chapter 1). These functions drive children to learn and participate in language events as equal and demanding partners. The more they spend time with others, with an agenda of their own and freedom to explore their world, the more children will become competent communicators. The classroom, where there is a great diversity of background experiences, family lifestyles, cultural mixes, and so on, provides a rich opportunity for developing communicative competence. Children learn to narrate, which is a fundamental way of making sense of the world (Rosen, 1984), to explain and inform, and to express their personal ideas and opinions. They learn to adapt their communication to the situation; to the age and status of the conversational partner, to whether this is a family member or not, to their familiarity with their partner, and to the physical location of the communication. In other words, a child speaks differently on the playground, than in the classroom, in the doctor's office, or at church or temple. The development of these competencies at school is the focus for the remainder of this book.

Oral Language in the Classroom

In the school years children must learn all of the competencies that allow them to be conversational partners in all walks of life with many different people, in many different contexts. The research cited earlier in this chapter suggests that if schools are to assist in this development, and facilitate children's abilities to communicate effectively in adult life as well as in childhood, then teachers must talk *with* children on topics that are of interest to children, and in a manner that enables children to participate as *legitimate conversational partners*.

Student and teacher discussion during science writing project.

We know that oral language skill is the foundation for literacy development. Children come into Canadian classrooms from a vast range of ethnic, racial, political, and social backgrounds. They bring with them a similar range of oral language abilities. Many children come to school with well-developed oral language. They ask questions, tell about themselves, engage in play, listen to and read stories, and know how to interact with teachers and other children in diverse situations. Other children are shy, have not been encouraged to ask questions, have not been exposed to books, or have different values about what is appropriate and acceptable than do children in white, middle-class classrooms. The studies by Loban, Wells, Heath, and Tizard and Hughes demand that educators examine current classroom practices and pay greater attention to listening and speaking, and the ways in which these facets of language are facilitated by instructional programs. The term "oracy" was coined to refer to auditory and spoken language, just as "literacy" refers to written language. The study of oracy in classrooms is a relatively new development.

Listening

Of all the modes of language used in the elementary school classroom, listening is undoubtedly the most prevalent. The success of storytime, providing instructions, organizing children and activities, as well as teaching concepts, all depend on the abilities of the children to listen and to understand. Much of what children listen to is not information as such, but directions regarding how to do something and what to do next. Children in the primary grades can easily be confused if they do not hear directions, or understand the teacher's instructions. Being able to listen attentively and respond appropriately accounts for a large part of a child's success in a primary classroom. Even in the upper elementary grades, listening remains important in coping successfully with schooling.

Listening consists of six stages (Freshour and Bartholomew, 1989):

- receiving—hearing the sounds in the environment
- attending—paying attention selectively to those sounds that are important
- understanding—creating pictures and mental images or making connections to concepts already understood
- analyzing—raising questions and interrogating the validity of what is heard
- evaluating—accepting or rejecting what is heard
- reacting—responding to what has been heard, either emotionally, physically, or cognitively

Listeners understand speech at about double the rate a speaker can produce it, and so the mind tends to wander away from the topic of conversation and onto something else. Passive listening is difficult. Research tells us the average length of time a listener can attend to one thing is only twenty seconds (Moray, 1969). In order to lengthen that attention span, most listeners learn how to listen actively by nodding, agreeing with the speaker, making notes on a paper, focusing on key words, formulating questions, and generally engaging in the stages noted above. When helping children to become active listeners, these six stages can be taught, and children can be directed to focus on one of them at a time. A teacher can establish specific items to listen for before beginning to read a story or give directions for accomplishing a task.

Wolvin and Coakley (1985) have distinguished five purposes for listening:

- discriminative—to distinguish sounds, especially nonverbal communication
- comprehensive—to understand a message
- therapeutic—to allow a speaker to work through a problem
- critical—to comprehend and evaluate a message
- appreciative—to enjoy a reader or speaker

The purpose for listening to a message, as with any other language act, drives the way in which the listening happens. If children understand why they are to listen to a message, a story, a poem, a list of instructions or whatever, they are more likely to listen effectively and focus on the appropriate element of the communication. In the above list of purposes for listening, only three generally apply to the classroom: comprehensive listening, critical listening, and appreciative listening. If educators can state reasons for listening and focus children's thinking on ways they can accomplish that task, then children's listening skills will undoubtedly be enhanced.

The English Language Framework (1988) suggests the following activities to enhance children's listening abilities: teach children to respect the opinions of others, be a considerate listener, negotiate rather than argue stubbornly, share discoveries and queries, interact in group discussions, recall facts, repeat instructions, and respond to what is heard. In addition, children engage in active listening when they participate in writing conferences with their peers, engage in group projects, take part in drama activities, and read to each other in shared reading experiences.

The classroom vignette in Chapter 9 describes an oral history project that Grade 4 children in Lunenberg County, Nova Scotia, complete each year with the guidance of their teacher. In this project the children interview local residents, tape-record the interviews, search archives and local libraries, and eventually write a history of one of the local communities. The project is a superb example of integration of all the language arts modes—listening, speaking, reading, writing, and viewing. The children complete individual work, group work, and whole class work as they produce the history book. Clearly, oracy plays a large part in the success of the project.

Talking

Oral language occurs in classrooms all day long. Oral language is used by children for all the purposes Halliday outlined—to have needs met, to regulate the actions of others, to express who they are, to interact with peers and teachers, to ask questions and wonder, to represent what is known, and to enter the world of the imagination. Oral language precedes much of the written language that takes place in classrooms, because children frequently need to talk their way into understanding before they begin a writing task. Children also talk while they are writing, and they talk in order to check out meanings and understandings with their peers. Teachers give most classroom directions orally, and the organization of classroom life is communicated to students orally. Children ask their questions orally, and establish and maintain their social relationships orally. It is clearly important that oral language be understood, and that children be encouraged to use it effectively. Many children can talk on the playground, but have difficulty expressing meaning in the classroom or school office. Some children feel comfortable moving from one language register to another and speak easily to different people in different contexts, while other children are limited by their experiences of language use.

While children are usually comfortable with oral communication in having their needs met or regulating the actions of others, they may not be as comfortable in school using persuasive language, giving directions, or making inquiries. These functions of language can be taught, so that children become more articulate, precise, and confident in their spoken language. Thoughtful teachers and adults working with children nurture and support children's oral language. If a child is having difficulty describing something, the teacher asks questions; if a child has difficulty explaining something, the teacher prompts and questions. Activities that promote the functions of language described in Chapter 1 also promote the development of oral language. In addition, most drama activities enhance oral language development—both talking and listening. The teacher's role is to provide challenges to children in their oral language capacities, and also to support children in their oral language efforts. Many adults can remember being corrected in their language as children, or remember being told that their dialect was not appropriate, and that they should not speak in a certain way. These kinds of comments silence children and are the equivalent to telling children they can sing in the choir, but must only mouth the words. This is not teaching, nurturing language growth, or encouraging children's self-worth. All children's language can be accepted and built upon, for our oral language is part of our familial and cultural heritage and an important part of who we are as human beings.

The following vignette describes an oral language project that developed children's communicative competence, their understanding of the world, and their abilities to articulate their ideas persuasively.

Inside **the Classroom**

Elizabeth Thomey, a Grade 6 teacher at Elwood Elementary in Deer Lake, Newfoundland, incorporates music, visual arts, drama, movement, and graphics into her oral language program in an interesting and purposeful way. In this vignette, Elizabeth describes how she was able to integrate oral language into the social studies lessons.

The activity initially was geared to be a culmination for the various activities we had been working on for the introduction to the "Canadian Experience" [a social studies unit in Newfoundland]. However, when I noticed there were advertising techniques to be used, I thought this would be a great time to instruct the Grade 6 social studies class on the various techniques that are used in advertising in an effort to make them aware of their roles as consumers. I asked the students to work in pairs to prepare a short radio advertisement that would attract visitors to Canada.

The first step in organizing this activity was to teach the various advertising techniques and then for me to videotape different commercials currently being shown on TV. I did this at home myself while watching TV. I showed the advertisements to the class and we discussed each, noting its characteristics and determining which technique it was using. The techniques used included the bandwagon approach (convincing audiences by implying that everyone is doing it), flattering generalities (using general words that describe the product in only the best light), testimonials (having a famous person talk about the product), transfer (using a good symbol or idea and connecting it with

continued

the product), and card stacking (picking only the best features to highlight and ignoring the worst).

The instructional period began with viewing a tape that Canada had produced for its 125th anniversary called "Canada on Top of the World." I then proceeded to talk to the students about the activity and began the instruction on advertising techniques. Following this period of instruction I asked the children to watch TV at home, over a one-week period, approximately one show per night, noting the commercials. They were to describe each in writing and then determine which techniques were being used to promote the product.

I then paired the students, choosing the pairs, since I didn't want buddies with buddies nor did I want strong writers with strong writers. Needless to say, some students were not happy with this. But I felt my arrangement was the better choice, so we continued. The students worked together preparing their radio advertisements and I helped them to correct their drafts.

I provided a blank tape and tape deck and let the students audiotape their advertisements. A number of weaknesses were apparent after completion of the project, and I would try to rectify these another year. The most glaring weakness was that I should have included the music teacher in my planning and instruction as she would have been able to help the children incorporate music into their ads to make them more appealing.

Elizabeth saw an opportunity to integrate oral language into her social studies program. In addition, she used material that was currently being shown on television, making it even more relevant for the children. It took Elizabeth considerable time to videotape appropriate advertising material to use in the classroom. However, this seems to have been highly successful, as it motivated the children to critically examine advertising techniques, rather than passively watch the advertisements. Elizabeth was well organized, and already had knowledge of current advertising strategies herself. She chose the partnerships in the classroom with care, and provided the time and materials the children needed in order to complete the activity successfully. She was also able to reflect on the activity and determine what she would do differently next time.

One of the advertisements created by the children in this classroom, and audiotaped by them as a radio commercial, promotes Prince Edward Island as a tourist destination. This is a transcript of the commercial, which was read chorally by three children:

Prince Edward Island—P. E. I. (*said with emphasis*)
Prince Edward Island. Come on down.
This is the place where fun is found.
With its rugged red cliffs and clear blue sea
Prince Edward Island is the place to be.
Green Gables house is green and white
And to us it was a big delight.
We visited a beach of the singing sands.
Where the sands sing in the palm of your hand.
A visit to Prince Edward Island could never be
Unless you visit Avonlea.
Prince Edward Island was fun for me.
It made my summer the best it could be.

Vocabulary development occurs when children use language purposefully, and are stretched to say new things in new ways. Children learn new words from reading, and from the constant oral language they hear around them. We each have a receptive and an expressive vocabulary. The receptive vocabulary is generally much larger than the expressive vocabulary—we can understand many more words than we actually use in speaking and writing. Young children depend heavily on the oral language they hear around them for their early vocabulary development, but as they get older, they depend increasingly on their reading (McKeown and Curtis, 1987). Teachers play an important role in children's vocabulary development as well. Teachers must not use vocabulary so complex that children do not understand, but it is up to teachers to use new words in their speech, and to occasionally draw children's attention to those words. We generally hear or read a new word and pay attention to it, and then we might use the word in speaking, if we feel confident enough. Only then do we usually use the word in writing, where it becomes more permanent. If a word is used incorrectly in speech it is not as glaring as a word used incorrectly in writing, where the reader has the opportunity to reread and ponder the use of the word. New words generally enter our expressive vocabularies slowly, for users must be confident about the meaning and context of a word before they can use them with ease in the general flow of language. Some words become fashionable for a while, and quickly move into the general lexicon; words such as "viable," "interface," "cognizant," and "explicate" are all words that have appeared in common academic usage in the past twenty years and then have faded somewhat. Similarly, children have their own language (or slang) in which certain words attain powerful meaning before becoming outdated. Vocabulary generally cannot be taught through word lists and definitions, since words have to be used to be meaningful. However, children certainly need to use a dictionary and check the meanings of words they are unsure of.

In promoting oral language growth in classrooms, it is helpful if children are given opportunities to talk with each other and with teachers, janitors, office staff, and visitors. Some of these situations will be unstructured, as when children play together at recess or chat while they set up activities. Other situations will be structured, such as the talk that occurs when children are discussing science activities, creating dramatic episodes in social studies, writing conferences in composition, and participating in reading workshops. Purposeful talk includes that which surrounds journal writing, and the inevitable talk that provides much of the basis for written composition itself, particularly in the primary grades. We must remember that oral language is the basis for much classroom learning, and for the personal growth that occurs in children. All children's talk is purposeful to the speaker. Whether it is about last night's hockey game or a classroom project, an intention is being realized. Children grow and learn through their talk, and there is room in the classroom for many kinds of talk on different topics. The only concern for most teachers is to discern and articulate to children what language and topics are appropriate in the classroom.

Inside **the Classroom**

Jewel Bondar, a school counsellor and special education teacher at Youngstown Elementary School in Edmonton had taken her primary adaptation students on a field trip to Fort Edmonton Historical Park. In Alberta, children in an adaptation classroom are usually at least two years below the accepted standard of competency in at least four subject areas. The Alberta Grade 3 social studies curriculum requires that students study the history of their community. During the visit to the 1846 fort, one of the last students to leave the ice house had left the door open. The tour guide reprimanded the students for this and raised questions about the consequences of such forgetfulness for residents of the fort in 1846. On returning to the school, Jewel decided to engage the children in a group drama session about this action. She worked in role as the mother of a pioneer family.

J = Jewel C = children B = boy G = girl

J: Are you ready to begin drama time?

C: Yeh!

J: When your father gets home he will whip you soundly—all of you!

[Silence]

continued

Was it you, John? Jake?

B: It was him. He got you, us all in trouble.

J: Do you have a name?

G: That guy there is Tom.

J: And you?

G: Rebecca.

J: Who did it?

C: Did what?

J: Look over there. What do you see?

G: Wolf tracks.

J: What else?

G: Trees and a cookhouse and water.

J: Good eyes, daughter. What else?

B: I see a door open over there.

J: Look children! A door is open!

[Stepping out of drama and into real life: Do you want to be frightened by this?]

C: Nope, pioneers were tough, a kid done it.

B: Somebody forgot to lock it.

J: [as teacher-in-role] I wonder what sort of person would go into someone else's...

B: I told him not to, but he done it.

J: What did he do?

B: A traveller came by in the night.

J: How do you know?

B: I told him where the food is, like when my brother tells me where the stuff, the good stuff is hid.

G: Look, mother, it is yucky. A door is open.

continued

J: What do you think is the problem? Why would that door be open?

B: He was hungry.

J: Who?

B: The traveller, so he stole some food.

J: Oh no! The door to the ice house has been left open and our meat for winter is sure to spoil.

B: I'll shoot a crow or somethin'.

B: A crow would not even fill you up and we got no guns.

G: There aren't no berries like we had for breakfast in winter.

B: Nope and a lotta snow.

G: Could we trap?

B: Trap what?

B: Buffalo.

G: Ain't no trap big enough.

G: I know, we could get beavers and rabbits and stuff.

G: We'll starve on small things like that. Do we have to feed all of us all winter long?

B: Of course, there ain't no Safeways.

G: You dumby.

J: [Out of role and in real life] Stop. Is this the way pioneer children would talk to one another?

C: Nope, they'd get beat, it's not appropriate, no put-downs remember?

J: Do you want to continue?

C: Yes, let's find out, come on you guys. I like this, yeah.

J: Any ideas on what to do about the meat supply? What might we do?

G: I got an idea, we could set a trapline like we did last day.

B: We'll starve on small things like that.

B: How much meat we got now?

continued

G: What meat? It stole and rotten, ain't it?

C: Pew! It stinks, there are bugs, it's green, yuk ew.

J: [In real life] Stop. Put your head down on the table and close your eyes. I want you to think about the ice house. What is it similar to today? I want you to think what rotten meat would smell like, look like, taste like. What would the pioneers do for food in the winter if the meat spoils? In your tables, groups, I want you to help solve the problem. Somebody has left the ice house door open. The meat is warming and sure to rot if a solution or answer is not found soon.

[Students brainstormed together for ten minutes and Jewel circulated among the groups. Table two needed assistance in focusing on the problem.]

J: Give me five! (Classroom control signal) I don't believe someone has been so careless. Well, can any of you suggest what to do before your father comes home from his voyage? [Several hands go up.]

J: I am going to ask each group to show the class how they think the ice house problem was solved. When I say freeze, I want you to stop like I expect in physical education class. In drama this is called a still image because it is similar to taking a picture, the people are in a pose. Kathy, can you stand over here, please? Brush your hair. Freeze—very good listening. Kathy brushed her hair and then when I said freeze, she gave a still image. Do you all understand freeze means to stop everything, not fall over or fall down?

C: Yes, we do.

And so the drama continued. All the groups shared their tableaux, still image and thoughts in the head (see Chapter 10). Clearly, the children were actively engaged with the drama activity and were generally using language appropriate to the situation. They engaged in problem solving, brainstorming and sharing their solutions. The children had to think as though they were pioneers themselves, and they quickly moved into role and took over the language and thinking of a family with a problem to solve. Jewel has found success working with drama and oral language activities in her classroom. The children are more focused and seem to learn more through these activities than they do through only reading and writing about them.

In order to facilitate talk, classrooms can be organized so that children can talk to each other easily without having to move from their desks or speak in loud voices. Grouping desks together or seating children around small tables works effectively. It is also important to consider the purpose of the grouping, and to group children differently at different times. Most of the time, heterogeneous grouping is most effective and allows children to express what they know and ask questions of each other. This kind of grouping enables children to help each other and develop expertise independently from the teacher. Maintaining a vital oral language curriculum means that classrooms cannot be quiet places. We have to distinguish between the busy chat and movement of actively engaged children and the noise created by off-topic talking and irrelevant behaviour. As teachers structure learning activities in their classrooms that engage children's interests, and as they respond to children's needs with understanding and compassion, oral language will be alive and stimulating. More drama activities to facilitate oral language development are described in Chapter 10.

Chapter Summary

In order to understand how children learn language, we must understand language itself. Language is probably the most complex and sophisticated of all human behaviours—many researchers maintain that the use of language sets human beings apart from the other animals. Language consists of five major elements: pragmatics, syntax, semantics, phonology, and morphology. Pragmatics refers to the ways in which language is used to communicate. Syntax is the way words are strung together so that meanings are created, while semantics is the meaning element of language. Phonology is the study of the sound system of language, and morphology is the study of the structure of words and morphemes (the smallest units of meaning).

Over the years, theories of language acquisition have developed and changed. It was once believed that language was learned through the purely Skinnerian model of behaviourism; children making an utterance, and learning through the reactive behaviour of those around them. It quickly became apparent that this explanation was not sufficient to account for the great range of words and sentence structures that children learn so quickly. It is generally believed that any sentence of more than twenty words has probably never been uttered before. Behaviouristic psychology cannot account for that kind of learning and thinking. Chomsky maintained that language structures are innately present in children, and that when children come into contact with spoken language, these structures are activated and language learning progresses. Today, an interactional approach to language development prevails, whereby language acquisition is the result of a child's interaction with caregivers and the cultural environment. No doubt some aspects of all three of these theories apply when children learn language, and it will be a fascinating journey of discovery as researchers probe further into language and its development.

The social context of language development has also received attention from researchers. Longitudinal studies by Loban, Heath, and Wells have demonstrated the effects of the social system, and especially the classroom, on children's language learning and language use. It was once believed that a school environment could provide a richer language environment for children than they were likely to experience at home. Research has shown that this is not so, and that children's language use in the classroom is generally suppressed.

Language and learning cannot be separated. Much of what children learn happens through the vehicle of language—both written and oral. The processing of thoughts cannot be separated from the use of language. How would we think if we didn't have language? Although the focus of elementary language arts is generally upon literacy development, a great deal of classroom communication happens orally. It is therefore important that oral language be nurtured and supported in classrooms so that children become effective listeners and speakers, both in and out of school.

Selected Professional Resources

British Columbia Ministry of Education. (1988). *Enhancing and evaluating oral communication in the primary grades: Teacher's Resource Package*. Victoria, B.C.: Author.

A comprehensive resource for teachers, these materials combine background information with specific, practical strategies. Resource packages are also available for the intermediate and secondary grades. The packages can be used to help plan and monitor oral language learning across the curriculum, make decisions about the oral language development of students, plan instructional strategies, and develop evaluation formats.

Department of Education and the Welsh Office. (1995) *English in the National Curriculum*. London: HMSO.

The document outlines programs of study for children ages six to fifteen and makes specific suggestions for implementation in the classroom. The document is not detailed, however, and needs to be supplemented with other resources.

Ministry of Education, Victoria. (1988) *The English Language Framework, P–10: Language for Living*. Melbourne, Australia: Author.
The book lists goals for the oral language curriculum from kindergarten to Grade 9, and describes the teacher's role, the context, and specific learning activities in some detail.

Children's Literature Noted in Chapter 4

Parish, P. (1963) *Amelia Bedelia*. New York: Harper and Row.

CHAPTER 5

Emergent Literacy

A kindergarten teacher shares a book with children in the reading centre.

OBJECTIVES

- to understand differences between reading readiness and emergent literacy
- to be aware of the components of emergent literacy
- to understand the development of language and literacy at home
- to understand general principles for planning literacy programs
- to know how to use shared-book experiences, language experience stories, functional print, and writing to foster children's literacy development
- to be able to adapt emergent literacy instruction to meet the needs of all children

Introduction

When the children arrive at Iris Li's kindergarten class each day, they meet together on the rug in one corner of the classroom and update the calendar and weather report. Iris has written the days of the week on cards, and the children select the card that shows what day it is, talking about what letter they see and what sound they hear at the beginning of the word. They describe the weather and Iris prints what they say on a white board. The children watch and listen to her say each word as she prints it. This type of activity has been taking place in kindergartens for decades. What is different now is that we are more aware of how this helps children understand the functions and nature of written language.

The rest of the day in this kindergarten, however, is very different from the kindergartens of the 1950s and 1960s. Gone are the worksheets and visual discrimination activities with shapes and pictures. In their place are a wide range of reading and writing activities. Every day Iris shares a story with the children, sometimes from a big book with print large enough so that all the children can see it as she reads. The children talk about the book before, during, and after the reading. Iris knows it is more important for children to interact with the book than to listen quietly while she reads. She points to words as she reads and she invites the children to read along with her on second and third readings. The book is placed in the reading centre and children are invited to read it individually or in pairs later in the day.

There is print everywhere in Iris's classroom. Not just decoration, the print helps the children to organize their day and belongings as well as their play at various centres around the room. In one corner is a store centre with labelled cans and packages as well as a cash register, pencils and paper for making grocery lists, and signs showing where different products are kept. As the children write grocery lists and identify products from their labels, they learn not only what print is for and how it relates to what they say but also how print works. There is also a writing centre in the room where children go to write stories, letters, and recipes.

Iris uses the term "emergent literacy" to describe the learning experiences in her kindergarten classroom. This term, which began to replace "reading readiness" in the late 1970s, signalled a significant change in the way literacy programs for young children were conceptualized and implemented.

Historical Overview

Reading Readiness

The term *reading readiness* first began to appear in the 1920s. Durkin (1983) traces its roots to the work of influential psychologists such as Stanley G. Hall at the beginning of the century. Hall emphasized the impact of heredity on development and indicated that everyone went through the same stages in the same order. Educators concerned about the number of first-grade children who had difficulty learning to read applied these notions to reading. They hypothesized that children who failed to learn to read were simply not yet at that stage of development. Since maturation rather than instruction was seen as necessary to move to the next stages of development, the solution to reading problems was to delay instruction.

The notion that children needed to reach a certain age to be ready to learn to read received increased credibility through the results of an influential study by Morphett and Washburne in 1931. They examined the relationship between children's reading achievement and their mental age and concluded that children needed to reach a mental age of six and one-half before they could profit from reading instruction. Although other researchers such as Gates (1937) found that whether young children learned to read was more dependent upon the nature of the reading program than the child's mental age, the concept of mental age continued to influence programs for young children into the 1960s.

Teachers had to do something with young children while they were getting ready to learn to read and the answer to this need was the reading readiness workbook. These workbooks were often part of basal reading programs and focused primarily on three areas—language development, visual-motor abilities, and auditory discrimination. Research showed that these areas were predictors of subsequent reading achievement (deHirsch, Jansky, and Langford, 1966). Hence, it was assumed that activities to develop these areas would get the children ready for formal reading instruction. Typical activities in reading readiness workbooks involved colouring pictures of words that rhymed, choosing pictures of objects that faced the same direction, arranging pictures in order, and drawing lines between pictures of objects related in some way, e.g., mothers and babies or shoes and feet. Almost none of the activities involved written language since the children were not considered ready for reading. Although some children already knew how to read when they arrived at school, it was common for all children in Grade 1 to complete reading readiness activities before beginning formal reading instruction.

In the 1960s, education came under considerable criticism after the launching of Sputnik I by the Russians. There were calls to teach more and to teach it earlier (Durkin, 1983). Initially, reading readiness tests and workbooks were moved into kindergartens, but by the late 1970s, an alternative view of early reading instruction was beginning to influence instruction in both kindergarten and first-grade classrooms. The term "emergent literacy" began to be used to refer to this early stage of literacy development.

Emergent Literacy

Emergent literacy is defined by Sulzby (1991, 273) as "the reading and writing behaviours of young children that precede and develop into conventional literacy." There is no sharp distinction between not being literate and being literate; instead, literacy development is viewed as continuous, beginning with children's earliest experiences with print at home. Hence, in contrast to reading readiness, which was associated with kindergarten and the first few months of Grade 1, emergent literacy is seen as encompassing a considerable period of time, roughly from infancy to age eight or nine for some children (Sulzby, 1991). Major distinctions between the concepts of reading readiness and emergent literacy are presented in Exhibit 5.1.

Whereas in the past parents were often cautioned not to teach their children to read and write, they are now seen as playing a vital role in literacy development. This change reflects the results of studies that have shown that most children who learn to read before school entry were read to by their parents, often for hundreds of hours, sometimes beginning very early in life. Doake (1988) describes how his infant son was read to in the hospital six hours after birth. Although Doake's home was exceptional in the

---

EXHIBIT 5.1

Major Distinctions between Reading Readiness and Emergent Literacy

Reading Readiness	Emergent Literacy
• is discrete, separate from reading and writing development	• is continuous, part of reading and writing development
• focuses on nonprint activities	• focuses on activities involving print
• begins at school	• begins at home
• occurs at the beginning of Grade 1	• occurs from infancy to age eight or nine

---

literacy environment provided, not all children who come to school already reading are from middle-class homes. In an extensive study of early readers, Durkin (1966) found that these children came from all ability levels and socioeconomic circumstances. In other words, not only bright middle-class children learn to read before school entry.

The term emergent literacy also reflects the view that reading and writing are interrelated processes. Young children sort out what print is for and how it works as they engage in a wide range of activities and experiences involving printed language. When they are read to by their parents, children not only experience the pleasures of a good story, but develop a schema for what stories are like. When they see their parents making lists to take to the supermarket and refer to these lists as they shop, children begin to understand that print carries ideas across time and space. In the morning as they eat breakfast, children become aware that there is a relationship between the words they say and hear and what is on the box. Although parents use the words reading and writing to describe what they and their children are doing, they frequently have little understanding of how these experiences contribute to the literacy development of their children.

Components of Emergent Literacy

There is a tendency to discount what young children do with print as cute or inferior in some way. Downing (1979), for example, used the term cognitive confusion to describe the thinking of young children about terms such as words and letters. However, it is increasingly being recognized that the achievements of young children in literacy development are quite remarkable. The following description, organized around major categories provided by Mason (1984), attempts to capture the complexity of what children learn in the emergent stage of literacy development. An overview of these categories is presented in Exhibit 5.2.

Functions and Nature of Written Language

Although young children may not recognize letters and words as such, they do understand that what they see written in books, or written by parents as lists, memos, notes, and cards, contains meaning. From the age of about two onward, as soon as children can grasp a pencil or crayon, they become involved in representing and expressing meaning. As children hear books read to them, they come to expect meaning from the encounter and try to make meaning as they interact with books independently. For example, five-

EXHIBIT 5.2

Components of Emergent Literacy

Functions and nature of written language

- Understanding that written language is meaningful
- Understanding why people read and write
- Understanding the relationship between oral and written language
- Learning the language of books (talking like a book)
- Matching words heard with those in print

Form and structure of print

- Understanding the difference between pictures and print
- Understanding how print works
- Segmenting sounds in words

Conventions of print

- Understanding terms related to books, reading, and writing

---

year-old Wendy in Julieбö's study (1985, 95) did not focus on individual letters or words when she independently read a favourite book (*In a People's House* by Le Sieg) to her mother. Instead, she reproduced the meaning as a whole.

Text	**Wendy**
"Come inside Mr. Bird,*" said the mouse. "I'll show you what there is in a People House."*	*"Come in," said* Mr. Mouse *to* Mr. Bird *in the people's house. "I will show you what there is in a people's house," said the mouse to the bird.*

Through these kinds of literacy experiences, young children learn that written language is meaningful.

Children see their mothers and fathers using reading and writing for a wide range of purposes. Their parents read manuals of directions to assemble new toys, furniture, and tools. They read items in the newspaper both for information and entertainment, and write letters to relatives and friends who live in other provinces or countries. By talking to their parents about what they are doing and pretending to be reading and writing alongside them, children learn why people read and write—for the fun of it, to find out something, to learn how to do something, to communicate with someone, and so on.

A major understanding that children develop from being read to involves the relationship between oral and written language. Temple and Gillet (1989, 113) indicate that children need to know "that the talk that is inspired by a text is not a free-form commentary on the pictures, nor a story that changes a little with each telling, but rather a sort of frozen discourse that must come out just so every time the text is read." The French writer Jean-Paul Sartre (1964, cited in Temple and Gillet, 1989, 114) wrote retrospectively about how he discovered that the stories told to him by his mother were actually in books. He recalled how as the servant girl read to him, he "grew sensitive to the rigorous succession of the words. At each reading, they returned, always the same and in the same order." While this seems self-evident to adults who know how to read, few of us can remember when we reached this realization. Nevertheless, children do need to figure out how oral and written language are related. Children demonstrate an understanding of this relationship when they become intolerant if their parents do not read every word in the text exactly.

It is not only experiences with books that contribute to awareness of the relationship between oral and written language. Torrey (1969) described a young boy who learned to read from exposure to advertisements on television. Others have documented the impact of **environmental print** on children's literacy development (Mason, 1984). In the supermarket, young children see products being named as they are selected, and they are frequently asked to find particular products. Television commercials, household products, and signs attract attention to print and help children become aware that words they hear are related to written language.

Children also become aware that there are differences between the language in books and the spoken language they use in their daily lives. We rarely talk like the three little kittens who cried, "Oh Mother dear, we sadly fear, our mittens we have lost." Doake (1988) refers to this as learning the language of books. He maintains that "children have to establish control over the oral dimensions of written language" (1988, 30) in order to learn to read as fluently and easily as they learn to talk. Clay (1972, 28) refers to this as "talking like a book." Knowledge about the language of books is reflected in the stories children tell and when they read. Applebee (1978) examined the stories told by young children and found that even as young as two years, children begin to differentiate storytelling from talking.

Children often ask their parents to read the same book again and again until they have virtually memorized the text. Sartre describes how he was able to teach himself to read by matching words in his memory with the written words on the page. This is frequently referred to as eye-voice pointing or speech-to-print matching. The child looks at each word at the same time as he or she is saying it. This is critical in learning to read because it enables the child to focus attention on the proper units of print as he or she attempts to read them (Temple and Gillet, 1989).

Form and Structure of Print

Perhaps the most basic knowledge children develop about print is that there is a difference between it and pictures. This is evident in children's writing when they begin to differentiate between what they write and what they draw (Harste, Woodward, and Burke, 1984). Understanding the difference between pictures and print is also evident when children answer questions about where to begin reading by pointing to print rather than to a picture.

However, this is only the beginning of what children need to learn as they figure out how print works. In alphabetic languages, a few symbols are arranged in different orders to produce all the words in the language, and these symbols are rarely repeated next to each other more than twice. Ferreiro and Teberosky (1982) studied the developing awareness of young children regarding the form and structure of print using a range of tasks. In one, they presented children with cards containing strings of printed symbols and asked the children to indicate which could be read and which could not be read. They found that the children tended to reject cards with less than three letters as readable, saying they were "too short" (29), and they also rejected those with the same letter repeated several times because "it's all the same" (32).

Early writing usually begins with scribble; large rounded gestures or scratchy straight lines. As the scribble develops in form toward print, letters and familiar shapes emerge that children repeat as they perceive a likeness to models in their own world. These developing scribbles have been the focus of much research. A great deal of the early work was conducted in New Zealand by Marie Clay, who has had a strong influence on how educators now regard emerging literacy. Clay says (1975) that "in the child's early contact with written language, writing behaviours seem to play the role of organizers of reading behaviours. Writing appears to help the child to come to grips with learning to attend to the significant details of written language" (3). Clay outlined eight concepts and principles of early literacy, presented here:

- **The message concept** is that the spoken message can be written down. Children hope that what they write down corresponds with what is said, though there is no basis whatever for establishing this correspondence. Children will write a string of letters and ask that it be read back to them. They may intend the print to say something, or once they understand the concept, they may write down whatever letters they know, wanting an adult to "read" it to them, fully aware that what they write controls what the adult says. Children are highly amused by adults trying to pronounce their strings of letters that run together across a

EXHIBIT 5.3

Beth's Writing

page, particularly if they have been generated on a typewriter or word processor. An example of the message concept is demonstrated in Exhibit 5.3. Here Beth is telling about the things that are important in her life; her writing is both representational and personal.

- **The sign concept** is that a sign carries a message. Children quickly become aware of the signs that have meaning for them, such as McDonald's golden arches (signifying French fries and hamburgers), Safeway signs (signifying a free cookie in the bake shop), cookie packages, and so on. Children learn the first letters of their names, and for a while this one letter might signify a child's whole name. If children see the letter in a different context they will frequently point to the letter and say, for example, "This says Beth." However, children have to go beyond working with signs to an understanding that these signs can be put together in different ways, and used to generate an infinite number of meanings.

- **The generating principle** is that letters and words can recur in variable patterns. Children come to understand that words are built out of letters (one form of sign), and can be generated by combining these signs in various ways. This is particularly important when children begin creating sentences. Learning that any meaning can be represented in print is an enormous step forward in literacy development. One little boy asked his teacher, "Can I write 'spiders scare me'?" Rather than asking for permission, he was asking if it was possible to write that sentence in print on paper.

- **The flexibility principle** is that children explore the boundaries of words and letters by writing them in various ways. Children frequently do this in writing their own names until well through adolescence. In their early writing, children seem to test the limits of a letter, wanting to find out when that letter will become something else, when it no longer signifies the same thing. So we see a child fill a piece of paper with different versions of the letter A, for example. We might see tall thin As, wide fat ones, upside-down As, and As with no stroke across the middle.
- **The copying principle** is that children seem to need to copy some words, letters, and phrases over and over again, in order to get them right, master them, and internalize their feel. Through this, they establish the first units of printing behaviour. Copying means practice, and more practice means a higher level of mastery of that word, letter, or phrase. This copying is self-initiated, not imposed by a parent or teacher. It is copying done by the child and for the child.
- **The directional principles** are that in English, print begins at the top of a page and continues to the bottom, that we read and write from left to right on the page, and that the front of a book opens on the right. These directional principles are different for other languages such as Hebrew and Mandarin. Directional principles are learned as part of our cultural understanding and heritage. It is important that we do not assume that children will know these principles when they begin school. Many teachers and parents express concern when young children write their names backwards or confuse the letters b and d. However, until children encounter written language, they have learned that directional orientation does not affect the identity of an object. For example, a cup is still a cup, whether the handle is turned toward the left or the right. We are still the same people whether we're lying down or standing on our heads! Directionality has not been used to differentiate objects in the child's environment, but with letters and numbers, all that changes. Nines and sixes are entirely different numbers, *b*s and *d*s are different letters, *on* and *no* are different words.
- **The recurring principle** is that children feel the need to repeat a word or phrase they have mastered. From this they achieve a sense of accomplishment. Therefore, children will fill a page with one sentence, word, or letter, written many times.

- **The inventory principle** is that children take stock of their abilities and take inventory of their own repertoire of letters and words. Sometimes children will make a box around each letter or word to distinguish it from other letters and words and signify its separate identity. Children will list all the letters or words they can write without copying.

These principles together mean that children must learn that print talks, they must learn to form letters, to build memories of words they can construct from the letters they know, and to use those letters and words to write messages. They also need to understand that there is a relationship between letters and sounds in written language. A first step in this understanding involves awareness that words can be segmented into phonemes or sound units (Mason, 1984). From her review of research on beginning reading, Adams (1990) concluded that phonemic awareness or segmentation is critical to success in learning to read. Children need to be able to hear the separate sounds in words in order to map sound onto letters to identify words or to map letters onto sounds to spell words. However, it is not clear whether children need to learn to do this *before* or *as* they learn to read and write.

Conventions of Reading and Writing

Although largely an artifact of reading instruction, children also need to learn the terms we use to talk about reading and writing. They need to understand what teachers mean when they say, "Find the word ...," "What sound do you hear at the beginning of this word?," and "Read the first sentence." (Mason, 1984). Many writers refer to terms about reading and writing as **metalinguistic** knowledge. Downing (1979) and Reid (1966) have shown that young children frequently have quite different concepts from adults about terms such as word, letter, sentence, and sound. Other conventions they need to learn involve our use of punctuation and the associated terminology, as well as words we use to describe books (e.g., front, back, author, cover).

Role of the Home and Society in Emergent Literacy

Parents are no longer told not to teach their children to read and write at home as they were in the middle of this century. Instead, it is now almost universally accepted that the home plays a crucial role in literacy development and parents are being urged to read to their children from an early age. Children's language and literacy learning at home is frequently referred to as natural learning, and some educators argue that the developmental model used in the home should be extended to the school.

Development of Oral Language and Literacy at Home

Holdaway (1979, 23) presents the following characteristics of the way children learn spoken language at home:

- *The learning begins with immersion in an environment in which the skill is being used in purposeful ways.*
- *The environment is an emulative rather than an instructional one, providing lively examples of the skill in action, and inducing targeting activity which is persistently shaped by modeling and by reinforcement.*
- *Reinforcement contingencies, both intrinsic and extrinsic, approach the ideal of immediate rewards for almost every approximation regardless of the distance of the initial response from the perfect "correct" response.*
- *Bad approximations—those moving away from the desired response—are not reinforced.*
- *What aspect of the task will be practised, at what pace, and for how long is determined largely by the learner. Practice occurs whether or not the adult is attending, and tends to continue until essential aspects of the task are under comfortable, automatic control.*
- *The environment is secure and supportive, providing help on call and being absolutely free from any threat associated with the learning of the task.*
- *Development tends to proceed continuously in an orderly sequence marked by considerable differences from individual to individual.*

Research on the literacy learning of preschool children has shown that many parents follow the principles of oral language learning outlined by Holdaway (e.g., Doake, 1988). Children who learn to read early are generally immersed in a literate home environment. They own books and are read to regularly by their parents. They see their parents and other people in their home and communities reading and writing on a daily basis. They are frequently invited to be part of these activities in the home, car, supermarket, and restaurant.

Research on the nature of the interactions between parents and their children as they engage in these literacy activities shows that parents reinforce children's early reading and writing efforts even when they are approximations rather than perfectly accurate responses. Doake (1988, 34) presents the following example of a mother reading *Brown Bear, Brown Bear, What do You See?* with her preschool daughter. Words the mother reads are presented in bold; what Adrienne says is italics.

Text	Adrienne and Her Mother
I see a blue horse.	**I see a** (mother pauses) ... **blue** (pauses) ...
Looking at me.	*horse*
	looking (pauses)
	look ... at me.
	Tail! (Adrienne points to the tail on the horse.)
	Yes. (Mother responds and continues reading.)
Blue horse	**Blue horse**
Blue horse	*Blue horse*
What do you see?	**What do you see?**
	see?
I see a gray mouse	**I see a** (pauses)
	gay mouse
Looking at me	**Looking** (pauses) ... **at me.**

Doake notes that the whole book was read in this manner and not once did Adrienne's mother correct any **miscues**. Instead, she invited her daughter to participate in the reading activity, modelling correct responses when her daughter was unable to respond and accepting approximations of correct answers.

Researchers have also found that children who learn to read and write at home frequently have considerable control over their own literacy learning (Doake, 1981; Juliebö, 1985). They decide when and how long they write and although they may not get their parents to read to them as often or as long as they would like, children often choose the book that will be read. They often select the same book day after day and by doing so, develop favourites that they virtually memorize. This gives them an opportunity to engage in eye-voice matching as they reread the books independently. This, in turn, helps them figure out how print works. They engage in as much practice as they want in order to develop control over whatever aspect of written language they are ready to handle. If parents attempt to involve children in some aspect they are not ready for, children often ignore the parents' questions or stop the activity.

Literacy Learning in Different Sociocultural Contexts

Most of the research that has led to calls for emulating home literacy learning in schools has been conducted in middle-class homes. Both the oral language and literacy learning contexts are quite different in other home situations, as shown in Chapter 1. While children from all three contexts studied by Heath (1983)—Trackton, Roadville, and Maintown—were immersed in literate environments, only the children in Maintown and to a lesser extent Roadville were involved in the kind of developmental learning described by Holdaway.

The children of Roadville were read to by their parents and involved in other literacy activities such as writing thank-you notes to relatives. They heard their parents talk about how important reading was but rarely saw them reading and writing. The children were expected to answer specific questions about what they had read and, when retelling a story, to stay with rather than embellish the story line. Roadville children were tended to, encouraged, talked to, and generally prepared for dealing with everyday tasks such as making cookies, mowing the lawn, fixing a bicycle, and so on. They were "given few occasions for extended narratives, imaginative flights of establishing new contexts, or manipulating features of an event or item" (352). Thus while they were ready for some aspects of school literacy and were successful in the initial stages of literacy instruction, they were not prepared for higher-level school work.

The children from Trackton had not been read to by their parents nor had stories been told for them by parents or older children. Instead, the children observed numerous group debates over what letters, notices, or bills meant and listened to adults tell stories to one another. Stories were rarely reflections of what actually happened or retellings of a story read. Rather, good storytellers based their stories on actual events and real people but creatively fictionalized the details surrounding the real event. The primary message was of accomplishments, victories over adversities or cleverness in the face of an enemy, and these stories had to be good in order to hold the audience's attention. This type of storytelling did not prepare children for the decontextualized story experiences of early schooling. Their "abilities to contextualize, to remember what may seem to the teacher to be an unrelated event as similar to another, to link seemingly disparate factors in their explanations, and to create highly imaginative stories" (353) were suppressed in the primary classroom, and Trackton children fell quickly into a pattern of failure.

Parents from all three communities in Heath's study had a strong desire for their children to get ahead and depended on the school to play a critical role in their children's future. However, only the Maintown people were able to provide their children with home experiences that matched the expectations of the school. While the principles Holdaway outlined for oral language and literacy development were reflected in many Maintown homes, the developmental sequences in the homes in Trackton were quite different. We need to be very careful that in building school literacy programs on the basis of child–parent interaction patterns in middle-class homes, we do not accentuate the disadvantage of children from working-class families. Instead, we need to plan programs that reduce the discontinuities children experience between their home and school learning.

General Principles for Planning Literacy Instruction

Writers who indicate that learning to read and write are as natural as learning to speak have contributed a great deal to our appreciation of what young children learn before school entry. They have also done much to foster meaningful literacy programs for young children. But there is a question whether rich descriptions of home literacy can or should lead to prescriptions for the classroom (Sulzby, Teale, and Kamberelis, 1989). There is a danger that focusing on the natural aspects of literacy learning may lead to literacy programs in which children are given opportunities to read and write but little more. Neuman and Roskos (1993) point out that this may not be sufficient; many children immersed in the type of home contexts described by Holdaway do not learn to read before school entry. Explicit instruction may not only facilitate literacy learning; it may be essential for some children to develop control over the functions, forms, and conventions of written language. Reading and writing are complex processes and when one adds the widely varied literacy backgrounds from which children come, the task of designing early literacy instruction becomes very complex indeed. Although there will be differences among literacy programs in different sociocultural areas, the following principles are recommended as general guidelines.

Children need to be immersed in a rich literacy environment.
Children are surrounded by print in their homes and communities, ranging from books to television commercials, signs, toys, newspapers, letters, and bills. They see adults and older children interacting with these print materials and they are frequently invited to become involved in these interactions, sometimes in ritualized ways such as in reading stories. Kindergarten and first-grade classrooms also need to be print-rich places where children are involved daily in meaningful, purposeful literacy activities. They need to see written language being used in authentic ways by their teacher and other adults and children at school.

The following examples help to distinguish between authentic literacy experiences and those that are more contrived. In one classroom, a teacher decides to increase the children's familiarity with signs in their community and to do so develops worksheets depicting frequently occurring signs such as stop signs, walk lights, restaurant signs, signs on washroom doors, and so on. The teacher asks the children to say what they think the signs mean and what they should do when they see each sign, and then puts the words on flash cards for the children to practise reading. Contrast this with another classroom where the children are planning to bake cookies and need to go to a local store to buy the ingredients. They first consult a recipe to determine what ingredients are needed and then make a list to take to the store. On the way to the store, they talk about traffic signs. Once at the store, they locate the products needed. The major difference between these two classrooms is that, in the first, the goal is the reading of signs for their own sake. In the second, which involves more authentic learning, the goal is to get to a store to purchase products in order to make cookies.

Children need to read and write everyday.

Children do not learn to read and write by cutting out or colouring pictures, although they may develop fine motor coordination. Similarly, children do not learn to read and write by working together to build a house out of blocks, although they may learn to work cooperatively and develop visual-motor perceptual skills.

Some writers have referred to what young children do with print as reading-like or writing-like behaviour to differentiate it from conventional reading and writing (Doake, 1988; Holdaway, 1979). However, as Harste, Woodward, and Burke (1984, 69) argue, even the term emergent reading implies that proficient language users engage in a process that is "psycholinguistically different from the process young children engage in." Working with young children from age three, they found no compelling evidence that this is so. For example, when young children sit down to write, they use marks on a page to communicate a message. Although the marks may not yet be conventional spelling, the process of encoding meaning through symbols is similar to that used by the proficient writer.

Using terms such as reading-like or writing-like to describe what young children do with print raises the question of just when it is appropriate to label what the child does as "real" reading or writing. What percentage of words do children need to identify correctly in order to call what they are doing reading? What percentage of words must be spelled correctly before we say the child is writing rather than engaging in writing-like behaviour? These terms create more questions than they answer.

We view reading and writing development as continuous, beginning with the child's earliest attempts to interact with print and progressing to proficient reading and writing. Hence, we refer to all young children's attempts to work with print as reading or writing (rather than as reading-like and writing-like behaviour), recognizing that over time these attempts will have more in common with conventional reading and writing.

In addition to being immersed in print-rich environments, children need to interact with books every day. For those who have been read to regularly by their parents before entering school, this will be a direct extension of home experiences, and they will know what to expect from and what to do with books. For other children, books and being read to will be far less familiar. These children will need lots of opportunities to play with and handle books as well as to be involved in book-sharing activities. Children also need to be involved in writing activities on a regular basis. Again this will be an extension of home experiences for some, but for others it will be relatively new. They will need opportunities to see others write, to have their ideas written by someone else, and to experiment freely with their own writing.

Children need to have control over their literacy learning.
Parents of young children frequently give their children considerable control over what is read, and they also answer the children's questions about print in their environment. Hayden (1985) describes bedtime story reading as reading with rather than to young children. Both parents and children ask and answer questions, and if a child is not ready to deal with a particular question, he or she is free to ignore it. The children basically choose what they want to do or learn and the parents help to facilitate their learning.

Although children will not have as much control over what is read in the classroom as they do at home, teachers can certainly encourage them to suggest books they would like to hear, particularly when rereading. Although group activities such as group language experience charts may be based on experiences of several children rather than one, children also need opportunities to dictate letters to guests or parents as well as individual stories. Ownership is important when children are learning to read and write; it is even more critical to their *becoming readers and writers*.

Parents are frequently surprised how long their children are able to spend on a writing or reading activity. They are also often dismayed at how often their children want to have the same book read over and over again. Teachers frequently do not reread books to children nor do they provide extensive opportunities for young children to reread the books that have been read to the class. But children need to achieve mastery over written language and only by having numerous opportunities to practise will they develop this mastery and control.

Children need to be reinforced for producing reading and writing responses that approximate the correct words.
Young children are given enthusiastic reinforcement by their parents the first time they say something that even remotely resembles mama or daddy. Parents are not concerned that the child does not articulate every sound correctly. Similarly when children are rereading their favourite books or pretending to write a letter to grandmother, parents rarely insist on accurate reading or spelling, partly because they do not view these activities as real reading and writing. However, once a child is receiving language arts instruction at school, both parents and teachers have a much more difficult time accepting approximate answers.

This seems to reflect the traditional notion that children need to engage in word-perfect reading and letter-perfect spelling right from the beginning, a notion that has come under considerable criticism in recent years. Learning involves exploration and taking risks. Children who learn to read and write before school entry seem to go through a series of stages in which their responses gain closer and closer resemblance to conventional reading and writing; they do not move from not being able to read and write one day to 100 percent perfect reading and writing the next (Doake, 1988). Children who are discouraged from reading or writing unless they can do it perfectly may become reluctant readers and writers. We are not suggesting that correct spelling and word identification are unimportant; rather we are arguing that this is not an appropriate goal until after a child develops an understanding of the functions, form, and conventions of printed language.

Children learn to read and write in an orderly sequence but there is considerable difference between individuals.

Although educators have described stages in reading development, stages in the preschool period are not well differentiated. Chall (1983) acknowledges that the prereading stage in her scheme (from birth to age six) covers a greater period of time and "probably covers a greater series of changes than any of the other stages" (13), but she does not describe the nature of these changes. Doake (1981) studied the reading development of young children and produced a model to describe the sequence he observed. Basing his model on Maslow's hierarchy of needs, he was able to identify and describe the first three levels in a hierarchy of reading needs. At the first level are attitudinal needs. By being read to and immersed in a rich literacy environment, the children in his study developed positive and powerful attitudes toward books. As their experience with books continued, they developed high expectations of books and moved into a period of disequilibrium, in which they wanted to gain independent access to books.

The second stage of literacy development grew out of this need as the children gained control over the oral dimensions of written language. By having favourite books reread to them, they were able to internalize or memorize what they heard and reproduce this independently on the basis of picture cues and memory. Fluent reading was evident at this stage. However, the children were limited to stories that had been read to them many times. At this point, they entered another stage of disequilibrium, in which they wanted to gain independent access to *new* books.

In order to do this, the children needed to gain control over the visual dimensions of written language. By matching the story they had memorized with words in the text, they began to develop a knowledge of sight words and letter names and sounds. Their reading became arhythmical at this stage as they focused on individual words and began to use sound-to-letter cues. This led to another stage of disequilibrium, in which they wanted to achieve their earlier fluent reading.

The implications of Doake's model for schools are clear. It is crucial that all children develop strong and positive attitudes to reading and writing in order for further literacy learning to occur. It is also clear that young children need to begin with making meaning rather than with the form and structure of print. Only when they understand the functions and nature of written language are they ready to deal with print.

Other researchers have studied the writing development of young children. Harste, Woodward, and Burke (1984) think that from the earliest stages of writing, children engage in intentional behaviour. They describe a child aged four who, when asked to write, made a series of marks on the paper and then looked up and asked, "What did I write?" They suggest that this child understands that people use "specific marks to sign specific meanings" (108) but that she does not yet understand how to do this. Sulzby (1991) notes that even after children begin to use conventional print in their writing, they are not always able to read the messages they write. Although the development of reading and writing are not parallel, there are some similarities. Children approach both from a sense-making perspective and they move from approximations of reading and writing to more conventional forms.

Sulzby has identified the following stages in the free attempts of young children to write. Children begin by using nonletter forms such as scribbling or drawing. Between ages two and three this often becomes differentiated into drawing and writing. Children typically begin to write with letters or letterlike forms at about age three to four, but this writing is generally made up of nonphonetic letter sequences until kindergarten or Grade 1 when **invented spelling** makes its appearance. Even then Sulzby notes that children move freely between different forms of writing, depending on the tasks they are completing.

There has been considerable focus in the literature on how children move from invented to more conventional spelling. Invented spelling has been a controversial issue for many years. Some teachers say they don't believe in it, but invented spelling is not something one can believe in or not. Children simply engage in invented spelling as part of their journey toward mastering orthodox spelling. What remains controversial is how long children should be encouraged to use invented spelling, and just when and how teachers should begin to teach conventional spelling. Invented spelling occurs as a result of children listening acutely to the spoken language they hear around them. Young children are particularly sensitive to the sounds of words, and as they attempt to encode words into print, they try to put the sounds they hear into symbol form (Read, 1975). During this process children move through five major stages in their growth toward conventional spelling. The process lasts from age three or four though to Grade five or six, and even later for some children.

1. **Prereading.** This stage consists of the random orderings of whatever letters children can draw. There is no awareness of sound–symbol relationship, and so strings of letters such as GJOEFNVMNKJ might appear on the page. Children may have their own "meaning" to go along with the letters, and may tell a coherent story to accompany them. An adult might transcribe this story onto the same page as the child's print (as in Exhibit 5.3). The child at this stage has no knowledge that specific configurations of letters and words

are needed to create meaningful print. However, the child does have a firm grasp of the message concept—that what is written on a page signifies a particular meaning.

2. **Prephonetic.** In this stage the child has a primitive concept of the alphabet and of letter names, and so letter names are used as clues in spelling. A child in this stage might write NHR for nature, or represent a whole word with one letter, usually an initial consonant. Rarely are vowels used; a child's spelling in this stage consists almost entirely of consonants. Ian, in Exhibit 5.4, is moving into the phonetic stage, but much of his spelling still consists of prephonetic elements as in GRL for girl and JWP for jump.

3. **Phonetic.** This is the stage most commonly seen in kindergarten through Grade 3. There is an understanding of sound–symbol correspondence, but the features of words are represented according to the child's hearing and articulation. This often leads to the omission of preconsonant nasals, such as the M in NUBERS or the N in SWIMIG. Exhibits 5.5 to 5.7 illustrate children's spelling during this stage.

4. **Transitional.** In the second through fourth grades, children generally include a vowel in every syllable, and familiar spelling patterns are used, though frequently incorrectly. The word MAKE may be spelled as MAEK, or WAS as WHAS. Rules are overgeneralized and the aspects of spelling a child is currently learning become obvious through error patterns in the writing. Children also use the meanings of words to help them to spell. One child wrote a note to his mother who was attending university at the time. He wrote, "I hope you have a good time at youknowvursdy." There is no doubt that he understood that university was a place where people come to know. Exhibits 5.8 to 5.10 show the writing of Grade 2 children. These students are exploring the nature of spelling conventions such as the use of *ch*, the *ed* suffix, *ck*, and silent vowels (coem for came) and developing a core vocabulary of standard spellings (I, my, the, on).

5. **Standard spelling.** At about Grade 5 or later, a more sophisticated understanding of spelling is demonstrated, and children understand the constraints of syntax and morphology on their spelling (i.e., the conventions of spelling). They use dictionaries to assist in correct spelling, and understand that correct spelling is a courtesy to the reader, as well as necessary for expressing meaning clearly to an audience.

Although these stages appear to be a natural progression for most children, the question remains how and when conventional spelling should be encouraged. The answer is that spelling always counts—but young children must first of all be encouraged to compose their own texts before they are required to learn to conventions. In addition,

EXHIBIT 5.4

Prephonetic Spelling

Stella is a nice girl
She can jump over the fence
Stella chewed the seatbelt in the car
To Granny
From Ian
Me and Stella go around the block

EXHIBIT 5.5

Phonetic Spelling

The one with the spider and turtle.

EXHIBIT 5.6

Phonetic Spelling

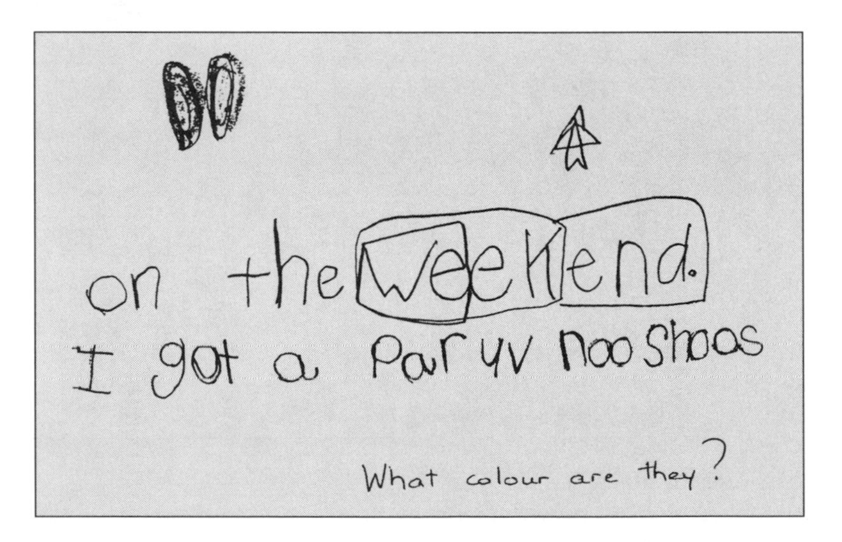

On the weekend I got a pair of new shoes.

EXHIBIT 5.7

Phonetic Spelling

I can write letters to my mom.

much spelling can be taught in mini-lessons, writing conferences, and the final editing of work before it is made public to a wider audience. When adults write in journals or letters to friends, even their spelling may not be 100 percent correct. What is important in these cases is that they make an effort to spell correctly so they can communicate with themselves (through the journal) or friends (through letters). When focusing on spelling in children's writing, we need to be aware of the audience and the purpose for the writing. There are many occasions when the message to be conveyed is more important than correct spelling, especially if the piece is to be read by a limited audience.

EXHIBIT 5.8

Transitional Spelling

My favourite part was when the witch kissed Thistle.

EXHIBIT 5.9

Transitional Spelling

When pig blew up and the family came out of the pig's stomach.

EXHIBIT 5.10

Transitional Spelling

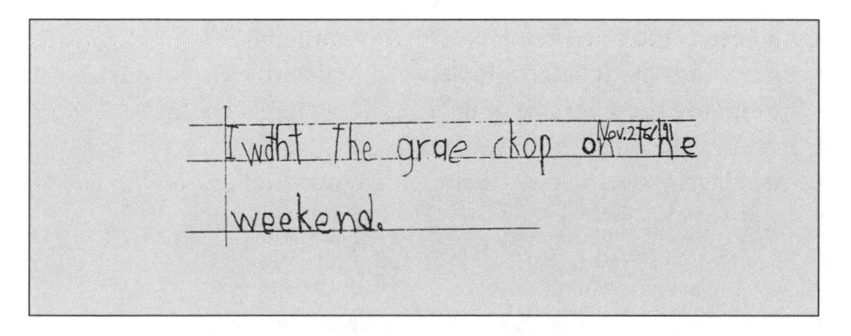

I watched the Grey Cup on the weekend.

School Experiences that Facilitate Literacy Development

The literacy experiences outlined in this section are effective for developing a range of learning outcomes. It is important to keep in mind that these are not seen as separate experiences; they often flow together in the classroom.

Shared-Book Experiences

Children's books provide the basis for a significant portion of the emergent literacy program. Young children need a wide range of experiences with books, including reading with their teacher, reading in a group, and reading independently. They also need exposure to a wide range of books including picture storybooks, **predictable books**, big books, nursery rhymes and poetry, information books, and ABC and counting books. A list of picture books is provided in Chapter 3. A list of predictable and big books is presented in Exhibit 5.11.

While teachers have been reading to children for decades, many have not been aware of all that this activity achieves. Sometimes teachers told children to sit and listen quietly so as not to interrupt the reading. Classroom reading was frequently very different from the interactive bedtime reading children had at home, and most writers are now suggesting that teachers read *with* rather than *to* children—hence, Holdaway's term "shared-book experience."

Children learn different things about written language from shared-book experiences, depending upon the literacy backgrounds they bring with them. Children learn through shared-book experiences to:

- develop a positive attitude toward stories and reading
- understand that written language is meaningful
- understand the relationship between oral and written language
- internalize the language of books (talking like a book)
- match words heard with those in print
- understand the difference between pictures and print
- understand how print works
- understand terms related to books and written language
- develop a sight vocabulary
- hear sounds in words and relate sounds to letters.

EXHIBIT 5.11

Predictable Books

*Available in big book form

Baum, A., and J. Baum. (1962). *One Bright Monday Morning*. New York: Random House.

*Ahlberg, J. (1978). *Each Peach Pear Plum*. New York: Scholastic Book Services.

Becker, J. (1973). *Seven Little Rabbits*. New York: Scholastic Book Services.

*Bonne, R. (1981). *A Dark, Dark Tale*. New York: Scholastic Book Services.

Carle, E. (1977). *The Grouchy Ladybug*. New York: Thomas Y. Crowell.

Carle, E. (1984). *The Very Busy Spider*. New York: Philomel.

Carle, E. (1983). *The Very Hungry Caterpillar*. New York: Scholastic Book Services.

*Cowley, J. (1980). *Mrs. Wishy-Washy*. Auckland, NZ: Shortland Publications.

*Cowley, J. (1983). *The Jigaree*. Auckland, NZ: Shortland Publications.

*Cowley, J. (1983). *Who Will Be My Mother?* Auckland, NZ: Shortland Publications.

Cranstoun, M. (1967). *1, 2, Buckle My Shoe*. New York: Holt, Rinehart & Winston.

Keats, E.J. (1971). *Over in the Meadow*. New York: Scholastic Book Services.

*Martin, B. (1972). *Brown Bear, Brown Bear, What Do You See?* New York: Holt, Rinehart & Winston.

Martin, B. (1970). *King of the Mountain*. New York: Holt, Rinehart & Winston.

*Martin, B. (1970). *Monday, Monday, I Like Monday*. New York: Holt, Rinehart & Winston.

Martin, B. (1970). *The Haunted House*. New York: Holt, Rinehart & Winston.

Martin, B. (1970). *When It Rains, It Rains*. New York: Holt, Rinehart & Winston.

Mayer, M. (1975). *Just for You*. New York: Golden Press.

*Melser, J. (1980). *Sing a Song*. Auckland, NZ: Shortland Publications.

*Morris, W.B. (1970). *The Longest Journey in the World*. New York: Holt, Rinehart & Winston.

Scheer, J., and M. Bileck. (1964). *Rain Makes Applesauce*. New York: Holiday House.

Sutton, E. (1973). *My Cat Likes to Hide in Boxes*. New York: Parents Magazine Press.

Tolstoy, A. (1968). *The Great Big Enormous Turnip*. New York: Franklin Watts.

Wing, H.R. (1963). *What Is Big?* New York: Holt, Rinehart & Winston.

Children who have been read to a lot at home will likely achieve goals in the second half of this list during story reading. However, the focus for children with more limited book experience might be on the basic attitudes and understandings about books in the first half of the list. In the classroom vignette later in this chapter, Becky Prins teaches differently based on what she knows about the literacy development of each child in her class.

It is rarely necessary to group children according to literacy background to share books with different groups. One book can be shared with everyone, but teachers will get—and reinforce—different kinds of responses from different children. For example, while one child is gaining control over the visual dimensions of written language, another might be just beginning to internalize the language of books. A repetitive book would be useful for both of these children, and they would both be able to engage in completion reading during the shared reading. However, only the first would be able to respond to the teacher's invitation to point to the words in a line of print while it was being read.

Holdaway (1979) outlines three basic steps in a shared-book experience: discovery (initial reading of the book), exploration (rereadings in the group), and independent experience (individual and small group rereadings and follow-up activities).

1. Discovery

Holdaway argues that the most critical goal of the teacher while first reading a new book is to provide an enjoyable experience for all children. This goal should not be sacrificed to any other purpose. The teacher encourages maximum participation of the children through talking about the book and asking and answering questions, as many parents do during bedtime reading. It is important for the teacher to hold the book so that all the children can see each page. Mason, Peterman, and Kerr (1989) present guidelines for teachers to follow before, during, and after the reading. These differ somewhat depending upon whether you are reading a story book, an informational book, or a predictable big book.

Before Reading

- For any book, teachers draw children's attention to the picture on the cover and have them predict what they think the book is about. The children are also asked to predict whether the book will tell a story or give information. Teachers also encourage children to talk about their own experiences related to the topic or story.

- For informational books, teachers may need to demonstrate key concepts in the book if it becomes clear that several children have limited knowledge to bring to the topic.

- For predictable big books, teachers may want to have some children predict words in the title as well, encouraging use of both picture and letter cues to do so.

During Reading

- While reading any book, teachers encourage the children to react to and comment on the story or ideas as they listen. Teachers also ask questions occasionally to monitor children's understanding of the story or ideas.

- For informational books, teachers may need to give demonstrations or examples of difficult ideas.
- When reading story books, teachers rephrase the text when it is clear the children do not understand something. They also ask the children periodically to evaluate their earlier predictions and to formulate new ones. It is important for children to evaluate their own predictions rather than having the teacher do it for them.
- When reading predictable big books, teachers point to words as they read in order to establish one-to-one correspondence between oral and written words and to emphasize the left-to-right and top-to-bottom directional nature of print. They also encourage children who are able to read along, and teachers stop reading at highly predictable places so that the children can fill in the text. The children are encouraged to use both context as well as letter cues to make and confirm their predictions. Teachers talk about aspects of the text using the terms children need to learn about reading, for example, "The first word in this sentence is..." and "There is a question mark at the end of this sentence so we need to sound as if we are asking a question when we read it."

After Reading

- For all books, children are asked to talk about what they have heard, relating the story or ideas to their own experiences.
- For stories, teachers often have children briefly retell the beginning, middle, and end in order to develop knowledge of story structure.

2. Exploration

Various group activities provide further opportunities for children to interact with the book. These include rereadings, innovations on literary structures, and interpretations of the story through dramatization or art.

Rereadings

Rereadings are often done at the request of children and frequently involve predictable big books. With this type of book, children are encouraged to join in the reading as much as possible to gain control over the oral dimensions of written language. Group choral reading of the book is encouraged, with the teacher pointing to words as they are read and reading along with the children when they need the support. By rereading the book several times, children are able to internalize the oral language they need in order to establish eye–voice matching when later reading the book independently or in a small group.

The teacher also uses the rereading time to focus on print and on sight vocabulary and use of letter sounds to identify words. The teacher asks children questions such as, "Where do I begin reading?," "Find words that begin with the letter m," and "What is this word?"

The teacher also begins to focus the children's attention on letter sounds. Predictable books such as *1, 2, Buckle My Shoe* contain rhyming words and children can talk about which words rhyme. The teacher also focuses on specific words in stories being read and articulates the words slowly while running a finger under the letters. It is important that this work on letter sounds is completed in the context of real reading rather than with isolated words or worksheets. There is little doubt that **phonological awareness** is important to learning to read, but it is recommended that this be an integral rather than a separate part of the literacy program.

Innovating on Literary Structures

Bill Martin Jr., who has written several predictable books, recommends that teachers have children innovate on literary structures in these types of books in order to help them develop greater awareness of written language structures. For example, near Halloween, the children can generate a Halloween book based on the structure of *Brown Bear, Brown Bear, What Do You See?* It might go something like this:

White ghost, white ghost, what do you see?
I see a black cat looking at me.
Black cat, black cat, what do you see?
I see a green witch looking at me.

As the children dictate, the teacher writes this story on large chart paper for them to illustrate. The story can be used both for group and independent rereadings.

Dramatizations and Art

A further and often deeper interpretation of stories is achieved through giving children the chance to dramatize or illustrate what they have read.

3. Independent Experience

Books that have been reread are placed in a reading centre for children to read independently or in small groups. Children reread the books as often as they wish, pointing to words as they read to more fully establish eye–voice matching.

Listening Centre

In order to increase the exposure of young children to story reading and give them control over the number of times they hear favourite stories, a listening centre with taped books is invaluable. Tapes can be obtained commercially or taped by volunteers or older children.

Two children share a big book.

Library

Young children need easy and continuous access to children's books. A classroom library is an important source of these books in kindergarten and Grade 1, but children also need to visit the school library regularly. This gives them an opportunity to use print to locate books and develop the habit of regular library use.

Inside **the Classroom**

Becky Prins was teaching kindergarten in Parkland Village School (outside of Edmonton) when we visited her classroom. Although she provided a range of emergent literacy experiences for children, this vignette focuses on shared-book reading.

As Becky Prins introduced *Monday, Monday, I Like Monday* to her kindergarten class, the children talked about the picture on the cover. Becky read the title of the book, pointing to each word as she read it. She then pointed to the word Monday and asked, "What's this word? We know this word from our calendar." Several children answered, "Monday." She then asked, "How did you know it's not Tuesday?" One child said, "Mmm." Another says, "Because of the M." Becky then said, "We've read a book about Monday before," to which several children replied, "*One Bright Monday Morning*." Becky then proceeded to read the book including the name of the author, and some children chimed in with her as she read. Others watched and listened. She encouraged them to talk about the pictures on each page and when they got to the page where the days of the week are presented in reverse order, "Saturday, Friday, Thursday, Wednesday,

continued

Tuesday, Monday, Sunday, a week," several children said, "It's backwards" without being asked.

Becky then reread the book, fading out when the children were able to read on their own and chiming in when they needed her help. At one point, she read, "Thursday, Thursday" instead of "Tuesday, Tuesday" to give the children an opportunity to monitor what they heard in relation to both meaning and print cues. One little boy immediately responded "It's Tuesday!" At the end of the group rereading, Becky told the children that the book would be available at the back of the room for them to read. The children also reread another big book with her, *Mrs. Wishy Washy*, dramatizing it as they did so.

Later that morning two children went to the back table where Becky had placed both the big book and a smaller copy of *Monday Monday, I Like Monday*. One of the children, Lisa, who was relatively advanced in literacy development, was able to point accurately to the words in the book as she read. On one page, she read two lines, realized that she had made an error, went back to the beginning of the page, and read it correctly. She was able to rely on both her memory of the text and the print cues to make this self-correction. Another child, Darren, was at the stage of literacy development where he was still learning to talk like a book and was not able to consistently attain an exact eye-voice match, even when listening to Lisa read.

Paul chose to reread *Brown Bear, Brown Bear, What Do You See?* independently and Becky came to listen. She saw that he was pointing accurately and asked him a question to help him understand more advanced concepts about print: "Is Redbird one word or two?" When the boy responded that it was two, she asked whether there was a space between red and bird. He thoughtfully replied that there was not but still maintained that redbird was two words. Becky did not pursue spacing further at that point because she knows it is a late-developing concept.

Throughout the shared-book experiences on the day of our visit, Becky provided opportunities for children to respond in different ways, depending upon their level of literacy development. Some, such as Paul and Lisa, were able to match speech with printed words and had developed considerable knowledge about how print works. Others, such as Darren, were just beginning to understand how oral and written language are related and to internalize the language of books through rereading predictable ones.

continued

Becky did not require the children to produce perfect reading because she understands the role of approximations toward the ideal in learning.

Becky, who is currently teaching kindergarten in another part of the province, continues to refine learning experiences for her class as her understanding of emergent literacy deepens. In a recent letter she wrote:

> In addition to the use of big books, I write simple poems and songs on sentence strips and use a pocket chart. We read and reread the selection several times. I mix up the lines and have the class put them back together, or I give them to small groups of children as a cooperative learning activity, where they put their own copy of the selection together.
>
> I use the song "Sing a Rainbow" to teach the colour words and to focus on print cues. I have a copy of the song for the pocket chart with the colour words written in their colour of ink, and the children match the black-ink copy with the coloured copy. To teach word boundaries, we play "I Spy" (e.g., I spy a word that starts with the letter *b* and ends with the letter *t*). The pocket chart is low enough that the children can play with the current selection on their own. It is very interesting to watch them imitate the activities we do in the large group.
>
> I also give the children more opportunities to write—daily journals, group experience stories, writing centres—and we use the house centre to encourage writing by changing it to an office, store, post office, restaurant, or other venue where children can engage in writing.

The children in Becky's classroom are clearly immersed in a rich literacy environment where they read and write on a daily basis. She provides centres and materials for children to work on cooperatively so that the children can control their own learning and succeed with more advanced literacy tasks than they would be able to handle independently.

Language Experience Approach

The language experience approach has been recommended for many years to help children understand the relationship between oral and written language. It builds on the children's own experiences and language as a source of material to be used for reading instruction. The teacher acts as a scribe, writing what the children say.

Understanding the nature of emergent literacy has led to an increased appreciation of the role of the language experience approach in literacy development. Through this approach children can learn to:

- understand that written language is meaningful
- understand the relationship between oral and written language
- match words heard with those in print
- understand how print works
- understand terms related to reading and writing
- segment sounds in words and learn letter sounds
- use meaning cues to identify words
- develop a sight vocabulary.

Language experience stories can be developed with the whole class, with small groups, and with individuals. Again, children at varying levels of literacy development can work effectively together on a language experience story, achieving different goals.

The following description of the language experience approach has been adapted from ideas presented by Hall (1981). The process of developing and using language experience stories is more important than the final product itself.

1. Experience

Language experience stories begin with a experience. Trips, pets, classroom events, wordless picture books, pictures, and television provide springboards for discussion. In the classroom described at the beginning of this chapter, the children visited another classroom in their school where chicks were hatching; the teacher saw that this created an excellent opportunity to develop a language experience story.

2. Discussion

This is an essential step in the language experience approach, providing children with an opportunity to develop both the vocabulary and sentence structures that will eventually be recorded. The teacher uses questions to expand and clarify as well as to elevate the children's language beyond a listing of ideas. Iris Li had the children show how they would peck their way out of shells and asked them to imagine the first thing they might see.

3. Recording

This involves two types of activities. Children select the ideas to be recorded and provide an oral composition. This helps the children understand some of the basic differences between oral and written language. Then, as children dictate ideas, the teacher records them without changes in large print on chart paper. As the teacher writes each word, the children watch to help establish the link between oral and written words. The teacher makes comments during this writing about where she or he begins writing, what direction the print goes, the use of capital letters and punctuation marks, and about special visual features of certain words, e.g., length, initial letter, and so on. If the children have some awareness of letter names and sounds, the teacher might have the children suggest which letters to include in some of the words being written to further develop phonological awareness. For example, when the children in Iris's class dictated a sentence about the chicks pecking out of their shells, she asked, "What letters do we need to write the word peck?" One child said "*p*" and another "*k*." Iris printed these letters and added the e and c herself, slowly articulating the sounds so the children would hear them as she wrote and commenting on the *ck* at the end of the word. She knew the children did not have enough knowledge of letter sounds to supply these letters without help.

A major dilemma the teacher faces when printing language experience stories is whether to write exactly what children say or to make changes. It is generally recommended that teachers use standard English spellings regardless of **dialect** (e.g., going to, not gonna) and use standard punctuation. However, it is important to use children's vocabulary and grammar in order for them to develop understanding of the one-to-one correspondence between oral and written words. For example, if a child said "Me and another chick saw a cow" and the teacher changed it to "Another chick and I saw a cow," the child would reread it as "Me and another chick," associating the wrong oral words with those on the page. Preserving children's language is also a matter of respect and acceptance.

4. Reading

Immediately upon completion of the story, the teacher reads it to the children, pointing to words as she or he does so. As an optional activity, the teacher may ask children if they want to make any changes in order to engage them in revising what they have already written. The teacher can demonstrate revision by using carets and arrows, crossing out, and writing in the margins. Once the children are happy with what they have dictated, the teacher and children read it together to ensure that their first reading will be successful. During subsequent rereadings, the children read more independently with the teacher providing support as needed. Finally, when the children feel ready, individuals can read the story alone.

5. Follow-Up Activities

A variety of follow-up activities are appropriate for both groups and individuals. Some examples follow.

- During rereading, the teacher asks children questions about where to begin reading, what direction to read, how to know to stop at the end of a sentence, and so on, to develop concepts about print conventions.
- Individual children are encouraged to read the story independently, pointing to the words as they read. Some teachers type the language experience story and make copies for the children to keep and read individually.
- Children are asked to find words containing a common letter, e.g., all the words that begin with the letter *m*. Discuss the sound at the beginning of these words and the fact that some of the words begin with an uppercase M and others with a lowercase *m*.
- Sentences are cut apart and children arrange the sentences in order, referring to the language experience chart if necessary. When the children are able to handle this task easily, individual sentences can be cut into words for them to put in order, again matching the words against an intact sentence strip if necessary.
- Selected words in the language experience story are covered and the children are asked to predict words that make sense and sound right in the space.
- Poetry, songs, and other material can be presented to children in large print on charts. By pointing to words on a chart as the children sing, further opportunities for eye–voice matching are provided. In addition, discussion of words on the chart can further develop knowledge of the form and structure of printed language.

Functional Uses of Print

Two kindergarten children read a chart.

Environmental print both inside and outside the classroom provides children with functional literacy experiences. Environmental print includes such things as signs, labels, calendars, charts, and lists that can be used to organize the classroom. Putting labels and signs up in the classroom is not, by itself, sufficient to achieve the following goals.

- understanding that written language is meaningful
- understanding why people read and write
- understanding the relationship between oral and written language

- matching words heard with those in print
- understanding how print works
- segmenting sounds in words and using letter cues to identify words
- understanding terms related to reading and writing
- learning to use context to identify words.

It is important that work with environmental print be authentic rather than contrived.

1. Labels can be used effectively in the classroom to identify children's cubbyholes and show where things belong.

2. Calendars are used to keep track of what day of the week it is and of children's birthdays. Attendance charts can also be used to help children learn to read each other's names.

3. Charts or lists on the blackboard can be used to indicate the daily schedule, classroom jobs, and who will be at which centre. Schickendanz (1989) describes how a teacher can use these types of lists to foster children's literacy learning. The teacher puts a list of activities the children may choose from on a chart and discusses them with the children, crossing each off after it has been discussed. If the activity is a familiar one, such as blocks, she asks, "Who knows what is next on my list?" When the children respond, "Blocks," she slowly says, "Yes, *b-l-o-c-k-s*" and runs her finger under the word as she does so (98). Once all of the possibilities have been discussed the children make their choices. If there are more children for one activity than there is room, the teacher makes a "turns" list.

   The children who choose the activity of making popcorn then consult a recipe chart. At the top is written "things we need," and with the teacher's assistance, the children read and locate the items on the list. The teacher then reads the "what to do" part of the recipe, pointing to the words as she does so, and the children carry out the instructions. When the popcorn is finished, one child comments that they didn't put salt on it and the teacher refers her to the recipe, which does not call for salt. The children decide that they want to use salt next time and so one child puts the word salt on the shopping list. The day continues with further opportunities for children to use written language to do things in their classroom.

4. The Morning Message is a technique in which the teacher writes a brief message telling about a significant event for the children that day. For example, "Today we are going to have a special visitor." Once the message is written and read, the children reread it and discuss the day's upcoming events. These Morning Messages are frequently written in minimal cues form once the chil-

dren have begun to read independently. In minimal-cues messages, the teacher leaves selected letters out of words and the children predict what the message is on the basis of the remaining cues. For example, "We are go_ _ _ on a treasure _ unt _ _ day." They predict the words and tell which letters should go in each blank.

5. Play centres can support literacy-related play. For example, a play post office involves a variety of props such as a mailbox, stationery, envelopes, pens, pencils, stamps, address labels, and signs about mailing. Other rich contexts for literacy learning include a cooking centre, store, doctor's office, and travel agent's office.

6. Field trips nearly always provide opportunities for children to use written language for functional purposes.

Writing

It is recommended that young children have daily opportunities to write (Sulzby, Teale, and Kamberelis, 1989). Writing can be integrated with all the experiences described above. However, the establishment of a writing centre in the kindergarten or Grade 1 classroom will provide further opportunities and incentive to write. Writing contributes to numerous aspects of children's literacy development including:

- understanding that written language is meaningful
- understanding why people write
- understanding the relationship between oral and written language
- understanding how print works
- segmenting sounds in words and matching letters with these sounds
- understanding terms related to writing.

A writing centre contains a variety of writing implements and materials: paper, pencils, crayons, chalk, small chalkboards, erasers, markers, scissors, and glue. Sulzby, Teale, and Kamberelis (1989) believe that all kindergarten children reared in a literate culture can and will write. First and most important, they suggest that in order to encourage young children to write, teachers must accept the forms of writing children use. Second, they recommend keeping requests simple, for example, "write a story" or "write a letter to your mother," and then asking children to read what they have written. Their third suggestion is to reassure children that their writing "doesn't have to be like grown up writing. Just do it your own way" (70).

At this stage of children's writing development, it is crucial that teachers respond to the content or meaning of what they are writing, rather than placing a heavy focus on letter formation, spacing, and spelling. Proctor (1986) found that first-grade children in meaning-focused classrooms scored higher on both mechanical and content measures than did children in traditional skills classrooms. Children in meaning-focused classrooms wrote more, they made fewer spelling errors, and their writing was characterized by a need to communicate ideas. They had a strong sense of audience and the ideas in their writing were more complex. Proctor concluded that when teachers focused on meaning, children not only developed their ability to express ideas with clarity and vigor but also mastered many of the mechanical aspects of writing as well.

This does not mean that teachers provide no spelling instruction at the emergent stage of literacy development. If children are trying to write phonetically, the teacher can use this as an opportunity to further develop phonemic awareness. There is considerable consensus in the literature regarding the need for young children to learn to hear individual sounds in words. What is not so clear is whether this is a prerequisite to reading and writing or if it develops as an outcome of children learning to read and write. Until this issue has been clarified, it is recommended that teachers include work on phonemic awareness as part of their language arts program for children in the early stages of learning to read and write.

In order to help children hear sounds in words they are trying to spell, the teacher slowly articulates the words and has the children repeat them slowly, listening for the sounds at the beginning, middle, and end of the word. It is recommended that words be articulated slowly rather than saying sounds separately to avoid distortion. While it is fairly easy to isolate sounds for letters such as *s*, *f*, and *m* without distorting them, it is far more difficult to produce isolated sounds for letters such as *b*, *d*, *g*, *p*, *t*, *k*, *j*, and *ch* without distortion. The sound for *b* often ends up with a *schwa* on the end and sounds a lot like *buh*. The goal of instruction at this point is to help children hear sounds in words rather than to spell words conventionally. It is also recommended that children be encouraged to represent each sound with one letter in the initial stages of writing. For example, the word *hammer* has four distinct sounds and a young child who has spelled the word as *hamr* has demonstrated the ability to hear all four of these sounds. When one focuses on what words sound like rather than what they look like, it is not surprising that children spell the word *hoped* as *hopt* or *dragon* as *jragn*. Other suggestions for developing phonemic awareness are provided in the next section.

Phonological Awareness

In order to understand the relationship between oral and written language and to be able to match words heard to those in print, children need to be able to segment sentences they hear into words. In order to map letters onto sounds and sounds onto letters, they need to be able to hear syllables and sounds in words. The activities in this section help children to hear separate words in sentences and match those words with those in print, and hear separate sounds in words and match those sounds with letters.

1. Speech-to-Print Match

Big books and language experience stories provide numerous opportunities for children to engage in speech-to-print matching. As preparation for this type of activity, the teacher can read sentences slowly and ask the children to clap once for each word they hear. Having blocks or bingo chips to use to represent words in sentences makes the task more concrete. With big books, charts, and language experience stories, pointing to words as you read them helps children to hear the words as separate units and to match them with printed words on the page. Children are also encouraged to point to words when rereading familiar books.

2. Hearing Sounds in Words

Reading nursery rhymes and other rhyming books and poetry to children helps focus their attention on the sounds in words. For many children, reading this type of material begins in the home but teachers cannot assume children have knowledge of common nursery rhymes such as *Jack and Jill.* By seeing these rhymes in big book format or on charts, children not only hear which words rhyme but also learn that when words sound the same, they often also look the same. Predictable rhyming books such as *Whistle, Mary, Whistle* can further develop children's awareness of rhyming words. When reading these books to children, teachers leave out the rhyming word so the children can predict them. For example, "Whistle, Mary, Whistle, and you shall have some bread. I can't whistle, Mother, because I'm standing on my ____."

Another way to promote phonemic awareness is by focusing on sounds during reading of books and writing of language experience stories. Teachers can encourage children to look at the first letter in words to predict the words. During the writing of language experience stories, children can tell the teacher what sound they hear first, next, and last in words. As they advance in literacy development, children can tell the teacher what letters they think she or he should write. Teachers can also encourage children to use letter sound cues to identify words around the classroom and in their play centres. If children experience difficulty doing these tasks, they may benefit by listening to the teacher slowly articulate words and clapping once for each for each syllable or sound they hear. Again, blocks or bingo chips make this activity more concrete. For a few children, hearing sounds in words is very difficult, and more explicit instruction, such as that described below, is required.

3. Elkonin Technique

Marie Clay (1985) suggests the following one-on-one modification of Elkonin's technique to help young children hear sounds in words.

1. The teacher prepares cards on which squares are drawn for each sound unit in words of two, three, and four sounds, e.g.,

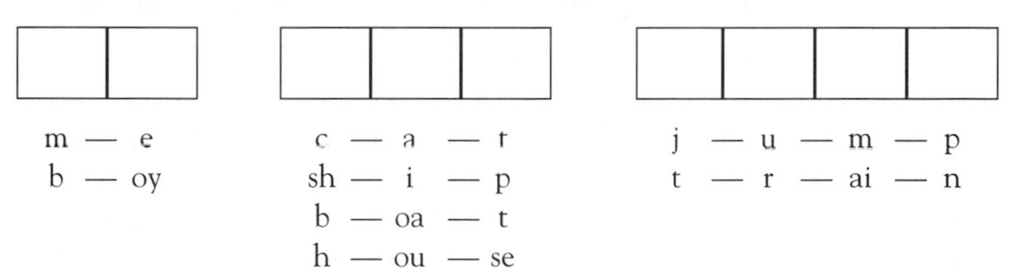

2. The teacher provides a selection of counters.
3. The teacher articulates a word slowly, encouraging the child to watch the teacher's lips and copy what the teacher says.
4. The child articulates the word slowly. (A mirror can be used if it helps children become more aware of what their lips are doing.)
5. The teacher articulates the word slowly, putting one counter into each box, sound by sound.
6. The child puts the counters into the boxes as the teacher says the word slowly, or the teacher puts the counters into boxes as the child says the word.
7. The child puts counters into boxes as he or she says the word.
8. Once the child is able to hear sounds in words, this activity can be applied to spelling words as he or she writes.

   - The child is encouraged to slowly articulate the word he or she wants to spell.
   - The teacher draws a box for each sound unit and asks, "What can you hear? How would you write it? Where will you put it?"
   - Initially the child writes the letters he or she is able to associate with sounds heard and the teacher writes the others.

B	i	ll

b	oa	t

t	r	u	ck

9. After the child is able to hear and record most consonants and some vowels correctly, the teacher gives him or her a box for each letter. Clay suggests using broken lines initially when two letters do not represent distinct sounds.

h	a	m	m	e	r

Meeting the Needs of All Children

As indicated in Chapter 2, differences among children in Canadian classrooms are greater today than in the past, both because of immigration patterns and the movement toward **mainstreaming** children with special learning needs. Regardless of cultural background or socioeconomic level, many children arrive at school with limited literacy experiences. Suggestions for these children are provided first, followed by suggestions for special needs children in the emergent stage of literacy development.

Limited Literacy

Some children arrive at school with limited literacy background. Some of them come from homes with considerable material resources where reading with children has not been a priority. However, many come from lower socioeconomic homes where there are neither material nor human resources to provide rich literacy experiences. Many parents work long hours simply to provide food for their children, with no money left to purchase books, crayons, or other literacy materials. Sometimes the parents themselves have low levels of literacy and cannot serve as reading or writing models for their children. The intergenerational nature of illiteracy is now being recognized and some school systems are beginning to provide family literacy programs involving both parents and children. The purpose of these programs is to improve the literacy levels of parents, as well as help them to provide appropriate literacy experiences for their children at home.

Children with limited literacy backgrounds need to be immersed in a rich literacy environment in the classroom. The teacher needs to provide shared reading, language experience stories, functional reading activities, and writing experiences on a daily basis. Teachers also need to show that they expect children will develop positive attitudes toward books and come to understand that written language is meaningful. Only after considerable exposure to books and other literacy activities will children develop control over the oral dimensions of written language and begin eye–voice matching. Teachers need to be particularly aware of the level of literacy reached by these children in order to provide appropriate experiences. In Exhibit 5.12, an intervention program for one Grade 1 child is described. The school is in an inner city neighbourhood and the child had just moved to live with her aunt and uncle at the end of September.

EXHIBIT 5.12

Amber Learns to Read and Write

When Amber arrived at Kathy Purkiss' Grade 1 classroom at the end of September, she appeared to have limited literacy background (Malicky, Purkiss, and Nugent, 1988–89). When asked to read predictable books (*Brown Bear, Brown Bear, What Do You See?* and *A Dark, Dark Tale*), she demonstrated very positive attitudes toward books and was able to "talk like a book." Her reading was meaningful although she was not yet able to match speech to printed words or to rely on print cues to identify words. In sharp contrast with her reading, she viewed writing as a process of mapping letters onto sounds and was very reluctant to write.

Amber was given one-to-one instruction for five months twice weekly using primarily shared reading, the language experience approach, and writing. Making steady progress in reading throughout the sessions, she was able to match speech to print by mid-November and had begun to make use of print cues as she read. She also began to take familiar books and her language experience stories to her classroom to read to the other children. This helped her to feel like a reader and gave her a sense of belonging to the literacy club in her classroom.

Developing Amber's writing was more problematic. She was reluctant to write on her own and when urged to try, produced short sequences of letters such as *I b swh* for *I like skipping*. These written products were far less rich than the language experience stories she dictated, indicating that she still viewed writing primarily as a process of mapping letters to sounds.

By late January, both of Amber's teachers were quite concerned with her progress in writing. Finally, the intervention teacher used a strategy recommended by Sulzby, Teale, and Kamberelis (1988). She assured Amber that her writing didn't have to be like grown-up writing, that no one else would read it. Amber then began to write, generating the piece reproduced on the following page.

When asked to reread what she had written, she read the alphabet first (the safe part) and then, pointing to the print line by line, read, "The elves made a castle for Santa to build his toys for the kids in the L. family. Santa likes to give out toys from the Christmas tree for all the kids." She smiled happily to herself when she finished reading. With reinforcement, Amber wrote another meaning-based story in the next session. She finally felt free

continued

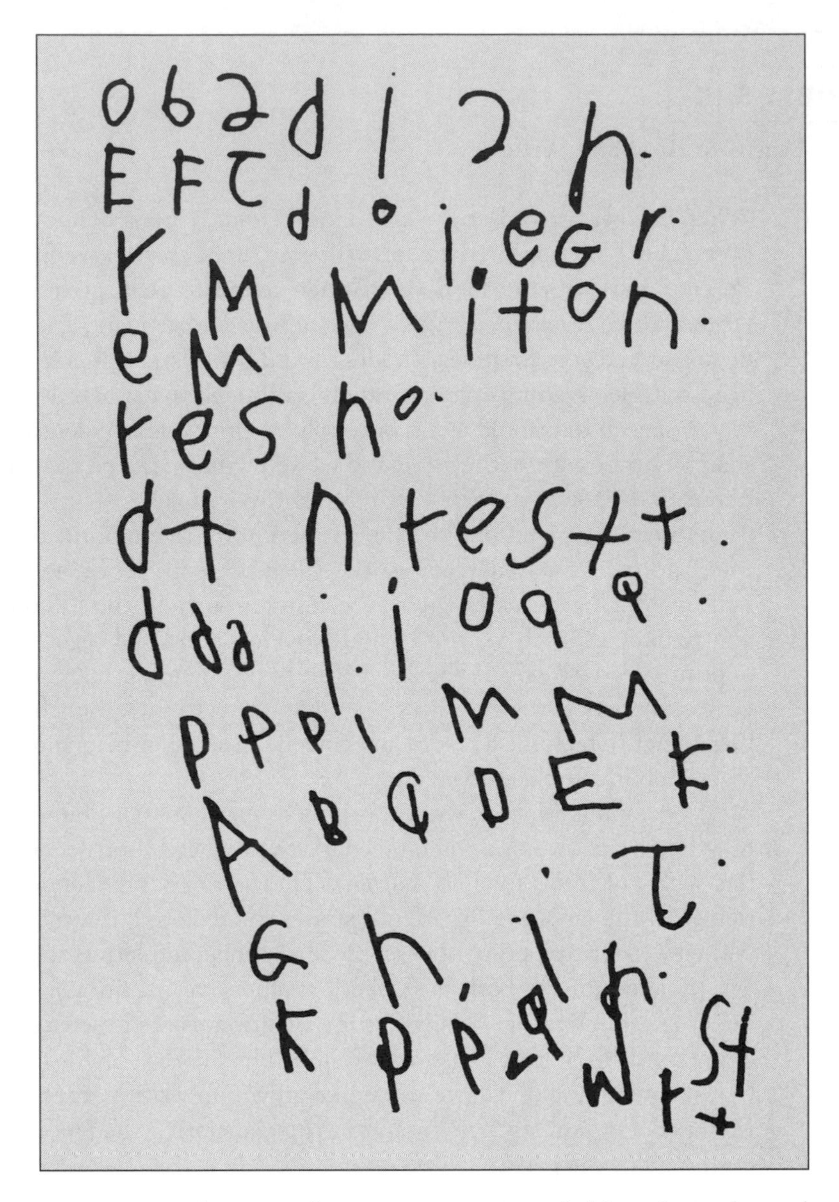

to engage in the type of writing most young children do in the early stages of literacy development, and this appeared to be a necessary step in her writing development. By the end of January, she was beginning to include inventive spellings in her writing, and then, unfortunately, she was gone—to the third school in her Grade 1 year.

Reprinted with permission of the Alberta Teachers' Association.

Special Needs

The general suggestions provided in Chapter 2 for children from different cultural backgrounds are appropriate for children both in the initial stages of literacy development and after they become more independent readers and writers. Perhaps most important is the need to understand and respect the culture of children in the classroom. When teachers incorporate books and other experiences related to children's culture, the children will feel included in the classroom community. It is also important to be aware of differences in storytelling and interaction patterns in different cultural groups, so that all children's stories are accepted and discontinuity between home and school is reduced.

The same general principles apply to most children with learning disabilities *or* mild mental handicaps. It is imperative to determine where they are in their literacy development and provide appropriate learning experiences. When teachers set appropriate goals for these children, they will achieve success and not become discouraged. Assessment techniques for determining emergent literacy needs are described in Chapter 11. Children with more severe learning problems, such as language delays, attention deficit disorders, and sensory impairments, which significantly interfere with their ability to profit from the literacy experiences outlined in this chapter, need to be referred to appropriate specialists for assistance in planning appropriate programs.

There is considerable similarity between the literacy needs of ESL learners in the emergent stage of literacy development and those of children whose first language is English. Both need to be immersed in a meaningful, purposeful literacy environment and to have numerous opportunities for meaningful interaction with written language. Hough and Nurss (1992) believe that early childhood classrooms are generally well suited to the needs of ESL learners. They provide numerous opportunities for concrete activities and small-group interactions, and the same types of literacy experiences are appropriate for both groups of children.

However, teachers of children with limited English proficiency need to make two major adaptations. First is the matter of ensuring comprehensible input. Teachers will need to make some changes in their language and use of gestures and visual aids for the ESL learner. Second, as with all children from different cultures, the teacher needs to ensure that ESL children feel they are part of the classroom group and that their culture is respected.

Shared-book experiences with picture books or big books provide a rich context for language and literacy learning. Predictable books are also well suited to the needs of children with limited English proficiency. The children can join in reading the repetitive parts of the story before individual words have become meaningful to them (Hough and Nurss, 1992). Rereading of both predictable and other picture story books is recommended for all children, including those learning English as their second language. This rereading will provide ESL children with further exposure to written English and also help these children internalize the structure of stories written by authors from Western culture.

Having children dramatize familiar stories will create further opportunities for language development and the internalization of story structures. Picture story books with lots of action and repeated sequences, such as *The Three Billy Goats Gruff*, are particularly appropriate for this type of activity.

The language experience approach is particularly effective with children learning ESL because it is easier to read what one has dictated than unfamiliar texts. The context, vocabulary, and language structures will be familiar to the children and hence, will support their initial reading experiences. Although important for all children, it is particularly important to record the child's language as dictated since they will read what they have said and it is crucial to ensure an accurate eye–voice match.

Chapter Summary

Until the last two decades, the concept of reading readiness influenced the type of reading instruction provided to young children when they arrived at school. Development was thought to proceed through stages and a mental age of six and one-half was viewed as necessary to learn to read. While children were getting ready to learn to read, they were provided with reading readiness workbooks focused on language development, visual-motor abilities, and auditory discrimination.

By the late 1970s, the concept of emergent literacy began to replace reading readiness in program planning. From this perspective, literacy development is seen as continuous, beginning with children's earliest experiences with print at home. Components of emergent literacy include the functions and nature of written language, the form and structure of print, and the conventions of print. Children need to understand that written language is meaningful, why people read and write, how oral and written language are related, what the language of books is like and how to match words heard with those in print. They need to understand the differences between pictures and print, how print works, and how to segment words into sounds. And they need to understand the terms related to books, reading, and writing.

Literacy experiences at home are seen as crucial to literacy development. Some educators argue that literacy programs at school should reflect the way children learn language at home. We need to be careful, however, that in designing literacy programs to reflect what goes on in middle-class homes, we do not increase the discontinuity many children from working-class homes feel when they come to school. Still, some general principles for literacy instruction appear to be appropriate for all children.

Children need to be immersed in a rich literacy environment and involved in meaningful, purposeful literacy activities. They also need to be involved on a daily basis in reading and writing, and to control their own literacy learning. Rather than requiring word-perfect reading and letter-perfect writing, it is important for teachers to reinforce children for producing approximate responses until they develop control over the visual dimension of written language. While children do learn to read in an orderly sequence, teachers need to take individual differences among children into account when planning instruction.

Shared-book experiences can be used to reach a wide range of learning outcomes, and predictable and big books are particularly useful for this activity. There are three steps in a shared-book experience: discovery or initial reading of the book, exploration or rereading, and independent experience. The language experience approach builds on children's own experiences and language and helps them develop a range of understandings about reading and writing. The four stages in development of a language experience story are selecting an experience, discussing the experience to develop vocabulary and language, recording ideas as the children dictate them, and reading the story. Follow-up activities foster specific aspects of emergent literacy development.

Environmental print both inside and outside the classroom also provides significant input for emergent literacy instruction. Labels, calendars, charts, lists, morning messages, play centres involving print, and field trips provide opportunities for children to use written language.

Daily opportunities to write also help children increase their understanding of written language. Initially, it is important to respond to the meaning rather than the form of young children's writing, although as children experiment with writing, they learn how to segment words into sounds and to map these sounds onto letters.

Many children begin school without a rich background of literacy experiences. The experiences described in this chapter are even more important for these children than for those from literacy-rich homes. In addition, there are children with learning problems, children from different cultural backgrounds, and children learning English as a second language. Teachers need to adapt programs to meet the needs of all of these different children.

Selected Professional Resources

Clay, M.M. (1975). *What Did I Write?* Portsmouth, NH: Heinemann.

Samples of children's writing and a description of children's early literacy behaviours are the core of this book. It is useful in identifying the level of development a child has attained and understanding early literacy in general.

Ollila, L.O., and M.I. Mayfield (eds.). (1992). *Emerging Literacy: Preschool, Kindergarten, and Primary Grades*. Toronto: Allyn and Bacon.
Experts from Canada and the United States present ideas to guide literacy development for children ages three through nine. Principles of literacy instruction and descriptions of classroom practices are included, as well as ideas on evaluation and working with parents.

Strickland, D.S., and L.M. Morrow (eds.). (1989). *Emerging Literacy: Young Children Learn to Read and Write*. Newark: International Reading Association.
This book presents many practical suggestions for fostering the literacy development of young children in daycare centres or classrooms. Considerable information is provided on shared-book experiences.

Doake, D.B. (1988). *Reading Begins at Birth*. Richmond Hill, Ont.: Scholastic-TAB Publications Ltd.
Doake describes the literacy development of young children from the perspective of both a researcher and parent. He also identifies instructional practices that are consistent with the way young children learn.

Children's Materials Noted in Chapter 5

Bonnie, R. (1981). *A Dark, Dark Tale*. New York: Scholastic Book Services.
Cowley, J. (1980). *Mrs. Wishy-Washy*. Auckland, NZ: Scholastic Book Services.
Cranstoun, M. (1967). *1, 2, Buckle My Shoe*. New York: Holt, Rinehart & Winston.
Le Sieg,T. (1972). *In a People's House*. New York: Random House.
Martin, B. (1972). *Brown Bear, Brown Bear, What Do You See?* New York: Holt, Rinehart & Winston.
Martin, B. (1970). *Monday, Monday, I Like Monday*. New York: Holt, Rinehart & Winston.
Martin, B. (1970). *Whistle, Mary, Whistle*. New York: Holt, Rinehart & Winston, Inc.
The Three Billy-Goats Gruff. (1963). New York: Holt, Rinehart and Winston, Inc.

CHAPTER 6

The Nature of Reading

This Grade 3 child is completely absorbed in reading a book.

OBJECTIVES

- to be aware of both psychological and social theories of reading
- to understand issues related to a social constructive view of reading
- to understand the nature of response to literature
- to understand the role literature plays in teaching children to read
- to learn a range of teaching strategies for working with literature in classrooms
- to understand the nature of critical literacy

Introduction

Nearly everyone has a theory of what reading is and how it should be taught. Because most people learned to read as children, they assume that the techniques used with them at school were effective and should continue to be used today. This view is often supported in the media, which often focus on the amount of attention that should be devoted to **phonics**. This controversy is not restricted to the public and media, but extends to experts in the field of reading as well. Some take strong positions in favour of teaching phonics in an organized, systematic way (Adams, 1990), while others recommend far less focus on phonics (Goodman, 1993). More important, however, are the questions that rarely get asked in the media—questions such as, Why do more poor than rich children fail to learn to read? Why do so many individuals who learn to read not become avid readers?

This chapter begins with a discussion of the nature of reading and general issues related to the teaching of reading. The remainder is devoted to children's response to literature and **critical literacy**.

Psychological Perspectives on Reading

Psychological perspectives have dominated the field of reading since the beginning of the century (Huey, 1908). Both behaviourist psychology, which focuses on skill development, and cognitive psychology, which focuses on the reading process, have been reflected in views of reading.

Skills vs. Process

Most of us learned to read using material reflecting a skills orientation to reading. **Basal reading series** of the 1960s and 1970s were generally based on development of a series of skills, often ordered hierarchically. For example, a certain number of sight words were introduced before letter sounds, and consonants were generally dealt with before work on vowel sounds. Comprehension was also broken down into component skills, with literal comprehension tasks assumed to be easier than those involving inferential and critical comprehension. Educators thought at the time that reading could be taught by breaking it down into component skills to be learned one at a time, often through drill and practice.

In the 1970s, there was a major shift to a focus on reading processes rather than skills. This has continued into the 1990s and is reflected to some extent in the current generation of basal readers being used in Canada. For example, the Nelson Networks series includes a *Reading and How* (Hughes and McInnes, 1983) book at each of Grades 4 through 6; these books focus on reading processes. The emphasis of the process perspective is on how the child is constructing meaning from print. The focus is on learning rather than teaching, the learner rather than the teacher, and the process rather than the products of learning (Malicky, 1991).

Bottom-Up, Top-Down, and Interactive Theories of Reading

There are three major variables in the reading process: the text, the reader's knowledge, and the process as readers interact with the text. The extent to which readers rely on the text as compared to their knowledge formed the basis for much of the discussion of reading processes in the 1970s.

Text, more specifically letters and words, has been the focus of theorists who view reading as bottom-up processing. According to this interpretation, readers begin with letters and, from them, identify words. As they identify words, they put them together to get the meaning of phrases, sentences, and passages. In other words, readers process information through a series of low-level to high-level stages (Laberge and Samuels, 1974). Gough (1972, 354) states that readers are not guessers. Although they appear "to go from print to meaning as if by magic," this is an illusion; readers actually plod through sentences letter-by-letter.

Laberge and Samuels (1974) note that for readers to become proficient, processing of letter level information must reach a level of **automaticity** so they can focus on meaning. Automaticity is the ability to carry out a process without conscious awareness, much as we steer a car on the highway without actively thinking which way to turn the wheel. With bottom-up theories of reading, reading is viewed as primarily a perceptual process, meaning resides in the text, and processing proceeds from parts to the whole (Lipson and Wixson, 1991).

While letters and words have been the focus of bottom-up theorists, those who view reading as top-down processing emphasize the importance of readers' knowledge. A proponent of this view, Goodman (1970) calls reading a psycholinguistc guessing game in which readers use their knowledge about language and the world to generate hypotheses about meaning, which are tested against the print.

From this perspective, readers are seen as problem solvers, and a complete analysis of print is not considered necessary, or even desirable, for the construction of meaning.

Before encountering text, readers have expectations about what they will read. As they read, they process text in relation to these expectations, and use this information to formulate predictions about the message. If the prediction sounds right and makes sense, readers continue reading, checking the meaning out with subsequent text. If the prediction does not sound right or make sense, readers reformulate their predictions and reread the text to check out these new predictions. Top-down processing can explain why most of us have so much difficulty proofreading our own writing. We have such clear expectations of what we will read that we do not see deviations from what we predict on the page. From this perspective, what readers know is more important that what they see. In top-down models of reading, reading is viewed as a language process, meaning resides in the reader, and processing proceeds from whole to part (Lipson and Wixson, 1991).

By the late 1970s, many writers (Rumelhart, 1977; Adams, Anderson, and Durkin, 1978) began to question whether either top-down or bottom-up models of the reading process were adequate. Bottom-up models were criticized for focusing on the minute analysis of words and for failing to account for either comprehension or the impact of meaning on word identification. The major criticism of top-down models was their vagueness in accounting for research findings and in generating practical implications for teaching. As a result of these criticisms, many educators began to ask how the two positions could be combined to produce a more adequate model of reading.

In Rumelhart's (1977) interactive model of reading, reading is viewed as neither top-down nor bottom-up but as a process of synthesizing information from all levels. Rumelhart hypothesized that processing occurs simultaneously across six levels (features of letters, letters, letter clusters, words, sentence patterns, and meaning). At each level, readers form hypotheses and share information for integration at other levels. From an interactive perspective, reading is seen as a cognitive process, meaning results from interaction between the reader and text, and processing proceeds from whole to part and part to whole (Lipson and Wixson, 1991).

A major advantage of interactive models is that they can account for different use of different information under different circumstances. For example, as good readers, we sometimes encounter material that is difficult to read, such as highly technical scientific material. When that happens, we adjust our reading to process the information much more carefully than when reading a novel or magazine article on a familiar topic.

Social Perspectives on Reading

While psychologists have been concerned with reading since at least the turn of the century, sociologists, anthropologists, and political scientists have had far less impact on how reading is viewed. This has resulted in a heavy focus on the individual child and on learning to read as an individual achievement. The social, cultural, and political nature of learning to read has largely been ignored. There is little wonder that when children do not learn to read in their first few years at school, the focus of attention is on what's wrong with the child rather than examining the child's home, school, or society. However, it is apparent from results of studies that we need to look beyond the child when reading difficulties occur.

In 1992, the National Anti-Poverty Organization (NAPO) released the results of a study examining the relationship of **literacy** and poverty in Canada. Large discrepancies in income distribution were reported, with the richest fifth of the population receiving almost half of all income and the poorest fifth receiving only 3.2 percent. NAPO maintains, "It is poverty and other forms of inequality that create the barriers to good education for many Canadians" (1). Low-income earners, the long-term unemployed, aboriginal peoples, seniors, prisoners, people with disabilities, and racial and cultural minorities all have higher-than-average rates of under-education and poverty. The school drop-out rate for poor children is much higher than average. NAPO reports that while 27 percent of all students aged fifteen to nineteen years drop out of school each year, the drop-out rate for poor children is 45 percent. In his book entitled *Savage Inequalities*, Kozol (1991) points out large disparities in the levels of funding for public education of middle-class and poor children.

Politics pervades all aspects of children's lives both inside and outside of schools. As Edelsky (1994) points out:

> *Politics is about who gets what, where, and how—who gets money, who gets jobs, who gets diplomas, who gets good health care, who gets high-quality literature in classrooms, who gets turns at talk, who gets listened to, who gets valued socially...(253)*

If we want schools to be a vehicle for social justice and democracy, Edelsky says we need to rethink reading education. **Transactional** and social **constructive** views of reading reflect an awareness of the broader context of education.

Transactional Theory

Ironically, much of the impetus for a movement toward social perspectives on reading came from the work of Vygotsky, a psychologist, rather than from sociologists or anthropologists. Vygotsky (1978) theorized that the ways we think are learned primarily through social interactions and that the ways we learn language develop as a result of our use of language in social contexts. Hence, we take on the thinking and language patterns of our social group.

The other major impetus for an alternative view of reading came from literary theory, specifically from Rosenblatt's (1978) transactional theory of reading. Rather than seeing meaning as residing in the text and the task of the reader as figuring out what this meaning is, Rosenblatt sees meaning as being constructed by the reader during the act of reading. The focus is on the reader's response. Readers actively create meaning, relying on the text itself, their knowledge of language and the world, their background experiences, and their world view.

Rosenblatt's work has resulted in a significant shift in the ways we view and teach reading. An extensive discussion of her theory is presented later in this chapter.

Social Constructive Theory

Social constructive theories maintain that "knowledge is socially patterned and conditioned, that coming to know is a result of social experiences and interactions, and that all knowledge and knowledge construction are essentially social acts" (Straw, 1990). The construction of meaning is dependent upon both the social background of the reader and the social context for the act of reading. As with transactional theories, reading is seen as a process of making, rather than getting, meaning. However, social constructive theories also place a heavy emphasis on the collaborative nature of meaning construction and learning. Bogdan and Straw (1993) describe education as a communal pursuit and indicate that reading instruction based on social constructive theory will avoid methods that require students to get the teacher's meaning in favour of providing opportunities for children to respond to texts in group contexts.

According to Straw (1990), a major difference between interactive theories of reading and transactional or social constructive theories is that interactive theories are grounded in the basic assumption that reading is communication, that reading is part of a larger language act that includes "the author as originator of meaning, the text as symbolic or representative of meaning, and the reader as receiver of meaning" (171). In contrast, transactional and social constructive models perceive reading as a "more generative act than the receipt or processing of information or communication" (171). In addition to the text and reader's knowledge, meaning is also constructed on the basis of the social background of the reader and the social context of the reading act.

Implications of Our Definition of Reading

In this textbook, reading is viewed as involving the active construction of meaning from cues in the text and from readers' background knowledge within a social context. Several important components in this definition have implications for teaching and learning reading.

Reading as a Constructive, Meaning-Making Activity

If we want children to view reading as a meaning-making rather than a meaning-getting process, we must be careful of what we say to them and the types of reading activities we ask them to complete. For example, if we constantly ask children literal questions such as, "What colour was the girl's dress in this story?," we give them the incorrect impression that reading is a meaning-getting process and that the meaning is in the text. We also need to be careful to accept and discuss alternative interpretations of the same text. Children will quickly learn that we do not really value their responses to literature if we always tell them the "right" meaning. A major portion of this chapter will focus on fostering the development of children's responses to literature.

Use of Text Information and Knowledge

Similarly, if we want children to understand that their own knowledge is at least as important as the cues in the text in constructing meaning, we have to be careful that most of the work we do on word identification strategies is done in a meaningful context. Otherwise the children may come to believe that the major purpose of reading is accurate identification of words and that meaning is secondary. We also need to take care that we present a balanced reading comprehension program including strategies for using both text cues and knowledge to construct meaning. The best program will be one in which most activities involve using a range of different cues, an integrated use of information sources. In addition to saying, "Look at the word," when children are having difficulty, we also need to say things like, "What would make sense? What would sound right?" In addition to literal comprehension questions, we need to ensure that children have opportunities to respond to inferential and critical questions as well. Chapter 7 will focus on instructional strategies for helping children learn to use text-based and knowledge-based information to construct meaning.

The Social Context of Reading

Finally, we need to view reading in relation to the child's home, community, school, and classroom contexts. The social nature of reading underlines the importance of social experiences and interactions in classrooms. Since knowledge is socially constructed, emphasis is placed on children and teachers talking and working together in groups rather than on individuals reading in isolation.

From a broader sociopolitical perspective, it is important to acknowledge that our classrooms are not neutral. They are nearly always more appropriate learning contexts for some children than others. The greater the discrepancy between the social background of the teacher and children, the harder it will be to reduce discontinuities between home and school. Our classrooms are also not neutral about maintaining or changing the status quo. We can either help children fit into existing sociopolitical structures or we can help them to critically examine inequities based on age, gender, and race to prepare them to engage in social action for change. Some ways to help children examine these inequities are discussed in the part of this chapter on **critical literacy**.

Issues in Reading Instruction

Some other general issues need to be considered when planning and implementing reading programs.

Reading Real Texts

One of the most important issues involves the need for children to read every day from real texts. They will not become good readers by reading lists of isolated words nor will they become good readers by reading books or other materials for only ten minutes per day. If we say to children, "You can select something to read after you finish the assigned workbook pages or chalkboard exercises," we are telling them that reading is not as important as skills exercises. We need to make reading a priority in the way we allocate class time. Providing children with time to read, by itself, will not be sufficient for most children to learn to read, but it is certainly a necessary condition.

Need for Explicit Instruction

Some children seem to develop strategies for using text cues and their knowledge to construct meaning with very little guidance from their teachers. Others, however, benefit from explicit assistance from the teacher. The nature of this explicit instruction is an area of considerable controversy. Some proponents of direct instruction recommend that reading be broken down into a myriad of subskills and each taught in turn, often in isolated drill-type activities. Some children are quite successful in these types of programs, whereas others learn each skill but do not use these skills in an integrated way when they try to read.

Most educators who hold a transactional or constructive view of reading recommend that strategy instruction be provided when needed, rather than according to a predetermined sequence. For example, if children are able to sound out most words but what they read does not make sense, they need to learn to ask themselves, "Does this make sense? Does this sound right?" Teachers need to help such children learn how to use **context cues** along with letter sounds to identify words. Teachers may model the strategy, they might support a child in using the strategy, or they might deductively talk about the strategy and then provide the child with opportunities to use it.

Metacognition

A major question related to explicit instruction is whether children need to become aware of reading strategies and when to use them in order to become proficient readers. Awareness and control of reading strategies is generally referred to as **metacognition**.

We have knowledge about factors that affect reading (Jacobs and Paris, 1987; Cross and Paris, 1988; Flavell 1979). For example, a reader may know that he or she is good at figuring out hard words but has difficulty finding main ideas. A reader may also know that he or she is a better reader than most of the children in the class, or that there is a limit to how fast most people can read. We know it is easier to recall the gist of a story than to remember it word for word. We also have knowledge about reading strategies (Flavell, 1979; Jacobs and Paris, 1987), for example, we know how to figure out difficult words or how to study for a multiple-choice test. And we know when and why to apply particular strategies. For example, it does not make sense for children to use a phonic strategy to identify a word they have already established as a sight word. It wastes time and takes attention away from meaning.

The regulative or control dimension of metacognition involves readers in planning and monitoring their reading. We plan what we will do as we read, for example, using the headings and subheadings to make predictions about what a passage or chapter will be about before we begin reading. We evaluate our reading to determine whether what we read makes sense, and we make corrections to what we are doing if what we read does not make sense. For example, if you reached the end of this paragraph and decided that the meaning you constructed did not make sense, you might decide to reread the paragraph. Alternatively, you might decide to read to the end of the section to see if that helped you to make sense out of what you had been reading.

Researchers have generally found that young children are less likely to display metacognition than are older children (Flavell, 1979; Brown, 1980). Yaden (1984, 34) concluded from his review of the literature on young children's **metalinguistic awareness** that young children "have disparate notions as to what comprises the act of reading." From their review of the literature on children's awareness of reading, Paris, Wasik, and Turner (1991) concluded that while young children have rudimentary understanding of the task of reading, they have incomplete concepts about the nature of reading, print conventions, and purposes and processes for reading. However, children's understanding and control of strategies increase with skill and age.

While some research tends to be more optimistic about the ability of young children to engage in metacognitive behaviour (Malicky, Juliebö, and Norman, 1994), there is still a question about the impact of metacognition on reading achievement. Ultimately, our aim is to help children achieve **automaticity** in their reading so they do not have to consciously think about how to figure out words or to make meaning as they read. Brown (1980) talks about this as being on automatic pilot. It is only when we experience difficulty reading that we need to consciously think about what we are doing.

Instructional Level

An area of controversy in the field of reading in recent years involves the notion of **instructional reading level**. It is similar to Vygotsky's (1978) **zone of proximal development**; children need to receive reading instruction from material that is just difficult enough to help them develop new strategies. If instruction is provided with materials that are too easy, the children will not need to develop any new strategies. If it is too hard, they will struggle and become frustrated.

Matching children with texts is not as easy as it once seemed. In the past most people believed that the difficulty of a book could be determined by considering factors in the text, such as word and sentence length. That was before we were aware of how significant readers' knowledge was in the meaning-making process. Now some people ignore factors in the text and say that readability is determined almost completely by the child's interest and knowledge. Clearly, both views are wrong. Regardless of how interested a child is in a topic or how much background knowledge she or he has, factors in texts, such as word difficulty, sentence complexity, and text organization, may negatively affect the meaning-making process to such an extent that the child becomes frustrated.

Some guidebooks for **basal** readers recommend that one way around this problem is to have all children work with the same text but to have different children do different things with it. For example, a particular text might be appropriate for some children to read independently, for others to read with help from the teacher, and for others to listen to as the teacher reads. This is acceptable practice as long as the children who do the listening also receive reading instruction in appropriate texts as well. Otherwise, some children may become good listeners but be denied the opportunity to learn to read. Therefore, children and teachers need to work together to select appropriate texts for reading instruction. Of equal importance is the need to have a wide range of texts available in any classroom so all children can receive at least some of their reading instruction in their zone of proximal development. Criteria and techniques for determining a child's instructional reading level are presented in Chapter 11.

Reader Response

In her work on reader response, Rosenblatt (1978) pointed out that people read different materials differently depending on their purpose for reading. When you were in elementary school, your teacher likely treated both stories and informational material in a similar way. You were likely asked to read and then answer a series of questions about what you had read. While this approach is appropriate for informational material since **efferent** reading involves "taking away" information from what you have read, it is a questionable practice with **narrative** material. Reading stories involves entering into and living through them rather than taking away information.

As an increasing number of teachers use **trade books** in their classrooms instead of, or in addition to, **basal reading series**, they frequently work with a response-based curriculum. Because this type of approach is so important for working with children's literature and because this practice has become so widespread, the next part of this chapter is devoted to a discussion of reader response.

Responding to Literature: Engaging Child with Text

People respond to all kinds of events in their lives; to a menu read in a restaurant, to a movie seen at the cinema, to news from a friend, to a television show, to international news on the radio, to a song, to a play, to an editorial in the newspaper. Response is part of the human condition; part of an individual's interactions with the people and the world around. It is part of the process of making meaning. Louise Rosenblatt (1978) maintains that text is simply squiggles on a page until a reader reads it. When a reader reads that print, something happens in a reader. That something is response. The response might be boredom, confusion, interest, sadness, empathy, or joy, but reading never happens without a variety of responses.

Rosenblatt (1978) refers to the reading experience as a transaction between text and reader that creates what she calls the "lived-through experience with the text." Readers respond to the transactional experience as they read, as well as afterward, when they reflect upon, or recapture their experience. Rosenblatt maintains that a response is shaped, to a considerable extent, by the purpose for reading, or in other words, by the stance (approach) the reader takes to the text. The approach can range anywhere on a continuum from efferent at one end, where the reader seeks information, to aesthetic at the other, where the reader focuses on appreciating what is read. Of course, readers can take both approaches at the same time. Responses also fluctuate along this continuum

EXHIBIT 6.1

Continuum of Reader Response

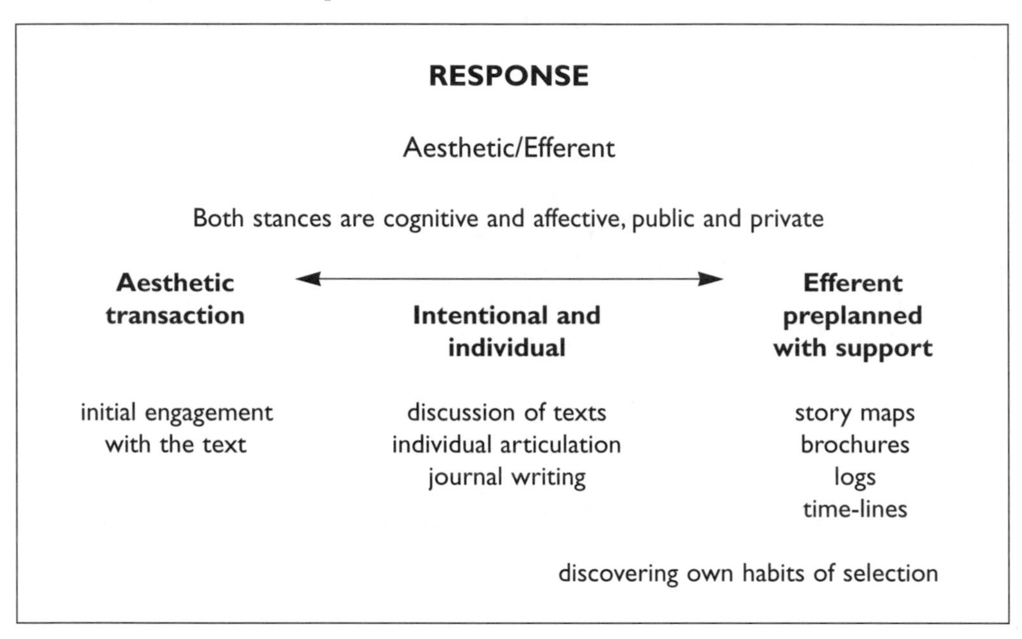

(see Exhibit 6.1). At one moment a reader may be reading for pure pleasure, and the next moment might notice something in the text that takes one's attention and that the reader relates to some other piece of information received in the past. For example, when reading *The Iron Man* (Hughes, 1968), a reader may be appreciating the artistry of the language and the metaphorical nature of the story, when her or his attention might focus on the issue of pollution of the environment, connecting the book with a newspaper article read the previous day. The reading experience thus moves from an aesthetic to a more efferent stance.

To show the extremes of response on this continuum, let us examine two different reading events. Reading a first-aid manual is efferent reading, at the far end of the continuum. The reading has very pragmatic results: to gain essential information that will directly affect the reader's behaviour in the immediate future. On the other hand, reading a novel is an aesthetic experience, at the other end of the continuum. The reader's aim is appreciation, and at some level, a deeper understanding of the human experience. As readers engage with a novel, they are likely to enter into its space and disconnect from their own existence in time. Whether a good book evokes angst or pleasure, it is almost certain to evoke deep personal engagement. Hence, children must be given the opportunity to respond aesthetically to any text, whether in a basal reader or a trade book. Rosenblatt maintains that "once the work has been evoked, it can become the object of reflection and analysis, according to the various critical and scholarly approaches" (Farrell and Squire, 1990, 106). Once the reader begins to reflect upon the experience of reading aesthetically, there is a move toward a more efferent response. For example, a reader may read a short story in such a way that he or she enters the story's time and leaves behind immediate worldly concerns. However, when reflecting on the story, the reader may create meaning (based on the text) that relates to other stories or poems, historical facts, information the reader possesses, or the reader's real life. Thus the reader has re-entered chronological time and has engaged in a more efferent response. A totally efferent response might involve paraphrasing or summarizing the story, retelling it, or analyzing the text.

The reader response that a teacher sees in a classroom is like the tip of an iceberg; most of it is out of sight (Purves and Rippere, 1968). What children show of their response in a classroom will depend upon their individual reading abilities and the level of trust they feel in the environment. People do not usually share something they feel unsafe about. Many adults learned in school that there is one right response to a piece of literature—the teacher's interpretation. These students engaged in a game of "guess what's in the teacher's mind," rather than offering their own personal responses and thoughts about a text. Literary texts then remain a kind of unfathomable mystery. It is therefore important in the elementary school years for teachers to encourage children to respond to texts and to talk with their peers and teachers about books. It is in these early years that many attitudes are formed and foundations laid for further, perhaps more sophisticated or analytical, responses during the secondary school years.

In encouraging children to respond to texts it is important that teachers understand why they are doing this, and what is being learned. Children come to understand how texts work, what constitutes a good book, and how language can be used in different ways to create different meanings and effects. In short, they learn how to become readers, not just people able to read. Children are more likely to take ownership of the reading process and come to understand that there is no "right answer" to literature when they are invited to respond to a text, although as Rosenblatt says, some responses are more legitimate or appropriate than others. Children use high-level cognitive abilities when they engage with, and respond to a text aesthetically, and they learn to respect and honour their own interpretations. Children appear to become more critical in their thinking about texts, more creative in their own writing, and much more capable language users and learners.

Literature can be the basis for an entire language learning program in the elementary classroom, for the nature of reading and response causes children to integrate their knowledge, make personal sense of it, and express it through movement, visual arts, music, drama, writing, and dialogue. When encouraging response to literature in the classroom, Thomson (1987) reminds us that "the development of a mature response to literature involves a progressive movement from close emotional involvement to more distanced reflective detachment, and from an interest in self to an interest in other people and the human condition" (153). This means that the process of response almost always begins with an aesthetic, personal experience of the text. It is this personal experience that a literature response journal is able to facilitate.

Literature Response Journals

Response journals are a place for students to reflect and think about what they are currently reading. These journals are intensely private and personal in that they reflect exactly how a reader responds to a text. It is essential, therefore, that the journals not be corrected for grammar, spelling, and so on, but be accepted by the teacher as a fellow reader and not as an authority on the text. This applies, of course, to oral discussions of books as well. If a teacher has chosen a book for the class to read, or to read to them, and it is a favourite of the teacher's, it can be difficult to handle the response of "I didn't think it was a very good story, really" (which happened to one teacher during a recent sharing of a picture book with a class of children). On these occasions, the teacher must take the utmost care to receive the child's response, to honour it, and to further the child's thinking by asking questions about her or his comments. These discussions can be extremely enlightening for a teacher and can be a springboard for finding alternative ways of exploring books. In the example above, the child went on to say that the author had not told the whole story and there was lots of information missing. As a result of that observation, the class moved into a hot-seating strategy (see Chapter 10) in groups of three. One child in each group took the role of the character in the book, and the other children asked him or her questions. Within half an hour, they had created many versions of the story, each group developing the missing pieces. Thus, these children engaged in a deeper and more expanded reading of the text. At the end of the session the children were so eager to reread the book that at least half the class went straight to the library looking for that book and for others by the same author.

Literature response journals should remain as open-ended and unstructured as possible. It seems that the more structure these journals have, the more contrived they become, and the less fluent and cohesive the children's responses (Pantaleo, 1994). We must not allow the book report, for example, to interfere with the format a journal entry might take. We must ask, "What are we teaching and what do we want children to learn?" Teachers have discovered that most children will eventually work through many of the structures and elements of literature if given the opportunity to ask questions and search for answers themselves. Educators have an unfortunate reputation for providing children with answers to questions that children have not asked. In other words, we still tend to be teacher oriented. Literature response journals are one place where instruction can be student oriented and text oriented, and teachers can genuinely work with children as they seek to understand how literature weaves its magic, how reading is accomplished, and how books work.

For children who need help in responding to a text in a journal, it is usually effective to talk about the book first, or to ask children questions about the book that might lead to a deeper or fuller response. For example, when working with *The Tunnel* by Anthony Browne (1989), we might ask, "How did you feel when you read that the brother was about to go through the tunnel and leave his sister behind?" Directing children to focus their response on some aspect of the text such as plot, setting, characters, or theme, does not appear to be as effective as leaving the response options totally open to the students, so it's wise to provide suggestions only where necessary. Response writing, like any other type of writing, has to be learned. Children who are not used to writing in the expressive voice (see Chapter 8) may need some time to get used to the idea that this is an acceptable form of writing. It is not a matter of learning what to write, but rather of learning how to write a response. This applies to adults as well as to children.

Any response to literature is shaped by the text itself. Some texts, such as *Gorilla* by Anthony Browne or *Julie* by Cora Taylor, invite immediate responses. Other texts, such as *The Dark Is Rising* by Susan Cooper (1973), may need to be read completely before a response can be shaped. Texts that have been described as writerly are ones where readers must make inferences, judgments, and interpretations, filling in the gaps and reading between the lines. Readerly texts, on the other hand, are very straightforward and leave little room for individual interpretation or inference (remember *Dick and Jane* and *The Bobbsey Twins?*) (Meek, 1988). In addition, readers deal with expressing their responses to texts in very different ways. As we have examined children's written responses to books, we have seen how the responses demonstrate what children know, what and how they think, and just exactly how they have comprehended a text. There is no need for retelling the story to see whether a child has understood the book or not, for response goes beyond retelling. Below are some examples of children's journal writing from a combination Grade 2/3 class, a Grade 5 class, and a Grade 6 class. The Grade 2 children wrote in peer dialogue journals (see Chapter 9), and so the two children's entries are written below each other in different fonts.

Melissa and Stuart (Grade 2)

Miss Rumphius by Barbara Cooney

Melissa This story reminds me of me becos I alwiys wanted to plant a garden over in they emtey lot acros from us but my mom sade it wood be to mush work, but I'm saving my alowince for some plants and flowers so I can plant some ther.

Stuart *I like planting flowers and vegebals but I hate it when I have to take a slug off a flower there so slimy and ugly but I kind of have a indoor green house that I got from Scholastic books.*

Two Bad Ants by Chris Van Ahlsburg

Melissa This reaminds me of wen I went to the mountins and I fownd a wered object it looked like a melted tin but it was verry hard to bend. at ferst I thot I wood end up richer than my parentes but I endied out not beaing rich atole. Do you think the ants were beaing gready or wanted to try their musteyris cristels that we know is sugar. It also reaminds me of the time my brother fownd a white rock and thot it was a cristel and he came in yelling mom—mom I fownd a white crustel.

Stuart *The rock your brother found probely had shiny minirels in it but doase your brother still have the rock.*

Melissa he still thinkes ther cristeles so he heas got tuns.

Jennifer (Grade 5)

Gloomy Gus by Walt Morey

I would and wouldn't like to be Eric. I would like to be Eric because he has a tame bear as a pet and it would be neat to have a pet like that. Also because of living in Alaska, with all the wildlife of beauty. Also because of all his good friends like Ten-Day and Charlie (who he met at the circus) would make me want to be Eric. I wouldn't want to be Eric because of Ned Strong. Ned pretended to be Eric's father and was mean to him and drank beer all the time and got drunk. Also I wouldn't want to be Eric because Eric had gotten taken away from his home and Ten-Day to join the circus which his "dad" made him do just for the money.

Jennifer has written a very personal response to *Gloomy Gus*, putting herself in Eric's situation and empathizing with him. The response reflects Jennifer's own love of the outdoors and her appreciation of nature and beauty. She can see two sides of the situation; the land, the animals, and the value of friendship, and also the abandonment and abuse that befell Eric.

Cathie (Grade 6)

Jasmin by Jan Truss

> I think that the end of this book was excellent because everything wrapped up well. Jasmin's clay animals were put in a box that had home-made forest surrounding them. She won second prize at the Science Fair. Her teachers decided Jasmin could go to grade seven as they were giving her another chance. Her parents talked to a family counsellor advising them to give Jasmin her own room. They also advised Leroy to be moved to a special home because he was getting too big for them to be looking after anymore. The good thing was that he could visit them on weekends. While Jasmin had run away, her whole family began to realize how much they needed her and when she was found, they showed love for her again. Jasmin realized she was pretty (someone had painted a picture of her) and could do useful things with her hands (example clay animals). Best of all she liked who she was!

Cathie has gone back to the text, in this response, to explore her reasons for liking the book. She has suggested why the ending was appropriate, and described how the author pulled together all the pieces of the story.

Ron (Grade 5)

The Dragon Children by Bryan Buchan

> I really liked this book because there were two mysteries in the whole book. One of the mysteries was if the crook would make it out of town in time, and if John, Scott, Cathy and Steven would get the crook or not. The other mystery was to find out who or what Steven really was. I figured out what Steven was by putting all the clues together. At the end of the book I found out who Steven was. At first I thought that Steven was a ghost (even though he was) that the crook had drowned in the river. I was half right about that.
>
> It was a surprise to me when John, Scott, and Cathy found out that the crook wasn't who they thought he was. It surprised me because when Steven told John that the crook was driving a green car with a license plate number 5K-206 it wasn't the crook driving it. Instead it was the man who had come with his family for their vacation. The man did seem like a crook though because when he was walking through the woods with his son, it looked like he had kidnapped the child.

> My favorite part, though, was when Scott sneaked up behind the real crook and poked the needle in his back-end. I liked it because it really made me laugh.

Ron has written this response about how he played detective as a reader and fit together all the pieces of the story, making meaning and unravelling the two mysteries. It shows how Ron engaged with the text; how he experienced a more distanced response to the book rather than a personal identification with the characters and their actions.

Mitch (Grade 5) (written as a dialogue journal with the teacher)

The Iron Man by Ted Hughes

> I think the Iron Man will be like the machine in the scrap metal yard that gets rid of the metal. The Iron Man will be happy, the farmers will be happy and Hogarth can visit the Iron Man all the time. Who were the people that had the picnic on the hill and will they show up again? If the Iron Man is controlled by something, who or what is it and what will it think to the Iron Man being so happy? If there is more Iron Men does the Iron Man we know about keep in touch with them? If he does, maybe our Iron Man will tell the others and they will come too. I like how the author called all the metal delicacies. I can see how the chain is spaghetti and maybe the knobs on the bed were chocolate covered candy. Brass covered iron. I don't understand how different kinds of metals have different kinds of tastes. What do you think the Iron Man's favorite kind of metal is? ... What will happen when the Iron Man runs out of food at the metal scrap yard? Will they bring him food from other towns? Do you think the Iron Man will ever go back to the sea? Maybe if he leaves the scrap yard all the townsfolk will look for him at the sea. Do you know if the farmers filled up the hole? I sure hope so. It would be disastrous if somebody fell down the hole. If somebody did fall down the hole, maybe the Iron Man will help them out and then he might not be hated so much. Is the Iron Man hated? I think it starts out in the story that the Iron Man was hated but now I think maybe he is more liked.

Mitch's response is more like stream of consciousness writing. He has put on paper the many questions he had as he listened to the story, and has highlighted some of the images in Hughes's writing. The response demonstrates how involved Mitch felt as he listened to the story, processing the many thoughts that went through his mind. Mitch moved quickly from one idea to another, not stopping long to reflect on one aspect of the chapter, but trying to capture the excitement and wonder that occurred as he heard the story.

Readers' Workshop

Readers' workshop is a term made popular by Nancie Atwell in her book *In the Middle: Writing, Reading, and Learning with Adolescents* (1987). A complaint frequently voiced by children is that they are given very little time in school to actually read. Instead, they devote most of their instructional time to activities about reading (Pantaleo, 1994). Atwell suggests that time be provided in school for reading books *and* learning about reading. She maintains that children read magazines, TV guides, and such material out of school, and therefore in school they need to be encouraged to select books that interest them (novels, biography, poetry, plays) and material that they may not normally choose. Alan Purves (1993) has emphasized that reading in school can never be like reading out of school, because in school it is the teacher's job to teach; to facilitate children's growth in book selection, reading skill, confidence, fluency, ability to express opinions, and critical and creative thought. He writes, "I urge us to see our task in schools as helping students read literature and understand the culture, to speculate on the ideas and the imaginative vision, and to speculate on the nature and the use of the language that is the medium of the artistic expression" (360). Atwell proposes a readers' workshop format where most in-class time is spent reading, and where minilessons help children to do what Purves suggests is the role of schooling in the teaching of reading and literature.

In readers' workshop, children come prepared with a book that they have chosen from the class or school library and that they are ready to read or are already reading. Readers' workshops are *not* a time for making book selections. For the first twenty minutes or half-hour of the workshop (the time will vary, depending on the age of the children), children read their books. It is important that they have a sustained amount of time: ten minutes is *not* enough. Children may not talk or disturb others, though they may sit or lie anywhere, depending upon the physical arrangement of the room. *Quiet time is important when reading.* Most readers cannot read fluently if there is noise around them, or if they are trying to pay attention to more than one thing. The second part of readers' workshop might consist of a minilesson: the teacher reading part of a book to the class, a book talk by the teacher or a student, or some other activity in response to a book. The teacher might make a presentation on a particular author and show the class a number of books by that author. Information on authors is easily available in libraries in publications such as

Two Grade 5 girls share a children's newspaper.

Something About the Author or in the newsletters some authors (e.g., Jan Brett) send out to readers who write to them. Alternatively, this time can be spent in further exploration of a book, or small group discussions of novels. The time might also be used for writing in a response journal. The main purpose of readers' workshop, however, is to give children time to read, to have them take ownership of their reading, and for them to respond in their own language to the material they chose.

Novel Studies and Response Groups

Novel studies might be conducted as part of readers' workshop. A study can include a whole class if class sets of novels are available, or they can take place in groups of four to six students. Multiple copies of novels are needed for a number of children to read one book over the same period of time. This facilitates discussion of a more personal and intense nature. Working with small groups means that the number of novels available for study can be larger, since fewer copies of each novel are required than when working with the whole class. It is less costly to have twenty sets of five books than twenty sets of twenty-five, and most classrooms have many more than twenty sets of novels. Many teachers choose to complete one whole-class novel study at the beginning of the year to set out the expectations of novel studies and to establish guidelines and procedures.

Inside **the Classroom**

Sylvia Pantaleo has taught in Grades 4, 5, and 6 in Olds, Alberta. One of the main goals of her language arts program is to develop a lifelong love of reading in her students. One approach Sylvia uses to accomplish this is literature workshops. She uses a class novel study to teach and model some of the strategies and activities expected of the children when they participate in these workshops.

Sylvia writes: "Regardless of the grade, students are assigned to groups of three to five members, based upon their approximate reading speeds. Each group of students chooses a book to read, and the group members meet daily to discuss three questions that each member has generated as a result of reading the text the previous day (or night at home). They read about twenty to forty pages daily, depending on the group. As well, the group discusses each person's "pizzazz" word (a word students encounter that they find interesting or are uncertain about). During discussion time, I circulate

continued

about the room, listening to the conversations. Once discussions are complete (approximately ten to fifteen minutes), each group sets a new reading goal (the number of pages or chapters to be read for the following day) and records it on a small chart posted at the front of the room. I monitor the reading goals to ensure they are appropriate for the different groups. The students spend the rest of the period reading their novels and/or writing a response. I read silently during this time or help individual students with their written responses. After three to four months, the groups disband and the program becomes individualized. Students work on their own, setting their own reading goals, and talking with me about the pieces of literature they choose to read.

As well as engaging in reading conferences, the children write responses to the books at the midpoint and upon completing the texts. The children are introduced to the process of response writing by talking and writing about their reactions to movies, music, clothes, tragic events, surprises, sounds, smells, and so on. I provide instruction through class discussions, modelling, class collaborations, and direct group instruction. I believe that response writing gives children opportunities to savour, reflect upon, and deepen their aesthetic experiences of books. The students decide on the content of their responses (i.e., there is no particular structure or format) but I encourage them to select and write in-depth about one or two ideas, images, feelings, memories, or thoughts they experienced during or after their reading. For example, some students relate the story to other books, movies, or experiences in their lives. Some evaluate a situation or a character, put themselves in a character's position, and discuss what they would feel or do and why. Others discuss the author's purpose, writing style, or techniques.

As well as the many instances of direct instruction outlined, I also teach individual students or groups who need help improving the quality of their questions, dealing with comprehension difficulties, selecting novels, or organizing themselves to meet their goals. In addition, the students need to be independent, since for most of the period they work on their own. Therefore, the children must be aware of when literature responses are to be written and handed in, signing-out procedures for books, and other classroom routines."

continued

Sylvia Pantaleo, who has run literature workshops in her classroom for many years, estimates there are probably 1 500 books in her classroom. She has read all the books in the multiple copies section of the classroom library, as well as many from her own collection. She feels very strongly that knowledge of the books is important to the success of the program so she can recommend novels, discuss books, and write literature responses to her students.

As mentioned in Chapter 2, many teachers have been accused of basalizing children's literature (Jobe and Hart, 1991), and this has caused much concern in the profession. Working with novel studies is different from working with a basal reader, since the children are reading an entire piece of work, and it is a literary work, not a text written for teaching purposes. If the same teaching strategies are used with a work of literature as with a basal reader, there is no point in using works of literature. We must understand why we are choosing to work with literature rather than a basal reader. If we want to work from an efferent stance, using detailed questions retracing the story line, focusing on main ideas, and monitoring children's reading strategies, then we should probably work with a basal series. If we want to work from an aesthetic stance, encouraging the appreciation of literature through students' questions and developing interpretations, as well as nurturing children's reading abilities, then we have to let go of some of the structure and many of the activities associated with basal readers (Langer, 1994).

The books for a novel study can be read at home. Atwell suggests that we encourage children to read in bed each night, since it is one of the few places children are undisturbed by family members, television, and so on. Readers' workshop can be used for reading novels if students choose to do this. Some teachers have individual groups decide how many and which chapters they will read before their next meeting. As children read a novel, there are many interesting activities that will help them to explore, interpret, and more fully understand the text. Chapter 10 includes many examples of activities that might be part of a novel study. Michael Benton and Geoff Fox's *Teaching Literature* (1985) also provides a rich source of activities for promoting children's explorations of books. Their suggestions for working with *Tuck Everlasting* (Babbitt, 1975) include creating a timeline, drawing portraits of the characters, "hot-seating" the characters, writing character sketches, interviewing characters for a talk show, making wanted posters for Mae Tuck, creating a map of Treegap and the surrounding area, and writing an imaginary diary entry as Winnie. These activities encompass the full spectrum of responses, from aesthetic to efferent. Michael Halliday's functions of language (see Chapter 1) can be enormously helpful in creating a diverse range of language activities for children as they explore novels.

A most important aspect of exploring a novel is the response group. It is imperative that children have opportunities for orally sharing and shaping their responses to books. This helps them to more fully understand the possible meanings of a book. As they share responses and listen to the ways that other readers responded to a book, children become aware that no two readers read in the same way. As children encounter different interpretations, their attention is called to details they might have missed, and they are forced to think about things that as individual readers they might not have thought about. Taking part in a response group can be a fascinating experience. It can also be frustrating if readers want everyone in the group to respond to a book in the way they did.

Donna Preston (1994), in her book *Whole Language: Novel Studies for the Intermediate Grades*, suggests the following questions for readers to think about before they meet in their response groups (8):

- Why did I choose this book?
- What made the writing easy or hard to understand?
- Did I have to force myself to finish it?
- Was it a good choice and why?
- What made it a good or poor choice?
- How would I compare it with other books I have read?
- Would I read other books on the same theme or by the same author?
- Would I want to share this book with someone else in the class?
- Did something happen in the book that I would like (or not like) to happen to me?
- Did I learn something from this book?
- What were the high points in the book for me?
- How real or fanciful was the writing?

Stanley Fish says, "Not only does one believe what one believes, but one teaches what one believes, even if it would be easier and safer and more satisfying to teach something else" (1980, 364). If we believe that teaching reading means asking children questions, and requiring children to retell almost everything they read, or pick out the main ideas from a chapter in a book, then our teaching will betray those beliefs. Langer writes: "The thought-provoking literature class is an environment where students [and teachers] are encouraged to negotiate their own meanings by exploring possibilities, considering understandings from multiple perspectives, sharpening their own interpretations, and learning through the insights of their own responses" (1994, 207). She goes on to remind us that response is based as much on the reader's own personal and cultural experiences as it is on the particular text and author. In closing, Langer says, "In instructional contexts of this sort, which treat all students as thinkers and provide them with the environment as well as the help to reason for themselves, even the most 'at-risk' students can engage in thoughtful discussions about literature, develop rich and deep understandings, and enjoy it too" (1994, 210).

Critical Literacy

Critical reading essentially means "arguing back with texts" (Gillet and Temple, 1994, 50) or, stated another way, "reading against the grain" (Temple, 1993, 89). One aspect involves critically reading advertisements so individuals will become wise consumers. Critical reading also involves analyzing books for hidden biases, particularly those that suggest one gender, race, or social group is superior to another. The first step in social change, according to Freire (1970), is critical awareness of the inequities and injustices around us. While critical literacy will not solve our social problems, it helps to create the conditions necessary for a more democratic and just society.

Edelsky is a strong supporter of education for democracy. While she believes that transactional and constructive theories are basically correct, she argues that they don't go far enough. They still "focus on individuals, but our goal (if it's democracy we're after) is societal" (1994, 255). As a beginning, she suggests that we need to revise our theories of language education to highlight the relationship between language and power. "It means figuring out and then spelling out how systems of domination are part of reading and writing, part of classroom interaction, part of texts of all kinds..."(255). It means that as reading teachers, we need to think about everything in the classroom in terms of power and domination. Who decides what is a "good" story? Who decides what meanings of a text are acceptable? Who decides what books are in the classroom? Whose view of the world is represented in these books?

Critical literacy also means that we need to think about the way we implement instructional programs in our classrooms. When we apply this concept to reader response, for example, it is not enough to have children respond to literature by relating what they read to their own experiences. We could start there, but we need to go much further. Edelsky (1994, 256) stresses the need for teachers to "encourage a sustained look at the societal issues that are suggested by so many pieces of literature and that languish unexamined in personal responses."

Temple (1993, 91) provides an example of how one teacher did this with a group of second- and third-grade children. The teacher asked several questions about *Beauty and the Beast* to help the children critically examine their assumptions about gender roles in society: "Suppose Beauty had been kind and clever but not prettier than her sisters? Do you think the author is suggesting that we should be more like Beauty or more like her sisters? Suppose Beauty had been a boy in this story, and the Beast had been a girl." As they discussed answers to these questions, the children dealt with issues such as the high value placed on outward appearance in our society, compared with inner qualities. One child said, "You don't judge people by how pretty they are. You judge them by how nice and kind and loving they are" (92). The children also talked about how some of the time they were like the "snotty" sisters and sometimes they were like Beauty, recognizing that there is good and bad in all of us. In relation to gender roles, one child summed it up with, "What bugs me is that in the fairy tales, the guys are always doing things outside, and the girls are just basking around in their beautiful dresses" (93).

Contrasting *Beauty and the Beast* with a book such as *The Paper Bag Princess* by Robert Munsch provides further opportunities for children to examine the focus of our society on outward beauty. In this tale, it is the princess who saves the prince through courage and intelligence. Other books such as *Tough Eddie* by Elizabeth Winthrop examine stereotypic portrayals of males. *Tough Eddie* is about a young boy who acts tough but has a secret—at home his favourite toy is a dollhouse.

Perhaps one of the greatest challenges we have to face in this work is what to do when a child's meaning is quite different from our own. Lewis (1993) describes the difficulty she had with one boy's response to *The Pelican and the Crane* (Lobel, 1980). In this fable, a pelican comes to tea at the crane's and is very sloppy and wasteful, all the time wondering aloud why nobody ever invites him anywhere. For example, when the pelican pours milk into his tea, he pours most of it on the table. When he is asked if he would like a cookie, he takes a large pile of cookies and stuffs most of them into his mouth, leaving a pile of crumbs. At the end of the story, the pelican says he hopes he will be invited back. The crane says, "Perhaps, but I am so busy these days," and calls for his maid to clean up the mess. The moral given by the author is, "When one is a social failure, the reasons are as clear as day." But one child, Rick, felt sorry for the pelican because he was a klutz. Rick focused on the crane, who told a lie, and decided his moral was "Give people a chance." What would you do if you were Rick's teacher? Lewis attempted to persuade Rick of her meaning because she felt it was her responsibility to help him understand texts in ways that match the expectations of those in power (the test makers, for example). However, she had limited success and hypothesized the following:

> *Perhaps Rick needed to know that he had formed a perfectly legitimate reading* before *he could listen for other voices as he read this fable. One way to legitimize his interpretation would have been to openly discuss differences between his moral and Lobel's (the author). Before having Rick read the fable, I could have asked him to read for a moral that made sense to him. Afterward, we might have*

> *compared his moral to Lobel's and discussed ways that readers might interact with this text to arrive at different conclusions. Encouraging Rick to listen for other voices while legitimizing his own would help him to begin to understand that in literature, as in life, these different voices create a tension we all have to acknowledge before we can find a place for ourselves, before we can take a position. (459–460)*

Children also need to critically examine the texts they are reading in other areas of the curriculum. Edelsky (1994) writes about a teacher who has her fifth-graders look at the social studies materials on the Pilgrims and Indians provided for the school and ask themselves: Who wrote this? Whose idea is it? Do you think this is the way the aboriginal people would tell it? Who benefits from this version of the story? How do they benefit from it? In the Canadian context, books about such topics as the Riel rebellion and exploration of the West by the French and English can be critiqued in a similar way.

Critical literacy also means discussing controversial issues that are not part of the curriculum. The children in one inner-city Grade 5 classroom in Edmonton dealt daily with such issues as racial identity, sexual abuse, and apprehension by government workers. However, these issues entered the curriculum only occasionally because the teacher and the children believed that they were best dealt with privately and individually. Few links were made between what the children were reading and what was going on in their lives (Leroy, 1995).

We are just beginning to figure out how to implement critical literacy in our classrooms. We know that the focus must be on groups of children rather than on individuals. We know that critique is at the heart of this type of reading instruction. And we know that the what and why of reading are as important as the how. We also know, as Ira Shor points out (*Liberation Education*, 1990), that it will not be easy to make the transformation from the traditional curriculum we were given to the democratic curriculum we need. If we do not try, however, we will perpetuate the inequalities that currently permeate language arts instruction and society.

Chapter Summary

Psychological theories have dominated the field of reading throughout most of this century. Behaviourist theories led to skills models, in which reading was broken down into component skills to be learned one at a time. Cognitive theories have placed the focus on the reading process. In bottom-up theories of reading, the focus is on print, and processing proceeds from parts to wholes. In top-down theories, the focus is on readers' knowledge and processing proceeds from wholes to parts. Interactive models of reading have combined ideas from bottom-up and top-down theories. Meaning is viewed as resulting from interaction between the reader and text, and processing of parts and wholes occurs simultaneously.

Recognizing the importance of social interactions and social contexts in learning underlies transactional and social constructive theories of reading. Transactional theorists see meaning as being constructed by readers during the act of reading, using the text, their knowledge, and their background experiences. Social constructive theorists also take a constructive view of meaning but give greater recognition to the social background of the reader and the social context for the act of reading. We define reading in this textbook as the active construction of meaning from cues in the text and from the reader's background knowledge within a social context. Issues that need to be considered when planning an effective reading program include the roles of "real" texts, explicit instruction, metacognition, instructional reading level, and reader response.

Using children's literature in addition to, or in place of, basal readers calls upon a whole different repertoire of teaching strategies. The purpose of working with literature in the classroom is different from that of working with basal readers. With children's literature we want children initially to have an aesthetic experience with the book, and from their response to that experience, learn about the book, about books in general, about authors and illustrators, and about what it means to be a reader. Novel studies, readers' workshop, literature response journals, and response groups are all part of the structure teachers can create for the effective teaching of reading through literature.

Whereas the focus of reader response is on the construction of meaning, critical literacy is more concerned with the social context of reading. Through critical reading, children become aware of social inequities and biases involving gender, age, social class, and race. This awareness is the first step toward social change and a more democratic society.

Selected Professional Resources

Benton, M., and G. Fox (1985). *Teaching Literature: 9–14*. London: Oxford University Press.
The authors explore many facets of working with children in the upper elementary and junior high-school grades. Many of their observations and ideas are also applicable to the primary grades. The book provides an overview of teaching the class novel, individual novels, poetry, plays, and nonfiction. Many activities are suggested for classroom work using specific titles, including Tuck Everlasting.

Edelsky, C. (1994). Education for democracy. *Language Arts*, *71* (4), 252–257.
This article is an excellent introduction to critical literacy as a tool for democracy. Edelsky also provides the name and address of a periodical that provides descriptions by classroom teachers of classroom interactions and activities to enhance critical literacy.

Children's Books Noted in Chapter 6

Babbitt, N. (1975). *Tuck Everlasting*. New York: Farrar, Straus, Giroux.
Browne, A. (1983). *Gorilla*. New York: Alfred A. Knopf, Inc.
Browne, A. (1989). *The Tunnel*. London: Julia MacRae Books.
Buchan, B. (1975). *The Dragon Children*. Richmond Hill, Ont.: Scholastic TAB Publications Ltd.
Cooney, B. (1982). *Miss Rumphius*. New York: Viking Press.
Cooper, S. (1973). *The Dark is Rising*. New York: Collier Macmillan.
Hope, L.L. (1904). *The Bobbsey Twins*.
Hughes, T. (1968). *The Iron Man*. London: Faber and Faber.
Lobel, A. (1980). *Fables*. New York: Harper & Row.
Mayer, M., and M. Mayer (1978). *Beauty and the Beast*. New York: Aladdin.
Morey, W. (1970). *Gloomy Gus*. Hillsboro, OR: Blue Heron Publishing.
Munsch, R. (1980). *The Paper Bag Princess*. Toronto: Annick Press Ltd.
Taylor, C. (1985). *Julie*. Saskatoon: Western Producer Prairie Books
Truss, J. (1982). *Jasmin*. Vancouver: Douglas (Groundwood).
Van Ahlsburg, C. (1988). *Two Bad Ants*. Boston: Houghton Mifflin Co.
Winthrop, E. (1985). *Touch Eddie*. New York: E.P. Dutton.

CHAPTER 7

Developing Reading Strategies

The children in this Grade 5 class read silently every day.

OBJECTIVES

- to be aware of traditional views of reading comprehension and word identification
- to know how to use instructional techniques to help children use text-based and knowledge-based information to construct meaning
- to know how to use instructional techniques to help children identify words by using cues both beyond and within words
- to be able to adapt reading instruction to the needs of all learners

Introduction

A group of children in Grade 5 have just finished reading an informational text on the Caribou Gold Rush and their teacher was leading a discussion to determine what meaning they had constructed. When she asked where gold was discovered in 1958, most of the children replied near the junction of the Fraser and Assiniboine Rivers but Daniel said, "I think it was in Alaska. I heard about that in a TV program." Daniel was relying too heavily on his own knowledge at this point and not enough on the text. At another point in the discussion, she asked the children to think about how the prospectors felt who did not strike it rich. Immediately, Heather answered, "It didn't say." In contrast with Daniel, Heather was not making enough use of her background knowledge.

In Chapter 6, reading was defined as the active construction of meaning from the text and the reader's knowledge within a social context. Both text cues and background knowledge are crucial to constructing meaning while reading. One important goal of reading instruction is to help children learn how to use these sources of information in an integrated manner. The major focus of this chapter is on instructional techniques to reach this goal.

The order in which these techniques are presented is arbitrary since instruction at any grade level will focus on both word identification and comprehension strategies as well as attempting to help readers develop **automaticity** as they read. Word identification and automaticity lead to increased comprehension; making meaning, in turn, leads to improved word identification. From a social **constructive** perspective, however, meaning is the essence of reading, and this is the reason for presenting techniques for developing comprehension strategies before those for word identification or automaticity. The use of any technique in this chapter is dependent upon the needs identified through the assessment of children's reading as described in Chapter 11.

Techniques for developing reading comprehension are organized according to information sources used by readers. Some techniques foster an integrated use of both knowledge-based and text-based information, whereas others focus more specifically on the structure of **narrative** and informational texts. Most of the techniques in these sections can be used to help children construct meaning from texts in social studies and science classes as well as in language arts classes. Some techniques are also included to help children learn how to study. The next part of the chapter focuses on word identification, and techniques are presented for helping children use cues both beyond and within words as they construct meaning. Following is a section devoted to helping children develop automaticity in reading. The final section of the chapter suggests ways to adapt reading instruction to meet the needs of all learners.

Reading Comprehension

Most of us received basic reading instruction in the elementary grades from a **basal reading series**. Two major techniques were recommended in these series for developing reading comprehension. One involved the teacher asking questions while and after students read stories. The other involved completing exercises (workbook, worksheet, and chalkboard) to develop specific comprehension skills such as finding the main idea, understanding sequence, drawing conclusions, and so on.

Considerable research has been conducted on the questions teachers ask during reading instruction, and the results show that these questions generally test rather than teach reading comprehension (Durkin, 1978–79). Rather than teaching readers how to construct meaning while they read, the questions check to determine whether the reader has constructed the teacher's meaning.

Another research finding about teachers' questions involves the level of questions asked. Hierarchies of questions, such as those based on Bloom's taxonomy (1956), have been provided to reading teachers for several decades. Although they vary, they commonly include at least three levels—literal, inferential, and critical—and are based on an assumption that meaning is a static or determinate reality that exists within the text. Literal level questions require the reader to read the lines to comprehend what the author says. Inferential questions require the reader to read "between the lines" to infer relationships among ideas and draw conclusions intended but not explicitly stated by the author. Critical questions require readers to use their knowledge to make objective or subjective evaluations of the ideas in the text. Research shows that teachers ask far more literal questions than ones involving inference, evaluation, or other higher-level thinking skills. A steady diet of factual questions communicates to children that the meaning is on the page. It is little wonder that when asked an inferential question, some children such as Heather in the example at the beginning of this chapter respond, "It didn't say."

Questioning can be a powerful technique for helping children learn how to construct meaning as they read and is involved in many of the techniques described in this chapter. However, questions can also use up a lot of instructional time on testing rather than teaching and communicate some unintended messages about reading if they're not carefully planned and formulated.

There is little support in the literature for teaching a series of reading comprehension skills. Pearson and others recommend instead developing many adaptable and flexible strategies for the construction of meaning. This chapter includes only a few of the many possible strategies, with others described in the Selected Professional Resources at the end of this chapter.

Integrating Knowledge-Based and Text-Based Information

The focus of these techniques is on helping readers use both their knowledge and text cues to construct meaning as they read. For these techniques to be effective, the children need to know why they are using them. They need to know that these techniques are designed to help them do what good readers do—use what they know and what is on the page together as they read. It is also important to help children apply these strategies to materials across the curriculum.

Most of these techniques help children activate prior knowledge before reading. If children talk about their knowledge of forests and forestry before reading about the lumber industry, they will find it easier to construct meaning from that text. For those children who have very little knowledge about forests, discussion of pictures, videotapes, and other media on forestry can help. In a classroom vignette later in this chapter, a teacher shares a technique she uses to get children thinking about what they know on a topic before beginning a new unit of study and to fill in gaps in their knowledge.

Directed Reading–Thinking Activity (DRTA)

This is an instructional method for use with narrative material, in which students first predict what they will read and then check their predictions through subsequent reading. Formulated by Stauffer (1975), the technique helps students to actively seek information from the material they read. The teacher acts as a catalyst to thought by asking such questions as: What do you think? Why do you think so? and How can you prove it? As readers predict what they will read, they rely on their knowledge, and as they check their predictions, they use cues in the text. Through this technique, children learn:

- to actively read narrative material
- to set purposes for reading narrative material
- to use knowledge-based and text-based information in constructing meaning while reading narrative material.

DRTA is most appropriate for narrative material with a clearly defined plot that can easily be read in one sitting. Short mystery stories are ideal for this activity. The basic steps in DRTA are outlined below.

1. Based on the title and illustration or first paragraph of a story, the teacher asks students to predict what will happen by asking questions such as:

   - What do you think this story will be about?
   - What do you think will happen in this story?
   - Why do you think so?

   This last question is particularly important because it provides an opportunity for children to refer to both their knowledge and cues in the title, picture, or first paragraph.

   During the prediction process, the teacher's role is not to evaluate predictions but rather to activate thought by asking students to defend their hypotheses. The teacher can write predictions on the chalkboard for later reference.

2. Students are then asked to silently read to a certain point in the material to confirm or disprove their hypotheses. It is particularly effective to have children stop at suspenseful points in the story.

3. After the students have read to the designated point, the children discuss which of their hypotheses were confirmed. The teacher asks for evidence from the text to support the plausibility and accuracy of the hypotheses.

   - What do you think now?
   - Find the part in the text to prove or disprove your prediction.

   Students might read aloud a sentence or paragraph to provide this evidence. Again, this helps to focus attention on both text-based and knowledge-based information.

4. After students have completed the three-step process (predict, read, prove) with one segment of the material, they go on to the next segment. The process continues until they have read the entire text. Throughout, the teacher serves as a mentor to refine and deepen the reading–thinking process, but takes care not to evaluate the students' predictions. It is also useful to emphasize the importance of evaluating and finding proof in the text rather than deciding who is right or wrong. DRTA is not a contest but rather a technique to make sure individuals start thinking before they begin to read.

Gillet and Temple (1994) suggest no more than five stops in one story in one sitting so as not to interrupt the students' reading too frequently. The DRTA is particularly helpful for those children who take a passive approach to reading and who appear to believe that the message is in the book.

KWL

This technique helps children when reading **expository** materials, and it models the active thinking involved in reading for information (Ogle, 1986). The letters K W L stand for the three basic steps involved: accessing what I *know*, deciding what I *want* to learn, and recalling what I did *learn* as a result of reading. KWL helps children:

- to actively read informational material
- to set purposes for reading informational material
- to use knowledge-based and text-based information in constructing meaning while reading informational material.

The children use a group or individual charts like the one in Exhibit 7.1. Then they follow these steps.

1. *K—What I know.* The children brainstorm information they know about the topic or a key concept in the material, e.g., wolves. The teacher records what the students brainstorm on the board or an overhead. The goal of this brainstorming is to activate whatever knowledge the readers have that will help them construct meaning as they read. Ogle suggests deepening students' thinking by asking questions such as:
   - Where did you learn that?
   - How can you prove that?

EXHIBIT 7.1

A KWL Chart

Topic:

K	W	L
What I *know*	What I *want* to find Out	What I *learned*

Categories
of information

The second part of this step involves the children in thinking about what general categories of information they are likely to encounter when they read. Ask them to consider the information they have brainstormed and group it together into more general categories, e.g., what wolves eat, where they live.

2. *W—What I want to learn.* As the children think about what they know on a topic and what categories of information might be included in what they read, questions emerge. After the group discussion, each child records his or her own questions in the W column to focus attention during reading. The children then read the material.

3. *L—What I learned.* After the children finish reading, they write down in the L column what they learned from reading. The role of the teacher is to have them locate this information in the text in order to discuss how they used both what they knew and text cues as they read.

   If not all of the children's questions were answered in the material, the teacher suggests further reading on the topic. This ensures that the children's desire to learn takes precedence over what the author has chosen to include.

Question–Answer Relationship (QAR)

Raphael (1986) has presented a method for enhancing children's ability to answer questions. Her method is based on Pearson and Johnson's (1978) taxonomy of textually explicit (answer in the text), textually implicit (answer involves use of both knowledge and text), and scriptally implicit questions (answer is in child's knowledge). This technique is designed to help children:

- to use information both from the text and from their background knowledge
- to determine which information sources are required for answering specific questions
- to answer text-based and knowledge-based questions.

QAR begins with two categories, which are the primary sources of information for answering questions: *In the book* and *In my head* (knowledge). Each of these two categories is subdivided into two question types as shown in Exhibit 7.2.

In the initial stages of instruction, the student's answers to questions are less important than being able to indicate which source of information (text-based or knowledge-based or both) is required and how this information should be used. Raphael suggests beginning by explaining to the children that they are going to talk about questions and the best way to answer them. Some questions ask for information that can easily be found in the book. Other times, they won't find it there and need to use what they know

EXHIBIT 7.2

Question–Answer Relationships

IN THE BOOK	IN MY HEAD
Right There The words in the question and in the answer are "right there" in one sentence. Find the words used to make up the question and look at the other words in that sentence to find the answer. **Think and Search (Putting It Together)** The answer is in the story but you need to find more than one sentence or paragraph. The answer comes from more than one part of the text.	**Author and You** The answer is not in the story alone. You need to think about what you know and what the author tells you, and fit it together. **On My Own** The answer is not in the story. You need to use what you already know.

to answer the questions. Each can be answered by figuring out where to get the information needed for the answer.

Initially, she recommends introducing students to the two major sources of information—*In the book* and *In my head*. Discussion focuses on where the children get information to answer specific questions asked by the teacher. The teacher then gives the children short passages and questions for which both answers and QARs are provided for further discussion. Next the children are given short passages with questions and answers and they tell which QAR each belongs to. Finally, the children are given passages and questions and identify both the QARs and the answers to the questions. The children then move to the two questions for *In the book* and *In my head* categories and to longer passages. Raphael recommends regular review and extension to content area texts.

Reciprocal Teaching

Reciprocal teaching (Palincsar, 1986) is a dialogue between a teacher and children to jointly make meaning as they read. It is designed to promote four comprehension strategies:

- summarizing a passage in a sentence
- asking one or two good questions about the passage

- clarifying parts that are confusing
- predicting what the next part will be about.

The teacher models these strategies using expository passages and then the students assume the role of teacher using segments of the text.

The teacher meets with a small group of students, each of whom has a copy of the same content area material, and models the four comprehension strategies while reading a paragraph from the material. The teacher summarizes the paragraph and the students decide whether or not the summary is accurate. The teacher asks questions about the paragraph and the students tell whether the questions involve important information in the passage and then answer the questions. The teacher identifies parts of the paragraph that could be confusing and, with the students' help, these parts are clarified. Finally, the teacher predicts what the next passage will be about and the students judge whether the prediction is logical.

After the teacher has modelled the procedure with several segments of text, he or she asks a student to be the "teacher." As the student "teacher" summarizes, asks questions, identifies confusing parts, and predicts what will come next, the adult teacher provides feedback and coaches him or her through the strategies. The other students are asked to judge the adequacy of the summary, the importance of questions, and the logic of predictions, as well as to help clarify points and support the student "teacher." The following steps indicate how reciprocal teaching is used after the children have become familiar with the technique:

1. The adult teacher presents the children with the title of the material they will be reading and asks them to use background knowledge they have about the topic to predict what they will learn in the material. A "teacher" is then appointed for the first part of the material and the group reads it.
2. The "teacher" asks a question that the other students answer and then summarizes what has been read. The students judge the accuracy of the summary and the importance of the questions.
3. This leads to a discussion of clarifications that the "teacher" and other students made while reading or of points that they think still need to be made.
4. Finally, the "teacher" and other students make predictions about the next segment of the material and a new "teacher" is appointed.

Throughout this dialogue, the adult teacher provides feedback and instruction on how to use the four strategies more effectively. For example, the teacher might help the students to produce shorter summaries or to ask questions about main ideas as well as details. At the end of each half-hour reciprocal teaching session, children may be given a passage they have not read before and asked to summarize it or answer a few substantial questions about it. Reciprocal teaching is more appropriate for students at the upper elementary level than for primary children.

Using Text Structure

As noted in Chapter 5, young children who have had stories read or told to them on a regular basis learn what stories are like, and the stories they tell reflect the structure of the stories they have heard. It's easier for children to make meaning from stories if they are familiar with the structures being used, because they will be able to organize ideas as they read and anticipate what comes next. Similarly, it's easier for children to understand informational texts if they know how authors structure ideas in these texts. Since few parents will have read as much informational as narrative material to their children, fewer children come to school with an awareness of how authors organize ideas in informational texts. This section deals first with helping children develop their knowledge of the structure of stories and then moves to informational or expository texts.

Narrative Texts

Story grammars are attempts to delineate the basic elements of a well-formed story (e.g., Mandler and Johnson, 1977). Nearly all contain a setting, which introduces the main characters and tells where and when the story takes place, and a series of episodes. Although episodes are represented differently in different story grammars, common elements include a problem, attempts to resolve the problem, outcomes, and resolution.

There is considerable controversy about using story grammars with children. One major problem has been teaching story grammar for its own sake rather than in order to make meaning. A second problem involves the often heavy focus on terminology related to story elements, such as characters, episodes, and so on. Rather than imposing our terminology on children, it is more useful for them to generate their own terms such as *who* and *what happened*. The purposes of instruction on story structure are to help children:

- to understand how narrative material is structured
- to use knowledge of narrative structure to construct meaning.

1. *Story reading*. The best way to build knowledge of story structure is to provide children with experiences with stories on a regular basis. However, some explicit attention to story structure will benefit children with limited experience with stories and those who do not appear to reflect this knowledge in their storytelling or writing.
2. *Story maps*. The teacher prepares a chart reflecting the structure of a typical story, such as the one in Exhibit 7.3.

EXHIBIT 7.3

Story Map

Setting	
When	
Where	
Who	
Events	
Problem/ internal response	
Attempt(s) and outcome(s)	
Resolution/ reaction	

a. Cochrane, Cochrane, Scalena, and Buchanan (1984) suggest that the best type of story to use for story mapping is a problem-centred one. The teacher reads the story to the children and, as a group, they analyze the story, filling in a large copy of the story map. This can be followed up with a range of activities, such as rearranging the parts of a well-plotted story in order and filling in a missing story element in a story.

b. Vacca, Vacca, and Gove (1991) suggest that teachers use story grammars to generate questions about stories.

Setting
- Where did the story take place?
- When did the story take place?
- Who is the main character?

Problem/Internal Response
- What is the problem of the main character?

- What did ____ need?
- Why is ____ in trouble?
- What does ____decide to do?
- How did ____ feel about the problem?

Attempts/Outcome
- What did ____do about ____?
- What happened to ____?
- What will ____ do now?

Resolution
- How did ____solve the problem?
- How did ____ feel at the end?
- What would you do to solve ____'s problem?

Informational Texts

The purpose of informational material is to inform, and it generally uses one of four types of organization, although occasionally narrative is used as well. For example, although the purpose of this book is to inform, we occasionally share a short story about a child or classroom event to illustrate a point. Most of this book, however, is expository writing.

The four most common types of organizational patterns for informational material are enumeration, sequence, comparison–contrast, and cause–effect. This paragraph uses an enumeration pattern, in which information about one topic is listed. In this case the topic is organization patterns for informational material and the four types are listed and defined with some examples provided for clarification. The sequence pattern, which presents information in time order, is commonly found in historical texts, recipe directions, and scientific experiments. Comparison–contrast and cause–effect patterns appear in a wide range of content areas, including this book. For example, in the first section of Chapter 5, concepts of emergent literacy and reading readiness are contrasted.

The techniques described in this section are designed to help children:

- to understand how informational material is structured
- to use the structure of informational material to make meaning.

1. *Enumeration (main idea/detail) pattern*
   Pearson and Johnson (1978) state, "We know of no aspect of comprehension so universally accepted yet so often confused as the notion of "Finding the Main Idea" (89). The term "main idea" is variously used to refer to the most important idea, the topic, the title, or the theme. In fact, main idea-detail is a "logical relation between more general and more specific propositions" (90). Main idea is the generalization; each of the details tells something

about it. Much nonfiction material is organized in this pattern, so constructing this type of relationship is particularly important for content area reading. Authors provide "signals" (connective words) to readers to help them construct relationships among ideas. Signals to the enumeration pattern include words such as *first*, *next*, *also*, and *for example*.

a. *Classification tasks*
Pearson and Johnson (1978) note the analogy between classification tasks with words and main idea-detail tasks with passages. For example, teachers can give children a list of words containing the classification label such as *jump ropes*, *kites*, *toys*, and *dolls* and ask them to indicate which one tells about all the others. A jump rope, a kite, and a doll are all toys so *toys* is the word that tells about all the others. They can then be given lists of words without the class label and asked to generate this label, e.g., for *screeching siren*, *crash of thunder*, and *booming gun*, they might say something like *loud noises*. Discussion of why the word or phrase selected is correct is essential to get the students consciously thinking about the general-specific relationship.

b. *Passage tasks*
Well-organized passages are then presented with the main idea in the first sentence. Students choose the sentence that is the main idea, i.e., the one that tells about the others. Again, discussion is essential. For example,

> *There are several good rules for bicycle safety. For example, always use hand signals. Another good rule is to ride on the right side of the street. Still others are not to go too fast and not to ride barefoot (McGuire and Bumpus, 1973, A4).*

Next, present well-organized paragraphs with the main idea unstated. For example,

> *Some seeds travel with the wind. Elm and Maple seeds do this. Other seeds are hitchhikers. Burrs stick to dogs, for example. Birds carry berry seeds, too. Still other seeds pop right out of their pods (McGuire and Bumpus, 1973, B3).*

An example of the kind of discussion that might ensue is presented in Exhibit 7.4 in an illustrative lesson for upper elementary students in an unpublished paper by Phillis Sutherland. The teacher then completes similar activities with less well-organized passages in which the main idea is explicitly stated and, finally, moves to those where the main idea is not stated.

EXHIBIT 7.4

Illustrative Lesson on Enumeration (Main Idea/Detail) Pattern

Provide students with copies of a short well-constructed paragraph, such as:

> *The moving ice did great things for Canada. It scraped a thick layer of topsoil off the Canadian Shield. This left the minerals near the surface where people could reach them. It carried good soil south to southern Canada where the climate is suitable for farming. Most interesting of all, it made Canada beautiful.*

The teacher says, "Read the paragraph in order to find out the writer's main idea. Underline the key words as you read. For example, what are the key words of the second sentence? Answers will probably be *scraped, topsoil,* and *Canadian Shield.* Students underline these words in the sentence. The teacher then asks the students to copy the answers and to read on, underlining key words, then listing them for each sentence.

Discussion will probably lead to this list:

1) ice did things for Canada
2) scraped topsoil Canadian Shield
3) left minerals near surface
4) carried good soil southern Canada
5) made Canada beautiful

Discussion should lead the students to conclude that sentences 2, 3, 4, and 5 are specific actions while sentence 1 contains a general action. This makes sentences 2, 3, 4, and 5 similar and sentence 1 different. That is, sentence 1 is the general overall statement arrived at by determining what the specific ideas have in common. It contains the main idea of the paragraph.

As a follow-up activity, students discuss the main idea of paragraphs selected from content area textbooks.

c. *Outlining and diagramming*

Pearson and Johnson (1978) suggest two techniques other than discussion to help clarify the relationship between main ideas and details, and these are outlining and diagramming. Generally, the teacher models these techniques to visually show the relationships before asking students to generate their

EXHIBIT 7.5

Diagrams for Enumeration Pattern

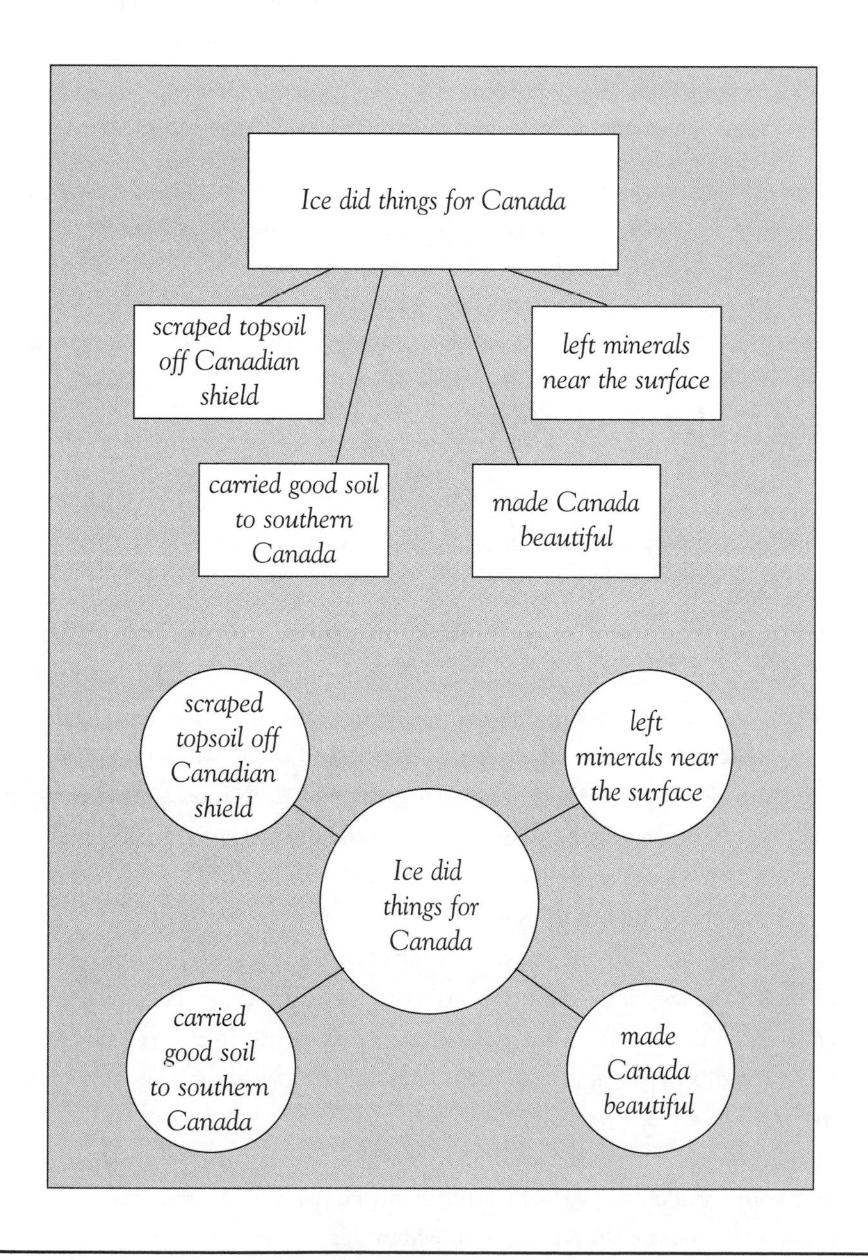

own outlines or diagrams. Examples of diagrams for main idea–detail relationships are shown in Exhibit 7.5 (Pearson and Johnson, 1978, 94–95). Both outlining and diagramming can also be used as processes for organizing ideas for written composition. Generally, once a topic is identified, a number of ideas related to it are generated through brainstorming. These are then organized through diagramming or outlining before the student begins to write.

d. *Semantic mapping or webbing*
Semantic maps or webs are diagrams showing the major ideas and relationships in a text. The map consists of nodes containing key words with connecting lines between nodes. These maps or webs are useful tools for brainstorming and organizing ideas for writing. Joyce Bodell describes how she uses semantic webs in the vignette below.

Inside **the Classroom**

Joyce Bodell spent seven years teaching at the primary level, and is now teaching Grades 6 and 7 at Mountain View Elementary School in Coquitlam, B.C.

Webs are a simple but effective strategy that serves a number of significant purposes for students, the teacher, and parents. Before beginning a new unit or theme, I have each of my students individually web everything they already know about the topic. I write the topic or idea on the board, read it aloud, and then ask them to take a minute or two to think of everything they know about it and write it on a piece of paper. Younger children can draw what they know, and invented spelling is always accepted. I encourage them to record ideas even if they aren't sure they are right. They will have many opportunities later to find out for sure!

This activity is done individually for two reasons. First, I want to know what level of understanding each child is bringing to our study. This informs my teaching and enables me to plan for content and lessons that meet the children's needs most effectively. For this reason, it is useful to do this activity a week or so before actually starting the study. Second, it helps children to recognize how much they already know and to raise questions about particular ideas or facts they are not sure about. It is possible that some students have very little or no knowledge on the topic. However, in my experience, most children come up with at least a few ideas. After they have finished

continued

their webs, I collect and read them, then store them until we have finished our study.

At this point, I usually do a whole-class brainstorming activity and record it on chart paper. This gives us a written record of our combined knowledge, which I leave posted somewhere in the room. I find that we often refer back to it in whole-class lessons when we learn something that validates (or invalidates) what we thought we knew, or when we find an answer to a question that someone raised.

At the end of the unit, I give their webs back to them, and I ask them to use a coloured pencil crayon to add their new knowledge to their webs. They can also cross out ideas that didn't really belong, but I ask them not to erase anything. The changes that they make are evidence of their learning.

The result is a two-colour web that provides the children with a powerful visual representation of all the learning they have accomplished. Often, children will ask for a second larger piece of paper in order to fit on all their new ideas. They glue the original web in the centre and branch out onto the larger sheet. In my experience, children tend to become really excited about discovering how much they have learned. Again, this activity is done individually. If a whole-class web was done, I also revisit this with the entire group, and together we build on our combined knowledge, adding all the new information we have acquired and making changes as necessary.

This second round of webbing offers the teacher a valuable assessment tool. It demonstrates the depth of understanding each individual student has acquired. It can also be used to note what has not been learned, either by individuals or by most of the class. For example, if an important concept seems to be missing from most of the finished webs, it tells the teacher that some additional instruction time needs to be spent on that area before the unit is finished.

I have successfully used this strategy with students from kindergarten to Grade 7. It is valuable to include in a student's portfolio for parent conferences, because it is such a tangible representation of each individual's learning. I have overheard many students saying to their parents, "Look, this is all that I knew before. See how much I know now!" To me, the greatest strength of this strategy is its potential to show to students how much knowledge they have acquired, and in this way, reinforce their concepts of themselves as learners.

continued

In Joyce's semantic web, shown in Exhibit 7.6, the ideas inside thick lines represent the children's prior knowledge about Canada; the remaining ideas are ones they learned. This vignette illustrates how one technique can be used for a variety of purposes. One of the most important is assessment, which is an integral part of language arts instruction in Joyce's classroom. It also shows the value of providing opportunities for children to evaluate their own learning.

EXHIBIT 7.6

A Semantic Web

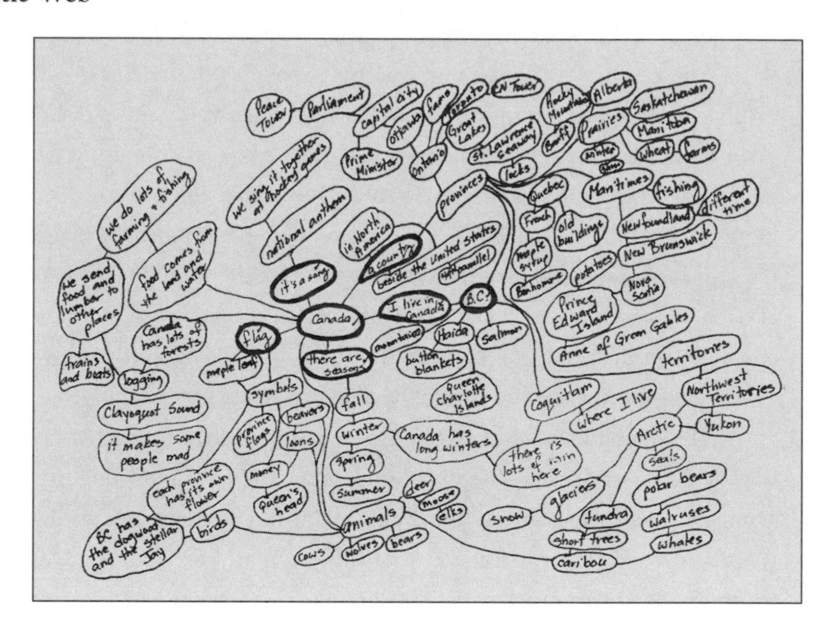

---

2. *Sequence pattern*

   Work in sequence patterns runs a close second to that on main ideas for causing students difficulty. The most common type of activity involves giving students several sentences that they are to order by placing a number beside each sentence. There are several reasons why this task is difficult, particularly for young children. First, we generally use numerals (1, 2, 3) to indicate quantity rather than sequence. When numerals are used to indicate sequence, they are generally transformed to ordinals, i.e., first, second. As well, there is often no real reason for one event to occur before another. In other words, the sequence is essentially arbitrary. Pearson and Johnson (1978) point out that primary children find reversible relationships more difficult to understand than irreversible or logical relationships (116).

- John watched television before he ate dinner. (reversible)
- John closed the door. Then he bolted it. (irreversible)

In addition, young children pay attention to the order in which events are presented rather than signal words (e.g., *then*, *before*, *after*) when sorting out sequential events. Hence, many young children might interpret the sentence *Before Mary ate dinner, she read a book*, as first Mary ate dinner and then she read a book. Finally, the sentences have to be reordered in the student's head, and this is too abstract for many children.

Pearson and Johnson make the following suggestions for teaching sequence patterns.

- Begin by having students understand the sequential relationships in familiar experiences before moving to unfamiliar material. Language experience stories are ideal for this.
- Have students read about irreversible events before reversible ones.
- Have students read material where the order of presentation matches the time order. Students need considerable instruction with temporal connectives before they can use them to aid comprehension.

A key instructional technique is discussion, with the teacher establishing signal words for temporal connectives. It is much more useful to have students recall the order in which events occurred than to have them order sentences unless the sentences can be physically moved and arranged in order of occurrence.

It is also useful to have the students use a time line to show temporal relationships among ideas. Again, diagrams can be one step in generating ideas for written composition when the topic involves a sequence of events.

3. *Cause–effect pattern*

Understanding cause and effect patterns is crucial to narrative and informational material. Plots often revolve around cause–effect relationships, and causality is important for understanding historical, social, and scientific issues. One aspect of causality that is difficult for young children to understand is the reciprocal relationship between cause and effect. Another aspect that causes difficulty is the chaining of causes and effects, i.e., a cause produces an effect, which in turn causes another effect, and so on. In addition, there is little evidence that young children understand the meaning of causal connectives such as *because*, *since*, *therefore*, *why*, and *as a result*. They often use words such as *because* as if they were causes themselves rather than words to link causes and effects.

In order to help readers understand causal relations, it is reasonable to begin with single cause–single effect relationships, then move to single cause–multiple effect and multiple cause–single effect relationships, and finally to chains of cause–effect relationships.

Discussion is crucial for helping readers understand these relationships. Throughout discussion, it is important to talk about the function of causal connectives, and to help children use these words in their own writing.

Charting cause–effect relations may help some readers conceptualize the relationships. Exhibit 7.7 shows such a chart. These charts may also help organize ideas involving causality for written composition.

4. *Comparison–contrast pattern*
Comparison–contrast patterns are used by authors in fiction when describing characters and settings, and in most content writing as well. Discussion should focus on common attributes of people, places, and things being compared, and on the features that differentiate those being contrasted.

Discussion should direct attention to specific words that indicate comparisons or contrasts, such as *however, on the other hand, both*, and *alike*. Charts are useful in helping readers see these relationships.

Teachers can give students a chart like the one in Exhibit 7.8 before reading to guide comprehension and fill in as they read. They can also use them after reading to guide recall or as a study guide. Students should internalize knowledge of this type of organizational structure and eventually use this knowledge to guide their own reading. In addition they can also use these charts to organize ideas when writing paragraphs comparing or contrasting places and people.

EXHIBIT 7.7

Chart of Cause–Effect Relationships

what happened	why it happened
the window broke the boy was "grounded"	the ball hit the window the boy hit the ball toward the window

EXHIBIT 7.8

Chart of Comparison–Contrast Relationships

	Major Product	Area	Type of Government	Population
Brazil				
Chile				
Argentina				
Peru				

Inside the Classroom

Lori Bosworth is a Grade 6 teacher at LaPerle Community School in Edmonton, Alberta. She worked with two other Grade 6 teachers and the school librarian to plan a science/language arts unit on endangered species that includes research and report writing. Previously she had used the KWL strategy to introduce this unit and it had worked well. However, this year her students lacked confidence and many did not have adequately developed library research skills. For each of the phases described below, the teachers modelled strategies before asking the children to use them in small groups or on their own.

Phase 1: Generating research questions

We used the otter as an example to generate research questions using 5 Ws and H (*who, what, where, when, why,* and *how*). Some of the thirty-seven questions the children generated included:

- What do they eat?
- How do they survive?
- Why are they called otters?
- Where can they be found?

continued

We then asked, "How can we classify and organize these questions?" The students then identified possible headings and used number codes, highlighters, and other means to organize the questions into categories. We encouraged the children to develop retrieval charts to house the various headings.

Phase 2: Possible sources of information

The next step was to identify possible sources of information that would help the children in finding the answers to the questions generated earlier. We began this discussion using the *Subject Guide to the Dewey Decimal Classification for Small Schools* (Alberta Education) and then had the children fill out an information plan to use as a guide for their actual research in the library as well as for recording bibliographic information.

Phase 3: Reading to identify key words

Modelling the RAP strategy (Read a paragraph, Ask yourself what you read, Put it in your own words), we identified key words, which could be transferred to the retrieval charts as important information. The children then worked in small groups, identifying key words and the appropriate headings they could be organized under.

Phase 4: Paragraph writing and topic sentences

The final process that we modelled was the effective use of topic sentences and paragraph writing. Together as a class we brainstormed words that can be used to label a category to use in an introductory sentence, e.g., habitat-home, shelter, environment, region, lives, found.

This classroom vignette illustrates how reading instruction can extend beyond the boundaries of language arts to reading across the curriculum. By studying language arts and science together, the children were developing reading and writing in the context of actually using these strategies to learn about endangered species. Reading and writing were not being taught for their own sake but rather as tools to learning.

The selection of strategies was not arbitrary but rather based on the teachers' observations that these students had developed few skills for handling content area materials or library research. Assessment of student needs is a necessary component of unit planning.

This vignette also demonstrates the effectiveness of teachers' modelling rather than telling children about strategies. Finally, it introduces several additional strategies and shows how they were combined to meet the needs of a particular group of children and the curriculum goals.

Studying

Studying is a special kind of reading. As with all reading, the major goal is to construct meaning on the basis of text-based and knowledge-based information. However, individuals also need to organize information in order to enhance retrieval. When asked how they study, many children say they just read the material again and again. Some of the instructional techniques described above can help children organize and retrieve information. For example, KWL can help children learn informational material in any content area. The techniques included on informational **text structure** are useful for helping children to organize ideas in content area texts, and we know that it is easier to remember related ideas than isolated details. In addition, Standal and Betza (1990) list the following strategies for both reading and studying.

- Scanning involves sampling the text. Readers rapidly search through the text in order to locate specific information or answer a specific question. They learn to focus on headings, pictures, summaries, illustrations, and key words rather than reading every word.
- Skimming is a quick survey of the text to get an indication of what it is about.
- Outlining helps children understand and retain relationships among ideas. Standal and Betza (1990) suggest that mapping can be used to teach outlining.
- Underlining and highlighting make it easier to refer to important points when reviewing information for an examination. Unfortunately, elementary children are rarely able to mark in their books unless the teacher provides them with duplicated material.
- Note-taking can be taught in the upper elementary grades to prepare the students for this activity later on.

These study skills are most effectively taught to children within the context of materials in the content areas.

SQ3R

This classic technique, developed by Robinson (1961), continues to provide students with an organized, systematic approach to studying. Students survey what they will read and ask questions before beginning to read in order to ensure that when they actually read, they are actively engaged in searching for answers. After they finish reading, they put what they have read into their own words or make notes about the questions generated from their survey of the material. Finally, they use these notes to review the major ideas and details in the passage. Throughout this process, they are continuously using information both from the text and their knowledge.

The steps in SQ3R are presented to students as follows.

1. *Survey*

   Glance over the headings in the chapter to see the few main points. This should take no more than a minute and will show the three to six core items around which the rest of the ideas cluster. If the chapter has a final summary paragraph, this will also list the ideas developed. This orientation will help you organize the ideas as you read them later.

2. *Question*

   Turn the first heading into a question. This will arouse your curiosity and so increase comprehension. It will bring to mind information already known, thus helping you understand that section more quickly. And the question will make important points stand out from details.

3. *Read*

   Read to answer that question. This is not a passive plowing along each line, but an active search for the answer.

4. *Recite*

   When you have read the first section, look away from the book and try to briefly recite the answer to the question in your own words. If applicable, give an example. If you can do this, you know what is in the book. If you cannot, glance over the section again. Another way to recite is by jotting down key words and phrases in outline form in a notebook.

   Repeat steps 2, 3, and 4 for each section.

5. *Review*

   When you have read through the chapter, look over your notes to get a bird's-eye view of the points and their relationships. Check your memory about the content by covering up your notes and trying to recall the main points. Then expose each major point and try to recall the subpoints listed under it.

   SQ3R is most effective when used with material students are actually studying for an examination. The teacher models the steps with part of one chapter from the text, thinking out loud. Students and teacher work through the next part together, with the teacher guiding students through the steps. Students then use SQ3R in small groups or individually.

Word Identification

Word identification has traditionally been taught from a skills perspective with skills arranged hierarchically. These skills have been organized into four major categories—sight vocabulary, phonics, structural analysis, and contextual analysis.

In this Grade 1 classroom, children get both reading instruction and lots of time to read.

Sight vocabulary refers to words that occur frequently and that readers are able to identify automatically. As skilled readers, we recognize ninety-nine percent of the words we read by sight. **Phonics** is the identification of words through the relationships between speech sounds and letters, and has been at the centre of the great debate about early reading instruction for the past three decades (e.g., Chall, 1967; Adams, 1990). Phonics has been broken down into more subskills than any other area of reading instruction. Structural analysis involves identifying words by larger more meaningful units such as prefixes and suffixes. Some people include syllabication as an aspect of structural analysis while others place it under the rubric of phonics. Contextual analysis involves use of meaning and grammatical context to predict unfamiliar words.

In most recent textbooks that take a **constructive** approach to reading, very little information is included on word identification in spite of the fact that nearly everyone recognizes that print cues are an important source of information for readers. Word identification has, quite simply, become unpopular as educators have moved toward **whole language** programs. We think that children need instruction on word identification including use of print-based information to identify words in order to make meaning as they read. The following sections are organized according to the source of information being used to identify words. It begins with cues beyond words and then moves to cues within words. The final section contains techniques to facilitate integration of both types of cues.

Using Context Cues

Some educators have championed the use of **context cues** as a way for children to use their language and world knowledge to identify words as they read. Other educators have denigrated it as encouraging children to guess. A more appropriate position is that context cues are one of several sources of information children have to help them identify unfamiliar words. They need to use context cues *along with* not *instead of* print-based information.

Cloze Procedure

In the cloze procedure, words are deleted from a written passage and readers fill in the blanks using their knowledge of language and the world, along with clues available from the context. Although some educators recommend beginning with cloze activities in which the reader can choose from among several possibilities the word that best fills the blank, this detracts from the meaning-making nature of reading. We engage in a process not of elimination but of construction as we read. The cloze technique is designed to help children:

- to be aware that language and meaning cues can be used to predict words
- to know how to predict words that make sense and sound right
- to be able to monitor predictions on the basis of meaning and language cues.

Material with a wide range of difficulty, and both narrative and informational, can be used to make cloze passages. For early readers or those experiencing difficulty, the teacher should initially delete few words and only those that are highly predictable from the context. As readers begin to make more effective use of meaning and language cues to make predictions, the teacher can delete more words including those that are less predictable. An easy way to make cloze activities is to cut up pieces of adhesive notes to cover selected words in texts. An example of a cloze passage created from a story in *Ranger Rick* (October, 1994) is in Exhibit 7.9.

When initiating cloze activities, the teacher might begin with a whole class activity focused on material presented on an overhead projector. The teacher should tell students to read through the entire passage before trying to fill in the blanks. Once all students have read through the passage, a student volunteer reads the first sentence and supplies the missing word. Other students who have responded differently read the sentence and provide their responses. Class discussion centres on such questions as:

> *Why did you choose this word? What do you know about the topic in this passage that helped you predict that word? What in the passage helped you to make this prediction? Is there a difference in the meaning constructed by different students? Why did different students predict different words?*

Later, the teacher can give students cloze passages to complete individually. The teacher asks each student to explain in small group discussions why he or she used a particular

EXHIBIT 7.9

Sample Cloze Passage

The first paragraph (not shown here) is left intact so children will already have begun to make meaning by the time they get to the first blank. In that paragraph, Scarlett Fox and Ranger Rick Raccoon are in a picnic area near the ocean, when they see a white shapeless form in the fog.

> *"Look, it's coming back!" Rick whispered in horror as the Thing came right toward them. Suddenly it _____ over their picnic basket and fell in a heap. Now Rick and Scarlett could see that the white thing was a _____ and out from under it crawled their friend Boomer Badger. He laughed gleefully between gulps of_____ as he tried to catch his breath.*

word, again focusing on knowledge and text cues. The small group discussions could then lead to large group discussion of some of the more interesting or controversial items.

It is not important in cloze activities for children to predict the author's exact word. As long as the predictions make sense and sound right in relation to the rest of the passage, they should be accepted. By insisting on exact replacements, the teacher will send the children the message that text cues are more important than knowledge when making meaning, and the task will be reduced to "guess what word the author used."

Using Cues Within Words

This section presents techniques to help children use both letters and word parts to identify words as they read.

Letter Sounds

No area of reading instruction is as controversial as phonics. Many people view it as a panacea—the key to teaching all children to read. Others see it as a problem—an area of instruction leading to confusion and word calling. We believe neither view is defensible. Although it is helpful for children to be aware of the relationships between letters and sounds, particularly when spelling, knowledge of letter sounds is certainly not enough for children to be good readers. It is more crucial that they be aware that reading is a meaning-making process and that mapping sounds onto letters is only one strategy to use as they engage in this process. We do not want children to think that reading equals sounding out words.

Several issues about teaching phonics need to be considered. One involves terminology. First, a brief overview of the language of phonics is presently followed by a discussion of its place in teaching children. Nearly all of you are familiar with the terms *vowels* and *consonants* although even this distinction is somewhat arbitrary (e.g., vowels are the letters *a, e, i, o, u,* and *y* when it is not the first letter in a word). The major difference between vowels and consonants is that there is one sound for most consonants, whereas there are several sounds for each vowel. The terms *consonant blends* and *consonant digraphs* refer to combinations of consonants. In blends, the two or three letters combined each retain their original sound (e.g., *bl, fr, sm, str*), whereas in digraphs, consonants that are combined produce a new sound (e.g., *th, sh, ch*). The letters *c* and *g* are different from other consonants in that they have both hard (e.g., *car, go*) and soft (e.g., *city, gem*) sounds.

The terminology for vowels is even more complex. First, there are long and short vowels (although there is nothing literally long about the sounds we call long, which linguists call tense instead). Whether a vowel is labelled long or short depends upon its location in a word and the presence of other vowels in the same syllable. As with consonants, vowel digraphs are combinations of two letters that have one sound—generally the long vowel sound of the first letter in the digraph (e.g., *coat, meat, wait*). Vowel blends are called diphthongs, and as in consonant blends, each vowel in the blend keeps its sound (e.g., *oi, oy, ow, ou*). There are also vowels influenced by consonants—*a* influenced by *l* (as in *fall*) and vowels influenced by *r* (e.g., *far, fir, for, burr, her*).

The terminology does not end there. Phonograms are letter clusters and often form the basis for word families (e.g., *at—cat, hat, mat, sat*). In phonograms, children map sounds onto larger parts of words rather than individual letters.

Although all these labels may appear in teacher's guidebooks, children are generally expected to learn only some of them. The most common terms that children learn in phonics programs are *consonants*, *vowels*, and *long* and *short vowels*. Even these few terms, however, appear to have limited utility for readers. Rather than telling children that the sound in a particular word is long or short or *r*-controlled, it is more important for them to know that there are three possible sounds for the letter *a* (as in *can, cane,* and *car*) and that if one possibility does not result in a meaningful-sounding word, they should try another.

Some people argue that labels and categories are necessary so children can use phonic rules or generalizations. Some of you may recall some of these rules from your schooling, such as, "When two vowels go walking, the first does the talking." One major problem with these rules is that they do not work often enough to make them worthwhile learning. There are many exceptions to the rule just given, including all the vowel diphthongs. Consider as well the final *e* rule. Many common words simply do not follow the rule (e.g., *give, love, some, come, live*). Another major problem with phonic rules is that children often know them but make no use of this knowledge. For example, a child may be able to describe in detail how the *e* at the end of the word jumps over the letter in front of it and kicks the vowel to make it say its own name, but that same child then identifies the word *mate* as *mat*. Memorizing rules is not recommended as an effective, productive way to help children learn to map sounds onto letters.

Another controversy about phonics concerns the size of unit that should serve as the basis of analysis—individual letters or larger units such as phonograms. Having children learn to associate sounds with individual letters and then blend these sounds into words is generally called synthetic phonics. A major problem with this approach has already been identified—it is very difficult to isolate sounds for many letters without distorting them. Another problem involves using this approach with words of more than one syllable. It is not uncommon to hear young children attempting to identify words such as *hammer* by saying, "huh,a,muh,muh,eh,er," but then having no idea what the word is.

Having children identify words by mapping sounds to larger chunks of letters is generally referred to as analytic or whole word phonics. As Vacca, Vacca, and Gove (1991) point out, there are several advantages to this approach. Children find it easier to identify words using phonograms than rules, phonograms are fairly consistent, and a relatively small number of phonograms are found in many of the words in primary reading material. Still, children do come across words in which they do not recognize a phonogram and hence, need to map sounds onto smaller units of words at times.

A final controversy about phonics involves the extent to which it should be taught as a separate entity. A few years ago, it was not uncommon for phonics instruction to be timetabled in a separate time slot and taught in virtual isolation from the rest of the language arts program. We still see children who are able to associate sounds with isolated consonants and vowels and to recite phonics rules, but who make almost no use of this knowledge when they read. We see others who are able to use the knowledge to identify words in lists, but when they are read connected texts, they are unable to make effective use of their phonics knowledge. Most of the children we see do not lack phonics knowledge (in spite of the fears of opponents of whole language); what they lack are strategies for using this knowledge to spell and figure out unfamiliar words. It is strongly recommended that work on letter-sound relationships be completed in the context of real reading and writing.

The purpose of phonics instruction is to help children:

- to understand that letters and sounds are related
- to know how to use letter sounds to identify words.

Letter sounds are generally introduced in conjunction with other activities such as language experience stories and big books. The teacher talks about words and about the sounds associated with letters in words. When children are rereading, the teacher encourages them to use developing letter-sound knowledge along with other cues to identify words. During writing, the teacher encourages children to write words the way they sound.

In Maureen Kelly's Grade 2 classroom, the first thing children do in the morning is read the morning message to find out what they will be doing that day. By omitting letters from some of the words, the teacher encourages the children to predict what would make sense and associate letters with sounds in those words. When she notes that several children in the class are having difficulty with marking long vowel sounds in their writing, her minimal cues message includes several words containing the final *e* (e.g., Today we will mak_ puppets and writ_ a story about something we lik_). As the children predict the words, they discuss what letter needs to go on the end of each word and notice that in all the words, the sound of the vowel in the middle is the same as the name of the letter. After the morning message has been completed and the children are working on group projects, Maureen calls together the six children whose writing reflects difficulty with final *e* and gives explicit instruction. She tells them what she has noticed in their writing, beginning with final *e* words spelled correctly and then focusing on those incorrectly spelled. She then gives them word cards containing words with long vowel sounds, and they sort them according to whether they contain the final *e* or not. Before they leave the group, she reminds them to think about this spelling pattern when they write later that morning. The morning message the next morning again includes final *e* words for review, but introduces two vowels together as well.

Other strategies for focusing on letter sounds in context are in the section that follows on integrating both context and print cues. Some children, however, need more systematic instruction on phonics for them to figure out relationships between letters and sounds and how to use this information as they read and write. For these children, the following techniques are suggested.

1. *Analytic phonics*
   Most teachers begin by teaching consonant sounds without isolating the letters. The children listen to words that begin with the same sound (e.g., *bicycle* and *ball*), are shown what letter goes with this sound, and then asked to say other words that begin with the same sound. The teacher often makes a key picture card. After the children have mastered several consonant sounds, the process of initial consonant substitution is used to present or analyze new words. For example, the teacher says and prints the word *cat*. Then the teacher changes the initial consonant and asks the child to identify the new word (e.g., *cat, bat*). When children encounter unknown words, teachers encourage them to determine if the word is similar to one they know and to use a process of substitution to identify the word.

The focus then shifts to final consonants and finally to vowels, always dealing with sounds in word context and encouraging the children to use their developing knowledge of letter sounds to identify words as they read and to spell words as they write.

2. *Making words*

In this activity, developed by Cunningham and Cunningham (1992), teachers give children letters on cards, which they use to make words. During a period of about fifteen minutes, children make twelve to fifteen words, beginning with two-letter words and working up to longer words until they make a target word. The teacher prepares a set of small letter cards for each child and one set of large cards to be used on the pocket chart or ledge of the board. Each card has the lowercase letter on one side and the uppercase letter on the other. The teacher begins planning a lesson with a target word (e.g., *spider*), which ties in with some aspect of the curriculum and contains letter-sound patterns the children need to learn. The teacher then generates a list of shorter words that can be made with the letters in *spider* and selects those that include common units (e.g., *side, ride, pride, Ed, red*). The teacher writes these words on index cards and orders the cards from shortest to longest and according to patterns. Once these materials are prepared, the steps in the lesson are as follows:

a. The teacher places the large letter cards in a pocket chart or on the board ledge.

b. Each child has corresponding small letter cards. The teacher holds up the large letter cards, names each, and asks children to hold up their matching cards.

c. The teacher writes the letter 2 or 3 on the board and says a word with this number of letters in a sentence. He or she asks the children to make the word, using the small letter cards.

d. A child who has made the word correctly using the small letter cards forms the word using the large cards on the pocket chart or ledge, and the other children check their word.

e. This continues for other words, with the teacher cueing the children when the word is a proper name, when they are changing one letter, and when they are changing letter order. Before telling them the last word, the teacher asks if anyone has figured out what word can be made with all the letters. If they don't know, the teacher tells them the word and they make it.

f. Once all the words have been made, the teacher places the word cards one at a time on the board ledge or in the pocket chart, and the children say and spell them. The teacher then picks a word and asks the children to find other words with the same pattern.

g. To maximize learning, the children use the patterns they have found to spell a few new words dictated by the teacher.

3. *Word sorting*

   Word sorting can be used as part of the making words technique or separately for older children. It is a technique to focus children's attention on particular cues in words (Gillet and Temple, 1994). Children begin by developing a word bank of several known sight words. The teacher asks the children to group words (the words all have to be the same in some way) and then asks them to tell how the words go together. In an open sort, the teacher does not specify how words are to be grouped; in a closed sort, the teacher specifies the feature (e.g., all words with the same vowel sound, all words with two syllables, all words with soft *g*).

4. *Compare/contrast technique*

   This is another decoding strategy for children beyond the initial stage of learning to read. Cunningham (1979) recommends teaching children to make analogies to known words when attempting to identify unfamiliar multisyllabic words. The steps are as follows:

   a. The teacher writes high-frequency one-syllable words on cards for students.

   b. The teacher presents unfamiliar two-syllable words (e.g., *problem*) on the board or a word card, and the students find the two words on their index cards that look most like the word presented (e.g., *Bob* and *them*). The teacher asks students questions that require comparing and contrasting (e.g., "Where are the two words alike?") and students pronounce both their words and the two-syllable word.

   c. Students practise the technique, adding words to their store of index cards and matching these words to two-syllable words.

   d. The teacher presents the students with more unfamiliar two-syllable words and asks them to try to recall words that look like the unfamiliar word, using their store of words on index cards only when they are unable to match words in their heads.

   e. This strategy is extended to three-syllable words.

Using Word Parts

Structural analysis is the term traditionally used to refer to the identification of words using larger more meaningful units than letters. It generally includes: compounds, roots, affixes (e.g., *ly*), and syllabication. This area has not received the widespread attention of phonics and much of the material available has limitations. First, the work on compounds, roots, and affixes focuses almost exclusively on the association of meaning to words containing these units rather than on how to use knowledge of these units to identify words. Second, much of the material presents words in isolation rather than in the context of reading. The tasks children are asked to complete, such as putting lines between syllables in polysyllabic words, frequently don't even involve them in identifying the words. Third, there is often considerable attention to labelling, also a problem in relation to phonics. Finally, rules (particularly for syllabication) are frequently taught by memorization. As with phonics, children may be able to say the rules but still be unable to identify the words to which those rules apply. Teaching structural analysis is designed to help children how to use larger meaningful units than letters to identify words.

The most effective way to help children use structural units to identify words is to show them how to organize polysyllabic words into units when they encounter difficult words in their reading. The teacher can write the word in parts on the board, thinking out loud about how she or he is analyzing the word into parts, pronouncing each part, blending the parts together, and then checking to determine that the word makes sense in its context. Teachers can encourage children to employ a similar strategy when they encounter unknown words. For most children, this will be sufficient to help them develop an understanding of how structural analysis works and an intuitive ability to organize unfamiliar words into parts. Precise syllabication is not necessary since context is available to check possible pronunciations.

For those children who require more explicit instruction, the following activities are recommended.

1. *Compound words*
   A logical starting point for those who have difficulty analyzing units larger than letters is compound words. Analyzing these words into two known real words is a concrete task and, as well, takes advantage of words the children already know how to identify. After a brief discussion of compound words, the teacher gives students a passage containing several compound words with the compounds underlined and asks students to read the passage silently and be prepared to talk about what they have read. When difficulties occur, compound words can be segmented on the board and discussed.

2. *Syllabication*
   The goal of this instruction is to have the student identify syllables by hearing and seeing places in words where structural breaks occur between syllables. Exact division in accordance with the dictionary is unnecessary until students reach the point where they begin to hyphenate words at the end of lines in their writing.

The first step in this work is to help develop a concept of what syllables are, and we recommend that teachers begin with having children hear them in words. The teacher pronounces polysyllabic words, accentuating the syllable breaks. The teacher and children repeat the word together in syllables (clapping sometimes helps, as does having the children put their hands under their chin and feel it move down for each syllable). The children then repeat the words in syllables without the teacher's aid. It is not important for the children to show how many syllables are in a word; rather they need to be able to pronounce words in syllables.

To relate this concept of oral syllable to written language, the teacher presents familiar polysyllabic words to the children with syllable boundaries shown (e.g., *rab-bit, fun-ny*). Since the children already know how to identify these words, the focus is on syllables and how the spoken syllables relate to the visual units.

The next step involves having the children silently read texts containing polysyllabic words, reminding them to organize words into syllables if they have difficulty identifying them. They might lightly underline words that cause them difficulty in order to discuss them after they finish reading. They discuss the meanings they have constructed, paying particular attention to confusion resulting from difficulty with polysyllabic words. The teachers or students write selected words on the board in syllables for identification and discussion.

Finally, children are encouraged to use this strategy to identify polysyllabic words when reading independently. It is important that flexibility be stressed. If the word identified does not make sense, they are encouraged to try it another way until they get a meaningful word.

3. *Affixes and inflectional endings*
   We do not recommend systematically working through all affixes or inflectional endings, but rather focusing on specific inflectional endings (e.g., *ed, es*) or affixes when they cause difficulty. Again, we recommend that this work begin with familiar words and move to unfamiliar ones, and that most of the work involve words in context.

Integrating Context and Print Cues

Most work on word identification should provide children with the opportunity to use both context and print cues. The most effective way to accomplish this is to model or teach minilessons when children run into difficulty as they are reading. In addition, the following techniques may be useful.

1. *Masking*
   Holdaway (1979) describes how to use masking to help young children use context cues, structural units, and letter sounds to identify words. Working with either a transparency or a big book, the teacher uses a strip of paper to mask text lines and slides it aside to gradually expose parts of words, words, and phrases. Children read up to the point where the next word is covered and predict what will come next. Then the teacher uncovers the word so the student can use print cues to check the prediction. Discussion focuses on how predictions are made and where cues come from.

2. *Minimal cue messages*
   These are a modification of the cloze procedure set up to encourage integration of the various cues and also aid spelling.

   The teacher writes a message to the children with some of the letters missing. Dashes are generally given to show how many letters are required:

   Tod_ _ is a _ery sp_cial d_ _. W_ are go_ _ _ to th_ m_seu_.

   The message must be relevant to the children, and the language must be natural and predictable. It is important to discuss with the children what cues they used in unlocking the minimal cues message. Discussion should focus on both meaning and print cues.

   Initially the teacher writes in children's predictions but gradually the children take over the writing. Children who have been exposed to this technique often begin to write minimal cues messages themselves.

3. *Oral reading*
   When children are reading orally, the way the teacher responds to their reading communicates a great deal about what cues and strategies the teacher thinks are important. If the teacher constantly says, "Sound it out" when the child has difficulty, the child may come to believe that reading equals sounding out. The following general guidelines are recommended.

   - If a child pauses during reading, wait to give the child time to use both context and print cues to identify the word. Encourage her or him to predict a word that makes sense, sounds right, and checks out.

   - If a child makes a substitution while reading that is consistent with the author's meaning, ignore the miscue. Research shows that even good readers do not read with 100 percent accuracy; instead, they make some meaningful slips because of the constructive nature of reading. Ignoring such miscues communicates to children that making meaning is the essence of reading.

- If a child corrects a mistake, reinforce this by commenting on the appropriateness of the correction, rather than focusing on the error.
- If children make miscues that do not make sense, ask them if what they read sounded right and made sense. Focus discussion on the meaning the children constructed from their reading.

Fluency/Automaticity

Although there has been considerable criticism of sight word approaches (often referred to as "look and guess"), it is now clear that a critical factor in skilled reading is the ability to recognize words effortlessly and automatically in order to pay attention to meaning. What is not quite so clear is how to achieve this goal of **automaticity**. Traditionally, sight vocabulary was taught using flash cards or word lists, and having children read controlled-vocabulary materials. More recently, the focus has moved to reading connected texts. Rossman (1987) estimates that children need to read for a minimum of three and one-half hours a week in order to achieve automaticity. Since good readers are more likely than poor ones to read outside the classroom, it is imperative that time be set aside in school for all children to read.

Sustained Silent Reading

This technique, developed by Hunt, is becoming more prevalent in schools. In addition to the opportunity it provides for increased exposure to reading, it helps create an atmosphere in which reading and books are extremely important. In the classroom, the child gains a positive image of reading by seeing the teacher and other children enjoying books.

The following steps are recommended for implementing sustained silent reading (SSR).

1. The teacher discusses SSR with the children so they know what they will be doing, why they are doing it, and what behaviours are expected of them (e.g., all students will read a book they have chosen, everyone will be quiet, no one will move around the room).
2. Children are given advance notice so that they will have books chosen beforehand.

3. Teachers provide children with some background for choosing what to read by acquainting them with all kinds of books and by talking about books with them. Teachers "sell" books to children by reading parts of an interesting or exciting book to them to entice them to finish the book on their own.
4. Both teacher and children settle into comfortable spots and read silently. Initially, the block of time should be short enough to ensure success, but gradually it can be increased to fifteen to twenty minutes per day. Initially a timer can be used to indicate that SSR is over. The teacher can terminate the period depending on her or his observations. It is important that SSR end on a positive note while children are still interested in what they are reading. Interruptions are not permitted. A sign on the door indicating SSR will minimize interruptions. It is essential that teachers read during this time rather than catching up on other work because of the power of modelling.

Paired Reading

Paired reading is a technique developed in England by Topping that involves a child reading with another reader from a book the child has selected. The other reader may be the child's parent, a volunteer, a teacher, or another child. The activity is meant to be done for ten to fifteen minutes for at least five days per week for eight to twelve weeks.

The steps in paired reading are as follows (Brailsford, 1991):

1. The child chooses a book to read.
2. Beginning with a prearranged signal, the child and other reader read aloud together.
3. It is important for the child to read each word correctly. If he or she doesn't, the other reader reads the word correctly, the child repeats it, and they continue reading together.
4. Using a prearranged signal (e.g., a nudge or tap) the child indicates that he or she is ready to read alone. The other reader praises the child.
5. The child reads alone until an error is made or a word is encountered that he or she cannot read in five seconds.
6. The reader immediately rejoins the child by saying the difficult word, having the child repeat it, and then they continue reading together until the child gives the signal again and the procedure is repeated or the session ends.

Tutors praise children for appropriate signalling, self-correcting, and fluent reading. Children are encouraged to talk about the reading materials, and this can be initiated either by the child or other reader.

Meeting the Needs of All Learners

Our reading programs are generally less successful with children from nonmainstream backgrounds (poor, recent immigrants, aboriginals, those learning English as a second language) than for those in mainstream homes. Still, there are many children from middle-class neighborhoods who have difficulty learning to read, with some estimates as high as 25 percent. As stated in Chapter 2, reading difficulties are primarily a social construct and the goal of reading instruction for all children must be the same, namely to maximize the match between each child's needs and the program provided.

Reading Difficulties

The first step in working with children who have been identified as having difficulty learning to read is assessment of both the child (how he or she is using background knowledge and print cues to construct meaning) and of the instructional techniques, classroom interactions, and materials provided for that child. It is important to look beyond the classroom context as well to determine aspects of the child's home and community that need to be taken into account when planning appropriate reading instruction. Chapter 11 focuses on assessment techniques.

The next step involves planning and implementing an instructional program that takes into account the cultural and home background of the child as well as the way the child is using information sources to construct meaning when reading. It is essential for the child to experience success in his or her encounters with texts. Failure is a common element in the past reading experiences of all of these children (that's why they have been identified as having reading difficulties) and they generally view themselves as poor readers and learners. Success can be assured by selecting appropriate texts (considering both the child's background knowledge and text features such as predictability) and by providing whatever support the child needs to construct meaning.

Selecting Instructional Techniques

It is important to help the child develop more effective strategies for making meaning from texts, and hence, the selection of appropriate instructional techniques is critical. Research on the experiences of children in high-level and low-level reading groups shows that instructional activities for poor readers tend to focus more on specific skill worksheets or management rather than on text comprehension (Johnston and Allington, 1991). However, there is little evidence that these types of programs are effective with poor readers. Pearson (1993, 505) notes that "the consequence of differentiated instruction for low-track students has been devastating, particularly for children of diversity." What we need is different instruction for different learners rather than one type of program for all children identified as having difficulties learning to read. The key is matching techniques to the needs of the children. Exhibit 7.10 summarizes some common reading difficulties and some techniques that are appropriate for use with each type of difficulty.

EXHIBIT 7.10

Reading Difficulties and Recommended Techniques

Type of Difficulty	Recommended Techniques
• Child is a word caller and needs to make more effective use of background knowledge along with text to make meaning.	• Select techniques from "Integrating knowledge-based and text-based information."
• Child relies too much on phonics knowledge to decode words and produces nonsense words as he or she reads orally.	• Begin with techniques from "Using context cues" and move quickly to those for "Integrating context and print cues."
• Child has few strategies for using cues within words and constructs a different meaning from text information or little meaning at all.	• Begin with techniques from "Using print cues," and as soon as the child develops some of these strategies, move to those for "Integrating context and print cues."
• Child can decode short words but has difficulty with longer ones.	• Select techniques from "Using print cues: word parts."
• Child uses strategies for processing cues within words but constructs a different meaning from text information.	• Select techniques from "Integrating knowledge-based and text-based information," emphasizing text-based information initially.
• Child can construct meaning from stories but has difficulty with informational texts.	• Select techniques from "Using text structure: Informational texts."
• Child seems to think the meaning is in the text and can deal only with factual questions.	• Select techniques from "Integrating knowledge-based and text-based information."

Developing Automaticity

One thing nearly all children with reading difficulty have in common is that they simply do not read very much. Perhaps the most important feature to provide in programs for these children is the chance for them to read real texts during the school day. Research has revealed that children in high-level reading groups tend to spend more time reading than children in low-level reading groups (Bloome and Green, 1984). The amount of time children spend reading increasingly differentiates good and poor readers during their years in school. The good readers read more both at home and school, while the poor readers read very little in either context. Stanovich (1986) refers to this as a Matthew effect—the rich get richer and the poor get poorer. The Matthew effect needs to be reversed for children with reading problems by increasing rather than decreasing the amount of time they spend reading.

Early Intervention

One of the problems with most programs for children identified as having learning disabilities is that the children cannot get special help until they are reading at least two years below expectations for their grade. By this time they have often lost confidence in their ability to learn to read and have developed ineffective reading strategies. An early intervention program that has been used for many years in New Zealand and is beginning to have some impact in North America is Reading Recovery (Clay, 1985).

Children making the slowest progress in reading after one year in school are identified (not labelled) and given one-to-one reading instruction for thirty minutes daily over a ten- to twenty-week period. Research results have demonstrated that most children make rapid progress in Reading Recovery programs (Clay, 1985; Ohio State University, 1988).

The first step in Reading Recovery is a detailed assessment of the child's reading, followed by what Clay refers to as "roaming around the known." For the first two weeks of the program, the child is engaged in reading and writing activities the teacher knows he or she can do. This is a time for confidence and relationship building. Then the teacher moves into instruction, and each thirty minute period includes the following activities:

- rereading two or more familiar books
- rereading yesterday's new book and taking a running record (see Chapter 11)
- letter identification
- writing a sentence (including hearing sounds in words as described earlier in this chapter)
- rearranging a cut-up story (the sentence is cut up and the child puts it back into order)
- introducing and attempting a new book.

While reading and rereading books, the teacher encourages the child to use both context and print cues and praises the child when he or she makes self-corrections. The difficulty of new books increases gradually, ensuring the child success, and rereading familiar books promotes automaticity.

It is important to note that inservice is an integral component of the Reading Recovery program. During this inservice, teachers watch and critique each other's teaching in addition to attending workshops. This adds to the cost of the program, which has been the major deterrent to more widespread adoption. When one considers the cost of long-term intervention for children identified as having reading difficulties, however, Reading Recovery is not so expensive (Dyer, 1992). Clay claims that once children have caught up to their peers, they will not require further intervention during their time in school. While there is some question about this claim (Glynn, Bethune, Crooks, Ballard, and Smith, 1992), the program is successful for most children.

A Final Word

Teachers are bombarded, on a regular basis, with people who claim to have found the answer to reading problems. It may be a diet, it may be exercises, it may be listening or visual devices, it may be a specific commercial program. But whenever someone presents one answer for all children with reading difficulties, alarm bells should sound. Reading is a complex process. Reading difficulties arise from a complex interaction of factors. There are no simple answers. Each may be part of the solution for some children; none will be the total solution for all children.

Nonmainstream Groups

It has been estimated that aboriginal people in Canada have illiteracy rates as high as 45 percent (National Anti-Poverty Organization, 1992). These children arrive at school excited about learning to read just like children from mainstream families. However, after a few short years in school, many have not only lost their enthusiasm but may even resist our efforts to help. What is happening?

There is general agreement about the inappropriateness of education for aboriginals in the past. From the 1890s to the late 1960s, aboriginal children were educated mainly in residential schools and the abuses of these schools have been widely publicized in the media in recent years. Although residential schools are now a thing of the past, their impact lives on in many aboriginal communities, and most aboriginal children still do not receive equal educational opportunities, particularly in schools controlled by non-natives.

While the most appropriate solution seems to be aboriginal-controlled schools, some aboriginal children will continue to be enrolled in other public schools, and it is crucial that teachers adapt reading instruction to meet the needs of these children.

There is often a mismatch between the literacy knowledge these children bring to school and the instructional program. The children may have been exposed to oral storytelling in their own culture rather than being read children's books written by members of Western cultures. They frequently have not developed the knowledge about the functions, nature, and form of written language upon which formal reading instruction is based. It is recommended that a more extensive emergent literacy program be provided for these children. This will help prevent the devastating effects of early and persistent failure when these children are given reading instruction.

It is also important that teachers recognize and respect the cultural knowledge these children bring with them to school and build on this knowledge in reading and writing instruction. Children's books written by aboriginal authors and about aboriginal people can be incorporated into the reading program. As teachers, we need to do a great deal of listening while children share their responses to these and other stories, since their meaning will often be different from ours. Different meanings can be discussed and understood in relation to the different backgrounds of the readers.

We also need to be sensitive to the different ways of interacting with people these children bring with them to the classroom. Although it is commonly believed that aboriginal students are passive learners, a more accurate interpretation may be that aboriginal people regard the display of knowledge quite differently from the way it is regarded in mainstream groups. Whereas we frequently encourage young children to display their knowledge by asking them questions to which we already know the answers, this is far less common in aboriginal homes. We need to be sensitive to these differences and find ways to invite aboriginal children into the classroom environment that are consistent with their cultural background.

The biggest hurdle aboriginal students face when entering school is the widespread belief that they will have difficulty learning to read. The most significant problem for aboriginal students may lie in us rather than in the children themselves. It is clearly our responsibility to weed out the stereotypes we have developed for aboriginal groups and to approach all children as potentially successful learners.

It is obvious that children from some minority groups fare better in our schools than those from others. Asian immigrants from Japan and India have greater success learning to read than do aboriginals. Ogbu (1993) partially accounts for this by distinguishing between the way immigrants (voluntary minorities) and aboriginals (involuntary minorities) respond to being denied access to quality education and to job opportunities that match their education. Immigrants to Canada believe they will find better overall opportunities and greater economic well-being, if not for themselves, then for their children. Their belief helps them to persist and overcome language and cultural conflicts with the school and to do well academically. Even in the face of discrimination, they see their situation as being better in Canada than in their birth country and some of them can go back if they want to. In contrast, aboriginal people see their situation as being worse than in the distant past and they know that they are relatively worse off than mainstream Canadians. They do not view the cultural differences they encounter in school as barriers to be overcome but as markers of identity to be maintained. There are social pressures against "acting white," and as children become more aware of their limited employment opportunities, they divert their energies into nonacademic activities.

All minority children experience some degree of discontinuity between their communities and school, and the main task of teachers is to develop as much understanding of minority communities as possible so that adaptations of both curriculum and classroom interactions can be made. In addition, many of these children will come to Canadian schools with very limited proficiency in the English language.

Many of the same general suggestions for teaching emergent literacy to ESL learners apply to teaching reading to older children as well. This is particularly true for those children who have not already learned to read in their first language. They need to learn about the functions, nature, and form of written language before they will be able to profit from most of the techniques recommended in this chapter.

For children who already learned to read in their first language, there is no need to delay reading instruction in English until they develop proficiency in oral English. Work in literacy facilitates competence in oral language and vice versa, and knowing how to read in one language facilitates learning to read in another, because reading concepts and strategies can be transferred from one language to another. The functions of literacy are the same regardless of what language is involved, even though the form may be different. Reading in any language involves the active construction of meaning, based on background knowledge and cues in the text. Even strategies for processing cues within words are similar across alphabetic languages such as Spanish and English, although some specific sound associations for letters may vary.

There is little doubt that the most crucial factor is for children to be immersed in meaningful reading rather than skills exercises. They need to read texts with natural language patterns rather than contrived texts with controlled vocabulary and grammar. The focus of all reading instruction, as for the English-speaking children in the class, should be on the construction of meaning. Studies of older ESL children show that many have a concept of reading that focuses on decoding individual words to such an extent that it interferes with meaning (Hough and Nurss, 1992). Hence, the focus on making meaning needs to be stronger for ESL learners than for other children.

As for ESL children at the emergent stage of literacy development, older ESL children also need numerous opportunities to interact with both adults and peers in the classroom. Having children work together in pairs and small groups on meaningful activities is beneficial to all learners. ESL learners not only acquire greater oral language proficiency but they also develop a sense of belonging in the classroom. In addition to using the instructional techniques described above with small groups, it is beneficial for ESL children to read and discuss books in pairs or in small groups, rather than reading independently. This provides more language input and an opportunity for these children to watch other children engaged in the meaning-making process.

As noted above in the section on aboriginal and immigrant students, it is vitally important that teachers promote respect for cultural diversity when there are children with limited English language proficiency in the classroom. This can be achieved by incorporating material about the culture of the ESL learners into the curriculum and by selecting children's books that illustrate significant aspects of their culture.

From a constructive view of reading, it is expected that all readers will make different meanings from a text because of differences in their social backgrounds. The background knowledge of ESL learners will often be more diverse than that of other learners in the classroom, and teachers need to work even harder to understand and respect the meanings they construct. Again, a critical approach to literacy will help children to understand the relationship between different backgrounds and meanings.

Chapter Summary

Two major techniques have traditionally been used to develop reading comprehension—questioning and comprehension skill exercises. Teacher questions tend to test rather than teach comprehension and more are literal than inferential or critical. There is little evidence for teaching a series of reading comprehension skills. Instead, this textbook presents instructional techniques to help children develop strategies for using both text-based and knowledge-based information as they read.

Several techniques can be used to help children integrate knowledge and text cues to make meaning as they read. Some of these include the directed reading–thinking activity, KWL, question–answer relationships, and reciprocal teaching. In order to help children use story structure to construct meaning, we suggest story reading and story maps. There are four major types of organizational patterns in informational texts—enumeration, sequence, cause and effect, and comparison/contrast. Discussion, charting, and diagramming can help children to understand relationships among ideas in these patterns.

Word identification has traditionally been taught from a skills perspective with a focus on sight vocabulary, phonics, structural analysis, and contextual analysis. Recently, there has been a heavy focus on using context cues to predict unfamiliar words, but children need to learn strategies for using both print-based and knowledge-based information to identify words as they read. In addition to using meaning and language cues to predict words, children need to process print cues. There are many instructional techniques to help children use letter sounds and word parts to identify unfamiliar words as they read. The most effective techniques are those involving integration of cues both within and outside words.

No one instructional strategy will meet the needs of all children. Instead, a major goal of reading teachers is to assess each child's needs and match the program as closely as possible with those needs. This is true for children from both mainstream and non-mainstream backgrounds, although more adaptation is often necessary for the latter group.

Selected Professional References

Tierney, R.J., J.E. Readence, and E.K. Dishner. (1995). *Reading Strategies and Practices: A Compendium (Fourth Edition)*. Boston: Allyn and Bacon.

Widely ranging instructional techniques to facilitate reading development are presented. The major focus is on comprehension, although attention is also given to study skills, word identification, assessment, and other aspects of reading instruction.

Froese, V. (1991). *A Language Approach to Reading*. Scarborough, Ont.: Nelson Canada.

This book provides practical classroom-oriented information on teaching and assessment strategies in reading. With a heavy focus on comprehension, Froese links reading to other areas of the language arts.

Wiseman, D.L. (1992). *Learning to Read with Literature*. Boston: Allyn and Bacon.

This book provides an introduction to teaching reading using children's literature, including suggestions for teaching strategies.

Children's Materials Noted in Chapter 7

Mealy, N.S. (October 1994). Adventures of Ranger Rick. *Ranger Rick*, 40–43.

CHAPTER 8

Teaching Writing

A Grade 1 student engaged in the writing process.

OBJECTIVES

- to be aware of the major forms of writing elementary school children use
- to understand the models of writing most prevalent in educational theory
- to understand the process of composing
- to be familiar with the teacher's role in facilitating and enhancing children's written compositions
- to understand how writing skills can be taught through minilessons and conferences
- to be familiar with strategies for the direct teaching of spelling and handwriting

Models of Writing

Writing is a complex set of processes and skills including the application of **syntactic**, **semantic**, and **graphophonic** knowledge, and the physical act of creating print. It is a generative rather than a receptive process. When we write we generate meaning using all the **cueing systems** of our language and culture. D'Arcy (1989) refers to the various elements of writing as processes (the thinking involved), products (the pieces of formatted writing), codes (spelling, punctuation, **grammar**, letters, words), and media (handwriting, word processing, notes, jottings, and so on). Each of these must be given due attention when teaching writing.

Not long ago, teaching writing meant teaching handwriting, or what was called penmanship. Almost all the writing done by children in school was copied from the blackboard or from a book. The emphasis was on creating beautiful copy, not on composition or critical and creative thinking. Special teachers of penmanship circulated among the schools in a district and children spent an hour or more each day working in their copybooks. Today, with the use of word processors, the emphasis on handwriting has diminished.

Today, we see writing as an act that is carried out with a specific purpose for a distinct audience. Writing involves command of the print code (grapho-phonics), grammar (syntax), and meaning-making devices (semantics). In order to fulfil their goals, writers need to know many formats: letters, memos, poems, reports, editorials, invitations, journal entries, logs, diaries, essays, plays, filmscripts, textbooks, novels, short stories, lists, recipes, instruction manuals, and so on. As writers, we can never separate a piece of writing from its form, function, or audience. Each one of these affects the others and shapes the piece of writing. We learn much of this from the reading we do every day—in bus advertisements, television listings, mailbox coupons, letters to friends, application forms for jobs, cooking directions on packages of food, articles in magazines, and novels. Each time we read we learn more about writing and what we need to know and do in order to be effective writers.

Most importantly, we must understand that each time we write, we do so for a specific purpose and audience. The purpose and audience dictate the format and voice or style of the writing.

James Britton (Britton, Burgess, Martin, McLeod, and Rosen, 1975) proposed a model of writing based on the stance or voice of the writer—the purpose, audience, and function of the writing. Britton identified three voices of writing: expressive, poetic, and transactional. **Expressive writing** is what we do when we write in a journal, write a personal letter to a friend, or write in a notebook about ideas that have lingered in our minds. It expresses who we are, and what we think and feel. In expressive writing, which usually uses the language of everyday speech, we articulate ideas that are close to us, that may not yet be fully shaped. **Poetic writing** is more literary and is used in stories and poems. Usually created for an audience other than the self, poetic writing is crafted and often contains an aesthetic element not usually present in either transactional or expressive writing. **Transactional writing** is the voice used when we want to convey information to others in a report, list, essay, or textbook. It is usually not personal.

Britton noticed that young writers frequently move from one voice to another as they write. When writing a report on a pet, for example, they may add a personal anecdote about their own pet, and hence combine the expressive and transactional voices. Similarly, they may shift from the poetic to the expressive voice when writing a story, adding themselves as a character and writing in the first person. Britton terms this the **transitional** voice. Usually, as writers mature, they are able to select an appropriate voice for their writing and remain consistently within that voice.

James Moffett (1979) proposed a model of writing that demonstrates a hierarchy according to the skills the writer needs. The first level is that of drawing or handwriting. This is the level at which children begin writing, as they struggle to make sense of the written language system, and replicate it. The second level is copying, where children are capable of copying from a model provided by someone else. They are not, at this point, generating their own ideas in writing. The third level is transcribing or paraphrasing, where writers put someone else's ideas into their own words. The next level is crafting, where children can generate meaning through writing in a conventional form. The final level is what Moffett calls "the revision of inner speech." Moffett claims this is the only true writing, for it involves expressing and shaping one's own thoughts. In any classroom, all these levels of writing should be happening, for indeed we use all of them in adult writing. If we confine children to copying from the board, they will not develop mature writing skills. Likewise, if we confine children to crafting polished pieces of writing with an aim to making them public in a writing workshop, they will not learn how to use writing as a way of exploring thought. All these levels are essential, and all must be engaged if children are to develop into thoughtful, articulate, and skilful writers.

Donald Graves (1983) conducted research with children that led to a major shift in the teaching of writing. This work, along with that of Lucy Calkins (1986), Nancie Atwell (1987), and others, promotes a workshop approach to teaching writing. This means that children work with each other and their teachers, composing, drafting, revising, editing, and making public their works. Graves's work enabled teachers to reconceptualize writing as a series of processes that a writer goes through with each piece of writing. The workshop approach demands that teachers engage in writing themselves so that they fully understand what a writer goes through in order to create a composition, making it clear and conventionally appropriate for an audience. The process requires time, thought, and reworking of multiple drafts. The focus is on composition and the thinking that must take place in order to develop a composition. Graves's work has fundamentally changed the way educators think about the writing process and the teaching of writing in schools.

Forms of Writing

Narrative

Narrative writing links a series of events either through chronology or through cause and effect. It seems an almost natural way for human beings to make sense of the world. Barbara Hardy (1975) says that narrative is a "primary act of mind." We seem to think in narrative—retelling events to ourselves to see how the pieces fit together, or telling ourselves how something works as we try to figure out a problem. We even create lists in narrative, although we don't write the list that way. "I need mayonnaise because I want to make salad dressing on the weekend. I noticed the paper towel roll was almost used up. I don't want to run out while I'm working in the kitchen. I must remember to get chicken breasts for the dinner," and so on. Narrative, then, is a way of linking thoughts together so that they make sense to us. It's the story we tell ourselves behind whatever it is we are doing.

When we write or tell a story we craft the narrative in a certain way. In Western culture a story needs an introduction, a middle section with a problem or conflict (sometimes a series of conflicts), and then an ending, which attains some resolution of the problem. This structure is not common to all cultures; for example, aboriginal Canadian and Caribbean stories often involve the same characters, who are familiar to the audience before the story begins. These stories, therefore, do not need the same kind of introduction common to most European or Western stories. Applebee's 1978 study of the development of children's concept of story suggests that children have to learn to do two things at the same time when they write or tell a story: chain events together and focus on a theme, problem, or character. Children begin to form stories from the age of two onward, but they learn to apply these two essential elements over time, mastering the story form (or story grammar, as it is sometimes called) over a period of years. As children mature, their stories become more complex and cohesive. Children become aware of an audience for their writing, striving for clarity and an engaging text. An example of a typical story written by Grade 5 children is shown in Exhibit 8.1. Unfinished at the end of the school year, this story was put "on hold" by the two girls who wrote it because they were not sure what to do with it next, and they had another piece of writing they wanted to start. This story will be referred to later in the chapter in the section about the importance of talk. At that point, the girls' struggle with the piece becomes more apparent.

EXHIBIT 8.1

The Wellington Story
Written cooperatively by Sharon and Erica (Grade 5)

"Hi I'm home! Yvette have you started dinner yet?" called Margaret Wellington from down the hall. "Yes, Mrs. Wellington. Dinner will be served shortly," replied Yvette. Mrs. Wellington walked into the kitchen and dropped two packages on the dining room table. "The guests should be arriving soon. I'll go put my new dress on my bed for the upstairs maid to iron and then take these paints to my husband," said Mrs. Wellington and went upstairs. Later that evening, Mrs. Wellington came downstairs to help Yvette with dinner. Just then Mr. Wellington came downstairs. "I'll be out in the paint house while you girls fix up dinner," he said and left.

Mrs. Wellington placed a bowl of cranberry sauce on the dining room table. Then she leaned over the bowl of cranberry sauce and put a candle on the center of the dining room table. "There," she said with a sigh.

Just then the doorbell rang. "Yvette, could you get the door please?" asked Mrs. Wellington. Yvette went to answer the door. "Good evening, Miss Murphy," said Yvette. "May I take your coat?" Miss Murphy handed Yvette her coat and went into the lounge.

After everybody arrived they all sat down for dinner. "Cheers to Mrs. Wellington for having this party," said Miss Murphy in a loud voice. Then they all lifted their glasses and clinked them together. "I'll go get my husband for dinner," said Mrs. Wellington and left. A few minutes later, Mrs.

continued

Wellington came back into the dining room. "My husband will be coming shortly," she said as Yvette started carving the turkey. After about ten minutes had passed Mrs. Wellington asked Yvette to go see where her husband was.

Yvette left the dining room and went to the paint house. There was a moment of silence and then Miss Murphy spoke. "The strangest thing happened to me yesterday," she said. I…Ahhhhhh." Miss Murphy was interrupted (loud scream). Mrs. Wellington dropped her fork.

"It's coming from the paint house," said Mr. McGregor. They all rushed out to the paint house and saw Yvette shaking, with a knife in her hand. Mrs. Wellington gasped and walked into the paint house. She saw her husband lying dead on the floor." "Yvette," she screamed.

"How could you?" Mrs. Landenburg walked into the room, looked at the body and fainted. "Somebody call the police," said Mrs. Hunt. Mrs. Wellington started to cry. Mr. McGregor called the police. About 5 minutes later they arrived. "We were in the neighborhood," they said. "Now what happened?" Mrs. Wellington explained the whole thing. "Then we walked in and saw her," she said pointing to Yvette, "standing there with a knife in her hand. She did it, officer, I know she did."

"Why don't you go into the house and rest while we look around and take the body away," said the police officer. Mrs. Wellington went into the lounge with the other guests. "It's all right Margaret. It had to happen sooner or later being a famous painter and all," said Miss Murphy. "He was such a kind husband to me," said Mrs. Wellington and then started to cry. Meanwhile in the paint house officer McCarther was searching around the floor when he spotted a loose floorboard.

He pulled back the floor board and saw a white dress with a red wine stain on it. "Hmm," he said. Then he put on a pair of rubber gloves, picked up the dress and placed it in a plastic bag. Then he took a second look, and saw the top of a broken wine bottle. He picked up the wine bottle and put it into a plastic bag. Then he walked over to where Mr. Wellington was lying and picked up the knife that Yvette dropped and went into the lounge. "I'll have to take finger prints," said officer McCarther and pulled out a stamp pad in front of Mrs. Wellington. "Are you accusing me of killing my own husband? Why would I kill him?" asked Mrs. Wellington. "You might kill him for his money and besides everyone in the room is a suspect," said officer McCarther. "Why didn't I wait until he dies?" asked Mrs. Wellington.

continued

The girls ended the story with the following note to themselves:

tired of story — change some parts
Stop story for now

want to start cat by-law — not doing a play
—yet at least!

(Used with permission of Catherine Lewis)

Expressive

Found in casual letters, diaries, and journals, this is the kind of writing we do informally as thoughts form in our mind. We rarely revise or craft expressive writing. (Britton's use of the word "expressive" to describe one of the three voices of writing differs from this use, though there is some overlap in meaning.) Expressive writing is done for an audience who knows the writer; sometimes the self. Expressive writing presents our ideas, thoughts, feelings, and interpretations of events. It includes our responses to books we have read, movies we have seen, and so on. Expressive writing is essentially the language of exploration, the language of learning. In expressive writing, just as in expressive speech, we speculate, hypothesize, predict, and generally articulate our thoughts. Exhibit 8.2 illustrates a Grade 4 child's expressive writing.

Informative or Expository

Intended to explain or expose something, expository writing must be well organized, clear, and coherent. This writing is not meant to convey feelings or personal observations, but to pass on information to an audience. Reports, textbooks, memos, and notices are examples of expository writing. The term paper is a form of expository writing with which most university students are familiar. It both informs the audience and demonstrates the role of the writer as an expert in the field. An example of a Grade 4 child's expository writing is shown in Exhibit 8.3 (Petite Rivière, 1993a).

Persuasive

Persuasive writing is used more often in our society than we realize. Advertising, editorials, political campaign literature, religious tracts, and much of the unsolicited junk mail that arrives in our mailboxes is persuasive writing. Someone wants to persuade us to do something, buy something, or believe something. Children use persuasive writing when they do a poster presentation about a book or a book celebration. They write persuasively when they want something very much and have to convince an adult to allow them to have it. At school, this can be channelled into writing to government agencies requesting changes. This might be part of a social studies or science project, and may involve a letter-writing campaign. An excerpt from a piece of persuasive writing by a Grade 6 child follows.

> *I think instead of having a curfew we should have police patrolling the streets at night as a pair. I think we shouldn't have a curfew at night because there are a lot of people out that are not vandalizing the streets.*
>
> *I would like to talk about why there should be two policemen in each community and how they should work the streets. In my area we have different sorts of gangs. One kid that I know was riding his bike down the street and one of the gangs called Devil's Knights, one kid threw a knife and almost hit the kid. I think the police should talk to different people and ask questions about the gangs and where they meet. I hope we can get the perfect president to run a place like this.*

EXHIBIT 8.2

Grade 4 Expressive Writing

May 24

I am okay in multiples. I think multiples are fun, espealy in number munshears. I understand multipes quiet alot. But with factors I don't understand. My dad does not ethier, My mom surt of does. So last night with the homework I was suck. But in the mornig I got it enuf figerd out I could do it. I need help on factors, not alot but.

Explaining about factors!

let's tack the number 18 if you count up to 18 in 6's. you can get up to 18. Factors are when you can count in something and get the the number you are doing.

EXHIBIT 8.3

Grade 4 Expository Writing
"Music in Crousetown"

The Anglican Church in Crousetown, has the oldest pipe organ in Nova Scotia. It still is used in 1993. Every Sunday music was a big entertainment in those days and it still is today.

Most of the music of long ago was made up for fun. Some children might take some spoons and clack them against their knees, or a little boy might put some beans in a can and shake the can.

At night some people might gather together in someone's house and listen to each other play fiddles and accordians.

In those days there were no heavy rock bands or electric guitars. In the old days some homes had pianos or pump organs and if there was someone who could play the piano or organ they would play for sing along songs. Instead of electric guitars some people would play wooden guitars.

They had just about the same fun the old fashioned way as we do with rock bands.

Descriptive

Descriptive writing is frequently part of a larger piece of prose, though descriptive pieces can stand alone. In descriptive writing the author tries to create a verbal picture of a scene or event, and tries to make the reader experience what the author is experiencing. Careful crafting of relevant detail can make a descriptive piece of writing particularly dramatic. Below is a piece of descriptive writing by a Grade 5 child, an excerpt from a story in chapters.

> *We'd been flying for almost an hour when a grotesque aroma floated from the back of the plane and filled the air. From experience, I knew that the meal was salmon and spinach pate. My stomach turned inside out at the thought of it. The old woman who I was sitting beside didn't help my stomach because she stank of Super Polly Grip, Efferdent and cheap perfume. The clickety-clack of her knitting needles was driving me insane as I tried to write a letter to my best friend, Brooke. I knew that she was going to be knitting for a long time because she had a pattern for a large sweater taped to the back of her tray and she was still on the first cuff!*

Another piece of descriptive writing from a child in Grade 6 also came from a chaptered story:

> *Then I saw her. She was massive, at least it seemed that way to me. Tall and sleek and black. I shut my eyes again until I felt soft breath on my back. She woofed softly and only then did I realize that she was my mother and meant no harm. I opened my eyes again and squinted as the light hit them. The interior of the large foaling stall was dimly lit and quiet. The walls were made of dark, rough wood and a light rope hung across the doorway. This was all so new to me that I lay my head down and let my mother lick my tousled coat.*

Poetry

Rather than being one specific form of writing, poetry is a style of writing that attempts to capture feelings, events, places, people, and so on in an aesthetically pleasing way. A few words or phrases convey a whole set of meanings in a particularly striking way. Poetry is not defined by a rhyming scheme or rhythm, but is uniquely artistic, although often disconcerting. Although young children often find difficulty writing poetry themselves—probably because of the discipline involved in creating it—children in upper elementary and junior high school seem to find poetry a singularly effective form for much of what they have to say. Children in these grades write much excellent poetry. A poem written by a child in Grade 2 is shown in Exhibit 8.4. The following poem was written by a child in Grade 3:

> **Cowboys**
> *Brave and dirty,*
> *Hazing,*
> *Roping,*
> *Digging their spurs into the horses.*
> *Riding,*
> *Racing,*
> *Branding the cattle -*
> *Cowpunchers.*

The Process of Composing

Writers often say there is no such thing as a finished piece. As we write we think, and as we think and receive feedback, we revise, develop new ideas, begin new pieces, share old ones, and continue our development. One aspect of the thinking process, writing both reflects and facilitates the exploration of ideas. It would be more appropriate to think of the composition process as a spiral, for we are never in the same place as before; usually we make some forward motion, developing new writing strategies, techniques, and ideas.

The first stage of composing is referred to as collecting, rehearsing, or pre-writing. At this point we collect ideas, memories, and experiences that help us to decide on a topic. We decide on what belongs in the composition, and what memories and recollections we can use to develop it. Our writing is almost always based on our own experiences, whether real or vicarious. We use mixtures of people we have known, places we have visited, and experiences we are familiar with. Writers of published work tell us that all their stories are about themselves, in some way. The children's author Katherine Paterson tells of her feelings of loneliness and alienation during her Grade 1 year in the United States (Paterson, 1989). She had spent the first six years of her life in China, and on her first Valentine's Day she did not receive a single valentine card. She maintains that all her books are about not receiving a valentine, and that theme is certainly discernable in *The Great Gilly Hopkins*, *Bridge to Terabithia*, and *The Flip Flop Girl*. We retain our memories and emotions, and these become the raw material of our writing. Children are just as capable as adults of choosing a topic and working with their experiences. They need help and encouragement, but the more they have ownership of their writing, and

EXHIBIT 8.4

Grade 2 Poetry

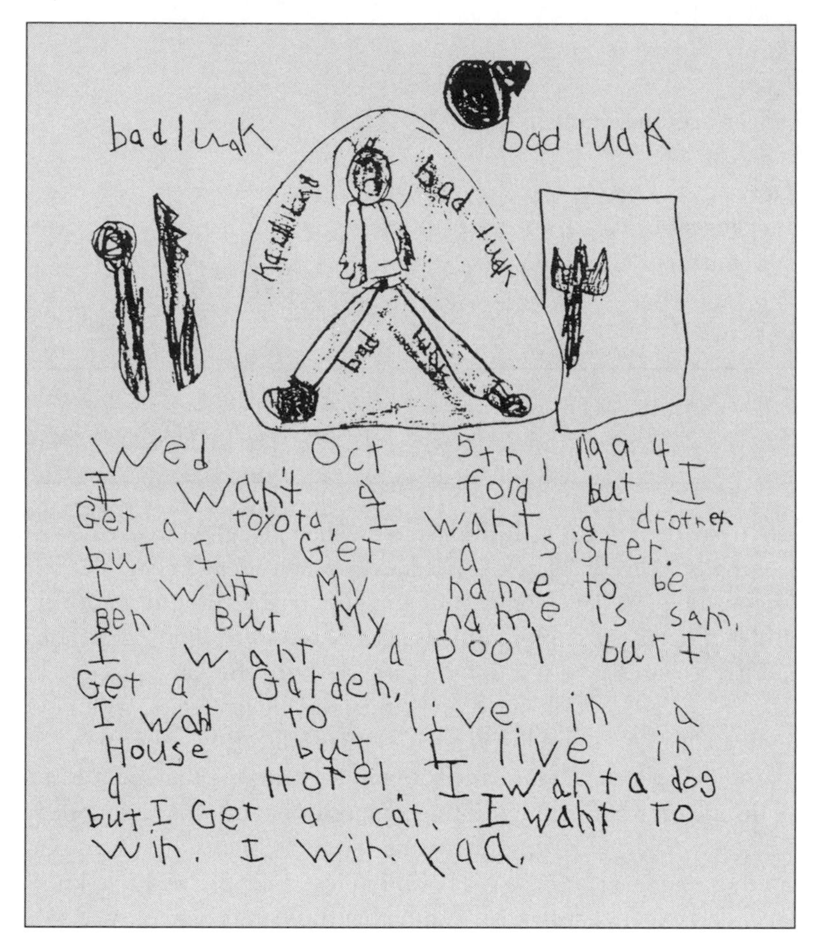

Bad Luck

I want a Ford but I get a Toyota.
I want a brother but I get a sister.
I want my name to be Ben but my name is Sam.
I want a pool but I get a garden.
I want to live in a house but I live in a hotel.
I want a dog but I get a cat.
I want to win. I win. Yaa!

write about topics that interest them, the more they are likely to work at their writing and improve it. We learn to write by writing.

Once a topic has been determined, the writer begins to draft a text, putting onto paper the intentions developed in the rehearsing stage. The text will go through many drafts, as it is modified and reworked, with the original intentions in mind. During this drafting stage, it becomes clearer what can actually be done, and what needs to be changed. We play with the drafts, changing words here and there, adding to it, deleting parts that are not effective, and rewriting parts that simply don't work. It is during this stage that the writer asks, "Am I meaning what I say and saying what I mean?" We strive for clarity, and try to maintain the interest and attention of the audience. Sometimes, thoughts do not fall into place until we start writing; the actual process of writing enables the ideas to flow. Writing seems to slow down our thinking, allowing time to capture it, reflect on it, and generate new thoughts connected to the old ones.

As a draft takes shape, the writer revises it many times, moving parts around, editing it and ensuring that it is ready for an audience. Much of this work used to be done with scissors and glue as we cut and pasted parts to make a text more coherent. Now, that work is often done on a computer, which facilitates revision like no other writing tool. Many classrooms have computers, and children often learn how to work on a computer, including keyboarding skills, in Grade 3 or 4. Editing and revision skills still need to be taught, but much of this can be done in minilessons or in the conferences that are an essential component of any writing workshop. When children are writing on paper, they must be taught how to prepare for revision by writing on one side of the paper only, and on every other line. These practices enable them to cross out, write over top, use carets to insert text, and make other changes without having to copy a whole piece over.

Some published authors, including Katherine Paterson, say they cannot share a piece of writing until it is completely finished, because it is so close and precious to them. Most of us, however, need feedback while we are in the process of writing. This is particularly so for children. Peer conferences, and group and one-on-one conferences with the teacher are all necessary so that children can get feedback on their writing when they need it, and not when it is too late to make changes. It is during these conferences that most of the teaching of writing occurs.

Sharing a piece of writing with others can be a celebration of work completed, or it can mean sharing a work-in-progress when help or feedback is required. Sharing writing with an audience can be a nerve-wracking experience, because the writing is very special to its author. It is a part of the writer, and is not to be belittled or demeaned in any way. Children must be taught how to receive work. They must feel safe before they can share, and they must learn how to give constructive feedback and positive comments as well as make suggestions for further work. A three-part response system usually works well for elementary school children. First, give a positive comment about the piece—what works well or sounds good. Next, ask questions about anything that is not clear.

Finally, make suggestions about what can be done to make it an even better piece of writing. The focus in a writing conference should be on the content until the final editing stages when language conventions must be addressed: correct spelling, punctuation, and capitalization must be ensured so that the meaning and feeling of the piece are communicated to the audience. Frequent misspellings or other errors can detract from the effectiveness of a piece of writing, particularly when children have reached the age where these conventions are expected (around Grade 2 or 3), and invented spelling no longer adds to the personal voice of the writer.

The very last phase of the writing process is publication or celebration. When a piece is finished to an author's satisfaction, the piece can be shared with a wider audience. It might be read aloud to a whole class or group, made into a book and placed in the classroom or school library, sent to students at a nearby college, shared with residents of a seniors' home, or sent home to family. At this point, the writing is to be celebrated. It is no longer a work-in-progress, and it is no longer appropriate to make critical comments or suggestions for change. The work will stand alone, ready for public scrutiny and the future enjoyment of reading audiences.

Establishing a live audience for children's writing makes a difference in how they go about the process of composition and revision, as the following story illustrates.

Fran Chalmers and her teaching colleague in Edmonton assigned a writing activity on the topic of dogs to their respective Grade 1 classes. The activity "bombed" in both classrooms. The two teachers shared their dismay and tried to figure out a reason for it. Had the students not had enough time to share their thoughts with a partner before beginning their writing? Did the children lack experience with dogs? Was there enough motivation in this activity? Was it relevant to the children's lives? Did the topic not interest them? As a result of their discussion, they decided to return to the classes with the news that the children were going to share their stories with their buddies in the other Grade 1 classroom. The announcement had a profound effect. The children tackled the writing with renewed interest and enthusiasm. Only thirty minutes later, twenty-seven pairs of children were excitedly reading their stories to each other. Awareness that a real audience was going to hear the stories made all the difference. This anecdote also demonstrates how teachers must be responsive to the students in their classes and must be willing to question their own teaching and change their plans at short notice when something is obviously not going well. The next vignette (Inside the Classroom) gives a further glimpse of the effects of audience on children's writing and motivation.

Poetic writing is not the only kind that benefits from having an audience. **Transactional writing** might also receive peer and teacher responses as it is created. In fact, any piece of writing we wish to do well may require input from others along the way. Letters to a business, letters to government agencies, reports, and scripts can all benefit from feedback. Writers may work on their ideas and original drafts alone, but at some point they usually require feedback to clarify and present those ideas to a reading public.

Inside **the Classroom**

Rhonna Jessome teaches in Dartmouth at Bicentennial School, and Jan Buley in Halifax at the Halifax Grammar School. The vignette they share here demonstrates the enthusiasm created through writing to a known audience. The awareness of audience causes a shift in focus in not only the content of the writing, but the conventions of written language as well. The Grade 3/4 classroom conversation about penpals began like this.

"Has anyone ever had a penpal before? What's it like?"

"I did. In Korea. Mine moved away, though. I don't know where."

"Did you ever meet the person you wrote to?"

"No. But our penpals are in Dartmouth. Maybe we could."

"How do you know your penpal is a boy? Jamie might be a girl."

"Will we ever meet them?"

"What will we say when we meet them?"

"Hey, I'm giving mine my phone number."

"There's a Michelle. The same name as me."

"Should we use pencils or markers?"

"What do you think?"

"Should we print or write the letter?"

"How did you make that envelope?"

"I'm making my penpal a book mark."

"Can I borrow some stickers for the stamp?"

"How do you spell sincerely?"

"S-i-n-s-e-r-l-y, I think."

To get things rolling, our classroom wrote penpal letters first. That was an interesting experience, since many of the children commented that they hardly ever wrote letters to people they'd never met before. It was heartwarming to brainstorm some content areas with them before they began writing.

"What sorts of things do you want to find out about your penpal? What kinds of things do you think they're wondering about right at this very moment about you?"

At first, the letters were simple and filled with all sorts of trivia—lots of small talk and inquisitive safe questions and comments. Many children asked "politically polite" questions about everything from favourite television programs to hair colour.

continued

Pets were also a hot topic. (Both classrooms have guinea pigs.) A few children asked questions in their first letters. "Do you like school? Do you like your teacher? When is your birthday?"

The flat, oversized brown envelope arrived, addressed to us in colourful marker. It took up a lot of room in the classroom mailbox and was seen right away. The name of the school wasn't spelled correctly—there was an *n* missing—but the children didn't notice.

"Hey, Michelle. There's one for you! It's from a Michelle, too!" Eager hands snapped forward to grab the letter. Everyone was curious and full of anticipation. Nobody needed a personal invitation to come to the carpet area.

"Is there one for me?" begged Stuart.

"Quit pushing!"

Twenty-three children were instantly captivated by this mysterious envelope. The suspense of receiving their own letter coupled with the reaction of their peers as they examined their mail was almost more than they could bear. They couldn't contain their joy and curiosity. Hands fidgeted, feet squirmed, and chatter filled the room. They were desperate to see who got what, who got a pencil taped onto their letter, a baseball card bookmark, a knock-knock joke. Who likes pizza with pineapple and who has a pet? The similarities jumped right off the paper at the children.

"Hey! They stay in for lunch every day!" shouted Josh.

"My penpal has the same birthday month!"

"She has two sisters, too!"

"Hey, everybody! Their guinea pig's name is Sylvester!"

"Knock. Knock."

"You've got the same paper as me," said Quinn, showing his letter to Monty.

"Look at that. It's a guinea pig on the paper," giggled Devon.

"Looks like they made it. Do you think they did?"

"Aw … lucky. You got a pencil."

"They used enough staples."

"I got an envelope and a bookmark," announced Laura.

"Look what Susanne got. She's got extra recess."

"Guess what! My penpal likes Goosebumps too."

"What's this word mean?" asked Rory, walking toward Devon with his letter.

"Did this really come in the mail? All this stuff?"

continued

Stuff, indeed. The envelope was literally stuffed full. And so was the envelope we sent back to our penpals a few days later. It resembled a giant ravioli pocket. The contents were bursting out and there was no hope of licking it shut; we had to resort to masking tape. Letters with and without wallpaper envelopes, coloured paper meticulously stapled to letters, odd artifacts made from egg carton bits and recycled greeting cards—all giving the semblance of cast-off items racing in front of a caretaker's pushbroom.

A new voice emerged in the letter writing this time—a much stronger, confident voice. Nobody told the letter-writers how to spell something or how to punctuate in a conventional way. Occasionally, a child would ask another child a question. Sometimes, the writer simply shouted out an observation for the rest of the class to consider.

"I can't believe she spelled my name with an *h* at the end. I told her it was just four letters—Sara."

"Lemme see. Lemme see. How did she spell it?" asked Michelle, leaning over Sara's table.

I overheard the conversation and put in my two cents.

"So what could you do, Sara?" I asked, tossing the ball plainly into her court.

Her head lowered and she began to write. The next time I ventured near Sara's table, I could see the opening line of her letter to her penpal, Robin:

"dear Robbin,

please don't spall my name with a h on the end.

it doesn't have a h on the end. it is just Sara."

It will be interesting to see how the exchange unfolds and see whether Robin reacts to the ironic spelling error in his name. This issue demonstrated clearly that Sara had a fairly good understanding of the power of language. She can competently use written form to communicate and complain. She is also offering a solution in her letter.

The children in our classes realize that they may be separated by Halifax Harbour, yet they share many interests, opinions, and questions. Most importantly, they have unending enthusiasm to write and tell each other more news. Whenever anything new happens in the classroom, a child invariably pipes up with, "Hey! We've got to tell our penpals about that!"

continued

When we began this penpal activity, the first envelope we exchanged was thin and skimpy. The enthusiasm for our new classroom friendship has expanded considerably, however. A skinny brown envelope is no longer enough to hold the messages from one classroom to another. The last time we exchanged mail, we needed a car for the delivery.

This vignette clearly illustrates the power of a real audience for children's writing. The excitement and anticipation was authentic and motivating. Children began to pay attention to the conventions of print as well as to the lives of their penpals—the differences and similarities of school routines, names, pets, brothers and sisters, and so on. Rhonna and Jan, like Jessie Haché in Chapter 9, understand the power of audience on children's writing and have captured the dramatic impact of it in their classrooms.

The next section of this chapter addresses some of the ways teachers can organize a writing workshop in their classroom.

Guidelines for Conducting a Writing Workshop

1. A writing workshop should have a predictable format so that students know when it is to occur, what is expected of them, and what they can expect from the teacher and the situation. Usually, teachers work out for themselves what feels comfortable, and what seems to work in their classrooms. Time should be provided for children to write, as well as respond to each other, and time must also be provided for teachers to respond to individual students' work. Some teachers create a schedule so that they meet with a particular group of writers on a rotating basis. Group members give feedback to each other, and when the group finishes work together, the teacher is able to work with individual students who need help that day. Some teachers also try to build into their schedules time for their own writing so that children can see them modelling the writing process themselves.

2. A writers' workshop is something like an artist's studio and should have all the necessary resources. Young children need different colours and sizes of paper, scissors, tape, felt pens, pencils, pens, and staplers so they can create their own booklets for writing and drawing. Older children need dictionaries, a thesaurus, reference books, rulers, white-out liquid, and staples.

3. There will be noise in a writers' workshop, since the children need to talk about their writing, but there must also be quiet times when all the students are writing. These various times can be agreed upon by the class as they begin to understand and articulate what they need as writers. Many children say that they cannot do any real writing or reading at school because it is too noisy. We must respect this need as well as the need for interaction. Catherine Lewis schedules quiet time in her Grade 5 classroom for writing only, when any conversation must be in a whisper. Catherine also schedules open time, when students can write or meet together in a response group on the floor in one corner of the room. In addition to this, she schedules planned group conferences where she interacts with the children in a more traditional way.

Student and teacher in writing conference.

4. A writing folder is essential for each person in the classroom, including the teacher. The folder doesn't have to be specially purchased; children can design and make their own. The important thing is that the folder be expandable in some way so that it can hold a stack of writing. Ideally, the folder needs two or three sections—for pieces that are just being started, works in progress, and completed writing. Rather than have children keep these folders in their desks, it is usually easier and neater if all the folders are kept in a filing cabinet or large cardboard box that is accessible to the children at all times. A box can be decorated and kept in a prominent place.

5. All pieces of writing should be dated with a draft number printed at the top. Students should save all writings, even those that "don't work." This allows them to see how their work is changing. Sometimes a writer will go back to an earlier draft of a piece because it is better than a later one. When Sharon and Erica created "The Wellington Story" (Exhibit 8.1), they were unsure what to do next. They had lots of thoughts, but needed time to distance themselves from the piece so they could return to it later with fresh ideas. The piece stayed in their writing folders with various dates on it at intervals as they worked on it over a long period of time. Eventually they agreed to

abandon the story, but they each kept a copy of it. Perhaps one day we might see a variation of it in print!

6. Students should generate a list of possible writing topics and keep them at the beginning of the folder—either on the cover or stapled to the inside cover. They should add to the list on a regular basis as they discover new topics and experiences that will make good stories. Teachers can encourage children to take a few minutes every few weeks to update their list of possibilities, and can discuss topics with the class that they have chosen to put on their own lists.

7. Writers should not erase their work. Instead, encourage them to put a line through changes and insert new material. Writing on every other line and on only one side of the paper helps this process and encourages children to make changes and insertions without having to rewrite the whole piece. When children compose on a word processor it is more difficult to separate drafts, as changes are made to a text on a continuing basis. However, it is helpful if children can print drafts at various stages of development, label them, and keep them in their folder. Alternatively they can be saved on the computer in the same way.

8. Writing conferences might focus on a piece's content, topic, or organization, clarifying the ideas and focusing the writing into a more cohesive whole. A writing conference should generally deal with only one of these elements at a time, since young writers cannot revise everything at once. The information given in a writing conference should be in small enough chunks that the writer can think about it and act on it.

9. Minilessons are taught as a result of specific points that come up in a writers' workshop, usually in the context of the children's writing. The minilesson is a vehicle for teaching many writing skills such as capitalization; the use of commas and periods; particular spelling that is difficult for a large number of children; clarifying ideas; and so on. The craft of writing is taught in these minilessons using the overhead projector and a piece of student writing or one written by the teacher. Grade 5 teacher Catherine Lewis often uses a piece of her own writing to demonstrate an idea to her students, or to ask them to suggest how the piece can be improved. The aim is always to improve the piece of writing, making it more interesting, effective, and enjoyable. Minilessons are described in detail in the section of this chapter about teaching spelling and grammar, and in Chapter 9 in the section on research and study skills.

10. In a writing conference, have the writer read the work aloud. Listen and encourage the writer to lead the conference as much as possible. The writer should be in charge of the piece. The role of the teacher and the peers is to make suggestions and share responses as interested listeners and co-writers. The conventions of writing can be attended to later in the process when the ideas and organization are in place.

11. In order to be authentic and to model the writing process, teachers must write—either with the children or at some other time if they are too busy during the writers' workshop. In addition, they must share their writing with the children. Children need to see that even adults struggle with creating good writing. Writing is hard work, and all authors labour over their compositions. It is especially effective to have published children's authors visit the classroom and speak about their work. Children find these visits inspiring as well as interesting, and they benefit from knowing that books come from real people who struggle with their work just as much as we do in an elementary classroom.

Social Interaction in the Writing Process

Although educators have long realized that learning to speak is a social process, it's only recently that we have acknowledged the importance of social interaction when writing. If, as Moffett (1979) maintains, true writing occurs only when we revise inner speech, then children must become aware of what the revision of inner speech entails. They must make their inner speech explicit and wrestle with the ideas they are attempting to articulate. Moffett says that teachers "have no choice but to work in the gap between thought and speech" (1979, 278). He also suggests that "writing cannot be realistically perceived and taught so long as we try to work from the outside in" (279). In other words, true writing comes from within the writer, who must learn to articulate thought and put it into print. When children work collaboratively in the writing process they explore the gap between thought and speech. If we listen to them, we can find out how they negotiate meaning and the structural elements of writing. The social context of writing in the classroom and the relationships among the students influence writing enormously. Through their talk, as Michael Halliday has said, they learn "how to mean."

The Importance of Talk

As children talk together or with a teacher, continual scaffolding is evident. Through constant interaction, the students become teachers and learners interchangeably. The following excerpt is a planning session where Erica and Sharon, in a Grade 5 classroom, considered each other's opinions and incorporated them into a written debate about the city cat bylaws (Lewis, 1989).

Sharon:	Want to do a debate?
Erica:	*Yes, then we can each have our own opinion.*
Sharon:	What's yours about?
Erica:	*My what?*
Sharon:	Your issue you want to debate. I want to do the cat bylaw. OK?
Erica:	*OK. I'll just put "Cat Bylaw" at the top of the page.*
Sharon:	OK. If I was in charge of the world I'd change the cat bylaw.
Erica:	*Do you want to do this one (pause) together? I don't have a cat, you do, so it makes a difference, doesn't it?*
Sharon:	Cats should be able to walk around.
Erica:	*And I'm going to write against that! Cats go to the bathroom everywhere and...*
Sharon:	Good, we disagree then—we agree on that. (laughter)
Erica:	*And it smells! Write on the top of the page "Cat Bylaw" again.*
Sharon:	Why?
Erica:	*Because we're going to do it together ... We'll put my opinions and your opinions so we know whose is what.*
Sharon:	I want to ask you a question. If you don't have a cat, would you still not like the rule as much? I still think it's dumb.
Erica:	*Ya, but you wouldn't like it as much, like it wouldn't be ... Even if you had a cat would you still hate it more?*
Sharon:	No, exactly the same.
Erica:	*What! I'm writing against you, right?*
Sharon:	Well, cats ... I agree that cats do that—go to the bathroom, I mean.
Erica:	*I agree in a way (writes this down slowly).*
Sharon:	Don't write this next part down till I figure it out.

Erica: *But dogs—dogs do that too (still writes slowly, thinking, pausing). Dogs do poop on our lawn.*

Sharon: Dogs usually have their owners with them.

Erica: *Not always. Some people let their dogs out 'cause we've had a lot of ...*

Sharon: Ya, but dogs don't come back.

Erica: *Yes, they do.*

Sharon: No, but cats always do—in the same place.

Erica: *Well, it depends on how far they go...*

In their continuing negotiation of meaning, the two girls found that they became very aware of writing for an audience. They began to negotiate meaning and work out details, where each sentence, and at times each word, was important. Disagreements were common, and they questioned the logic of each other's ideas. The following excerpt, from a discussion Sharon and Erica held while writing a mystery story together, concerns the phrases *looked closer* and *looked again*.

Erica: *He looked closer into the hole...*

Sharon: He looked again, *sounds better.*

Erica: Well, Sharon, if you looked closer, would you stick your head right into the hole?

Sharon: *It doesn't mean that.*

Erica: Well it does to me!

Sharon: *Closer isn't sticking your face into the hole but* looked again *just sounds better.*

Erica: Sharon, you don't listen!

Sharon: *So, we don't use "closer" or "again." We say "he looked into the hole and saw the top of the wine bottle."*

Erica: No, "he looked closer"—a bit closer—know what I mean?

Sharon: *Why would he look closer to see the wine bottle?*

Erica: 'Cause the dress might have covered it up, you know. Then "he looked again" doesn't mean "he looked closer."

Sharon: *Yes it does!*

Erica: Sharon, I don't know. It's the way—the sentence—the way

Sharon: *The way you put it sounds dumb.*

Erica: Well, where did he actually look?

Sharon: *Under the floorboards.*

Erica: Well, I don't think he needs to get closer to see under the floorboards—that's what I really mean.

Sharon: *When you say "looked closer," it doesn't necessarily mean you looked closely right in the hole—it means you sort of took a second look.*

Erica: Ya—that's it—he took a second look!

Sharon: *Oh, wow, we got it!*

Erica: Phew!

The following group conference was initiated and conducted by four students who relied on strategies their classroom teacher had taught them. The transcript, taken from Lewis (1989), shows how they used these conferences to further their own writing development. Erica began by reading the unfinished Wellington story quoted in Exhibit 8.1 at the beginning of the chapter.

Erica: "It's coming from the paint house," said Mr. McGregor. They all rushed out to the paint house and saw Yvette shaking, with a knife in her hand.

Sharon: That's as far as we've got.

Craig: I have a question. Who's Yvette?

Erica: The maid.

Craig: What's her husband's name?

Erica: The maid? She doesn't have one.

Dana: No, Craig. Mr. and Mrs. Wellington.

Craig: Oh, right.

Dana: All of a sudden you brought in that Mr. McGregor. Who's he supposed to be?

Sharon: One of the guests. When it says—well, we didn't want to just list them all.

Dana: You could say, "Mr. McGregor, one of the guests ..."

Erica: Good idea.

Dana: Where do you guys go from here?

Sharon: Well, we're not sure. We have to have the loose floorboards so the police can find the ...

Erica: We also think we want it to be a play and we talked about highlighting the speaking parts except Sharon wants to write it all out so ...

Dana: Hey, you guys, we forgot to say our favourite parts. The part about the paint house really catches my eye. Is this guy a painter—a famous one?

Erica: Ya, and that's why Yvette kills him because he painted a picture of her and she is afraid that Mrs. Wellington will find out.

Dana: Wouldn't it just be easier to destroy the painting than to kill the guy?

Sharon: Well, another idea we had is that it's not Yvette. It's the wife and she kills him for his money. We aren't exactly sure about that part yet.

Craig: I like the part where they find her holding the bloody knife.

Erica: We didn't say it was bloody.

Craig: Well, it would be, you know.

Because of the importance of talk, and the amount of learning that takes place in group conferences, it is important to encourage and facilitate this kind of dialogue as part of the workshop. Through interaction, students become more aware of their covert writing processes, and of the conventions necessary to communicate with an audience. Sharon said,

> *I like to talk about all my ideas and I like to figure it all out with someone else. It got kind of hard, you know, because I get really excited and I yelled at Erica—she's so picky, though, you know (smiles).*

The statements that follow illustrate the students' thoughts on writing conferences:

Dana: Some days it's easy—all goes well, and some days it's bad—it's really hard.

Erica: *Well ... it's both actually—easy and hard. Maybe at different times it's harder...*

Craig: It helps me—I love talking to someone.

Sharon: *She helps me about quotations and ... other things, too.*

The extensive use of this expressive language enables students to clarify and extend their thoughts as they write. Children must be allowed to talk through their understanding at every stage of the process. Some days, there is more talk than writing, but it is through this talk that children make explicit their understandings of what writing is, and what writing can do. They also articulate their understandings of literary structures, and what it is that makes a piece of writing work. In "The Wellington Story," (see

Exhibit 8.1), Sharon and Erica demonstrated a command of the mystery story genre, and of the conventions of story writing. Carefully crafted with an audience in mind, their story undoubtedly reflects some of the reading they have both done.

The Conventional Aspects of Print

Teaching Spelling in the Context of Writing

Most children develop competency in standard spelling through reading, writing, and sharing their writing with an interested audience. However, standard spelling does require effort to master; it is a discipline to be learned. An awareness of the need for correct spelling must be taught from Grade 2 onward. It is easy for any writer to become lazy about spelling, and writers must make obvious efforts to adhere to conventional forms. Habits formed in childhood often persist into adulthood, though usually as adults we have only one or two major error patterns in our spelling. For some the error pattern will be confusion over double consonants, for others it will be problems with the reversal of letters, or omission of letters in a word.

Teachers can deal with many spelling errors by simply conducting a minilesson on the overhead projector, focusing attention on common misspellings and encouraging children to watch for these specific words in their spelling this week. More idiosyncratic misspelling can be addressed in the writing conferences, but usually not until a piece is ready for a final draft. This also applies to errors in capitalization, punctuation, and grammar. In elementary school, teachers no longer focus full lessons on these aspects of writing, though the issues are addressed in context, usually through minilessons.

Minilessons of five to ten minutes are more effective than drills and worksheet pages of exercises. It is the context of the usage and the relevance to the child that make an impact. We know that skills learned out of context are rarely transferred to writing completed in workshops or writing done across the curriculum. If a particular number of children have problems in one specific area, a group can be formed so that the teacher can give direct instruction to those who need it. There is no point in teaching to a whole class if only a few children really need to learn that skill. Through reading children's writing, and through listening to the talk children engage in while they write, the teacher can gain much useful knowledge about who needs to be taught certain skills and who has already mastered them.

There are some specific strategies that can be used with or taught to students:

- Don't circle spelling errors, but let children know if there are mistakes and ask them to find them themselves. Children can frequently recognize incorrect spelling, and doing so encourages them to remember the words they have difficulty in spelling.
- Have children write on every other line so that they can make changes without rewriting or erasing.
- Encourage writers to leave a blank space for words they do not know how to spell. It is important that thoughts continue to flow; omitted words can be inserted later. Children can be encouraged to write the first few letters of the omitted word so they will have a greater chance of remembering which word they meant.
- Encourage children to have paper at their desks so that words they are unsure of can be written down for them.
- Do not just orally spell a word to a child; always accompany it with a written model. Spelling is essentially a visual memory activity that is only carried out in writing. Therefore, it is important that children see the word they need help in spelling.
- Teach children how to use dictionaries and other word books effectively and encourage their use. Many alphabet games (including having second- and third-graders line up in alphabetical order according to first name) are helpful in enabling children to see how dictionaries and encyclopedias are organized. These activities also help children to use telephone books and other reference aids.

Direct Teaching of Spelling through Word Lists

We know from research studies that new and different words are always entering the language. Dictionaries are updated on a regular and ongoing basis. Many of these new words appear in children's writing. Ves Thomas (1979) showed that *more* words were used in children's writing in the late 1970s than were used thirty or forty years previously. Since that date we have seen the advent of microcomputers, computers, and video games, and with them a whole new vocabulary that children use as part of their everyday life. In addition, the past fifteen years have seen a shift in the way writing is taught in the elementary school. Children are encouraged to write about what they do and think about, so more of the child's personal world has entered the classroom. Characters from video games appear in stories and reference is frequently made to these games and to various computer programs that children have access to at home or at the video arcade. Teachers have to contend with a vocabulary in children's writing that is expanding and changing. This expanding vocabulary obviously causes an equal increase in the number of words children must learn to spell correctly. It may appear that children do not spell as well today as they did in the past, but it is also probable that children are using more words, are writing more, and are attempting to spell a greater range of words than in earlier times.

Spelling is one of the most heavily researched areas of the curriculum, with research dating back to the very first part of this century. Spelling is easy to test; a word list can be dictated to a student and the examiner can check to see if the words are spelled correctly or not. However, it has been discovered that words spelled correctly on a word list do not necessarily transfer to the context of a piece of writing. It appears that unless the words have been internalized and have become part of the stored knowledge a writer possesses, the spelling remains in doubt. Spelling a word correctly on a test list is no guarantee that the same word will be spelled correctly in a shopping list, a journal entry, a letter, or an essay. One of the chief findings of this body of research (well documented by Loomer, 1978) is that teaching words through a spelling program in a textbook is generally ineffective. It is not the use of a word list, as such, that is ineffective, but the selection of words included on the list, and the activities suggested for learning the words. In four different spelling series examined by the authors of this textbook, words appeared randomly at different grade levels. For example, the word *party* appeared at a different grade level in each of the series, ranging from Grades 3 to 6. Many activities in the books are repetitious and do not enhance children's learning of correct spelling (Loomer, 1978). The only real way to become an effective speller is to do lots of writing for audiences other than oneself, read widely, and check spelling in a dictionary whenever there is doubt.

Children's motives for correct spelling must stem from communicative needs rather than a desire to please the teacher. If children have something important to say, and they have an audience they wish to address, then they must learn how to spell correctly, in order to convey their message clearly to the reader. Correct spelling is not only a courtesy to the reader, it is important in transmitting a clear message and it adds to the writer's credibility. This is especially important for teachers, who are generally perceived as role models. Teachers are expected to spell every word correctly, and certainly teachers should not send to parents or the public any of their writing that has not been checked for correct spelling.

The following are the major components of a program of direct spelling instruction:

- a reliable word list created from either the words children in the classroom have difficulty spelling or from a reliable resource book
- a self-corrected pre-test of ten to twelve words

- a study procedure to ensure that children learn effective strategies for memorizing words
- check-tests with a buddy throughout the week
- a mastery test of the entire list of words provided on day one
- a record of spelling achievement (on a chart at the back of the spelling scribbler).

When a teacher has observed children's writing and identified those who need direct spelling instruction (which would rarely be more than half the class), a word list approach can be used. A good word list to work with is one compiled by Ves Thomas, found in his book *Teaching Spelling: Canadian Word Lists and Instructional Techniques* (1979). Although this book may be considered dated, it still stands as one of the most reliable and thorough resources for teachers today. The lists are based on the frequency of usage of words in writing, so that the most frequently used words are on the word list for the youngest children (Grade 2), and so on up through the grades. It is suggested that word lists and study procedures not be used with children before Grade 2.

When selecting words for a word list, teachers can use either an already existing list, such as the one suggested above, or they can create lists themselves, based on the spelling errors they notice in children's writing. Both approaches provide relevant lists for children to work from. It is not suggested that children learn lists of words from current units of study across the curriculum. Words on such lists are usually used for only a short period, when the unit is being studied, and they are not the most frequently used words in writing. The most important factors in creating a word list are that the words be relevant to children's lives and be used regularly in their writing.

Many studies have been conducted on the most frequently used words in both adult and children's writing. It has been found that the most common 100 words used by elementary school children in their writing make up about 60 percent of all the words children write. The most common 500 words make up 70 percent of words written, and 2000 words make up 83 percent of words written (Simpson, 1980). The average elementary school program teaches between 3500 and 4500 words over a five-year period. It is therefore essential that the words taught on those lists form part of a child's core spelling vocabulary. The remainder of the words used in writing have to be learned by memory from the simple experience of writing them and checking for correct spelling in dictionaries and other word books. Thomas's research (1979) finding that Canadian children are using an increasing number of words in their writing has implications for the teaching of spelling, since it is not possible to teach all these words by memory in the five years of a school spelling program. Exhibit 8.5 is one well-known list of the 100 words most frequently written by children in elementary school (Carroll, Davies, and Richman, 1971).

EXHIBIT 8.5

100 Most Frequently Written Words

The 100 words most frequently written by elementary school children, according to Carroll, Davies, and Richman (1971) are:

a	find	like	over	up
about	first	little	people	use
after	for	long	said	very
all	from	made	see	was
an	has	make	she	water
and	have	many	so	way
are	he	may	some	we
as	her	more	than	were
at	him	most	that	what
be	his	my	the	when
been	how	no	their	where
but	I	not	them	which
by	if	now	then	who
called	in	of	there	why
can	into	on	they	will
could	is	one	this	with
did	it	only	through	words
do	its	or	time	would
down	just	other	to	you
each	know	out	two	your

A word list should always be used along with a self-corrected pre-test. All the children in the spelling group are given a test before the words are presented in list form to them. This allows children to identify which words they actually have difficulty spelling correctly. As children self-correct the pre-test, they become aware of the spelling errors they have made, and this feature alone allows most children to correctly spell the word the next time they use it. The self-corrected pre-test is probably the single most effective strategy for improving spelling ability. It provides each child with an individualized list of words that need to be studied. The words spelled correctly can be put aside until the end of the week when a mastery test of all the words provided on day one will be given.

It is essential that children correct their own pre-test, for much learning occurs during this process. Sometimes only two or three words are incorrectly spelled and other times, there may be as many as five or six. If a child is presented with more than five or six words to study in one week, it is usually not as effective as a shorter list. Children who experience difficulty in spelling need to work with small amounts of material and short lists of manageable words. In the early grades a pre-test of ten words is usual. In upper elementary school, the list may include from ten to twelve words. The incorrectly spelled words must be written out correctly and used as a model for the study procedure (see Exhibit 8.6). This procedure can then be followed and on the next day the children can work in pairs and give each other a buddy test of their own personal spelling words.

All children should learn a study procedure for spelling. There are many variations of study procedures for memorizing the spelling of words. For most children, the study procedure is a "key to the door." Spelling requires visual memory and a study procedure provides weak spellers with a concrete structure for learning. A suggested study procedure is outlined in Exhibit 8.6.

EXHIBIT 8.6

Spelling Study Procedure

1. Look at the word, pronounce it, and say the letters. (Auditory and visual stimulation)
2. Listen to the sounds and notice how they are represented.
3. Close your eyes and try to see the word as you pronounce it. (Recall—Visualization)
4. Keep your eyes closed and say the letters in order.
5. Open your eyes and check
6. Write the word without looking at the model. Check writing. (Kinesthetic Recall)
7. Write the word a second time and check it.
8. Write the word a third time. If it's correct, consider it learned.

A final mastery test given at the end of the week consists of the complete pre-test list given at the beginning of the week. Spelling scores can be recorded on a chart at the back of a spelling scribbler, so that children can track their own progress.

The simple procedure outlined above eliminates irrelevant and time-consuming activities sometimes found in spelling textbooks (especially older ones). It focuses the energies of the children on the direct learning of specific words that the individual finds difficult. There will be occasions in the classroom when other methods of teaching spelling are necessary. Children with special needs may require alternative strategies for learning how to spell correctly.

Over the years, educators have become aware of some strategies that have not proved helpful in assisting children with spelling. Pointing out the hard spots in words, for example, may be helpful to only a small number of children, not most of the class. The self-corrected pre-test should make hard spots apparent to each individual. Teaching spelling rules is also to be avoided, since very few spelling rules can be applied regularly. Such sayings as "*i* before *e* except after *c*" may be very useful to most writers, but if they are taught as rules, then words that do not follow the rules must also be pointed out (such as *weigh* and *neighbour*). It is more effective to teach how to add suffixes (e.g., *baby* becomes *babies*) than it is to teach specific spelling rules. Most rules have almost as many exceptions as adherents (Clymer, 1963). Teachers should also avoid having students copy spelling lists as a punishment. The practice establishes a negative attitude toward spelling that is not helpful to children's feelings about writing in general. Spelling is one of the written language conventions that has to be mastered in order for writers to be effective. Educators should not do anything in school to detract from this, or to make children dislike spelling or writing in any way.

Teaching Grammar, Capitalization, and Punctuation

The teaching of grammar, once perceived as a core feature of the elementary school curriculum, is now relegated a very minor role. Memorization of grammar rules, as well as poetry and quotations from plays, was once believed to be good for the mind. The mind was conceptualized as a muscle, and memorization as good exercise for that muscle. But the mind is no longer seen as a muscle. Today, grammar is not taught as an end in itself, but in the context of writing. Knowledge and control of grammar enables writers to strengthen their writing and clarify meaning. Studies in language development have shown that many concerns about grammar are mostly concerns about usage, and usage depends upon the dialect learned when children are young. A person's dialect can change when he or she moves from one area to another, or works among people speaking a closer approximation of standard English. However, the basic rules of grammar learned in childhood usually persist throughout life, and most of those rules are correct. By the age of six, when most children enter school, they have already mastered most of the grammar of the language, described in Chapter 4.

Controversy has arisen in the past about whether dialect is part of a child's cultural heritage, and therefore to be protected and respected, or whether educators have the responsibility to teach children standard English so that all children will have a greater opportunity for success in higher education, business, and the professions. However, it is generally agreed that grammar should be taught in school so that children learn to become effective writers and have the opportunity to move between dialect and standard English in speech. One of the reasons grammar is a concern to educators is that correct grammar facilitates effective and precise communication. Grammar is part of what makes for effective composition and clarity of meaning, and so it is generally taught in the context of writing.

It has been acknowledged for many years that teaching grammar in isolation from a child's actual writing is ineffective (Braddock, Lloyd-Jones, and Shoer, 1963; Elley, Barham, Lamb, and Wyllie, 1976). Teaching units and providing worksheets on grammar have little effect on children's writing and speaking. More effective learning occurs when grammar is taught as part of the editing process of composition, and in minilessons, when necessary. Children can sometimes detect grammatical errors in their compositions, especially if the flow of the language or meaning is disturbed by the error. However, much of the time, children cannot detect their own grammatical errors because the writing makes sense to them. As members of language communities, we accept certain phrases and incorrect usage as the norm, and it is very difficult to teach children to change that usage. This is where a minilesson is useful, because the whole group can focus on that particular item of grammar and there is more likelihood that children will retain an awareness of it.

A minilesson on the differences in usage between *taught* and *learned*, *lent* and *borrowed*, or *seed* and *saw* might be necessary in some classrooms. A minilesson on misplaced participles can be fun for children in the elementary years, as they can see the humour in sentences such as "I saw the lady walking down the hill with purple hair," and they enjoy figuring out why the sentence is ambiguous and how to fix it. It is through meaning that grammar can be taught most effectively, not through parsing sentences or learning definitions of parts of speech.

Knowing labels and definitions of parts of speech allows writers and speakers to talk about the language they are using. It is in this context that these items must be taught. In writing conferences and during the editing process, labels such as noun, adverb, and clause can be used. Through minilessons they can be taught. A brief five-minute presentation, using examples on an overhead projector and involving the children in discussion, can be very effective in reminding children about grammar and usage, or in introducing certain concepts to children for the first time. Full lessons with exercises on worksheets are generally not necessary. It is necessary, though, for children to learn these labels, and the meaning of them, so they can talk about their writing and hence improve it.

Punctuation and capitalization are usually taught in much the same way as grammar. These are the mechanics of writing, which intonation takes care of in oral language. Writing conferences and minilessons are the most effective and appropriate ways to teach these skills. Punctuation and capitalization can be taught in the editing stage. During such times, it is also useful to refer children to the novels they are currently reading. Novels provide a quick reference for checking how direct speech, paragraphing, and capitalization of names are dealt with. Children often remember rules of capitalization and punctuation for a short time after they have been taught, but then forget to use them when they are composing and focusing on ideas.

Minilessons must have a context that children can relate to. It is therefore useful to use examples of writing done by children in the class, or to begin with questions children have raised. It is a good idea to refer to these questions and honour the intent of them. Children who ask questions are the ones who want to learn. A mini-lesson on the use of quotation marks might begin with a problem raised by a student. Anne is writing a story and wants to use dialogue for two of the characters. She stops in her writing at "Who's going to run for help and who's going to stay here she asked." Anne does not know where to place the quotation marks. An overhead transparency of a comic strip can be used to demonstrate how quotation marks are used. Whenever the actual words spoken by a character are shown in a comic strip, they are inside a balloon. In a story, quotation marks are used instead of a balloon. Only the actual words spoken belong inside the quotation marks. The teacher can demonstrate this with a section of a story that includes dialogue printed on an overhead transparency. Working through it with the class, putting in the quotation marks where they belong, is usually helpful for the children, since they are working together as a group rather than in isolation. Instead of a follow-up exercise to see if the children have understood, it is more effective to observe the children's writing and remind them, when necessary, about the minilesson. Minilessons can be repeated, using different examples, whenever necessary.

Teaching Handwriting

It might appear that handwriting is a lost art. Certainly, the fine penmanship we recognized in our grandparents is not evident in the handwriting of children today. In fact, the focus of instruction has shifted from penmanship to composition. Yet legible handwriting is essential in today's world of computers just as much as it was fifty years ago. Although much writing today is completed on a word processor, a great deal of what we write on a daily basis is still done by hand. Notes, jottings, journal entries, memos, and letters to friends are usually written in personal handwriting. We still need to teach handwriting in elementary school in order that children can produce legible script with a minimum of time, effort, and concentration. We need to be able to read our own handwriting, and we need to be able to read the handwriting of others.

The process of handwriting must be fluent, easy, routine, and comfortable. A teacher who pays little attention to handwriting is suggesting to students that handwriting is not important. When children are required to write for an audience they must be given enough time to do a good job. However, the true test of handwriting is in situations where it is used on a day-to-day basis. Here good teaching is essential, not just in the early grades, but throughout elementary school.

Handwriting lesson in Grade 3.

The Perceptual Motor Approach

Handwriting is more than simply a motor skill, fine muscle coordination, and practice. Children must remember letter forms, somehow internalizing them. That is where the term "perceptual motor skill" originates. Each child has to build a perception or mental image of each letter form. It is a thinking process as well as a fine motor process. The research in this area goes back to the 1960s and the work of Bea Furner (1969). Furner believed that a child must first have a clear concept of how each letter appears, saying out loud how each letter is formed, while at the same time drawing it. The same process can be used for teaching **cursive writing** and for **manuscript printing**. Furner outlined the steps in this process as follows:

- The teacher models handwriting instruction on the board or overhead projector.
- Clear lines are drawn on the board so that children can see the spacing of letters, and the lines on which they are positioned.
- The teacher uses a writing vocabulary such as baseline, midline, headline, and tail-line.
- As the teacher draws the letter on the board, she or he describes where the letter begins, the direction the hand moves, and the place where the letter ends.
- The children describe aloud the strokes the teacher is using, as the teacher draws the letter again.

- The children draw the letter, saying aloud the description as they write, while being guided by the teacher.
- After the letter is completed the children compare the letter they have drawn with a model already on paper at their desks (see Exhibit 8.7).

EXHIBIT 8.7

Writing Model

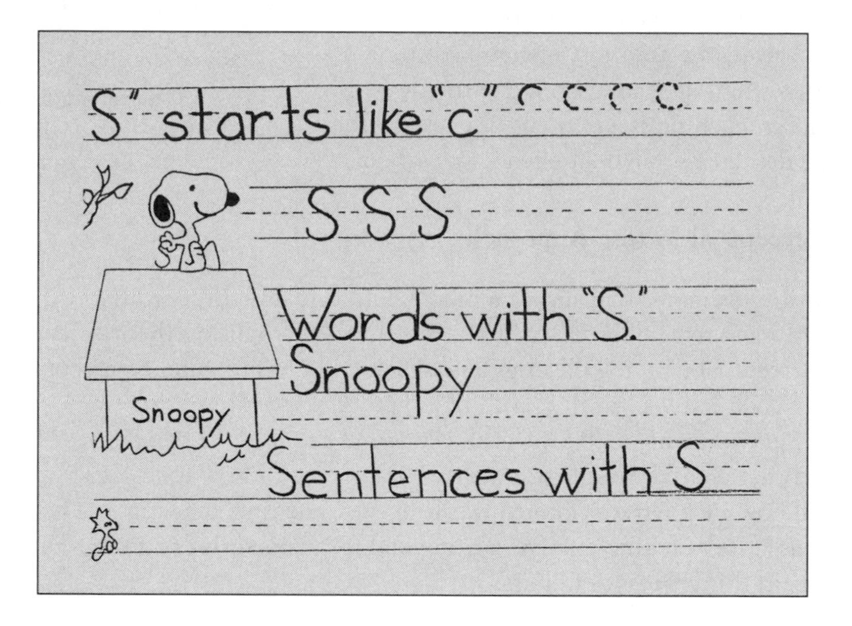

A guided practice of the manuscript letter *d* might go as follows: "Pencil on the midline, go counterclockwise, round to the baseline, back up through the midline, up to the headline, retrace down to the baseline. Stop." This would be repeated a number of times until the children begin to master this letter. The teacher must pay attention to the number of strokes, the starting and stopping points, the direction of the strokes, and the size of the letters. The process should not be repeated more than five times, for after five "tries," handwriting begins to lose quality—a good reason for not having children write lines or copy tedious work as a punishment.

In the intermediate grades, children do not need handwriting lessons every week, but they do need them from time to time, when the teacher can see that some children are having difficulty with a certain letter. A minilesson on the overhead projector can result in improvements in children's awareness of their handwriting and in penmanship legibility. These minilessons are sometimes referred to as maintenance lessons.

Evaluation of handwriting should consider:

- the form and size of the letters
- the spacing of letters and words
- alignment according to headline, baseline, and so on
- uniformity of slant.

There are many handwriting scales available, but these do not allow for individuality in writing style.

Left-handed writers have many problems with handwriting, and so it is important to give them much support in the early years. They usually need more one-on-one attention from the teacher than right-handed writers. Left-handed writers cover up their writing as they work and thus have no clear image of what they have just written. In addition they tend to smudge the work they have completed. They cannot read their writing as they go, but have to stop and move their arm to reread their script. Suggestions to help left-handed children are:

- Make sure they are holding the pencil correctly—about 3 cm from the point and with the correct grasp by the fingers.

- Position the paper so that it is tilted downward at the right-hand side. This allows for an even slant and for seeing what they have already written.

- Try to prevent a "hook"—the habit that many left-handed children develop of hooking their wrist around the writing so they can see what they have written.

- Seat the children so that light comes over their right shoulder, and hence the shadow of their hands will not fall on their work.

- If possible, seat all the left-handed children together for handwriting instruction so that they can take advantage of the light and share teacher instruction.

- Some children may need a lower desk surface to write on, or a cushion so that they can have a clearer view of their work.

Printing and Cursive Handwriting

Two styles of handwriting are taught in elementary school: printing (also called manuscript writing) and cursive writing. Children begin with printing and toward the end of second grade or the beginning of third grade move into a cursive hand. The specific styles of each vary according to region and country. In North America there are a number of popular cursive styles including D'Nealian (see Exhibit 8.8) and Alberta Education's model of cursive script (see Exhibit 8.9). Most provincial and state curricula have a model of handwriting to be followed. These curriculum guides should be consulted before teaching any handwriting style, as it is important to have consistency in handwriting style across the grades in any school.

EXHIBIT 8.8

D'Nealian Script

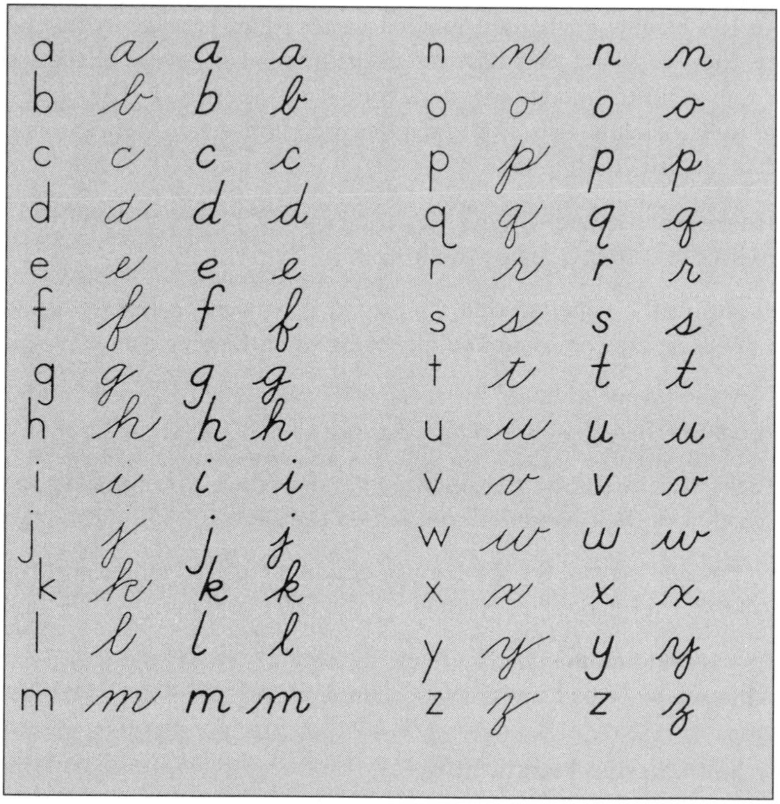

From D'Nealian® ALPHABET. Copyright © Scott, Foresman and Company. Reprinted by permission.

EXHIBIT 8.9

Alberta Education Cursive Script

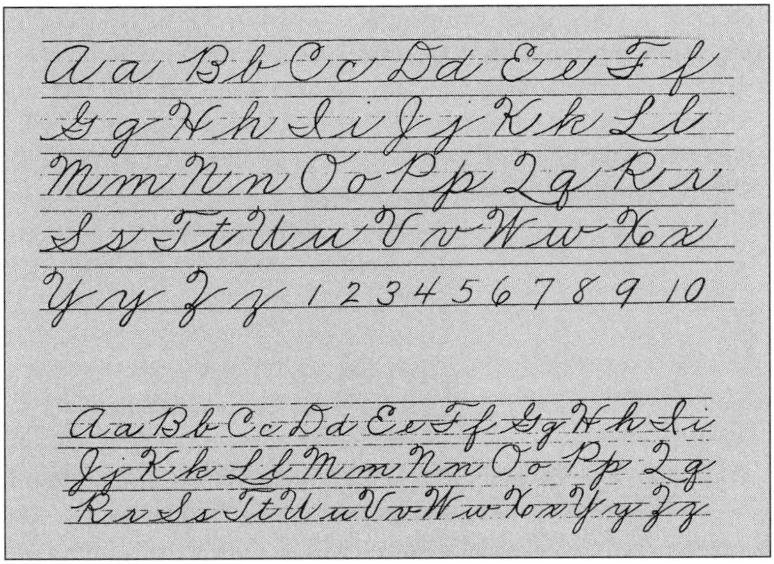

Reprinted with the permission of the Minister of Education, Province of Alberta, Canada, 1995.

Toward the end of Grade 2 children are often eager to begin cursive handwriting and will begin to make the transition on their own. Other children will not be comfortable with cursive script until well into Grade 3. Cursive handwriting is not usually taught until Grade 3. Increasingly children are expressing a preference for continuing to print. There is no particular reason why they should move into cursive handwriting other than that it is an accepted adult convention. One of the advantages of D'Nealian script is that it was developed specifically to make the transition from printing to handwriting easier for children. Children working with D'Nealian script usually move into using cursive writing toward the middle of Grade 2. A simplified form that flows from manuscript to cursive with little change in letter forms, it is extremely legible and easy to use. Other styles are more difficult for children and specific lessons on individual letters have to be taught.

The perceptual-motor approach can be used for teaching cursive writing in much the same way as outlined earlier with printing. A new vocabulary has to be used in order to describe the strokes necessary. Children beginning cursive writing must become familiar with terms such as undercurve, overcurve, downcurve, and horizontal curve. These are the strokes necessary for linking letters to create a fluid handwriting style. The most difficult aspect of learning cursive handwriting for most children is the formation of capital letters. This is the area in which children generally need most guidance and practice. It is not unusual for adults to use a simplified version of cursive capital letters (they often print them). Handwriting habits formed in the early years of schooling frequently persist into adulthood. It is therefore essential that handwriting be taught effectively in the elementary school, with a maximum stress on legibility and comfort in writing. The model the teachers provide in their own handwriting will have a great impact on children. Writing on the chalkboard must always be clear and legible, for just as with spelling, the teacher is the primary model.

Chapter Summary

Writing is a skill we must develop if we are to function effectively in our lives. Most of the writing we do is not the creative kind, but is of daily use in our lives. Britton wrote about the expressive, transactional, and poetic voices in writing, and in any classroom all three of those voices must be fostered and taught. Teachers must teach skills that range from drawing the letters and words (handwriting), to transcribing, paraphrasing, crafting, and revising inner speech.

When composing and crafting a piece, writers need feedback from an interested audience. Writing conferences help writers learn how to draft and revise their thoughts until they say exactly what they want to say. This in turn leads to better writing.

The code aspects of print must be taught—the conventions of the written symbol system such as spelling, handwriting, punctuation, capitalization, and word usage. However, we must not teach them as ends in themselves, nor at the expense of having children create their own pieces of writing and retain ownership of those pieces.

Spelling, punctuation, capitalization, and grammar can be taught as part of the writing process during editing or during writing conferences. Alternatively, these skills can be taught through minilessons using the children's own writing and based upon their questions and problems. Handwriting must be taught, especially in the primary grades, but even students in the intermediate grades must have regular maintenance lessons. A perceptual motor approach can be used throughout the grades, with children verbalizing letter descriptions or saying them silently as they draw the letters.

If writing is a tool of empowerment, then it is imperative that children be taught the skills of writing so that they can communicate effectively in writing as well as in speech. Young children bring a vast store of knowledge to school about language and how it is used. In the classroom teachers must plan programs that allow children to use this knowledge to communicate with a wide range of audiences and for a variety of purposes. But the conventions of written language must also be taught. Without a working knowledge of these conventions, compositions cannot be as effective as their writers would like. Much of the empowerment of writing comes from its precision, clarity, and imagery, whether in a novel, journal, song, or letter.

Selected Professional Resources

Atwell, N. (1987). *In the Middle: Writing, Reading, and Learning with Adolescents*. Portsmouth, N.H.: Heinemann.

A superb resource to help in organizing writing workshops in the classroom, the book establishes rules of conduct and processes of interaction. Although originally intended for Grades 6 to 9, it includes many useful suggestions that can be implemented from Grade 1 onward.

Thomas, V. (1979). *Teaching Spelling: Canadian Word Lists and Instructional Techniques*. Toronto: Gage Publishing.

It is an excellent source of word lists and strategies for teaching spelling. In addition, Thomas summarizes previous research findings and presents them in an accessible format.

Children's Books Noted in Chapter 8

Paterson, K. (1977). *Bridge to Terabithia*. New York: HarperCollins.
Paterson, K. (1978). *The Great Gilly Hopkins*. New York: Thomas Y. Crowell.
Paterson, K. (1994). *The Flip Flop Girl*. New York: Lodestar Books (Dutton).

CHAPTER 9

Writing across the Curriculum

A Grade 1 student writes in her journal.

OBJECTIVES

- to understand the nature of writing across the curriculum
- to be aware of alternative ways of using writing to consolidate learning
- to become familiar with strategies that help children to represent the learning they have accomplished

Writing and Learning

Writing across the curriculum can take many forms; journals, notes, letters, diaries, scripts, commercials, brochures, invitations, reports, posters, and so on. Writing can be done in all areas of the curriculum for many purposes. It can be a way for teachers to assess what students know about a subject, what they have learned independently, and how they are making sense of the material being taught. As exploratory writing, it can be an important vehicle for learners coming to understand a concept. As expository writing, it can be a way for learners to consolidate what they know and to present those ideas to others. Writers move from expressive to expository writing, moving from what James Moffett has termed "the revision of inner speech" (1979) to crafting or polishing a product for an audience. The process of re-examining, refining, and reorganizing ideas appears basic to learning, and particularly important in writing across the curriculum.

Newkirk (1987) found considerable evidence, in his research, of an emerging hierarchical organization in the development of expository writing abilities in children from kindergarten to Grade 3. He discerned eight structural types in children's non-narrative writing, beginning with labelling and list making, moving through attribute series, reason lists, couplets, and hierarchical attribute series, and concluding with basic paragraphs and ordered paragraphs. He concluded that "the abilities shown by the students are probably closely tied to the knowledge they possess on their topics and to the collaborative community in which they work." He went on to say that writers should not suddenly be expected to write expository prose in upper elementary school. They should first be encouraged in the early years of schooling to label, write lists, and generally sort and make sense of what they know. Young children need to write in their own voice in ways that are meaningful to them. Newkirk's data suggest that young children develop organizational skills as they write. He believes that children must feel their way through the concrete world they know before they can begin to represent their understanding abstractly. This very important idea must be kept in mind as we work in all areas of the elementary curriculum. Children need to write in many forms, and for many purposes from the very beginning of schooling.

In the mid-1960s, when James Britton and the team of researchers from the London Institute collected their data on *The Development of Writing Abilities, 11–18* (1975), they found the majority of the writing had been done by students as evidence of what they knew. "Writing was unquestionably regarded as a mode of expression chiefly to indicate what had been learned, not as one to learn through" (D'Arcy, 1989, 105). Writing to make sense of the students' own world, perceptions, or feelings was rare. Today, we are acutely aware of the need to help children make their thinking visible, to develop their confidence in their ability to think, and to value their thoughts. One way to do this is through dialectic journals, dialogue journals, think books, or learning logs, where a child's thinking can be shared in a nonevaluative way with a teacher or peers. These will be described in the next part of this chapter.

Fulwiler (1987) outlined five basic assumptions about language and learning, approved by the National Council of Teachers of English. Three of these are particularly important with regard to writing across the curriculum. Firstly, when people articulate connections between new information and what they already know, they learn and understand that new information better (Bruner, 1966). Secondly, when people write about new information and ideas—in addition to reading, talking, and listening—they learn and understand them better (Britton, Burgess, Martin, McLeod, and Rosen, 1975). Thirdly, when people care about what they write, and see connections to their own lives, they both learn and write better (Moffett, 1968).

Dialectic Journals

D'Arcy (1987) writes that **dialectic (learning) journals** provide the space for reflecting, rehearsing, reshaping and redrafting what we know. She quotes the Children's Learning in Science Group in the United Kingdom when she says, "If a pupil's own picture of how the world works is ignored, her ability to make sense of someone else's picture, the teacher's or the textbook writer's, is seriously impeded" (1989, 3). The writing we do as we learn—half-formed ideas, insights, thoughts, and reflections—is part of our own picture of how the world works. Because it is a constantly changing picture, this writing is not in the process of becoming a finished product, but is part of the process of helping us to see more clearly and develop new understandings. This kind of writing acts as a platform on which other ideas can be built. We can go back to the writing and re-examine the ideas we captured there, reflect upon them, refine them, and build on them, as we integrate new knowledge into the old. In the past we have frequently thought of writing as something that is done after the ideas are complete, but writing for learning is an intrinsic part of the total learning process. It makes learning personally meaningful and creates what we might call "action knowledge" rather than "book knowledge" (Barnes, 1976).

While academic prose is supposed to be clear, conventional, organized, assertive, and objective, the writing in a journal is conversational in tone and reads much like talk. It begins with what the learner already knows and tries to build on this knowledge (Shuy, 1987). The journal entry in Exhibit 9.1 (by a confused student) shows what is meant by writing for understanding; it contains half-formed ideas and reflections written as the student struggled to make meaning from new learning. Douglas Barnes (1976, 76) says that writing is a means by which writers can take an active part in their own learning: "as pupils write they can—under certain circumstances—reshape their view of the world, and extend their ability to think rationally about it." James Britton (1982) refers to this same process as "shaping at the point of utterance." The advantage of writing about our ideas as we are processing them is that we are forced to focus on them to a far greater degree than when we simply talk about them. Our talked-over ideas are easily lost; we are easily distracted and lose the thread of our thoughts. But writing gives us a record of where we have journeyed in our thinking, and points to where we might travel next.

EXHIBIT 9.1

A Student Confused about Learning

Multiples of 2,3,4,5,9,10 Dec.20/89

All multipels of 2 are even - 2,4,6,8,10 12 14,16,18 and so on, and multpels of two can be put into group. The last dight of multpels of two are even.

Multipuls of 3 are odd for exampel 3x7=21 and 21 is odd.

the last Multipels of 4 can be formed by 2 digits that are divisble by 4.

divisabelt is just Eaxctact.

MacAlister, Kydd, and Jones (1988, 3) explored the value of writing in science. They wrote:

> *The chances are that most teachers think of science notes in terms of lab write-ups, diagrams and graphs, and specialized vocabulary ... They all have a place in science, but there are other kinds of writing that can be useful in an activity oriented classroom ... The idea of science notebooks that blended expressive writing with occasional forays into poetic writing appealed to us. We had already agreed that "worksheet science" was detrimental to developing complete thoughts. It tended to fragment concepts as well as demanding little original writing from students. We also agreed that the formal lab write-ups required of students in higher grades were too abstract for young learners.*

These science consultants suggest the following four questions as prompts for children's writing in science:

> *What did I do?*
> *What happened?*
> *What did I observe?*
> *What was the most interesting thing that happened today in science?*

In their booklet, *Writing and Primary Science*, they provide examples of the writing completed by children in Grades 1 and 2. They maintain that these pieces of writing and the drawings and charts that accompany them are a rich source of evaluative and diagnostic information for teachers. "Reading an explanation written in a child's words tells the teacher more about their level of concept development than any multiple choice test" (1988, 27). The specialized vocabulary of science, or any discipline, becomes important to children only when they understand the concept. The talk that goes on when writing a dialectic journal, as well as the actual writing, provide a forum for the sharing and clarification of ideas that leads to understanding the concept and internalizing the specialized vocabulary. Exhibits 9.2 and 9.3 are examples of science journal writing from children in Grade 1 (Ozdoba, 1992).

Much has been written about the role of talk in mathematics learning at the primary grade levels (see *Math Talk*, 1987) but little research has been done on the role of writing in mathematics and science learning. Linda Wason-Ellam studied journal writing in mathematics with one group of Grade 1 children. She discovered that the journals basically fulfilled four distinct purposes for the children: self-questioning, organizing information, assimilating new learning, and making guesses or hypotheses. She concluded that the writing was a worthwhile venture and enhanced the children's mathematical abilities and understandings. Her concluding remarks were: "writing to learn

EXHIBIT 9.2

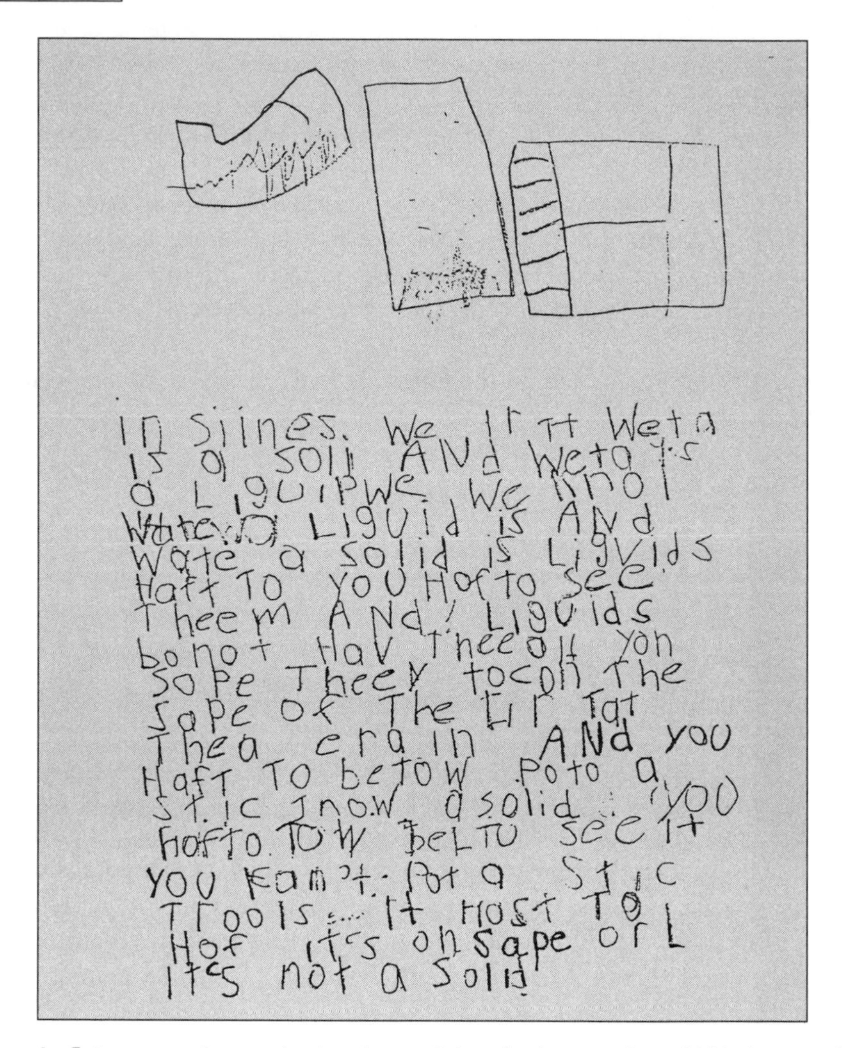

In Science we learned what is a solid and what is a liquid. We know what a liquid is and what a solid is. Liquid has to, you have to see them. Liquids do not have their own shape. They take on the shape of the jar that they are in. And you have to be able to put a stick through. A solid you have to be able to see it.

You can't put a stick through it. It has to have its own shape or it's not a solid.

EXHIBIT 9.3

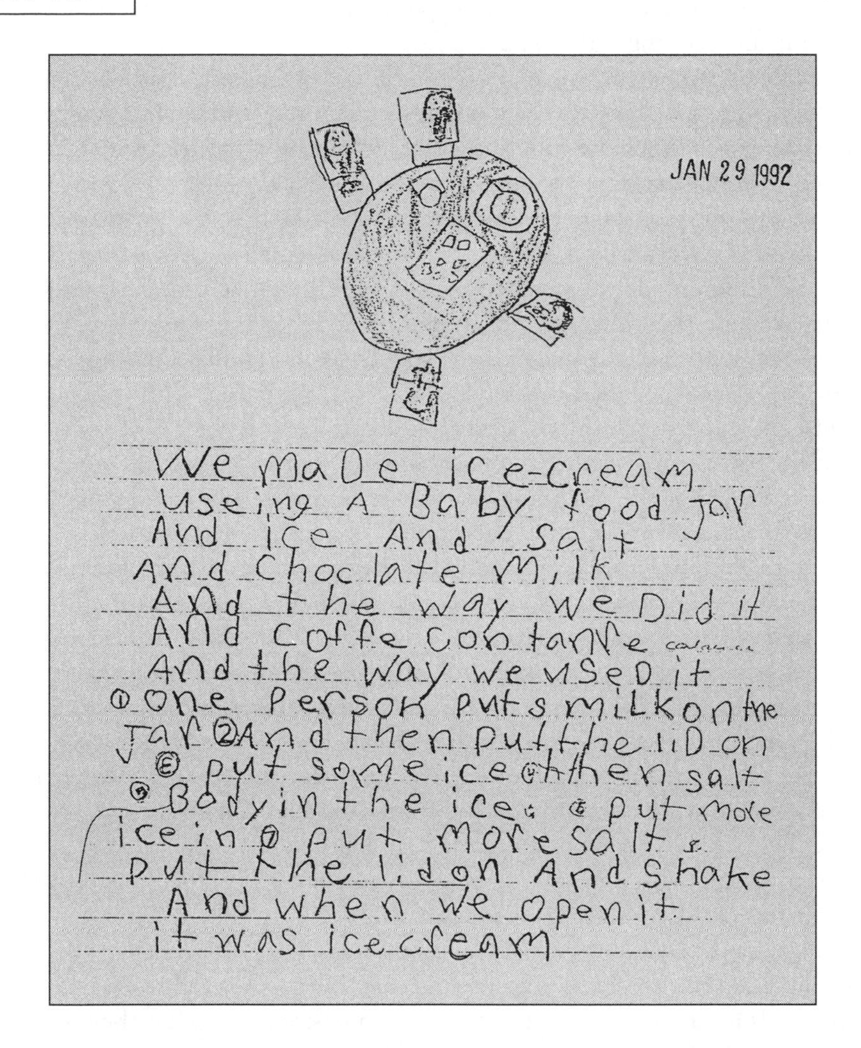

We made ice-cream using a baby food jar, and ice and salt and chocolate milk and the way we did it. And coffee container. And the way we used it. (1) One person puts milk in the jar (2) and then puts the lid on (3) put some ice in the salt (5) baby food jar in the ice (6) put more ice in (7) put more salt (8) put the lid on and shake.

And when we opened it, it was ice cream.

demands a view of learning which is active and personal. The students created their own language through interaction with mathematical experiences. ... Knowledge was a personal possession based on the knower's experience. This was different from memorizing, transcribing and reciting" (1987, 22).

Further research by Edwards (1992) on the use of dialectic journals in mathematics in Grades 2, 4, and 6 showed that journals can be a safe and challenging environment where students can enjoy the full satisfaction of knowing that they know what they do, and come to comfortable and fruitful terms with what they do *not* know. The journals took the focus off other people's learning and marks and correct answers, and focused instead on what individual children understood and could clearly articulate. It was, for most of the children and the teachers, a growing experience that gave them an opportunity to examine their own areas of strength and weakness as learners. It also allowed them to open up to other people's ideas, experiences, and understandings. It meant that the children were recognized as individuals in the classroom, with unique confusions, problems, and expertise. It encouraged children to work in their own style of language, while at the same time pushing the boundaries of that language and challenging them with the language of the discipline, the textbook, the teacher, and other children—a kind of language they may not have felt totally comfortable with at first.

The children reshaped and redrafted as they struggled with their learning (D'Arcy, 1989). It was also evident that some children seriously reflected on their learning, and through that *reflection*, engaged again in *reshaping* and *redrafting*—what D'Arcy calls the three Rs of learning. It's a cycle of learning that we repeat throughout our lives. Shared meaning remained at the heart of these dialectic journals (which were also dialogue journals), and this "stream of meaning" (Bohm, 1990) flowed among children and teachers, as all learned from each other. The journals were not only beneficial learning experiences for the children, but were powerful vehicles through which teachers could examine their teaching and knowledge base in mathematics education.

Reading the math journals focused the teachers on complex mathematical questions that the children asked; the teachers realized that they did not always know as much about math as they thought they did. They also realized that they needed to be very explicit in their teaching. They found that journals proved to be one of the most effective tools for assessing what the children understood and what they did not understand. In turn, this knowledge informed the specific teaching content, methodology, and grouping of students in the classroom. In short, it promoted individualized instruction.

Working with dialectic journals takes a considerable commitment of time and energy on the part of teachers. Writing in the journals takes a great deal of class time and a teacher who embarks on such a project must be willing to allow for this time, and must guide the children through the process so that it can be successful. Teachers recommend that math journals be used from Grade 1 onward. Over time, communication skills improve, especially in the area of **expressive writing**, which in turn leads to **expository**

writing. The teachers in the Edwards study realized that they needed to be flexible enough in their planning to encourage the children to use the journals at odd moments in the week, sometimes when the teacher least expected it.

D'Arcy (1989, 150) says, "I have a hunch that some of us need to verbalize our understandings of a non-verbal system like maths if we are to pin down patterns of significance." Children, especially, must feel their way through the concrete world of the known before they can begin to represent their understandings abstractly. It is possible that dialectic journals allow children to do this.

Dialogue Journals

In a dialogue journal, the writing helps to create a partnership with the person being addressed; a partnership based on compassion, acceptance, and a sincere interest in the other (Roderick and Berman, 1984). Dialogue journals are sometimes called response journals, but we use the term response journal only for those journals where the children are writing in response to their learning—a piece of literature or a science activity—not in response to each other. Where children are writing to a partner (whether a parent, teacher, or peer) we call these journals dialogue journals. A journal can be both a dialogue journal and a response journal, but the two terms are not synonymous.

> Logos *means "the word," or in our case we would think of the "meaning of the word." And* dia *means "through"—it doesn't mean two. A dialogue can be among any number of people, not just two. Even one person can have a sense of dialogue within himself. ... This derivation suggests ... a stream of meaning flowing among and through us and between us. And this* shared meaning *is the "glue" or "cement" that holds people and societies together (Bohm, 1990, 1).*

Bohm (1990, 2) maintains that in a dialogue, unlike a debate, nobody is trying to win. "In a dialogue, there is no attempt to gain points, or to make your particular view prevail. Rather, when a mistake is discovered on the part of anybody, everybody gains. ... In a dialogue everybody wins." In school, however, with the very best of intentions, we often place the learner in the role of passive receiver, waiting to be told. Dialogue is not common. As Carswell (1988) noted, studies on the role of language in learning have emphasized the need for learners to find meaning in the world through the use of language as a tool of exploration. Vygotsky (1962), Polanyi (1969), Britton (1970), and Halliday (1975a) have all argued for the use of language in a **heuristic** or exploratory way, by students as well as teachers, so that they may make greater personal sense of their learning. Dialogue, either spoken or written, is one way for students to pursue inquiry and create personal meaning in their learning.

Dialogue journals can be written with the teacher, parents, or a peer. The aim of a dialogue journal is to clarify and explore meanings in collaboration with a partner. The adage "two heads are better than one" pertains in this situation. We know what happens when we work in a small group to discuss an issue or try to solve a problem; it may take longer but we usually learn from it. We know what happens when we discuss a book or movie with a group of friends. Our original responses are modified, and we find our understanding changing (sometimes becoming more confused at first), as we challenge ourselves to expand the meaning we have created, and finally experience a broader or deeper interpretation.

In the math project cited previously (Edwards, 1992), the children worked in dialogue journals and responded to each other regardless of their level of writing ability or mathematical understanding. Enthusiasm for the process did not flag during the year. In Grade 6 the children often made a number of entries back and forth on one topic with their partner before the dialogue ended. On other occasions, there was only one entry and one response. The children enjoyed the opportunity of writing to, and getting responses from, many different people, and the process was set up so that they changed partners every few weeks. Jasmin, for example (see Exhibit 9.1), when writing in her journal, would often express confusion. However, she would read her partner's writing and consistently understand it, regardless of who that partner was. However, Jasmin often needed oral dialogue in order to become totally clear about a concept. She would have many questions to ask her partner before the pair were satisfied that Jasmin really had understood. At this point Jasmin would then be able to articulate the process, either orally or in writing, much more clearly herself. Whether it was the peer explanation that made more sense than the teacher's, or whether it was simply the dialogue, we do not know. Margaret Donaldson (1978) speaks of the distance between learner and teacher and says that it is often more difficult to teach when the gap between the two is wide. In this case the gap between teacher and learner was small—a point in favour of cooperative learning. The teachers reported positive class dynamics—the students were caring, compassionate, and genuinely engaged in a process of learning together.

In the Grade 2 class, the students left spaces in their logs so that the teacher could provide feedback or answer a question. Frequently, the children drew a line on which the teacher was expected to respond. For example, Julia wrote, "I get up at 7:30. What time do you come to school? ___." A further journal entry from this class is shown in Exhibit 9.4. The children in this class were also making their own connections with their prior learning and consolidating it into a more holistic understanding of the world. For example, children noticed that words used in one context could be used in a completely different context. Billy related his new knowledge of temperature and thermometers with prior knowledge in science, and observed a rule of capitalization:

EXHIBIT 9.4

Grade 2 Journal Page

We learned about time. It was fun. We learned 60 minutes is 1 hour and 30 minutes is a half hour. 24 hours is 1 day. I like time very much. Math is fun. Did you know time is math?

Today we learned about temperature and Celsius and Mr. Celsius. A thermometer is something that tells the temperature. Do you know what the grey stuff is in a thermometer? It is called mercury. There is a planet named Mercury. The grey stuff in a thermometer is spelled with a smaller m and the planet is spelled with a big M. Mr. Celsius is now dead. He was called Mr. Celsius! He invented the thermometer! He named the thermometer after him.

Dialogue journals do not always proceed smoothly, and experience has shown us that teachers play a very important role in the process even if they are not directly engaged in the dialogue. In one Grade 6 class, problems arose with motivation and with the meaningfulness of the journals. In that instance the teacher gave very little guidance to the students other than telling them to write. Often, a child's entry did not receive an appropriate response from the partner. For example, Marianne wrote,

The only part I don't get is when Mrs. Armstrong told us that when you have a question like this:

40.8
x 80.4

that the numbers in the ones place make up two decimal places. Then the decimal is two spots from the end.

This was met with a response from the partner about something entirely different. On the next entry, Marianne repeated her question.

Math is pretty easy, but I still don't understand why, when you have a question like this.

40.8
x 19.9 – 92.72

why the decimal would be two places after the decimal in the answer.

This time her partner did respond, and said,

I don't really understand why there has to be a two decimal place in the answer either. I wish I could do my social report on a typewriter ...

Marianne was remarkably persistent and in her third entry she again came back to the same question. Once again, she did not receive an appropriate response. Since this was a common occurrence in this particular classroom, we learned that there must be some guidance given to the children if dialogue journals are to be of value. In addition, it is essential that teachers read the journals regularly to see how they might facilitate the children's learning.

Teaching children what constitutes an appropriate response in a dialogue journal appears to be crucial. In the above example, Marianne's partner needed to be encouraged to look at the question posed and consider it thoughtfully. Perhaps the girls needed talk time to figure out an answer to Marianne's question. The journals did, however, help the teacher, who completed a minilesson on the topic and cleared up a very important math concept that many children had not fully understood. Modelling responses on the overhead projector is an effective way of helping children to become comfortable with a dialogue journal. The purpose of the modelling is not to tell children what to say, but to demonstrate a variety of ways in which they might respond to each other. Eventually, children can safely respond to their partners with comments such as this one from a Grade 6 class:

> *This is really confusing. The top part and bottom I don't understand. If I didn't know how [to do multiplication], it would take me longer to learn.*

In other words, the entry was more confusing than clarifying! Children can be encouraged to begin each response with a compliment of some kind, and follow this with a comment or a recommendation. This is a response pattern suggested in the writing process that seems to make sense for children to follow in dialogue journals as well. The following example demonstrates this twofold response pattern:

> *Jeremy, I like the way you explained it. It really makes sense. I also liked the way you showed an easy and a hard problem. You should talk about the remainder and tell people about estimating.*

Some children like to take their partner's journal home with them and make their responses there. We suggest that this only be done when the children realize that this is a privilege, and that taking someone else's private work home involves trust. Students can also be given ten minutes before math time to read their partner's response and talk about it if necessary. The talk that goes on around journal writing is a very important part of the learning process and must be facilitated in the classroom. Quite often, when journals are exchanged, children continue the dialogue with their partner at their desk, going over the tricky parts, repeating an explanation to one who didn't quite understand, trying to find a different way of explaining something, and discussing how an explanation or description could have been fuller for the reader.

Dialogue journals are an extension of cooperative learning. Each child becomes a teacher as well as a learner, learning together and from each other. Most children feel good about writing and responding in dialogue journals. With carefully established procedures, and the occasional reading by the teacher, dialogue journals can be an effective and enjoyable means of learning across the curriculum.

Writing to Consolidate What Is Known

Many forms of writing serve to consolidate what is known, including journal writing and notebooks. As we wrote many drafts of the manuscript for this book, we rethought our understandings, worked through difficult ideas, and finally consolidated what we know about teaching and learning in language. We went through all the stages that D'Arcy outlines of recollecting, reflecting, reshaping, and redrafting. Writing that consolidates what we know is basically meeting the representational function of language that Halliday wrote about; it uses what Britton has termed the expository or transactional voice. Writing that consolidates knowledge is a reflection of what the writer knows at the time of writing, and acts as a kind of summary of the learning journey. It is a little like a ship's log. It deals with the facts and not with opinions or explorations of intriguing questions.

Exhibit 9.5 demonstrates how one child in Grade 3 consolidated her knowledge of homesteading in a social studies class.

In a Grade 6 math class the teacher had spent a couple of weeks teaching about scale and its uses. At the end of the unit, she asked the children to write down very briefly what they knew about scale. Here is a selection of the classes' entries:

What I know about scale!
Scale is used for maps, to tell you how far it is from one place to another. Scale tells you the distance and how many kilometers or miles it takes to get from one place to another.

◆

The first thing you need to know how to work on scales you need to have the mm. and the cm. in order because then you can go from cm. to km. and then you can get all your answers right. When you have a test it's not hard when you go one space up like 2m.=20cm. by adding the zero in the order
I'm not finished

◆

1. *Measure the length and width of tables in nearest metres because we want to find the actual measurement.*
2. *We have to decide what the scale will be because we have to shrink it.*

EXHIBIT 9.5

October.29.1991

GETTING A
HOMESTEAD

Many people came to ALBERTA to get a homestead. A homestead is peace of land you can farm on. To make the homestead yours you had to live on it six month of three years. You got the peace of land free but you had to pay $10.00 for the registration fee. After you pay while you live on the peace of land you had to get thirty acres planted into crops. You also had to build a house worth at least $300.00 dollors. By the way the people looking for homesteads look for water near by. They also look for people near by too. THAT'S HOW THEY GOT HOMESTEADS 100 YEARS AGO.

3. *We look at the graphing paper because we have to find out how many centimetre squares there are.*

◆

Scale is anything that you can measure in linear instead of drawing the real size of whatever it is! You have to do this because if you don't it could take the rest of your life to draw it the real size!

◆

I know scale a little better now because I know some questions I didn't know before like who does scaling? People who build houses and cartographers. Now I know that you can measure scale with anything. What do you measure money and time with?

These five entries reveal the range of meanings children created from the unit on scale, and the ways in which they were able to apply that knowledge to the world. The writing shows how some children grasped the concept of scale very well, while others were limited to trying to manipulate numbers to make scale work for them. The writing provided excellent feedback for the teacher (who did some reteaching as a result) and also enabled the children to discover for themselves what they knew and how well they knew it. The children who were struggling to articulate their learning began to realize that they did not fully understand the concept, and some were more open to revisiting the topic as a result.

Research Projects

If children are given research projects, they must be taught how to do the research and writing. Too often, children in Grades 3 and 4 are required to complete research projects with very little instruction from a teacher, and very little class time devoted to it. Expository writing is a form that most children find foreign. Expository writing is often done for a broad and unknown audience. For many children, the only audience for expository prose is the teacher (and that means the teacher as evaluator). Children's early writing is usually in the expressive voice, but as Newkirk has said (1987), children learn to organize their ideas and their writing through actually doing it. Children learn as they write, and through this writing we see them acquire the transactional or expository voice. This is seen in some primary grade dialectic journal writing, and also in early reports. Exhibit 9.6 shows a Grade 1 child's report on the topic of seasons. The writing is well organized and includes information that the child found to be personally intriguing. The child talked a lot about the topic with her parents and teacher as she was writing the piece. Thinking about and being intrigued by the idea was her initial motivation for it. Thinking led to writing, which led to more thinking, reorganizing, and so on. Some early reports can be dictated to the teacher or adult helper, and the child can accompany the transcription with a drawing.

The developmental aspect of children's writing, moving from expressive to transactional (sometimes creating a combination of the two, which Britton termed transitional), does not mean that teachers have little influence on the process. On the contrary, teachers can show children how to do research. They can teach them how to use library resources effectively, including getting information from books, encyclopedias, pictures, magazines, charts, graphs, videotapes, and audiotapes, how to paraphrase what they read, make notes, and put what they read into their own words, or into visual form on a chart, graph, or diagram. Finally, children can be taught how to organize their findings into a more traditional report. This teaching can usually be accomplished in minilessons, showing how things can be done at the precise time when the children need the actual skill. To teach a lesson on using the encyclopedia one day, and then go to the library to use an encyclopedia the next day is not usually effective for enhancing children's learning. Working with children as they need the information, for example, using an overhead from a page in an encyclopedia in a minilesson, and actually working with a set of encyclopedias in the classroom, is much more effective. Likewise, developing a report collaboratively and finding information together as a class is much more effective with young children who are just developing the abilities to conduct library research and write exposition. The more children are shown how to do library research and the more they are actively involved in doing it themselves, the more effective the learning will be.

Teachers in Grades 1 to 4 sometimes provide students with an outline, matrix, or web to help them to organize information once they have located it. These devices also enable children to decide which information is relevant and which is not. Some also have room for children to make their own notes in the spaces provided. These outlines, matrices, or webs are not like the typical outlines many of us were required to write in high school, but are blueprints to help children make sense out of their research. They are, in effect, graphic organizers. Not all children will need a graphic organizer; some may find them constraining. However, graphic organizers do provide a sense of direction to children who need some structure and guidance in putting together a

EXHIBIT 9.6

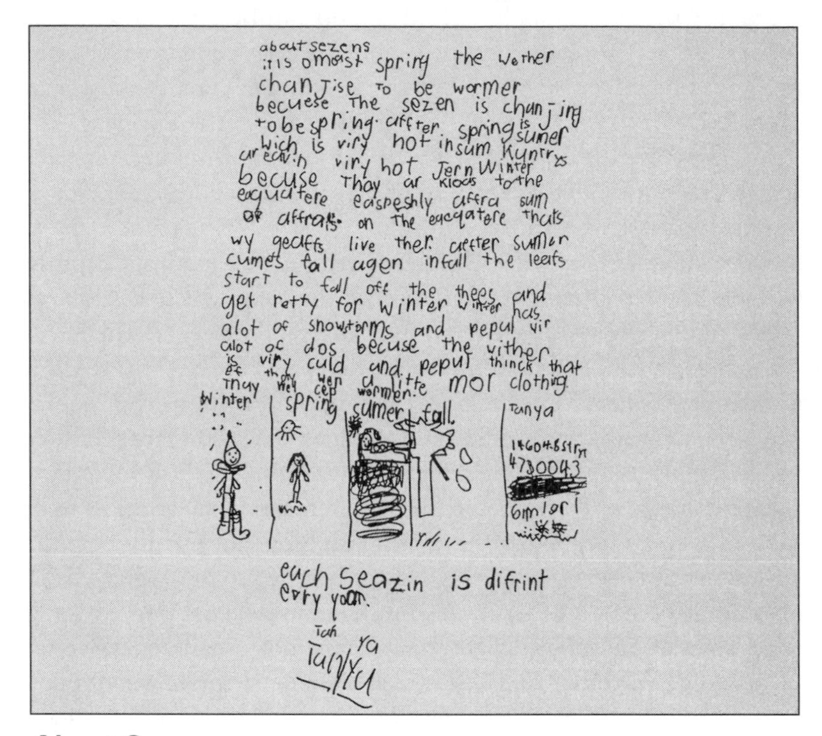

About Seasons

It is almost spring. The weather changes to be warmer because the season is changing to be spring, after spring is summer which is very hot.

In some countries are even very hot during winter because they are closer to the equator, especially Africa. Some of Africa is on the equator. That's why giraffes live there.

After summer comes fall again. In fall the leaves start to fall off the trees and get ready for winter.

Winter has a lot of snowstorms and people wear a lot of clothes because the weather is very cold and people think that if they wear a little more clothing they will keep warmer.

Each season is different every year.

EXHIBIT 9.7

Data-gathering Chart, Community Services, Grade 2

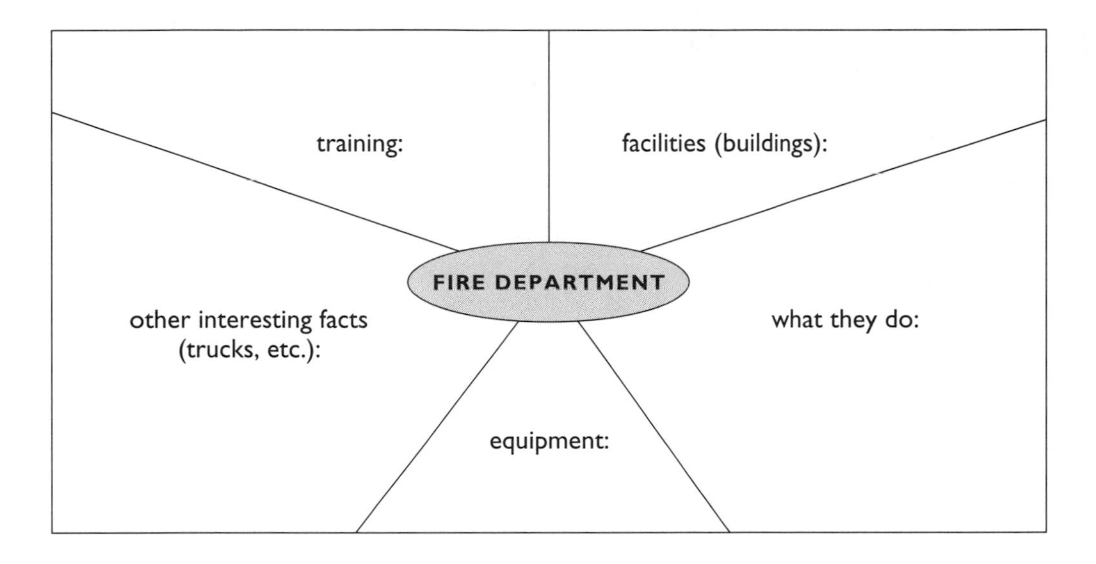

report. An example of one graphic organizer—a data collection chart—is shown in Exhibit 9.7.

A Grade 3 report on animals might include the following headings for the students to work with:

- introduction
- physical appearance
- habitat
- food
- enemies
- migratory patterns
- summary or conclusion.

These headings are meant not to dictate how a report must be written, but to provide structures for children's developing sense of organization. Children will still need individual conferences with a teacher, however, if they are to have their individual needs met, and be assured that they are on track with their work.

Student and teacher at work on animal report in Grade 3.

Jared, in Grade 4, was completing a report on fish that was to be made into a book and put in the classroom library. Jared had chosen to focus on the Mating Ritual Fish. The teacher felt quite sure there was no such fish, but Jared was adamant about his findings. The teacher sat with Jared as he went over the books he had used as resources. There, on one page, was a photograph of a school of fish and beneath it the caption "mating rituals." Jared and the teacher together carefully reread this section of the book, but it took some persuasive talk before the teacher convinced Jared that this was not a breed of fish, but what fish do to reproduce themselves. Jared wrote his report on tropical fish, and seemed pleased with the outcome. However, if the teacher had not carefully monitored the children's research, Jared's error might not have been discovered until it was embarrassingly late, and the book already well in progress. It would not have been helpful to Jared's self-esteem, his understanding of fish, or his confidence about library research, to produce a book based on an error in his comprehension of the resource material.

Traditional report formats often give way today to more interactive, visual, or imaginative presentations of research. Expository prose should not be dull or lifeless. On the contrary, it should be full of the enthusiasm and excitement we feel when we discover something new and want to share it with a wider audience. An excerpt from a booklet on the solar system written by a Grade 5 student is shown in Exhibit 9.8. The student chose to write this report in a format that would actively engage the reader, asking the question, "Is this fact or fiction?".

Alternatives to the Research Report

One fascinating research project completed each year by Grade 4 children at Petite Rivière Elementary School, in Lunenburg County, Nova Scotia, is a series of books about the local area. Conceived by their teacher, the project involves more than simple library research. The students go into the community and interview residents and businesspeople, as well as search archives, complete correspondence, and write the material in a

EXHIBIT 9.8

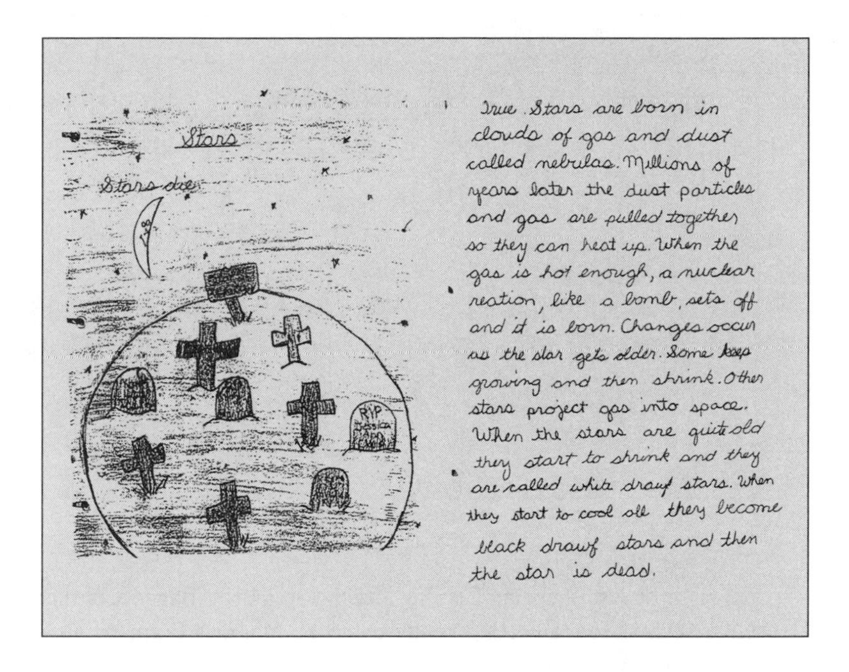

final form that is accessible and interesting to the general public. The books are printed (complete with ISBN number), bound by a local company, and sold by the school. Stories, drawings, biographies, history, lists, poems, recipes, directions for games, minutes from meetings, maps, and posters are all included. An excerpt from *History of Crousetown* (1993a) is in Exhibit 8.3 and an excerpt from a story in *Tales of Crousetown* (1993b) is in Exhibit 9.9.

It is important that children understand what they are writing about before they begin **expository writing,** and that they understand they are writing for a general, unknown, audience. The following vignette demonstrates how children learn to write expository prose. In this classroom, the children become "experts" in their local history before they begin writing the project. They know they are to publish a book that will be sold in the community. They therefore begin to develop an awareness of the clarity required of their writing in order to make sense to readers who do not know the writer or the story being described.

EXHIBIT 9.9

The Sunday Drive

It was a beautiful spring Sunday afternoon as the Baggett family of Crousetown were getting ready to go to Martin's Point to visit their Uncle James Baggett.

"It's NOT FAIR!" screamed Mildred as she helped put the shoes on her baby brother, Malcolm. "I think we should be able to go to see Uncle James, too. How comes Johnny gets to go?"

"Because he's older and can sit still longer in the car," Violet, their mother, patiently answered.

"Yeah, and I'm more intelligent too," teased nine year old Johnny, with a grin on his face.

At that moment, Charlotte Baggett walked into the kitchen. "Where's my black bonnet? I'm not going anywhere without my bonnet!"

"Grandma, I think it's in the dining room," said Johnny.

Freddy came in the kitchen door saying, "Violet, Violet, come on, hurry up! Dad is waiting in the car. We have to get going and drop Mildred and Malcolm off at your parents' house. Where's Ma?"

"She refuses to go to Martin's Point without her bonnet. She should be out in a minute," said Violet.

They all went out to the shiny new 1925 Starr Touring Car that was parked in the garage. Mildred hopped up on Violet's lap and Malcolm

continued

crawled up on his grandmother Charlotte's lap. Johnny squeezed in the seat between the two women. The two men sat in the front seat with Freddy driving.

"Can we stop at Mr. Crouse's store for a penny candy?" asked Mildred.

"No, child," said Frederick, "you can't eat in Grandpa's new car. And besides, the store is not open on Sunday."

In a short time Freddy turned the car into Solomon and Emma Brown's dooryard. Emma came out to greet them and took Malcolm in her arms while Mildred took her by the hand. "Can we have a cookie, Nanny?"

"Yes, Mildred dear."

The Baggetts set off again for Martin's Point. They drove through Conquerall Mills as the wind blew through their hair. The birds were chirping and there was very little snow left by the side of the road. The car bumped noisily along.

"We have not seen my brother, James, for a long time," said Frederick. "He will be glad to see us."

"Yes, and he'll be surprised to see our new car," said Charlotte.

"I think I've got the feel of this car, Pa. It drives quite easily but it's too bad the roads aren't in better condition," said Freddy.

continued

"They should be better in the summer. It was a hard winter on the roads," added Frederick.

They laughed and joked as they drove along and they soon arrived in Bridgewater. There were lots of cars parked along the river between the large elm trees. The Baggetts were rather arrogant driving their new car down the mainstreet of Bridgewater with everyone watching them. They crossed the bridge and headed up Aberdeen Road.

Inside **the Classroom**

Jessie Haché teaches Grade 4 at Petite Rivière Elementary School in Lunenberg County, Nova Scotia. Jessie provides this background on the oral history book project she completes with her students each year.

The oral history projects in Grade 4 at Petite Rivière Elementary School involve the students in researching the history of a local community and then writing and publishing a history book and companion storybook about that community.

Each student chooses several topics that will become part of the history book. They research their topics in the following ways: I take a group of students to the Public Archives in Halifax to research the old newspapers of that community. People from the community bring in artifacts and information to our classroom museum (a collection of old items from the community). I take the students, four at a time, after school to interview older citizens in the community (the students are prepared for the interview with questions from the whole class and a release form for each person interviewed). These interviews are videotaped and used for reference in the classroom by the students as they write their reports. The students check these reports for grammar, spelling, and punctuation. The students then discuss their finished report with the teacher and proceed to put their information and artwork together in the format for the history book.

As the oral history project gets into full swing, the class decides whether to write a chapter book about one main character or a collection of short stories about several characters.

continued

The storybook is different from the history book in that it is written collaboratively. For the storybooks, each child writes his or her version of each chapter. I then read all the chapters and underline in red the best sentences and paragraphs in each child's writing. I read all these chapters to the class and tell each child to make sure his or her sentences are included in the story as we write it. We start writing the story collaboratively with the children enthusiastically discussing each sentence. All students focus on making sure that they have some of their sentences in the finished chapter. I write the story on the blackboard and all students copy it in their best handwriting for writing copy practice. Then, in pairs, they type each chapter or story on the computer. After it has been typed, the story is photocopied and an overhead transparency is made and then the class collaboratively edits and revises it. At this point, the dictionary and thesaurus are in constant use. While the class is editing the story and the teacher is making changes on the overhead transparency, the two students who typed that chapter are at the computer, making changes as they are being suggested by the class. The stories are reviewed several weeks later and final revisions, including decisions about which artwork to use and where to place it, are made before the storybook is published.

The final stage of the project is an evening presentation in the community hall for everyone in the community. The children send special invitations to the people they interviewed and present their finished books to them that evening. They prepare an evening of entertainment based on the project (readings, drama, and an old-fashioned singsong) and then serve food prepared by their parents. I cannot overemphasize the importance of this celebration for the community and its impact on all the people gathered together for this special evening.

Jessie Haché integrates many aspects of language arts into this project each year. The children interview, discuss, listen, make notes, read, and write as part of the project. They work collaboratively in some areas and individually in others. Jessie provides guidance and structure, while at the same time providing the children with the opportunity to make the books truly their own. All the students have parts of their work included in the final books, and the purpose of the project is clear to the children from the very beginning.

The Grade 4 oral history project at Petite Rivière has become a tradition, and each year's class looks forward to it. As the children move into Grade 5, they take care of marketing and promoting the book, and of the accounting required for publication and sales. Jessie and the children select a different local community to study each year, and so the books and the project remain unique and interesting for both the children and Jessie, as well as community members.

Children frequently find designing and drawing posters a satisfying vehicle for representing what they have learned about a topic. Children in the 1990s are acutely visual in their learning, and have an ability with visual forms that generally surpasses that of adults. They watch television and movies and engage in video games to a degree that develops skills that less visually astute people do not have. The combination of artwork and writing can provide striking demonstrations of what children know, and these frequently are more attractive to children than the more traditional forms. Similarly, charts, graphs, maps, and diagrams can often provide children with a challenging alternative or addition to a report. In adult life we are far more likely to have to write a memo, letter, diary, or journal than we are to write a report. This is not to detract from the importance of report writing, for it is a major format for organizing and presenting information to others. There are, however, other ways of fulfilling this purpose. As with every form of writing, children and teachers must examine the purpose for the project as well as its audience and context.

Chapter Summary

Writing across the curriculum is not a simple matter of copying notes from the board or writing reports to demonstrate what has been learned. It is an opportunity for learners to write as they are learning, and to process that learning, making greater sense of what they know. It is a time for questioning, hypothesizing, predicting, and sometimes consolidating knowledge. Writing across the curriculum can be done from Grade 1 onward, as shown by the samples of young children's writing in this chapter. Writing for learning must be taught and modelled by the teacher, just as all other writing is modelled. In addition, research and study skills must be taught so that children can become independent learners, feeling confident in locating and using learning resources through card catalogues and computer databases. Many of the skills needed to complete research involve organizing information. This important ability has to be taught collaboratively in the early grades, and children must be shown how to use webs, grids, and charts to facilitate their learning.

All writing is purposeful. For every purpose there is an ideal format. Letters, reports, journals, lists, essays, scripts for plays, notes, and stories are all part of the repertoire of writing formats that enable us to effectively live in the world and communicate. Being able to write our thoughts on paper is a way to remind ourselves of what we know and think. It is also a way to communicate those thoughts to others. When children can read and write they can take control of their own learning and ensure that their lives move in the directions they desire. Writing is a central part of our learning, and it must be taught by teachers who care about it, and about the children they teach. When we teach children to express themselves in writing we are providing them with a skill that will be invaluable to them throughout their lives.

Selected Professional Resources

Atwell, N. (1990). *Coming to Know: Writing to Learn in the Intermediate Grades*. Portsmouth, N.H.: Heinemann

A very practical approach to writing across the curriculum, Atwell's book describes specific classroom activities and lists many resources. Easy to read, the book is an excellent reference for beginning teachers as they plan units and look for ways of incorporating writing across the curriculum.

D'Arcy, P. (1989). *Making Sense, Shaping Meaning: Writing in the Context of a Capacity-Based Approach to Learning*. Portsmouth, N.H.: Heinemann.

This British book explores and describes the many different types of writing children in an elementary school can do. The book is rich in samples of children's writing, and comments on the writing process. D'Arcy's focus is on writing across the curriculum, and she particularly examines the writing–thinking connection and the role writing plays in stimulating thought as well as capturing it on paper.

CHAPTER 10

Drama

Grade 6 students doing a tableau.

OBJECTIVES

- to be aware of the range of drama activities that can be used in the classroom
- to understand the different types of drama
- to know the different forms of dramatic expression that can be used to interpret literature
- to understand that drama can be used to create contexts for purposeful use of language
- to use drama as a medium for making meaning and learning
- to appreciate that all classroom teachers can use drama

What Counts as Drama?

Drama is like language in that one uses it to learn about events, issues, and relationships. Because drama is not a subject that is taught so that students become better at doing drama, but a way of coming to understand the world, it can be used across the curriculum. As students become engaged in drama activities, and become familiar with a variety of strategies, their drama skills do improve. Like language, drama skills are taught in context as the students explore meanings of stories, poems, issues, and events. The term "drama" applies to a wide range of activities; from the informal dramatic play of a young children's tea party, to the informal classroom presentation of a puppet play, to the more formal production of a school play with an audience. The first part of this chapter maps out the drama territory, and the second part provides examples of dramatic forms and strategies that enable teachers and students to journey into the "as if" world of drama.

> *Drama is practical, immediate and engages the emotions as well as the intellect... Drama brings a dimension of action to classroom learning through the imagined use of time–space–people (Neelands 1984, 6).*

How these elements of time–space–people are structured determines the shape of the action. Following are descriptions of several classroom scenarios that:

- illustrate the range of dramatic activities
- provide a context for examining different forms of drama and different strategies
- highlight the role drama can play in language learning
- demonstrate the use of drama as a way of learning in a variety of curriculum areas such as language, literature, and social studies.

First, an overview of the various scenarios is presented in Exhibit 10.1. Each scenario is analyzed according to the attributes noted by Neelands. A glance at this analysis quickly highlights the diversity of drama activities that can be used in the elementary classroom. This overview is followed by a more detailed description of each scenario. Each description has a brief analysis, which identifies the dramatic form and the teaching strategies. These strategies are also highlighted in the written description of the activity.

EXHIBIT 10.1

Analysis of Drama Scenarios

	Form of drama	Context	Roles taken
1.	Choric drama	Outdoors	Self
2.	Readers' theatre	Ship Grandfather's house	Immigrants, captain, Grandfather, grandson
3.	Puppetry	Grandma's house	Red Riding Hood, Wolf-as-Grandma
4.	Dramatization	Houdini's house, Town	Houdini, his mother, brother, friends, participants in the circus parade
5.	Dramatization	Forest	Monkeys, peddler
6.	Story theatre	Lake, tree, pond	Anglers, villagers, firefighters
7.	Contextual drama	Zoo	Zookeepers
8.	Contextual drama	Staffroom, classroom	Teachers, character from the story
9.	School concert, various forms of drama	Various contexts	Various roles
10.	Dramatic playing	Castle	Drawbridge keeper, keeper of the castle

Classroom Scenarios for Dramatic Forms

All these scenarios count as drama because they share common elements.

Scenario 1. Students in a Grade 1 class have learned the poem "One, Two, Buckle My Shoe," which they present to the class. Each student recites a line accompanied by dramatic movement.

Dramatic form: Choric drama
Strategies: Movement, recitation

Scenario 2. In social studies, the Grade 6 students are studying immigration. They have read a passage about the deplorable conditions on immigrant ships. Their task is to present this information to the class by transforming this expository passage into action and dialogue, using a script. The class defines the space to represent the ship by placing two tables in a V shape. The students huddle together under the table, "beneath deck," and one student ("the captain") stands on top of the table. The captain's authority is shown by his posture, relationship in space to the rest of the group below, and speech. The following dialogue ensues, using the script the students have created.

Captain:	I wonder how much of this human cargo will arrive in Canada? My ship's doctor will be busy...they look like a sickly lot.
First Passenger:	I feel so weak.
Second Passenger:	We need food.
All:	Water, give me water.

The scene continues, punctuated by the choric chant, "Water! Give me water." One of the passengers moves away from the ship and takes a role as a grandfather, talking with his grandson, another student in role:

Narrator:	Because of the conditions on the ship, many people died. The survivors had many stories to tell.
Grandfather:	So you want to know what it was like?
Grandson:	Yes, did you get seasick?
Grandfather:	We all got sick. Every night you could hear the passengers crying, "Water, give me water."
	The interview continues.

Dramatic form: Readers' theatre moving into contextual drama
Strategies: Scripted dialogue, chanting, defining space

Scenario 3. A Grade 1 class has completed a unit on fairy tales. In pairs, the students are asked to choose one small scene from their favourite story and present it to the class, using finger puppets and improvised dialogue. One pair chose to portray the scene of Red Riding Hood meeting the wolf as grandma. The dialogue is taken from the story: "Oh Grandma, what big ears you have."

Dramatic form: Puppetry
Strategies: Construction of the puppets, improvised dialogue

Scenario 4. A Grade 5 class has been reading a story about the life of Houdini. The class is divided into groups, and asked to select a scene from the story and represent it as a photograph, a frozen picture. In dramatic terms, this is called a *tableau*. The groups do tableaux, including such scenes as young Harry at home, Houdini performing tricks with his friends, a visit to the circus, and a circus parade. These tableaux are then sequenced and the characters speak their thoughts aloud. This strategy, *thought tracking*, combined with tableaux is a way of summarizing the story.

Dramatic form: Dramatization
Strategies: Tableau, thought tracking

Scenario 5. The teacher has read the story *Caps for Sale* (1947) by Slobodkina, which involves a peddler and monkeys. The peddler who is selling caps rests in the forest, and the monkeys, hiding in the trees, steal the peddler's caps. The peddler gets angry. He shakes his fist, stamps his foot, and throws his cap on the ground. The monkeys imitate him, so he retrieves his caps. As a literature response activity, the teacher dramatizes the story with the whole class.

Teacher narrates: So the peddler went to sell his caps, he packed his tray.

(All the children portray the peddler and enact the story, adding limited dialogue as the teacher narrates.)

Teacher: The peddler went back to town shouting...

Children: Caps for sale...

Dramatic form: Dramatization
Strategies: Narration, movement, dialogue

Scenario 6. A Grade 6 class was asked to do a presentation at the school assembly. The students created a slide tape show based on *The Three Sillies*, a traditional folktale retold by Paul Galdone (1981). Outlined below are the steps involved in the presentation:

1. They read and discussed the story.
2. They created *tableaux* of the major scenes, using *action* and *dialogue*.
3. They linked the scenes through narration. Example:

Narrator: A long time ago, there lived a man, a woman, and their daughter.

The first tableau depicts the family crying in the cellar, watched by a young gentleman, a prospective suitor for the daughter. After the narration, the tableau comes alive as students enact the scene using action and dialogue. The scene ended in tableau.

Narrator: This gentleman (pointing to the character in the tableau) refused to marry the daughter (pointing) until he had seen three sillies, sillier than these three (pointing to the family).

This process of narration, tableau, and improvisation continues until the end of the story.

4. Using the same dramatic strategies—tableau, improvisation, narration—the students composed their own stories patterned on this folktale. The new stories involve an angler on a lake trying to use a straw to bail out a boat, firefighters attempting to lure a cat out of a tree by singing to it, and villagers trying to catch the moon in a pond using fishing rods and nets.

5. The students used a storyboard technique to transform their drama stories into slides and a taped script. They acted out their story, photographed the tableau, and tape recorded the dialogue to produce a slide/tape presentation.

Dramatic form: Dramatization
Strategies: Tableau, improvisation, narration, writing, drawing, tape recording, photographs

Scenario 7. After reading the story of *Caps for Sale* described in scenario 5, a Grade 2 teacher moves into *role* as the zookeeper by announcing, "My monkeys have escaped from the cage. Have you seen them?" From this beginning, the students are involved as assistant zookeepers, in taking care of the monkeys and the other zoo animals. To establish the life of the zoo, the students engage in many language activities. They create signs, menus, and reports on the various animals. The teacher, in role as head zookeeper, introduces a problem in the form of a letter from the town council stating that funding to the zoo has been reduced. "How will we be able to take care of the animals?" This *dramatic tension* prompts the students to generate a variety of solutions to this situation: send a letter of protest, increase admission, advertise a special rate to increase attendance. These *literacy* activities are folded into the drama.

Dramatic form: Contextual drama
Strategies: Role, problem solving as a result of dramatic tension, variety of literacy activities

Scenario 8. A Grade 6 class is reading the novel *The Great Gilly Hopkins* by Katherine Paterson (1978). Gilly has sent her teacher, Miss Harris, who is black, a racist card. Miss Harris handles this situation by ignoring it. The Grade 6 teacher uses the following activity to help the class appreciate the character of Miss Harris.

Teacher narrates: You are a teacher in the school and you join your colleagues in the staffroom for lunch. You see the card that Miss Harris has left on the table, you begin to discuss what you would do with Gilly.

The students, in role as teachers, begin their discussion. The classroom teacher stops the talk and asks one group to continue while the rest of the class listens. This stopping and starting of the conversation continues until all groups have been overheard. This drama strategy, *overheard conversation*, gives each child a chance to participate in a small group and is an efficient means of sharing group ideas with the whole class. After the novel has been read, the students write down a list of questions they would like to ask the characters in the story. The teacher goes into role as one of these characters and the students have the opportunity to ask their questions. As members of the class become familiar with this hot seat strategy, they are able to move into role and take the hot seat.

Dramatic form: Contextual drama
Strategies: Overheard conversation, hot seating

Scenario 9. The school has organized a concert with a program of plays, songs, dance, and poetry. Lighting, props, and costumes are used and the general public is invited.

Dramatic form: Various forms are used
Strategies: A variety of strategies can be used but unlike the other scenarios, rehearsing is an integral activity

Scenario 10. Two children in a kindergarten class are playing with large interlocking construction blocks.

Richard: Let's make this into a castle (points to the structure she has built).

Pat: *Yes, and this (placing skipping rope around the structure) can be the water and this (placing large block over the rope) can be the bridge.*

Richard: What are you going to be?

Pat: *I'm going to be the bridge keeper.*

Richard: I'm going to look after the castle. (They continue plotting their play.) Come and let's eat.

Pat: *Okay. I have to put up this first ... a dragon might come. (Makes the noise of the bridge going up as he imitates a winding action.)*

Richard: Dinner is ready (uses the rest of the blocks to create a table).

Pat: *Hey, I want those blocks for my bridge.*

Richard: No, they're mine.

The squabble terminates the cooperative dramatic play.

Dramatic form: Spontaneous dramatic play
Strategies: Defining space, role, improvised dialogue, movement, sound effects

Common Elements of the Dramatic Forms

When children participate in drama, they:

- suspend belief in the here-and-now world of school and enter the world of the imagination
- construct meanings in a variety of ways
- cooperate with their peers to create a collaborative group project
- construct meanings about a variety of events, issues, and relationships from a variety of sources.

Suspending Belief

When children suspend their belief in the here and now of school, they are able to enter the "as if" world of drama time. This shift to the imagined world allows them to explore a variety of different contexts, roles, actions, and language registers. This variety is represented in Exhibit 10.1. When students suspend the belief in the here and now (school time), and move into the world of drama, these imagined contexts—managing a zoo, surviving a difficult journey, exploring the life of a famous person—are created in the classroom.

Constructing Meaning in a Variety of Ways

When students suspend belief in the here and now, they first have to construct the meaning of the dramatic context before they can work within it. (Examples of teachers establishing the context are provided on pages 429, 434, and 436.) Meaning is conveyed in a variety of ways including sounds, speech, gestures, actions, use of space, symbols, pictures, and written language. Several ways of conveying meaning occur simultaneously, which allows students to read the situation rather than relying only on language. In scenario 2, the misery of the poor immigrants is conveyed through gestures and facial expression, and use of space, as they huddle together below deck and the authority figure stands above them. One glance at this scene and the observer can read that all is not well with the group, and that one person has some sort of power over them. The captain's first sentence, "I wonder how much of this human cargo will arrive in Canada?" confirms this reading. Although these students have not likely experienced a dark ship, they have probably experienced overcrowdedness, sickness, misery, and travel of some sort, so they can generalize from their personal experiences to this one (Donaldson, 1978).

It is this creation of dramatic contexts that supports the language development of elementary students. While the drama is being enacted, students are using language in context, language that is embedded in the situation. The meaning conveyed by words is supported by action, gestures, and space. When the drama is over and the students talk or write about it, they have to use words to represent the meanings previously conveyed in other ways. Their language becomes decontextualized. A student may use only the words, "water, give me water," when participating in the drama. But in talking or writing about the experience she might say, "We were squished on the dark, dirty ship. Everyone got sick and was moaning, "Water, give me water." Within a dramatic context, students who have difficulty expressing meaning through words have other options—gestures, actions, facial expressions, and use of space. Drama helps them to construct meaning and convey it through language.

Cooperating with Peers

All forms of dramatic activity involve cooperation and collaboration. To move from school time to the "as if" world of drama time presupposes that the students will agree to take up a role in a dramatic situation and behave as if they were in that situation. If you think of drama as a game with agreed-upon rules, the game can only proceed if the rules are followed. The game ceases if the rules are broken. For example, if children are playing hide-and-go-seek and the seeker's eyes remain open, he sees exactly where all his playmates are hiding. The tension and excitement is lost and the game is spoiled. In the same way, the drama game can be spoiled if the rules are broken. For example, in scenario 2, when the students in role as immigrants are crying out, "Water, for God's sake water," they have agreed to the "rule" of being a passenger on a ship who is thirsty. This "rule" governs what they do and say. If one of the students cries out, "Water, water, no I want coke," and everyone laughs, the context is shattered and the drama collapses into silliness. Most children report that drama is fun; paradoxically, it can only be fun when the agreed-upon rules are given serious and concentrated commitment. As in other areas of the curriculum, these rules need to be negotiated with the class.

Constructing Meaning from a Variety of Sources

As noted in the introduction, drama is like language in that one uses drama to learn about events (scenario 2), issues (scenario 7), and relationships (scenario 8). The sources for drama ideas are numerous: poems, pictures, reports, stories, objects, newspaper clippings, questions on the board, teacher-in-role, and music.

Inside **the Classroom**

These common elements of drama activities—suspension of belief, cooperation, and construction of meaning in a variety of ways about a variety of topics—are demonstrated in the teaching of Lois Willis, a Grade 6 teacher in Malmo Elementary School in Edmonton, Alberta. In this vignette, she guided the students from school time to drama time to explore literature and social studies.

What was the most striking thing about this book for you? Write your response in your journal," said Lois Willis after reading Anthony Browne's *The Tunnel.* The students shared their responses with the class.

"It reminds me of my relationship with my brother. We used to fight, now we are friends," responded Jean.

"I loved the illustrations. Look how the author creates mood. As Jack turns back from the stone statue to life, the circle of stones around his feet change from dead things to living daisies," commented Elsie.

Adam noted, "Using a tunnel, which is dark and gloomy, is a good way to show the beginning of change ... it kind of starts a journey."

"That's an interesting idea, let's explore it," said Lois. "Push back the desks and make two lines facing each other. Take your partner's hands and raise them above your head. Now we have a tunnel. I'm going to be Jack and as I walk down this tunnel, make the sounds Jack might hear."

As Lois walked down the tunnel, she commented on the sounds. "That sounds like mice, but I'm not afraid of mice. I can't wait to see what's at the end." The students

continued

had many suggestions to make the tunnel darker and gloomier. Jill noted, "I was once picking berries in a wood, when suddenly a storm came. The wood became very dark and the wind was eerie. It seemed as if the trees and bushes were saying, 'We are coming to get you'..."

The students laughed. Bill said, "Let's have the walls of the tunnel talk."

"What might they say?" asked Lois.

"They would say different things for Jack, who was brave, than for Rose, who was scared," said Bill. Mrs. Willis (in role as Jack) walked down the tunnel and the "walls" (students in role) said, "Go for it, Jack," "You are so brave," and "Keep going Jack—nothing to be scared about." Returning down the tunnel as Rose, the teacher heard, "Go back, Rose," "You don't know what you'll find at the end," and "It's slimy in here!" As she walked down the tunnel, the teacher in role as Rose, repeated "I am scared but I must find Jack." The drama activity sparked further discussion about change and how such a concept is portrayed in stories by some sort of journey, in this instance down a tunnel.

Later in the week, Lois Willis and her class were studying the topic of immigration. She introduced the lesson by showing a slide of an immigrant ship. "I would not like to travel on that, it looks so small, it might sink—scary!" said one of her students. At this cue, Lois moved into the following drama activity. She began, "Stand quietly behind your desks and close your eyes. This week we explored how it felt to go on a journey. We talked about how journeys involve change, and that change is difficult. The pioneers took a journey on this ship, leaving the old for the new. Open your eyes. Look at this ship that you are about to board. What are your thoughts?

Lois moved slowly around the room and the students shared their thoughts as immigrants. After the drama, she wrote on the board, "Many people travelled from Europe to Canada." She said to the class, "You can imagine how these people must have felt, leaving friends, family, home, and country to travel to the unknown country of Canada. If these people had not risked that journey, some of us would not be sitting here now."

Lois Willis uses drama as a context for learning about literature and social studies, with no rehearsal, no performance, and no audience. The purpose of the drama is to engage the students emotionally, physically, and intellectually in their learning. If you refer back to scenario 2, you will see how Lois Willis continued her social studies lessons using other drama strategies.

Having explored the range of activities that count as drama and reviewed the common elements of these activities, we will now examine the differences between these activities.

Classification of the Dramatic Forms

Bolton (1979) classified dramatic activity into four major types. This classification has been modified to explain the difference between the various drama activities used in school and is summarized in Exhibit 10.2. Scenario 9 described the school concert, *drama-as-theatre*. This form of drama places great demands upon students as actors and the teacher as director. A great deal of time and energy is spent in rehearsing and the educational gains may be minimal, although such an enterprise probably strengthens home and school relations. This chapter will not address drama-as-theatre other than to provide a few general suggestions in selecting material and preparing a class for performance.

Scenario 10 portrayed the spontaneous drama of two young children playing with blocks. This *drama-as-play* is a very important type of activity as it fosters the social and intellectual development of the young child. As Vygotsky (1978) says, "children at play are always above their average age, above their daily behaviour; in play, it is as though they were a head taller than themselves."

This type of drama places the least demand on the teacher, who simply provides time and space for the play to occur. The students decide how long they will play, with whom, and what the play will be about. The analysis of drama-as-play in Exhibit 10.3 shows how some of the strategies used in the classroom are more structured versions of the ones that have their genesis in children's play.

For young children's play to work, they tacitly agree to abide by certain rules related to time, space, and people. These rules shape the dramatic play. The rules of this situation are: "We agree to be in a castle" (space); "Our story happened a long time ago" (time); "We agree to take on the roles of a drawbridge man and a castle keeper" (people); and "We agree to do and say what we think those people did and said in that time and place." The first part of this dramatic play is concerned with negotiating the rules of the drama game, so the play can begin. In order to sustain belief in their play, the children use a variety of strategies. The play terminates when a rule is a broken. The drawbridge keeper comes out of role and the young child demands ownership of the blocks.

This type of drama-as-play should be encouraged in young children. Classrooms in kindergarten that support this activity will have a designated space and props box for dramatic play. Sometimes teachers will structure this space to support the themes they are studying. The space may become a house, restaurant, hospital, post office, or store. Dramatic play fosters social skills, verbal abilities, cooperation, and symbolic representation.

EXHIBIT 10.2

	DRAMA AS Playing	Context for Learning	Interpretation	Theatre
Critical attributes	• spontaneous • no specified end • no practice required • duration of the play determined by students	• context is created through negotiation by students and teacher who take roles to explore an event, issue, or relationship. • dramatic tension is necessary to move drama forward • it appears spontaneous but the language and actions are prompted by demands of situation, which is carefully structured by teacher • reflection is crucial	• author's ideas are re-presented • a variety of different modes of expression used. Dramatization, story theatre, readers' theatre, choric drama, puppetry	• parts assigned • lines memorized and rehearsed for an audience
Examples	Playing at hospital	Looking after the zoo	Dramatization of stories and poems	High-school drama performances
Age	Young children, 3 to 6 years	All ages	All ages.	Older students
Teacher's role	Provides space and time in the classroom for playing to occur	• negotiator—helps students create the context • facilitator—helps students understand their roles • provides tension • guides students to seek a solution	• selects literature to be interpreted • teaches specific drama skills • coaches students to improve skills	Director: chooses play, auditions, organizes rehearsals to polish skills to performance level
Educators	Vygotsky	Heathcote, Bolton, Booth, O'Neill, Neelands	Stewig, Moffett	Corrigan

EXHIBIT 10.3

Emerging Drama Strategies

Strategy	Examples
1. Use of objects to build belief	Use of interlocking blocks. "Let's make this into a castle."
2. Defining space	Skipping rope represents water. "This is the water... this is the bridge."
3. Use of role	I'm going to be a drawbridge keeper.
4. Narration	They did their work and then it was time for supper.
5. Movement	Does the actions of making the supper, winding the drawbridge.
6. Soundtracking	Imitates the noise of the bridge being lifted.
7. Dialogue	1. Dialogue to negotiate rules: "Let's make this into a castle." 2. Dialogue in role: "I have to put up this bridge."

Probably the least familiar form of drama illustrated in the scenarios and the one used in the classroom vignette is *drama-as-a-context* for learning or **contextual drama.** This form of drama is the pioneer work of Dorothy Heathcote, a British drama educator. As its name suggests, this way of working with students involves using drama as "an important means of constructing and experiencing the social contexts within which the different functions and uses of language can be identified and developed" (Neelands, 1992).

In this form of drama, the teacher often works in role and facilitates the action from within the dramatic context. For example, in scenario 7, the teacher, as head zookeeper, worked with the assistant zookeepers (students in role) to overcome the issues and concerns. Rather than acting out a story with a defined beginning, middle, and end, this form of drama is more concerned with creating dramatic contexts within which teacher and pupils explore themes, issues, and relationships. As in dramatic play, the participants construct the meaning of the dramatic situation. Contextual drama appears outwardly spontaneous like drama-as-play, but is carefully structured by the teacher to help students achieve new insights and understanding. This structuring was exemplified by Lois Willis. This activity encouraged the students to reflect upon similar issues and themes in their own lives. Their understanding of change and journey that was related to their personal experience was then generalized to a new situation, that of immigrants. Another example, from a lesson on feudal times, also illustrates this generalization of experience. After reading a Robin Hood story, the class explored several drama activities that demonstrated the power of the lord of the manor over the peasants. After an unsuccessful peasants' revolt, the lord exacted more grain from the peasants as punishment for disobedience. One student confronted the lord, saying, "You are taking our bread, our children are dying ... You are killing our children. Murder is a sin in the eyes of God." This scene stimulated further discussion of the "might is right" concept. During this discussion, one child said, "My Dad says that the government is like that ... they do what they want." This comment sparked further discussion about power distribution past and present. The students experienced the abstract concept of powerlessness in the concrete, specific dramatic situation. The pupils had abstracted their understanding from this experience through talk. They then applied these insights to their own lives, government, school, police, army, and gangs. Instead of enacting stories from beginning to end or being plot driven, contextual drama involves students creating their own stories to understand the world. Sometimes the teacher structures the drama from within the situation, as when Lois Willis played the roles of Jack and Rose going down the tunnel. At other times the teacher may be more of a storyteller to link events and provide information. Lois used narration to link the pupils' experiences from the literature lesson on *The Tunnel* with the social studies lesson about immigrants.

Scenarios 1 through 6 are examples of the kind of drama most often used in the classroom drama-as-interpretation. Transforming text into a drama presentation is a means of helping students understand and compose stories. This form of drama is used as a way of re-presenting ideas from a story or poem. Students are encouraged to interpret literature through a variety of dramatic modes of expression: dramatization, choric drama, readers' theatre, story theatre, and puppetry. Most often, these forms are shared with classmates. When they are polished and rehearsed for a general audience-school assembly, or school concert, they move toward drama as theatre.

The first part of this chapter explored ten drama activities. Each of these different forms of drama makes different language demands upon the students. For example, in scenario 1, the students memorized language for choric presentation. In scenario 7, the students were involved in creating meaning for a variety of purposes. They used language orally to give reports on the welfare of their animals, they composed written advertisements to encourage patrons to come to the zoo. Language was used for different purposes in these various contexts but these contexts had common elements. All required students to suspend belief, construct meaning in a variety of ways about a variety of topics, and to do this in collaboration with their peers. These scenarios presented many ideas for dramatic exploration that were drawn from many sources: poetry (scenario 1), stories (scenarios 3, 4, 5, 6, and 8), current events (scenario 7), and history (scenarios 2 and 4). The classroom vignette illustrated how the drama strategies could be used across the curriculum to explore issues, events, and relationships.

The various forms of drama presented in the ten scenarios were classified into four major groups in order to clarify the concept of drama and to illustrate the significant role each of these dramatic forms can play in education. The remainder of the chapter explores further teaching strategies to implement drama in the elementary classroom.

Teaching Drama: Interpretation of Literature

Many forms of dramatic expression interpret stories and poems: dramatization story theatre, readers' theatre, choral speech, choric drama, and puppetry. Each of these forms of dramatic expression is illustrated using specific stories and poems.

Dramatization

Dramatization is an activity where students are guided to improvise an informal drama from a story or poem. The following lessons illustrate dramatization in the classroom.

Primary: Three Billy Goats Gruff

Strategy

Storytelling

Chant

Reading the teacher's signals.

The teacher has read the story to the children before the lesson. The class sits around her in a circle. She invites them to help her retell the story by joining in the refrain, "Who's that trip-trapping over my bridge?" This invitation to join in the story is signalled by the teacher's posture, voice, tone, and pause. "Class, when I raise my hand like this, you say, 'Who's that trip-trapping over my bridge?'" When the students have listened to the retelling of the story, the teacher moves into the dramatization.

Teacher: Find a space. Lie on the floor. As I count to ten you become more and more relaxed. Eyes closed. One ... two ...

(Teacher moves around the room to see if the children are following directions and then continues with the story.)

Relaxation	Teacher:	You are beginning to wake ... stretch ... put on your trousers ... etc. ... (The teacher narrates the process of getting dressed and children mime the actions.)
Movement (parallel action)	Teacher:	You walk slowly and heavily out of your house. You are so, so big ... (When the teacher sees the children have attained the movement quality of a giant she continues.)
Narration Chant	Teacher:	Stop Mr. Troll and listen. Trip-trap-trip-trap. Troll, you say ... (Teacher signals ... and class respond in unison.)
	Class:	Who's that trip-trapping over my bridge?
		(This dramatic sequence is repeated for the three goats.)
Role (as the big billy goat)	Teacher:	Mr. Troll, I am going to butt you with these horns. (Moves out of role which is signalled by change in posture and voice.) On the count of three you are butted in the stomach and fall into the river. Let's practise that part. (When the students have practised the teacher moves back into role.) Move, Mr. Troll, I am warning you. I have very dangerous horns. I will count to three ... one, two ... three. (The children collapse on the floor and the teacher moves out of role and narrates the ending of the story.) The goat joined the other goats and they lived happily ever after.

Upper Elementary: *King O' Cats* by J. Jacobs

Strategy

Story synopsis: The sexton's wife is sitting by the fire with her big black cat, Tom. Her frightened husband returns home from work. He tells her that while he was digging a grave he saw six black cats carrying a coffin covered with a purple pall with a crown on top. As the sexton watched the service, the leader of the cats turned to him and said, "Go, tell Tom Tildrum that Tim Tildrum is dead." When he spoke these words, their cat Tom flew up the chimney never to be seen again.

Teacher:	The sexton was digging the grave and when he looked up he was so scared. If he had taken a picture of that scene, what would it look like? I would like you to get into groups of seven and create that picture. (Students create the tableaux: one tableau depicts the cats entering the churchyard, another shows the cats kneeling around the grave).

Tableau	Teacher:	Let's look at these different frozen pictures. Look at the tableaux and tell me one thing you really liked. Give one suggestion for improvement.
	Sally:	They are not being silly. All their faces and bodies are sad like this (demonstrates). They could make it better by all holding the coffin at the same height.
Reflection on the drama	Teacher:	Can you try Sally's suggestion? You did well to stay so serious for so long. Well done! We've really improved at staying in drama time. (The process continues and the teacher reinforces the improvement in drama skills and helps the students to incorporate the suggestions. The improvement in the movement quality of the frozen pictures reinforces the commitment to the drama.)
Thought tracking	Teacher:	Move into your tableau. As I come around and tap you on the shoulder, tell me one thought. If you can't think of anything to say, just put your head down and I'll move on. The teacher moves to the first child, Mary, who whispers, "I'll miss you, Tim." Rather than spotlight the child by asking her to repeat the sentence in a louder voice, the teacher encourages a choral response. "Excellent Mary, say after me, class, 'I'll miss you, Tim.'" The process continues.
	Responses:	"I'll remember the time you helped me win the alley fight." "You looked after me when I was sick." "You helped me find Dick Whittington, my master. Thank you, Tim."
Individual memory	Teacher:	Some very interesting thoughts, lots of great stories there. Let us now add movement and dialogue. You will begin in tableau, come alive for a few seconds, and then freeze again.
Improvisation, action, and dialogue		The Grade 4 students practise their short improvisations and share them with the class. The sharing is important, since drama skills are taught in context. The students practise the skill (slowly picking up the coffin), in order to clarify the meaning of the story. Shaping the movement quality deepens the aesthetic experience for the students.

The following story has been dramatized by different classes and the interpretations have varied.

Music

- One class focused more on dramatic movement and music, and the story became a dance drama.

Writing

- Another class folded in different literacy activities: stories, eulogies, résumés for the position of king.

Meeting

- One class moved into contextual drama and had a meeting to decide the next heir apparent.

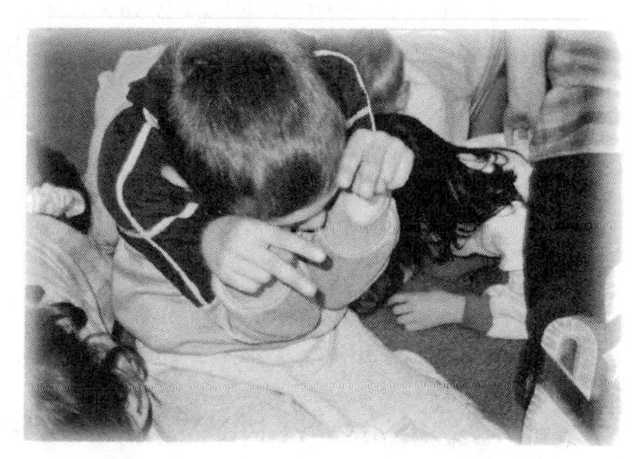

Class are being the billy goats hiding under the bridge.

Drawing

- One class, at Halloween, made the story into a shadow play. They used cutouts placed on the overhead projector and recorded the dialogue and sound effects.

When dramatizing stories with students, the key to success is to select a small part of the story with strong action qualities. Many folktales have this characteristic. With primary children, parallel action is more appropriate than tableaux. Young children like to move and tableaux are too static. In the stories of *The Three Billy Goats Gruff* and *Caps for Sale*, the same strategies were used. The teacher:

- selected a story with a strong line of action
- chose one or two short scenes to be enacted
- analyzed the movements of the characters and included these descriptions in the narration: "Troll, you walk very slowly to the bridge"
- gave all children the same role and chose scenes in which the characters were clearly defined
- folded in simple dialogue such as, "Caps for sale!" and "Who is trip-trapping over my bridge?"

Strategies common to the dramatization of stories presented in this chapter are: storytelling, tableaux, movement, thought tracking, improvisation, and extension activities. These same strategies can be used for story theatre.

Story Theatre

Story theatre is the dramatization of a *narrative* where the action, relationships, and theme of the story are represented visually through movement, mime, and characterization. The storyteller provides the links between the scenes dramatized by the players. The storyteller remains "on stage" throughout the presentation, while the players enter and exit at appropriate cues. A Grade 3 class prepared the following story for presentation to a Grade 1 class.

The Elves and the Shoemaker

Cast: Shoemaker, wife, (possible customers, elves), storyteller
(approximately 8 to 10 players)

Organization of Physical Space in the Classroom

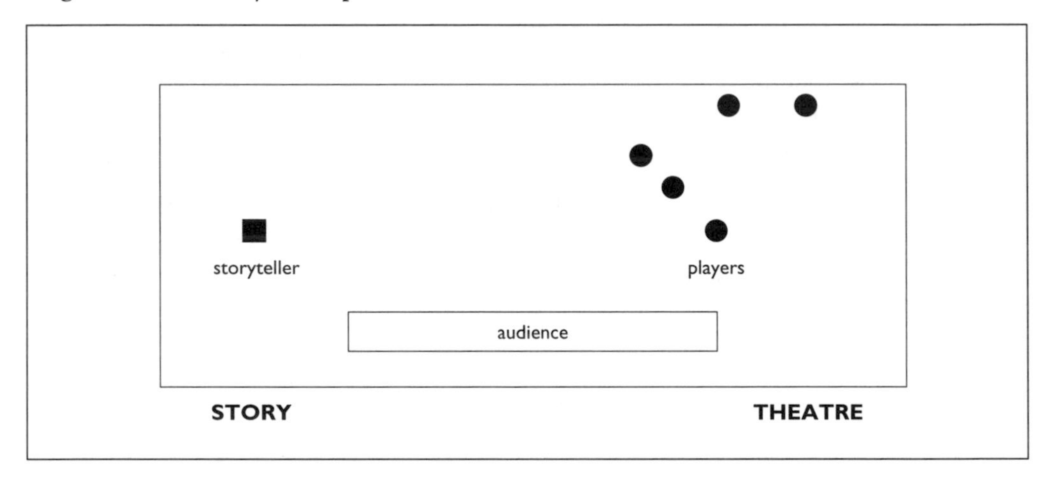

Storyteller: Once there was a shoemaker, who, through no fault of his own, became so poor he had only enough leather to make one pair of shoes. (Stop.)

Storyteller: While they were asleep, the elves visited.

(The scenes have been improvised and practised. No scripts were used.)

Scene I *Shoemaker*: Come, wife, let's go to bed. (Wife and shoemaker exit. Elves peer round the corner and tiptoe in.)
1st elf: Let's help this poor man.
2nd elf: I'll cut the pattern.
3rd elf: I'll sew them.
4th elf: I'll put on the design.
1st elf: We'll sing while we work.

(The students create a song patterned on the familiar, "Here We Go 'Round the Mulbery Bush." They include actions as they sing, "This is the way we cut the cloth." Elves exit.)

Preparing the students for this activity, the teacher would use the strategies outlined for dramatization. When the students are familiar with the story, the teacher could divide the class into groups and each group could enact the story. The teacher may take the role of storyteller creating and presenting the text. Older students can create their own text.

> *For any narrative, what improvisation does is to translate* what happened *into* what is happening, *thus making the abstraction of the story come alive in the present moment (Moffett, 1983, 114).*

The preparation for story theatre involved students moving between these different levels, from *what happened* to *what happens*. This process becomes internalized and shows up in their written stories as dialogue (present tense) and narrative (past tense). This same process is also practised when students translate a story or poem for presentation as readers' theatre.

Readers' Theatre

Readers' theatre is a form of oral interpretation in which a group of readers perform written texts using a script. The previous story, *The Elves and the Shoemaker*, would become readers' theatre if the teacher had scripted both the storyteller's part and the dialogue. The students would be assigned parts. Time would be given to practise speaking the lines. This activity provides a meaningful context for practising reading aloud. There are commercially prepared scripts, but students can prepare their own scripts. Guidance from the teacher is needed to facilitate this task, since children need assistance with:

- choosing a story—the story needs to be short, with lots of dialogue and a variety of characters
- organizing the cast—the class needs to be grouped according to the number of characters involved in the story
- transforming story to script—Initially, the teacher may model this process with the whole class. As the students become more proficient at transforming story to play, they can create their own scripts. This transformation of text to script involves students in a close reading of the text, which is an excellent context for developing comprehension abilities. Readers' theatre is more akin to a radio play, except that the readers are visible and can utilize gestures and facial expressions to portray meaning. This form is more appropriate for older students (Grades 3 to 6).

The texts that students transform are usually stories and poems, but they can be expository pieces. For example, a Grade 5 class created a readers' theatre piece from a news incident.

Narrator:	The World Series is here. The Toronto Blue Jays of Canada are playing against the Atlanta Braves of U.S.A.
1st commentator:	Here come the two teams behind their respective flags. They are about to begin. I am Mike Jones, NBS, New York, and with me is Gord Smith from CTV, Toronto. Hello, Gord.
2nd commentator:	Hello, Mike. It's good to be here. Oh no!
1st commentator:	What's the matter?
2nd commentator:	Look at the Canadian flag!
1st commentator:	What's wrong ... Oh, it's upside down.

The play continued, ending with:

Mr. President:	On behalf of our country, I apologize to Canada.
Prime Minister:	We accept the apology and the win! Thank you for calling, Mr. President.

Readers' theatre provides practice in reading aloud with an emphasis on oral interpretation. Oral interpretation is also a major focus of choral speech and choric drama.

Choral Speech

Choral speech is the art of interpreting text as a group. The following nursery rhymes have been selected to demonstrate the variety of ways poems can be interpreted. Older students can use these same strategies with more age-appropriate poems. Choral work can be as informal as students chanting repetitive phrases while the teacher reads a story, or as formal as performing a poem for an audience, to be judged at a drama festival. For more formal presentations, four basic ways to approach text for choric work can be used to achieve variety.

Line-by-Line Arrangement

The first scenario at the beginning of the chapter "One, two, buckle my shoe," is an example of arranging poetry in this manner. Each child, or group of children, chants one line.

Antiphonal

The class is divided into two groups: one group recites the first verse, and the second group recites the following verse. This process is continued throughout the poem.

Group 1:	Pussy Cat, Pussy Cat Where have you been?
Group 2:	I have been up to London To visit the Queen.
Group 1:	Pussy Cat, Pussy Cat What did you there?
Group 2:	I frightened a little mouse under the chair.

Cumulative

One voice begins and others are added throughout the poem.

Student 1:	For want of a nail a shoe was lost.
Students 1 and 2:	For want of a shoe a horse was lost.
Students 1, 2, and 3:	For want of a horse the general was lost.
Students 1,2, 3, and 4:	For want of a general the battle was lost.
	[Pause]
Student 1:	All for the want of a nail.

Unison

All students say all parts. Unison is not very appropriate for elementary children because the meaning of the text is obscured by the singsong pace of the group. It takes practice to effectively interpret a poem in unison. Students prefer to spend time adding action, dialogue, and props to their choral interpretation. With these additions, choral speech becomes choric drama.

Choric Drama

Choric drama is a combination of dramatization and choral speech. A simple illustration using "Little Miss Muffet" follows.

The class is divided into four groups. Each group says one line while two students role-play Miss Muffet and the spider, who add their thoughts between the lines.

	Choral speech	**Dramatization**	**Thought tracking**
Group 1	"Little Miss Muffet sat on a tuffet." (teacher cues the stopping and starting nonverbally)	Miss Muffet sitting down.	"Oh! I am so hungry."
Group 2	"Eating her curds and whey."	Begins eating.	"This is delicious."
Group 3	"There came a big spider."	Spider moves toward a frightened Miss Muffet.	"I'm scared." "*Give me some of that.*"
Group 4	"And sat down beside her."	Spider sits down and puts his arm around Miss Muffet.	"Go away!" "*Give me some of that.*"
All	"And frightened Miss Muffet away."	Miss Muffet runs off. Spider eats.	"Help! Help" "*This is delicious.*"

This poem also lends itself to puppetry for younger students. It has minimal characters, lots of action, and the thought tracking can be used as improvised dialogue.

Puppetry

When using puppetry in the classroom it is important to simplify puppet construction. The puppets help the students into the imaginary world of drama. Many shy children find security in this form of drama. They can hide behind the puppet theatre as attention is focused on the puppet. Puppet plays should not be scripted as students find it difficult to read scripts and manipulate the puppets. To organize students for puppetry:

- Provide guidance and materials for puppet construction.
- Help students select an appropriate part of the story. Select a small part with strongly defined action.
- Provide practice time. Put a time limit on the practice and then evaluate. At this point, the first attempt can be appreciated and improved. Group process

skills can be reinforced. It is often these procedural concerns that deter teachers from drama work—"It takes too much time and energy" (Edwards and Payne, 1994).

- Celebrate puppet plays by inviting another class to watch the polished performance.

All these forms of drama can be used in the elementary classroom to help students develop an appreciation of literature. These forms can also be used in conjunction with music, art, social studies, science, and health. In the process of transforming text to drama, students use many skills that support the comprehension and composition of stories.

In the next section, text and drama will be explored. This exploration is not concerned with transforming written text into a dramatic form. It is concerned with using drama to interpret text, using drama to understand the text more fully.

Teaching Drama: Contextual Drama

Contextual Drama

A brief overview of *contextual drama* was provided earlier in this chapter. It was noted that outwardly, contextual drama appears spontaneous, like dramatic playing, but unlike dramatic playing, it is structured through careful planning. Planning for this structured spontaneity involves an understanding of the recent insights generated by such drama educators as Heathcote, Bolton, Booth, O'Neill, Neelands, and Verriour.

At this point, it would be helpful for the reader to see the 1972 film *Three Looms Waiting* to experience the power of contextual drama. It illustrates very effectively some of the principles that are fundamental to contextual drama. Although this film is dated, it shows Heathcote, the pioneer of this work, demonstrating these concepts very effectively. If this film is not available, Wagner's 1976 publication, *Dorothy Heathcote: Drama as a Learning Medium*, provides rich descriptions of Heathcote's early work. First, *the learning contract*—the rules for the drama game—are established through the process of *negotiation*. Using a variety of strategies, the students *build belief* in the specific *role* in that specific *context*. With the *teacher in role*, the students are helped in their *commitment* to the drama. Once commitment is established, dramatic *tension* is injected into the drama creating a dilemma. The urgency to release this tension by *seeking a solution* propels the

EXHIBIT 10.4

Language Forms

Drama	Oral	Written
Old Henry (1987)	Informal Discussion Gossip Formal Introductions and presentations	Drawings Maps Legal documents Reports Letters News reports Diary
Bo-Peep	Interview Song Lists	
Gorilla (1983)	Meeting	Charts Business letters Reflections on learning

students in role to think, speak, and act in new ways. They may use the language of the interview, the gossip, the meeting, or any other dimension of the real or imagined world they have constructed. Exhibit 10.4 is a list of some of the language forms used in the contextual dramas described in the following pages of this chapter.

The film *Three Looms Waiting*, not only illustrates these basic principles, but also demonstrates the powerful affective quality of this kind of work. The intensity is akin to that experienced by small children who are deeply absorbed in dramatic play. Following is a written description of a contextual drama, where the students involved achieved this kind of intensity. Their work had the spontaneous quality of dramatic play. Although this spontaneity was achieved through using several drama strategies, it was carefully planned.

Contextual Drama: An Example

The book *Old Henry* by Joan Blos (1987) deals with a social studies theme. This drama was used with a Grade 2/3 class and represents three hours of instruction.

Phase 1—Establishing the life and activity of the village (context building)

Strategies	Classroom Sequence
Read story (provides a shared context)	The teacher reads the story up to the episode where the men try to help Henry.
Imaging **Discussion** **Drawing** (The class begin to concretize context as a way of building belief ... a way of helping the class to step into the imaginary world of Old Henry.)	Children are asked to close their eyes and imagine what Henry's house might look like. They share their ideas and the teacher draws Henry's house as they provide the detail.
Imaging (about themselves in role ... an invitation to take on the role) **Drawing** of their house (further concretization of context and enticing students into role)	The teacher continues imaging exercise. "Close your eyes ... You also live in this community ... Who are you? What does your house look like? ... Draw your house."
Mapping **Subtle questions and responses**	The teacher rolls out a large piece of paper, places Mr. Henry's house at one end, and asks the students to place their house on the map and draw the other important buildings. As the children are working on the activity the teacher walks around feeding information and using a "subtle tongue." "I wonder who lives here?," "Maybe I can find information about Mr. Henry from the shopkeeper?" As children begin to accept the lures, the teacher reinforces their roles. Child says: "Mr. Henry comes into my shop for his parrot seed." The teacher: "Oh, so you know something about him then?"

Phase 2—Establishing the community

Strategies	Classroom Sequence
Gossip strategy (Building the character of Mr. Henry, giving the students a chance to move into role.) **Teacher in role** **Gossip strategy—form of storytelling**	The teacher asks the class to sit around the map. "There seem to be a lot of stories going around our community about Mr. Henry ... Maybe we could share these? It may help us to know how to deal with him. Please introduce yourself and share a story if you have had dealings with Mr. Henry. I am the mayor and I know he's honest because he pays his taxes." Students share their stories about Mr. Henry.

Defining space	The mayor calls a town meeting.
Use of ritual (slows down the drama and provides students time to deepen belief)	Chairs are set up in a formal manner. A child is selected to role-play the clerk of the court. The mayor asks each person to introduce themselves and say what they do. This process is done very formally. The teacher uses the role as mayor to control, "Order, please."
Teacher in role (formal manner represents authority figure)	The mayor says, "Clerk of the court, please read out the charges."
Use of documents (These documents can be prepared by the teacher alone or with the children out of drama time.) Use of formal language sustains belief.	The clerk reads. City bylaw 99: Failure to keep town tidy. City bylaw 11: Failure to shovel snow. City bylaw 63: Failure to pay fines. "I, the mayor of this town, am hereby opening the floor for discussion."
Storytelling	Children provide eyewitness accounts.
Mantle of the expert (Students become "experts" on solving problems as members of the task force.)	The mayor closes the meeting with the following statements:
Meeting	a) "I am hereby appointing special community task forces to find a solution to our problem." The class is divided into groups and the groups discuss their ideas.
Report (written out of drama time)	b) "Please have a full written report to present at the next council meeting."
Teacher in role	Town meeting—the groups present their solutions. (Teacher/mayor leaves the room and comes back as Mr. Henry.)

Phase 3—Injecting the tension

Improvisation	Mr. Henry rejects all proposals. He tells the community they are intolerant and informs them of his departure.

Phase 4—Seeking a solution

Letters to Mr. Henry
Newsreports
Diary entries
(These documents are written out of drama time.)

The community members modify proposals and generate other solutions.

During the reflection on the drama, the students discussed the impact of their solutions on themselves and Mr. Henry. The class reflected on the similarities of the dramatic situation to a local political issue. "We've done our best; we've been responsible. Mr. Henry needs to cooperate. It's just like what's happening with our hockey team. Let them go, the hockey team and Mr. Henry." This example once again illustrates the generalization of experience from one situation to another. After the reflection on the drama, the class compared their handling of the situation with that of the author, Joan Blos.

Planning a Drama

In this drama, the planning was broken down into four phases (Littledyke and Baum, 1986). These phases overlap and the boundaries are not rigid.

Students in role as the mayor's task force generate possible solutions to deal with Mr. Henry's problem.

Phase 1: Establishing the life and activity of the village

- creating the context and roles

Phase 2: Establishing the meaning of village life

- sharing stories about Mr. Henry
- coping with the problem

Phase 3: Injecting the tension

- Mr. Henry rejects the village proposals and calls the citizens intolerant

Phase 4: Seeking a solution

- villagers modify proposals
- they decide Mr. Henry has to take some responsible action

In the first phase, the emphasis is on building belief in the drama through tasks—imaging, drawing, and mapping. In the second phase the tasks become less important and the students are asked to reflect on village life. They share their stories about Mr. Henry and review his status—gossip strategy, ritual, role, use of documents, eyewitness accounts, reports. In phase 3, the villager's suggestions are rejected and Mr. Henry leaves.

Sometimes the threat is introduced gradually. "I hope Mr. Henry accepts our proposal because his art shop brings many new people to the village. They spend a lot of money." In phase 3 of this drama, the element of surprise was used: the teacher switched roles from the mayor to Henry instantly. Phase 4 follows the logic suggested by the students. In this drama, students put their own solutions into operation, writing letters, news reports, and diary entries. These solutions were put into the context of their own lives during the reflection phase. In each of these phases the teacher plans for certain events to occur. However, the outcome of these events is not so predictable, as the students create their characters and make suggestions. It is this unpredictability that gives this work its energy. The students feel empowered when their suggestions are translated into action. For the teacher, it involves using a variety of strategies to structure their suggestions.

Many of the strategies used in this drama are familiar to teachers. The least familiar is probably the teacher in role. The following comments by Lois Willis, a teacher beginning this work at Malmo School in Edmonton, express some concerns about using role.

> *I wanted to use role because I have seen how effective it can be....but I am not an actor, I have no theatre skills. One day I was watching my son and daughter play "Star Trek"—then it struck me! They are in role. Role is not performance skills, role is a stance—thinking and acting "as if." If my four- and five-year-olds can do it, I can—and so can my class. If the drama does not work, there is no penalty. There is no audience to throw rotten eggs. I can stop the drama and say, "This lesson is not going well. What can we do to improve it?" Getting rid of the notion of teacher as actor and drama as performance, freed me to take the next step.*

In *contextual drama* the teacher makes explicit the strategies that young children use implicitly in dramatic play. A return to the dramatic play episode (scenario 10), illustrates that what children can do spontaneously in dramatic play, they can do in contextual drama, provided they have appropriate support. A comparison of the strategies used in the dramatic play situation and the *Old Henry* drama is given in Exhibit 10.5.

Teachers at Work

Following are examples of two dramas that were planned and taught by teachers beginning this work. They are included to illustrate the planning process, the range of strategies, the implementation of contextual drama at various grade levels, and the teacher's reflection on the implementation. These drama plans outline the possibilities for each phase. There was neither time nor need to complete all the activities listed, but planning these options reduced the teacher's anxiety in this new situation. The possible solutions were not used at all because the students created their own.

EXHIBIT 10.5

Relationship between Strategies Used in Dramatic Play and Contextual Drama

Phase	***Dramatic play*** Strategies	***Contextual drama*** Strategies
Phase 1 Establishing the context	Objects (bricks) to build belief Space defined (use of a rope)	building belief by: imaging discussion drawing space defined mapping
Phase 2 Establishing the meaning	moving into role e.g., "I'm going to be the drawbridge man." movement and sound to establish meaning	moving into role by: gossip, ritual, role, use of objects (documents), meeting, writing proposals
Phase 3 Injecting the tension	Possible tension is suggested: "a dragon might come"	Teacher in role as Mr. Henry, "I am leaving. You are unfair."
Phase 4 Seeking a solution	no solution since drama terminates when children step out of role	solution achieved through: news report, diaries, letters, reflection

The first example, a Grade 1 drama, began with the nursery rhyme "Bo-Peep." In the second example, a Grade 6 teacher used the story *Gorilla* by Anthony Browne (1983). These examples identify the strategies used, briefly described the strategies in action, and provide examples of reflection. These plans were selected to show that teachers beginning this work can plan for structured spontaneity, which propels students to use language in new ways.

These following four phases of planning were used by the Grade 6 teacher in "Example 1: Bo-Peep" below. The teacher's reflections reveal both her excitement and anxiety about her first attempt at contextual drama. She wrote, "I was amazed that no one needed any help with what to write," and "I understand more fully now this idea of letting the drama develop and giving up control. It's a bit unsettling at first." Her comments are representative of teachers who are beginning this type of drama work (Edwards and Payne, 1994).

*Example 1: Bo-Peep (Grade 1)**

Objective: **To provide students with a variety of contexts to use oral and written language.**

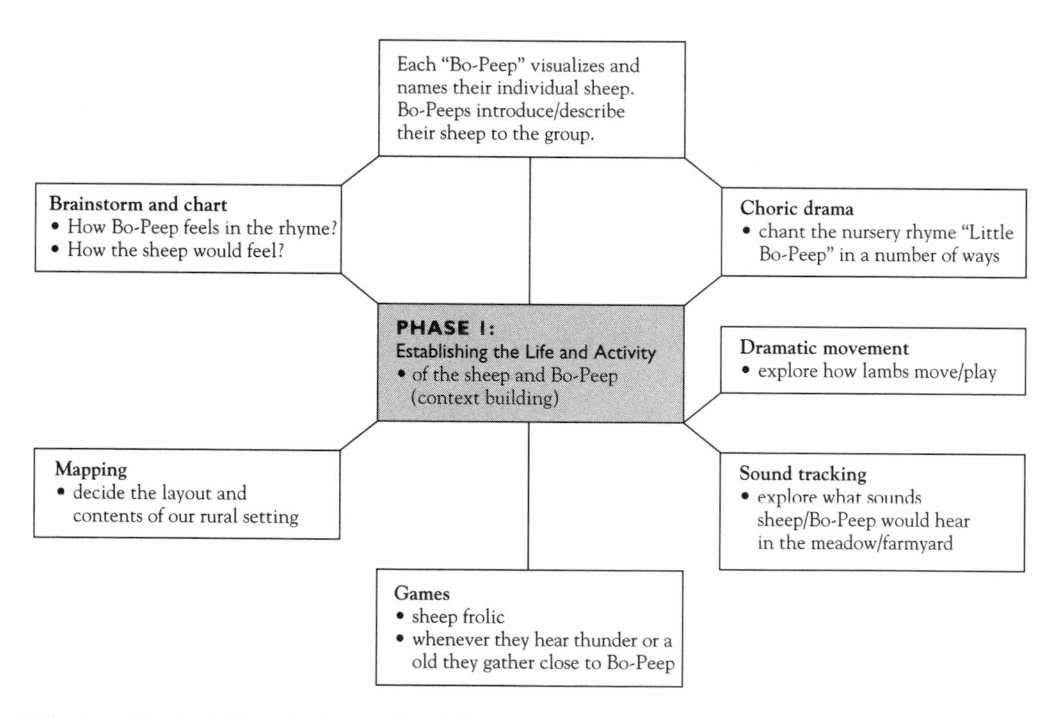

**Thanks to Heather Miller, Grade 1 teacher, Edmonton, Alberta.*

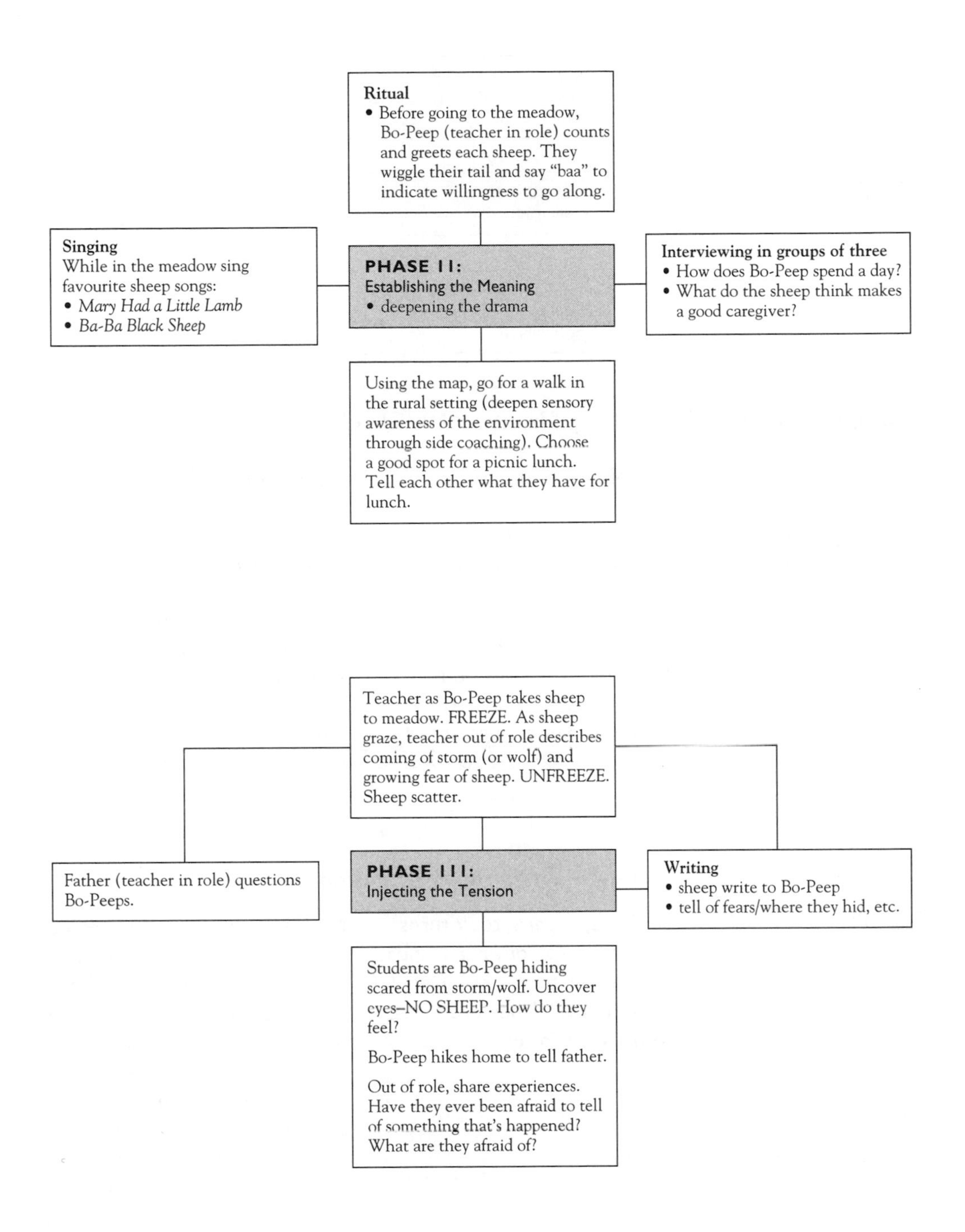
Ritual
• Before going to the meadow, Bo-Peep (teacher in role) counts and greets each sheep. They wiggle their tail and say "baa" to indicate willingness to go along.
Singing
While in the meadow sing favourite sheep songs:
• Mary Had a Little Lamb
• Ba-Ba Black Sheep
PHASE II:
Establishing the Meaning
• deepening the drama
Interviewing in groups of three
• How does Bo-Peep spend a day?
• What do the sheep think makes a good caregiver?
Using the map, go for a walk in the rural setting (deepen sensory awareness of the environment through side coaching). Choose a good spot for a picnic lunch. Tell each other what they have for lunch.
Teacher as Bo-Peep takes sheep to meadow. FREEZE. As sheep graze, teacher out of role describes coming of storm (or wolf) and growing fear of sheep. UNFREEZE. Sheep scatter.
Father (teacher in role) questions Bo-Peeps.
PHASE III:
Injecting the Tension
Writing
• sheep write to Bo-Peep
• tell of fears/where they hid, etc.
Students are Bo-Peep hiding scared from storm/wolf. Uncover eyes–NO SHEEP. How do they feel?
Bo-Peep hikes home to tell father.
Out of role, share experiences. Have they ever been afraid to tell of something that's happened? What are they afraid of?

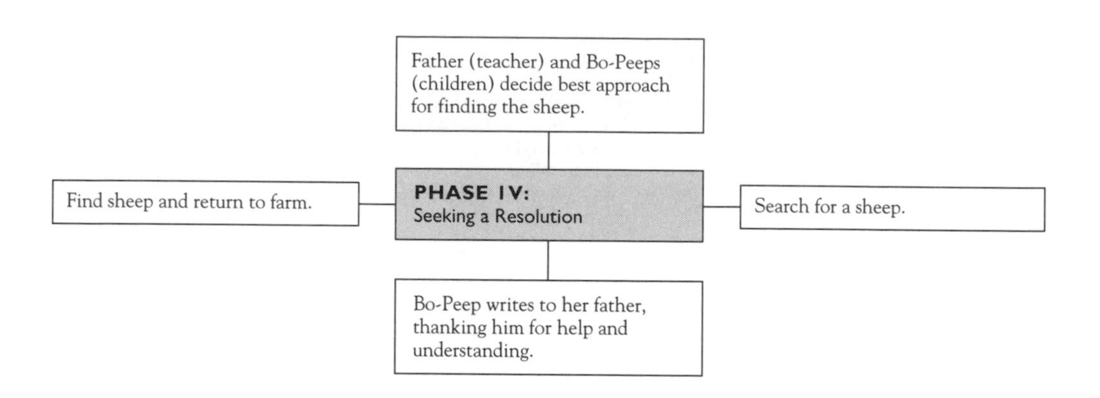

Example 2: Gorilla *by Anthony Browne (1983) (Grade 6)**

Phase 1—Establishing life and activity (context building)

Strategies	Activity	Reflection
Teacher in role	As Anthony Browne, the author, I talked about Hannah's father, a busy man trying his best to raise her, but working long hours. I suggested that perhaps Hannah had not talked to him enough about how important the zoo was to her.	In our previous dramas we had considered the zoo from the viewpoint of the gorilla, so with this role I wanted the students to look at the zoo from the perspective of a child whose only chance to see a gorilla is at the zoo.

Phase 2—Establishing the meaning

Role-play	Students, in pairs, took turns as Hannah to convince her dad to take her to the zoo. Dad did not speak. They presented to the class in turn.	Not as many reasons for going to the zoo came out as I had hoped. They did mention the love of animals, and the chance to see unusual or endangered ones. They concentrated more on pleading than on actual reasons. Perhaps the role of Hannah was too prescribed by the story. I might try a different way of developing this section next time.

**Thanks to Molly Benfield, Grade 6 teacher, Edmonton, Alberta.*

Teacher in role	I returned to a previous drama activity as the gorilla. I raised the bars (wire shelf from the school stove) in front of my face and challenged the students by saying, "You said you would do something for me, you said you cared."	My objective was to review the other aspect of zoos as places that keep wild animals in cages, away from their natural habitat.
	Phase 3—Injecting the tension	
Teacher in role	As a concerned citizen, I said I'd been hearing rumours about the zoo closing. The zoo board had called a meeting to discuss the problems.	The students joined in enthusiastically with "oh no" and "aaah."
Charting	I asked who might be concerned about or interested in this problem. Who would want the zoo to close, what people would want it to remain open? Who would be concerned about the animals and conditions of the zoo?	The students contributed well, and came up with a variety of people. Their suggestions sparked each other, and they were very serious about what they suggested and why. I felt this brainstorming was much more effective than others we have done in other subject areas.
Teacher in role Role-play Writing business letters	I read a letter from a concerned citizen about the zoo closing. I asked each of them to choose one of the people that we had listed and write a letter to the zoo board, as that person, expressing their concerns about the zoo.	The class got right down to the letter writing. I was amazed that no one needed any help with what to write. They were all motivated and interested. I put my letter on the overhead and they used that to format their business letters.
Sharing the letters	The following day I read two of the letters. I asked if they would be interested in finding out what might happen at the next zoo board meeting as a result of this influx of concern.	The class was enthusiastic about attending the zoo board meeting. By asking if they were interested I left the choice of continuing up to them, thereby getting some commitment on their part.

Decision making Defining space Making name cards	The class suggested nine board members and that the names be drawn out of a hat. I wrote these names on the chalk-board in order to define where the board members would be seated. They moved their desks accordingly. Board members and concerned citizens were asked to make name cards for the meeting, thinking about their position on the issue and their concerns as they did so.	I had originally thought of five board members but was pleased that the class had their ideas and stepped right into the decision-making process. They also suggested picking the names out of a hat. They really enjoyed choosing names but did need to be reminded to pick acceptable ones.
Gossip	The board members were asked to meet together and discuss the rumours informally and to clarify their beliefs about the zoo. The citizens (rest of the class) were asked to gossip around town about their concerns and whether they would attend the meeting or not.	The class needed some reminders to stay on task. They were very enthusiastic about the gossiping. I wanted to give them a chance to prepare for speaking at the meeting.
	Phase 4—Seeking a solution	
Ritual	Board members were asked to line up outside the boardroom with their name cards. Citizens were lined up at another door. As president of the board I welcomed each citizen, shaking their hands and thanking them for coming. I commented on their concern and invited them to sit down. I then went to the other door and announced each board member by name and added comments about their excellent contributions to the board. We applauded for each member as they took their seats.	The ritual really helped the students accept the drama and take it seriously. I whispered that I wouldn't announce inappropriate names and that was enough to have some kids make changes as they waited their turn.

Meeting	I (chair of the board), called the meeting to order and invited the citizens to express their concerns by speaking at the "microphone" placed in the centre of the room. A secretary was appointed to record suggestions and ideas.	At this point I wasn't sure how we would continue. (I understand more fully now this idea of letting the drama develop and giving up control. It's a bit unsettling at first.) Our drama evolved with the speakers indicating which board members they would like to address their concerns and questions to. This worked very well. I was very impressed with the students' expression of their concerns and with the answers the board members gave. It was most effective for me to be in role as the president. I found I could intervene very effectively as part of the drama.
Written reflection	The students were asked to stay in role and write what they thought of the meeting and what the zoo board should do next. I then asked the students to write how they felt about this experience with group drama.	I arbitrarily chose the time to end the meeting at a point I thought where interest was still very high. I wanted the students to have a chance to tie the ideas they had shared together. Their written reflections expressed their enthusiasm for the meeting and gave some good directions for the board. Their comments were very positive. Many suggested we do this again using other issues and concerns.

These sample plans illustrate the ample opportunity for using purposeful language in a variety of contexts.

Research has shown (Schaffner, 1985) that this type of drama supports language development. A special education teacher involved in a drama research project reported that her students showed significant improvement in oral and written language, standardized test scores, and classroom behaviour as a result of the drama work completed

(Edwards and Payne, 1994). Despite such research, there is still some hesitancy to use drama as a regular part of the elementary program (Neelands, 1992).

Teacher Concerns Related to Drama

Edwards and Payne (1994) were involved with teachers in a drama support group for two years. During this time many concerns regarding implementation were raised. An outline of some of these concerns follow.

Learning the Language of Drama

The teachers experienced the most difficulty with the terms used to label concepts in the contextual drama approach. Change brings new insights and requires new labels to identify these concepts. For example, "reading readiness" has replaced the term "emergent literacy." The first label represents a behaviouristic perspective, the second a developmental one. Such new terms represent new understandings, and this knowledge shapes classroom practices. Similarily, contextual drama has a variety of new labels to distinguish it from drama-as-interpretation-of-literature. The various labels used to describe this form of drama are: group drama, process drama, drama as a medium for learning, drama for understanding, role drama, and the label used in this chapter, contextual drama. These labels signify a new understanding of drama that shapes what teachers and students do in the classroom. Contextual drama often requires the teacher to take a role and work within the drama to facilitate the meaning-making process. The other form of drama, drama as interpretation of literature, requires the teacher to be a guide and director. The teacher coaches the students through a series of procedures until the dramatic product is complete. These procedures assist the students in translating text into a dramatic product, such as a puppet play.

Consider the statement, "I did drama using Browne's *The Tunnel.*'" For a teacher who views drama as interpretation, this sentence summarizes certain strategies and procedures: dividing the story into scenes, assigning characters, practising the scenes, and then sharing the presentation with peers. For a teacher who sees drama as contextual, this statement would mean the type of strategies and procedures outlined in the previous drama lesson on *The Tunnel.* One form of drama places the teacher outside the play as director, guide, and coach. The contextual approach to drama places the teachers inside the play as they take on various roles to support the work. This strategy—teacher in role—often causes some concern for preservice and inservice teachers beginning this work.

Using Role

Initially, the teachers in this study had some difficulty stepping into role. They found it helpful to pattern their role on a character from literature (Mr. Henry, Bo Beep) or to take on a role endowed with authority (such as a mayor or president of a board). These roles have a similar stance as the teacher role and permit the teacher to have some degree of control over the dramatic events.

Management

For the teachers in the study, management issues arose initially when they introduced drama into their classrooms. The following rules alleviated these concerns.

1. Have a signal for stopping. This can be a verbal command, such as "freeze," or some other signal.
2. Clarify the boundaries of the drama space. Avoid the gym.
3. Establish cooperation. Review the classroom rules.
4. Use a drama "eye."... This term represents the rule "we agree to enter this 'as if' world of drama." Following is one teacher's description of how she developed this rule.

I role-played a short sequence and then asked the students to describe my actions and to explain how they arrived at their meaning. Through discussion these young students could articulate the difference between using your real eye and using your "drama eyes"—between school time and drama time. The students practised using their drama eyes by demonstrating various activities, for example, eating their favourite food. They also practised identifying my actions as being in school time or drama time. It is important to remind students, particularly young students, of this distinction. At times, the emotions experienced in drama seem very real, and it is imperative that students can step out of drama time into school time to reflect on these feelings. Obviously, I want my students to be involved with, but not overwhelmed by, the drama experience. My students always have the choice of stepping out of drama time. I usually place a chair outside the boundary of the drama space and the students can go there if they feel uncomfortable during the drama. I have noticed when I use the term "drama eyes" rather than "pretend," off-task behaviour is minimized. (Jewel Bondar, special education teacher)

These rules can be reviewed with the class at the end of each lesson.

Time

Many of the drama strategies in this chapter can be used as part of the regular curriculum. Drama does not need a special time or place. Finding time to implement drama was perceived as a difficulty by the teachers in the study. This concern is not specific to drama, but to all meaning-centred approaches. In classrooms where pupils are actively involved in learning, there will be lots of talk and writing, which are crucial for the clarification of meaning. If one takes the talk out of reading, writing, social studies, math, and science, it is possible, though not desirable, for students to be engaged in some kind of silent, independent activity. But take the talk out of drama and it disappears.

Preparing for the Concert

During this two-year study the teachers were perceived by their staff as the drama experts and were responsible for the concert. The following guidelines facilitated this task.

- Use a presentational mode of drama. The forms presented in the section "Teaching Drama: Interpretation of Literature" would be appropriate.
- Where possible allow the students to improvise dialogue and practise until they are fluent. This avoids scriptwriting and memorizing.
- Make the presentation as visual as possible since most auditoriums have poor acoustics.
- Limit the amount of individual dialogue since young students cannot project their voices sufficiently. Dialogue for a play can be recorded and the actions mimed. Choral work can be used.
- Allow students to choose how they will participate: as performers, props makers, scriptwriters.

Chapter Summary

The first part of this chapter outlined a wide range of activities. These activities were classified into different types of drama and their common qualities were explored. The differences between drama-as-play, drama-as-a-learning-medium, and drama-as-theatre were explained to show the relationship between drama and language learning. Specific lessons and strategies were described for two approaches to drama: drama-as-interpretation-of-literature and contextual drama. These approaches highlighted the possibilities for language development. Drama in the elementary classroom, like language, has seen a shift in focus, from form to meaning. This change mirrors the development that has taken place in the theories and practice of language learning. Drama provides opportunities for using purposeful oral and written language, deepening response to literature and creating appropriate learning contexts across the curriculum.

Selected Professional Resources

Barton, B. (1980). *Tell Me Another*. Markham, Ont.: Pembroke Publishers Limited/Portsmouth.
This book is an excellent introduction to storytelling.

Booth, D. (1986). *Games for Everyone*. Markham, Ont.: Pembroke Publishers Limited.
This book outlines a variety of practical drama games to develop cooperation, problem-solving, and movement. Each game is clearly described with suggestions for follow-up activities.

Neelands, J. (1992). *Learning through imagined experience*. New York: Cambridge University Press.
This book integrates the theory and practice of contextual drama very effectively. The relationship between drama and language is illustrated throughout, with many examples of drama strategies along with units of study related to various curriculum areas.

O'Neill, C., A. Lambert, R. Linnell, and J. Warr-Wood. (1977). *Drama Guidelines*. London: Heinemann Educational Books.
This book is a classic, not only for its content, but also for its format. The lessons presented in this chapter are modelled on this text. Difficult ideas are made accessible through clarity of language and sample lessons.

Schwartz, L. (1988). *Drama Themes: A Practical Guide for Teaching Drama*. Markham, Ont.: Pembroke Publishers Ltd.
This is an excellent resource for teachers beginning work in drama. It contains many practical suggestions for using literature and drama in the language arts program.

Tarlington, C., and P. Verriour. (1983). *Offstage: Elementary Education through Drama*. Toronto: Oxford University Press.
This is a comprehensive text containing games, drama exercises, examples of role dramas and suggestions for drama as performance.

Children's Literature Noted in Chapter 10

Browne, A. (1983). *Gorilla*. New York: Alfred A. Knopf, Inc.
Browne, A. (1989). *The Tunnel*. London: Julia MacRae Books.
Blos, J. (1987). *Old Henry*. New York: William Morrow.
Slobodkina, E. (1947). *Caps for Sale*. New York: W.R. Scott.
Paterson, K. (1978). *The Great Gilly Hopkins*. New York: Thomas Y. Crowell.
Galdone, P. (1981). *The Three Sillies*. New York: Houghton Mifflin.
Jacob, J. (1973). "King O Cats," in *Starting Points in Reading*. Canada: Ginn and Company.

CHAPTER 11

Assessment

This teacher and child evaluate her work together.

OBJECTIVES

- to understand the difference in the nature and purpose of standardized and informal assessments
- to be aware that different purposes for evaluation require different assessment methods
- to learn current evaluation strategies for oral communication, emergent literacy, reading, and writing
- to know how assessment strategies can be completed

Introduction

The major purpose of assessing language learning is to determine how children talk, listen, read, and write to serve as a basis for planning appropriate instruction. In other words, we need to assess children's language in order to figure out if what we are doing is working and to decide what to do next. The ultimate goal in assessing any child's language learning is the improvement of instruction and the improvement of the children's learning. This sounds simple enough—figure out where the child is and go from there—but it gets complicated by all kinds of political agendas from government, business, and parent groups. Although the needs of parents, government agencies, and business are important, it is the needs of children that should drive assessment in language arts classrooms. Parents have a right to know how their children are learning and functioning in schools, and school systems have the right to know how their students are learning. The central question, however, should be what kind of information do we need to serve as a basis for program planning and for enhancing children's learning? And what are the best tools to gather this information?

Standardized Tests

A major issue in assessment involves the relative merits of formal as compared with informal tools. Standardized reading tests have been used in North American schools for many decades as one way to gather information about children's reading readiness and reading. Although reading readiness tests are rarely used in Canada today, they were widely used in the past to determine children's readiness to learn from formal reading instruction. These tests traditionally assessed areas related to reading achievement such as vocabulary development and visual and auditory discrimination. Some readiness tests produced more recently, such as the *Linguistic Awareness in Reading Readiness (LARR) Test* (Downing, Ayers, and Schaefer, 1983), reflect concepts of *emergent literacy* rather than traditional notions of reading readiness. The LARR test assesses children's ability to recognize literacy behaviour, their understanding of literacy functions, and their knowledge of the technical language of literacy. However, the major purpose of the test is like that of more traditional reading readiness tests—to predict a child's readiness to learn from formal reading instruction.

Most people who attended public schools during the past thirty years will recall year-end reading tests, and this practice continues today. Teachers are generally required by the school systems or provincial ministries of education to give these tests, which generally measure both vocabulary and comprehension. Two tests with Canadian norms that have been used extensively are *Canadian Tests of Basic Skills* (King, 1976) and the *Gates-MacGinitie Reading Tests* (Canadian Version, MacGinitie and MacGinitie, 1992).

Although the use of standardized measures of writing has been less widespread than the use of reading tests, the number of published language/writing tests has grown steadily over the years. They are about equally divided between those that are components of multi-test achievement batteries, such as the *Canadian Test of Basic Skills* (1976), and those that stand alone as writing tests, for example, the *Test of Written Language-2* (Hammill and Larsen, 1988). The tests are composed mainly of mechanics and usage items. Only a few higher-order skills such as organization and composition are covered in the older tests, but the most recent tests developed for elementary school are designed increasingly to measure the ability to recognize good sentence structure and to organize information. There has been a decline in emphasis on spelling and mechanics in these newer tests, and more complex composition skills are being examined.

Purpose of Standardized Tests

The primary reason school systems and provincial governments administer **standardized tests** is accountability—to show that the programs provided in the school system or province are working. From the results obtained, administrators are able to compare the scores of one class, school, or system with those of the standardization sample and with other classes, schools, and systems. Sometimes scores are even compared across nations.

Standardized (sometimes called norm-referenced) tests are developed by selecting items at a range of difficulty levels and administering them to children at various grade and age levels. Tables of norms are then developed providing teachers with percentiles, grade equivalents, and/or standard scores corresponding to the number of items a child completes correctly. When a standardized test is administered, it simply determines how well the children in the class perform on the test in relation to the children in the standardization sample.

Uses of Information on Standardized Tests

To the extent that a standardized test is consistent with the curriculum of the language learning program in a particular school or classroom, it can provide one indication of the overall effectiveness of that program. The results indicate how the children in the program rank in relation to other children who took the test.

Most standardized reading tests contain at least two subtests—vocabulary and comprehension. Results can be used to determine the relative strength of the children in a classroom in these two areas. From the following results obtained on the Gates-MacGinitie Reading Tests in a Grade 2 classroom (Exhibit 11.1), it is evident that many of the children are achieving at a higher level in vocabulary than in comprehension. Their teacher may want to examine the reading program and give greater emphasis to comprehension. This will be particularly important for those children who have a significant discrepancy between vocabulary and comprehension as indicated in the test manual. When children score low on the vocabulary subtest on tests such as this, the implications for instruction are less clear. Unless the teacher goes back over the test items with individual children, there is no way of knowing whether the low score reflects inability to identify the words or difficulty with word meaning.

Results on *standardized tests* can also be used to indicate the need for more in-depth assessment for some children, although the teacher will likely already have identified these children from observing their work in class. From the results presented in Exhibit 11.1, at least two of the children (3 and 25) are significantly below the others.

Critique of Standardized Tests

It is important to critically examine the items used on standardized tests to see if they are consistent with the language arts program being assessed. Clearly, a test needs to measure what has been taught in order to use the results to evaluate program effectiveness. A common criticism directed at standardized reading tests involves the nature of the passages used to assess comprehension. They tend to be short, contrived passages rather than quality children's literature. In spite of the movement away from skills models of reading to more holistic, **constructive** views, standardized tests have changed little in the last few decades. It is questionable whether the items on most standardized reading tests are appropriate for assessing the effectiveness of the type of language learning program being recommended in this textbook.

Standardized tests are also largely unsuitable for the assessment of writing at the elementary school level because they generally involve multiple-choice questions rather than actual samples of the children's writing. Hence, they primarily measure editorial skills such as choosing the best sentence and recognizing correct usage, punctuation, and capitalization. It has long been realized that *recognizing* good writing is not synonymous with being able to *create* it, and that the content of writing—ideas and their development—does not lend itself to the format of an objective or short-answer test. Identifying a complete sentence is a different task from creating one. The one is a writing task, while the other is simply an identification or memory task. Likewise, identifying a correctly spelled word is a totally different skill from being able to correctly spell that word from memory. Identification of a correctly spelled word may be a predictor of the ability to spell that word correctly, but although moderate correlations between scores on these

EXHIBIT 11.1

Results of a Grade 2 Class on the Gates-MacGinitie Reading Tests

Child	Grade Equivalents*	
	Vocabulary	Comprehension
1	2.0	1.5
2	3.9	1.5
3	1.7	1.4
4	3.1	3.4
5	4.4	3.1
6	3.6	3.1
7	3.6	2.7
8	3.9	3.1
9	4.4	4.0
10	3.3	1.8
11	4.8	2.8
12	3.7	3.1
13	4.1	3.4
14	3.1	1.9
15	3.6	3.4
16	4.3	2.5
17	4.6	3.7
18	4.1	3.1
19	3.3	3.4
20	2.7	1.7
21	4.4	2.5
22	2.7	2.6
23	2.0	1.9
24	3.1	2.2
25	1.5	1.7
26	3.6	2.1

A grade equivalent score of 2.0 means that a child scored like the average child in the standardization sample at the beginning of the Grade 2 school year.

two types of tests have been found at the high-school and college levels, a much lower correlation has emerged for children in elementary school (Moss, Cole, and Khampalikit, 1982). Research has shown that at the third-grade level, the relationship between the two is very low and may not be valid (Arrasmith, Sheehan, and Applebaum, 1984).

Rather than standardized tests measuring what is taught, the opposite is often the case. What is taught is determined by what is tested. In other words, teachers teach children what is measured on the tests, thereby narrowing the curriculum and letting the tests drive the curriculum, rather than the other way around.

There are also other problems with standardized tests. Field (1990, 108) notes that test items are deliberately selected "to produce failure among some and success among others." How does this happen? When items are being selected for inclusion on a particular test, those items that all students get right or all students get wrong are eliminated because they do not help to differentiate among children. In other words, unless some children fail an item, it is not included. And by linking scores on these tests to grade equivalents, it is predetermined that some children will be at grade level, some will be above and some will be below. In other words, when we use these types of tests, we predetermine that half of the children will succeed and half will fail. On the one hand, most people believe that an appropriate goal of schooling is to ensure that all children are able to read and write at a level appropriate to their grade; on the other hand, the use of standardized tests means that this will never be achieved. Instead, some children will be identified very early as reading and writing below expectations, emphasizing what they cannot do rather than what they can do. This is by far our greatest concern with standardized tests—the potentially negative impact that test results can have on individual children by marginalizing them, by telling them that they are not good enough.

A relatively minor but widespread misuse of standardized test scores involves the way in which grade equivalents and other scores are interpreted. When someone says that a child is reading or writing at a particular grade level (e.g., 2.3), it is important to realize that this score should be interpreted as a range of scores around grade 2.3. Every child's performance on a particular test will vary to some extent depending on factors such as how the child feels, what the testing conditions are like, and how lucky the child is on the multiple-choice items that particular day. Variability in a child's performance on a test across time is referred to as the standard error of measurement; an individual child might obtain a score on the same test of 2.3 on one day, 1.9 on another, and 2.6 on yet another. Because of this range, and also because of how grade equivalents are calculated (by comparing children with one another), grade equivalents can only be used in a very rough way to determine the appropriate level of materials for any particular child to read.

There are also misunderstandings surrounding the interpretation of percentile scores, largely because many people confuse them with percentages. Percentile ranks, which range from 1 to 99, indicate the proportion of students in the standardization sample who achieved raw scores higher or lower than a particular student. For example, a child with a percentile rank of 55 has performed as well as or better than 55 percent of the standardization sample. In other words, the child has performed better than half of all the children in the sample, and hence, is well within normal expectations for his or her grade and age level.

Still, it is important to keep in mind that all these scores tell about an individual child is how he or she performed on one particular day compared with other children who completed that test. The scores tell little about how the child talks, listens, reads, or writes, or about his or her specific instructional needs. In the eyes of many educators, the only justifiable use for standardized tests is for placement or prediction—and even then, more **direct assessment** techniques are preferable (Cooper and Odell, 1977). The information needed for daily planning of instruction can only be obtained through the use of more informal types of assessment, which will be the focus of the remainder of this chapter.

Informal Assessment

Informal assessment is frequently recommended to teachers as an appropriate means to decide what children need next. Indeed, we all engage in informal assessment constantly whether we are aware of it or not, and we constantly make decisions about what to do next based on the information collected. This assessment generally reflects our views of talking, reading, and writing. For example, whether we view oral reading **miscues** as errors to be corrected or as clues to how a child is reading depends on whether we hold a skills or constructive view of reading. Similarly, whether we view inventive spellings as errors to be corrected or as clues to how a child is relating sound and spelling patterns depends on whether we think product or process is more important in writing. Hence, informal assessment will only be appropriate for assessing the effectiveness of the language arts program recommended in this book or for determining what to do next with a specific child *if* it reflects a constructive, holistic view of language learning.

Advantages of Informal Assessment

Several advantages of informal assessment have been identified (Teale, Hiebert, and Chittenden, 1987). First, this type of assessment, in contrast with formal testing, is part of instruction. It is not separate from the teaching/learning process and, hence, does not take time away from instruction the way standardized testing does. Another major difference between informal and formal assessment involves the variety of instruments used in informal assessment. It focuses on all the things the child does in the language arts classroom rather than what the child does on contrived test passages or individual words. It occurs across the entire language arts program including talking, reading, and writing.

It also occurs continuously to provide a basis for daily lesson planning rather than at one or two points in the year.

Types of Informal Assessment

Four major types of informal assessment have been described in the literature. The first three involve informal assessment by the teacher; the last involves student self-assessment.

A few years ago, Yetta Goodman coined the term "kid watching" to refer to the ongoing observation by teachers of children in classrooms. She suggests that this kid watching is likely not as conscious as it needs to be for teachers to "gain the greatest insights from it" (1991, 58). For example, the fact that most teachers are unaware that they acknowledge the talk of boys more than that of girls in classrooms demonstrates the need for conscious awareness. One of the purposes of this chapter is to help to develop greater conscious awareness and control over classroom observations so that the information gathered through kid watching can enhance children's growth in language learning.

Teacher questioning has been a very common part of instruction in reading comprehension, and as Durkin (1978–79) has pointed out, this questioning has been primarily to assess rather than to enhance children's understanding. In order to maximize insights from children's answers, however, it is crucial that we go beyond assessing them as right or wrong to determining what they tell us about the way children use background knowledge and text-based information as they read. Interviewing generally refers to more structured interactions between teachers and children than those that occur in the classroom on a daily basis. Questions are generally organized around a specific topic or aspect of language learning, and the teacher uses the questions to gather information from children on an individual basis.

A third type of informal assessment involves gathering samples of children's work. This is not a new idea but has recently received considerable attention through the movement to **portfolio assessment**. (The term "portfolio assessment" comes from artists' portfolios in which they collect and display their best work.) While portfolios of children's reading and writing may not be restricted to their best work, Valencia (1990), a strong supporter of portfolio assessment, describes it as authentic, continuous, ongoing, multidimensional, and collaborative.

One of the major advantages cited for portfolio assessment is the potential it has for children to become involved in self-assessment. It is frequently recommended that children both select what goes into the portfolio and collaborate with their teacher in assessing what is in the portfolio. But does informal assessment and the use of portfolios reflect a real change from standardized measurements in how language learning is assessed?

Issues about Informal Assessment

To the extent that informal assessment continues to focus on individual accountability and on language learning as individual skill accumulation (Bloome, 1991), it may not accomplish much more than standardized testing. We may tell children that it is important for them to work together and provide opportunities for them to work in groups, but if all our assessment focuses on individual learning, they will know we really don't value collaboration.

To the extent that the focus is on how well the child talks, listens, reads, and writes rather than on how he or she does it, there is not much difference between informal and standardized assessment. It is easier to collect products of children's language use, e.g., writing samples, rather than language actually in use. There is already pressure on teachers to develop standard criteria for evaluating material in portfolios. If these criteria were correlated with age so that by a certain age, a child's writing is expected to meet specific criteria with respect to grammar, spelling, punctuation, capitalization, and handwriting, we would be no further ahead. We would simply be exchanging the norm tables on standardized tests for norm tables based on our own opinions of what is good or bad. For informal assessment to achieve its potential, we must resist pressure to use it to evaluate whether a child has met the expectations for his or her age or grade. Instead, the focus needs to be on using the information gathered to describe a child's talking, reading, and writing in order to help plan appropriate instruction to maximize growth.

To the extent that teachers continue to determine what counts as good reading and writing, the collaborative potential of portfolios will not be achieved. When children are asked to participate in the assessment process, they are frequently asked to judge their progress toward goals set by the teacher. In peer editing, for example, children frequently end up using the teacher's criteria to judge each other's writing. Seldom are children asked to set their own goals for language learning and to determine how progress toward those goals will be met. In order for language learning classrooms to achieve goals of democracy and social justice, we need to relinquish some of our power over assessment and pass it to our students.

Oral Communication

"In an increasingly oral society, success in interpersonal relationships, in learning, in the community and in the workplace is closely related to oral communication skills. Research suggests that these skills are developed through modeling and through practice—that students learn about language and how to use it effectively through opportunities to interact with different people in different contexts to accomplish different purposes" (British Columbia Ministry of Education, 1988, 1.1). For most people, speech is the primary means of communication. Through oral language and nonverbal gestures, we communicate most of our needs, fears, and dreams to the people we encounter in our day-to-day lives. Through oral language we frequently work out our ideas, "bounce" ideas off colleagues and friends, and communicate the most prosaic, yet necessary, messages to those closest to us. It is therefore of utmost importance that children's oral language abilities be fostered and monitored throughout elementary school. Oral language should not be taken for granted or ignored. Yet too often in the elementary grades, it is given very little attention.

The British Columbia Ministry of Education developed a resource package, *Enhancing and Evaluating Oral Communication in the Primary Grades* (1988), to assist teachers in developing and assessing children's oral communication skills. It is a comprehensive document, which serves as a central source of information for this section of this chapter. The document lists seven areas of communicative competence: affective behaviours, language awareness, listening comprehension, speech communication, critical/evaluative behaviours, social and interpersonal strategies, and oral language codes. It suggests that these areas can be assessed in three ways: observing students as they communicate; listening to what students say in conversations, group conferences, and other classroom activities; and reading what students write.

Affective behaviours are those aspects of communication that reveal attitudes and values. They usually have to be inferred, but they can be uncovered by asking appropriate questions, such as: Did the students participate in a certain activity? Did they participate willingly and enthusiastically? Given a choice of activities what do the students choose? Do they choose listening, speaking, or collaborative activities? What activities do the students remember? Do the students display emotional responses to specific experiences? Can they articulate these responses in a diverse range of media (writing, drawing, mime, puppetry, artwork, dance)?

Language awareness entails the actual knowledge students possess about their own language use and learning. This can best be uncovered by asking students direct questions about their learning, such as: How did they do something? Did they feel it was easy for them? How did they decide on certain strategies? What did they learn? What was the most important thing they learned?

Listening comprehension involves the students' abilities to construct meaning from what they hear. Teachers can assess students' abilities to construct meaning by listening carefully to their comments, by asking direct questions, and through observation. Children may sometimes give an inappropriate response if they do not understand the reason for doing something, and so it is essential that students know why they are listening and what they are listening for. Listening comprehension can be assessed according to whether or not the students meet the function of the task, Did they follow directions appropriately? Did they accomplish the task set out for them? How much support did the students need from the teacher or from peers? Can the students recall what they have heard? Can they recall the important features of what they have heard? Can they predict the unfinished parts of a message? How do they respond to literary material they hear? Do they ask questions about what they have heard? Are these questions relevant?

Speech communication is simply the assessment of how successful the students are in accomplishing the objectives of their speech. How much support do they need in order to accomplish their speech goals? How much control do the children have over their speaking strategies? Do the children attempt to expand their repertoire of speaking strategies by experimenting with new forms?

Critical/evaluative behaviour involves the students' abilities to monitor their own speech and the messages they receive from others. Are they aware of whether their message has been understood? Are they able to question and clarify messages received from others? Are they able to self-question: Was I a good person to work with today, and why? What was the best thing about my report to the class and did the students listen to me with interest?

Interpersonal strategies are those behaviours that allow students to create relationships with others. Children learn how to do this through their play and work in school. Interpersonal strategies include conversing, solving problems, sharing stories, and participating in drama activities—all of which fulfil Halliday's interactional function of language.

Oral language codes are those aspects of language that allow us to communicate effectively to different people in different situations. Children learn a wide repertoire of language codes as they participate in relationships with a diverse group of people—grandparents, parents, friends, teachers, salespeople, and so on. Children have to learn to be aware of their audience, what must be communicated, and the most appropriate ways to communicate their thoughts and feelings. Children learn to pay attention to auditory perception and discrimination, voice skills (articulation and expressiveness), and vocabulary and **syntax**. Questions teachers can ask include: Do the students attempt to extend their range of language codes? Do the students pay attention to the aesthetic qualities of their speech? Do the students possess a range of language codes that work for them in different situations?

A further resource for the assessment of language abilities is the *English Profiles Handbook*, which provides a series of assessment strategies for oral language. Published by the Department of School Education in Victoria, Australia, the document outlines nine "bands" of proficiency in oral language, and provides descriptions and assessment practices for each. The *English Profiles Handbook* emphasizes the importance of talking with and listening to students, and involving them in drama, listening to songs, poems, and stories, choral reading, share time, cooperative writing, group activities, designing instructions, readers' theatre, improvisation, cooperative cloze activities, storytelling, role-playing, group discussions, cross-age tutoring, and reporting.

The assessment records in the *English Profiles Handbook* (1991, 33) are organized into two categories: use of oral language and features of oral language. Spoken language band D (approximately Grade 4) lists the following attributes.

Use of oral language

- Tells personal anecdotes, illustrating in a relevant way the issue being discussed
- Recounts a story or repeats a song spontaneously
- Retells scenes from film or drama
- Offers predictions about what will come next
- Recites poems
- Asks questions in conversation
- Has a second try at something to make it more precise
- Arouses and maintains audience interest during formal presentations (e.g., report to class, announcements)

Features of oral language

- Uses range of vocabulary related to a particular topic
- Maintains receptive body stance in conversation
- Speaks in a way that conveys feelings (while keeping emotions under control)

One can see how this list of features could be made into a straightforward checklist that would be easy for a teacher to use, and that could be augmented with comments on the oral language behaviours of each individual child. The assessment of oral communication abilities relies heavily upon the teacher listening to children—not only listening to *what* children have to say, and responding appropriately, but also listening to *how* children create and communicate meaning. The above lists of features are helpful in tracking children's abilities and growth in this very important area.

One other source of information on assessing children's oral communication is *English in the National Curriculum*, published by the Department of Education and Science in the United Kingdom. Attainment targets, statements of attainment, and examples are set out for speaking and listening for ages six through fifteen. At age nine, for example, the statement of attainment is that children shall (1990, 4):

> *a) give a detailed oral account of an event, or something that has been learned in the classroom, or explain with reasons why a particular course of action has been taken*
>
> *b) ask and respond to questions in a range of situations with increased confidence*

c) *take part as speakers and listeners in a group discussion or activity, expressing a personal view and commenting constructively on what is being discussed or experienced*

d) *participate in a presentation.*

An example of a) would be to report to another class on a scientific investigation or the progress of a planned group activity. An example of b) is to guide other pupils in designing something; or to conduct an interview on a radio program devised with other pupils. An example of c) is to draft a piece of writing with others, on a word processor; or to contribute to the planning and implementation of a group activity. An example of d) is to describe the outcome of a group activity; or improvise a scene from a story or poem of the pupil's own devising.

Again, these attainment statements are descriptions of how children might be able to communicate orally at specific ages. In order to record each child's development and abilities, the teacher needs to make anecdotal records, keeping in mind the above criteria. One also needs to be familiar with the statements of attainment for children both younger and older than nine, for in any one class there will be a wide range of oral communication competencies.

Emergent Literacy

Some children arrive at kindergarten with very little understanding of what written language is for or how it works. Others come to school already reading and writing. Hence, right from the first day of school, children show considerable differences in their literacy development. Teachers need to know where children are in order to plan and provide appropriate literacy experiences. In this section, suggestions will be presented for informal assessment of both emergent writing and emergent reading.

Observing Children

As teachers, we cannot avoid gathering information every time we interact with children. However, much of the time these observations are left unrecorded even though they might still influence our decisions about what to do next. Some teachers keep anecdotal records, jotting down what they see and hear during or at the end of the day. For example, a teacher may note what books a child selected during free time or that a child was able to find the word *cat* in the language experience story that day.

At times you will want to be more systematic in gathering and recording information: one way to do this is by using a checklist. Chittenden and Courtney (1989) recommend that observations be organized according to the contexts in which children learn language. The learning contexts described in Chapter 5 involve shared-book experiences, language experience stories, functional uses of print, and writing. Chapter 5 also includes an indication of learning goals that could be achieved in each of these instructional contexts. The checklist in Exhibit 11.2 is organized around the learning outcomes of **emergent literacy** activities. For each learning context, specific behaviours are listed that indicate the learning outcome has been achieved.

The checklist can be used either as a general guide for unrecorded observations or in a more systematic way to record information on some or all of the children in the class. Used at regular intervals, it can provide an indication of a child's progress toward each of the learning outcomes and would be a very useful component in the portfolios of children who are not yet reading independently. The right-hand column in the checklist is a space to record examples of the child's relevant literacy activities. For example, if the teacher has checked *chooses books as free-time activity*, this column could include information on what types of books the child chooses (big books, animal books, familiar books), how frequently this happens (every day, once a week), whether the child reads alone or with another child, and so on.

Information gathered on a checklist such as the one in Exhibit 11.2 leads quite directly to instruction since specific learning contexts are used as an organizer for the information collected. For example, children who are beginning to point globally at print as they read or reread books are showing that they understand the importance of print (as compared with pictures) in reading. They are ready for speech-to-print matching activities when they point to words as the teacher reads, or they read a familiar book or language experience story as the teacher points. Similarly, children who have achieved the speech-to-print match when rereading familiar books or language experience stories show that they understand the one-to-one relationship between written and oral language. This knowledge is an important prerequisite to being able to identify the same word in different contexts. It signals readiness for instruction involving identification of specific words, first in familiar books and language experience stories, and later in less familiar materials.

Interviews

Parents can provide important information on their child's literacy development to serve as a basis for planning instruction. They can provide information about *who* reads and writes at home, *how much* they read and write, *what* they read and write, and *why* they read and write. Children learn a great deal about the uses of written language by watching their parents as they read newspapers, read and write letters to relatives, read

EXHIBIT 11.2

Emergent Literacy Checklist

Learning goals	Learning contexts	Behaviours	Comments and examples
Positive attitude to books and print	Shared-book/ language experience	___ enjoys group storytime and language experience activities	
	Shared-book experience	___ chooses books as free time activity	
	Language experience	___ rereads language experience stories in free time	
	Functional print experience	___ shows interest in print around the classroom, school, community	
	Writing	___ chooses to write during free time	
Written language is meaningful	Shared-book experience	___ makes comments or asks questions during story reading	
		___ predicts meaningful words during completion reading or when words are covered	
	Shared-book/ language experience	___ reproduces meaning as a whole during rereading	
	Language experience	___ contributes ideas during story writing	

continued

	Functional print experience Writing	___ responds meaningfully to labels, calendar, charts in classroom ___ produces meaningful message when reading what has been written	
Message stays the same	Shared-book/ language experience Functional print	___ chimes in during reading ___ knows when teacher/child makes a mistake during rereading ___ responds to labels/words same way each time	
What written language sounds like	Shared-book experience Language experience/writing	___ memorizes favourite books ___ "talks like a book" when rereading ___ "talks like a book" when dictating/writing stories	
Story sense	Shared-book experience Language experience/writing	___ predicts what will happen in a story ___ retells beginning, middle, and end of stories ___ is able to draw or dramatize stories ___ includes beginning, middle, and end in stories	
Importance of print	Shared-book/ language experience	___ points to print during reading/rereading	

continued

	Functional print experience Writing	___ points to print in classroom, school, and community ___ makes letters or letterlike forms when writing	
Directional aspects of print	Shared-book/ language experience Shared book Writing	___ begins reading at top of page ___ points from left to right when tracking print ___ reads left page before right page ___ writes from top to bottom of page ___ writes left to right across page	
Speech-to-print match	Shared-book/ language experience	___ points to each word while saying it during reading/ rereading	
Terms and concepts of print	Shared book/ language experience Writing Shared-book/ language experience/writing	___ uses terms *letters* and *words* while reading, e.g., "What's this word?" ___ leaves a space between words ___ uses terms *letters* and *words* while writing, e.g., "How do you spell *on*?" ___ uses terms *author, page, sentence* while reading and writing	

continued

Decoding/ encoding strategies	Shared-book/ language experience/ functional print Writing	___ identifies same word in different contexts ___ uses initial letter sound to help identify words ___ verbalizes letter sounds while writing ___ bases spelling on letter names or sounds	

cookbooks, read directions for assembling a new piece of furniture, read books for pleasure, read books to write a research paper, write lists of groceries to take to the store, and so on. Parents can also indicate how often the child is read to, who reads to the child, what books are read, what the child's favourite books are, how many books the child regularly has access to, the child's attitude toward books and being read to, what the child does when being read to (e.g., mumbles along, asks questions, wanders away, etc.), and what the child does independently with books. Similarly, parents can indicate what types of writing behaviours their child exhibits (scribbling, using single letters for words, spelling some words phonetically), how often they write, and what kinds of questions and comments they make when they are writing.

Children are able to provide some of this same information about home literacy. It is useful, for example, to ask them who reads and writes at home, what they read and write, and why they think these people read and write. Children are also able to answer questions about who reads to them, how often they are read to, and what their favourite books are. It is also informative to ask them if they read and write at home and have them talk about what and how they read and write.

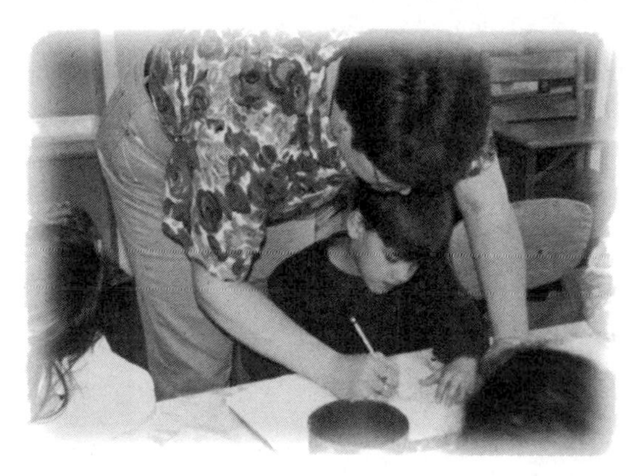

A kindergarten child receives feedback from the teacher.

Although the teacher will gain considerable information about children by observing them during shared-book experiences, there will be times when further information is desired about an individual child's concepts and knowledge about story reading. Several people have developed interview schedules for this purpose; the one in Exhibit 11.3 incorporates questions and concepts from book handling interviews suggested by Clay (1985), Doake (1981), and Alberta Education (1993).

EXHIBIT 11.3

Book-Handling Interview

Questions	Literacy concepts and knowledge	Comments
1. *How books work* • Can you show me the front of the book? • Where is the title? What does it tell you? • Open the book so we can start reading at the beginning of the story.	___ identifies front of book ___ identifies title ___ identifies first page of story	
2. *Importance of print* • Show me with your finger where to start reading.	___ points to print	
3. *Directional aspects of print* • Show me the top/bottom of this page. • Show me which page to read first. • Show me with your finger which way I go as I read this page.	___ identifies top/bottom of page ___ reads left page before right ___ points left to right across line of print	
4. *Speech-to-print match* • Point to the words as I read.	___ partial matching ___ exact matching	

continued

5. *Terms and concepts of print* • Point to one letter/word • Point to the first/last letter in a word. • Point to an upper/lower case letter.	___ one letter ___ one word ___ first letter ___ last letter ___ upper case letter ___ lower case letter	
6. *Letter/word identification* • Point to the letter __ (name two letters on the page). • Point to the word ___ (name two high frequency words on the page).	___ letter names ___ words	
7. *Meaning in written language* • Tell me the story.	___ retells by naming pictures ___ retells part of story ___ retells beginning, middle, and end	

Information gathered through interviews can be used to supplement that gained through daily classroom observations of children as they read and write. It can be used to fill in gaps in what the teacher knows about a child: Does a child who rarely joins in during the rereading of big books have regular story reading at home? Is he or she aware that print plays a special role in reading or are pictures still the primary focus of attention? What has the child learned about the directional aspects of print from watching the teacher's hand during reading of big books? This information helps the teacher ask the child to respond in ways during shared-book experiences that are consistent with the child's literacy concepts and knowledge. It does not make sense to ask a child to find a specific word on a page in a big book if the child does not yet understand the significance of print or know terms such as *word* and *letter*.

Collecting Samples of Children's Work

Emergent Writing

It is much easier to gather the artifacts of children's writing than their reading. Writing samples are frequently collected throughout the school year and kept in a child's writing folder or portfolio. These samples are then analyzed to describe the development of the child's writing.

Generally, the following stages can be used to describe young children's development of knowledge and concepts related to written language (Neuman and Roskos, 1993):

- uses drawing for writing
- uses pictures and scribble for writing
- uses scribble for writing
- uses letterlike forms for writing
- uses letters (not based on sound) for writing
- uses letter names for **invented spelling**
- uses letter sounds for invented spelling
- uses conventional spellings.

Not all children go through all these stages in this order but a child who is still using scribble for writing is clearly not ready for a heavy focus on conventional spelling. Children also demonstrate growing awareness of directional principles in their writing (Clay, 1985), moving from scribbles placed in no particular order on the page to some awareness of directional patterns to the correct directional pattern (top to bottom, left to right, spaces between words). The writing in Exhibit 11.4 was collected in May from David, a Grade 1 child identified by his teacher as having difficulty learning to read and write. The teacher provided David with the words *troll*, *live*, and *mushroom*, and David talked to himself as he wrote. At one point he printed the letter *d* at the top of the page to ask if that was right before writing a word in his story. This sample clearly indicates that he is using letter sounds for spelling but that he also used the arithmetic symbol to represent the word plus.

Although much of the focus of research has been on the forms of emergent writing, it is also important to look beyond these forms to determine what children think they are doing when they write. Even when children scribble, they are indicating that they realize writing and drawing are different. As they begin to use letter or letterlike forms, they show an awareness of a concept of sign and that we use signs when we write (Clay, 1985). They begin to talk about what they have written (or ask someone to tell them what they have written), indicating that they are aware that written language holds meaning. Usually by the end of Grade 1, they are producing invented spellings and are

EXHIBIT 11.4

David's Writing Sample

aware that a message is encoded in the words they write. David, whose writing is in Exhibit 11.4, was clearly aware that he was encoding a message in print, talking out loud to himself as he wrote. He also reviewed what he had written at one point before writing more.

Although these general developmental patterns are useful to teachers in assessing children's progress in learning to write, Sulzby (1991) has pointed out that many children, even until mid or late Grade 1 move between forms and understandings of writing. Whereas a child may write a short sentence using invented spellings and be able to read this sentence accurately upon request, this child might revert to scribbling on a more difficult task such as writing a whole book. From her research she feels that this movement between more and less sophisticated writing is part of normal development. Hence, we need to be careful about placing too much emphasis on any one sample of a child's writing in our assessment, but instead should look at many samples produced in a variety of contexts.

Emergent Reading

When children read orally or silently, no permanent record remains of their reading. While some teachers tape the reading of their kindergarten or first-grade children, it is still not easy to use these to assess growth. It takes a great deal of time to listen to tapes of children reading and it is difficult to remember what the child did on one tape when listening to the next. It is far more convenient to make a written record of the child's reading. Clay (1985) recommends that teachers take running records of their children's reading. For children in the emergent stage of literacy development, it is more useful to use books that the children have some degree of familiarity with, although it is useful at times to see what they do with a completely unfamiliar book.

To take a running record, the teacher has a child read a book and as the child does so, the teacher notes in writing what the child says and does. This can be done either by making a copy of the text the child will be reading and marking what the child says on that copy, or by using a blank sheet of paper and putting a mark for each word the child reads correctly and noting any deviations from the text. These two options are shown in Exhibit 11.5.

One way of analyzing children's running records is to examine their reading in relation to stages reported in the literature. The following stages are based on the work of Sulzby (1985) and Neuman and Roskos (1993):

- pays attention to pictures, labelling objects rather than forming a story
- pays attention to pictures, making up a story from the pictures
- pays attention to pictures, telling a version of the story
- pays attention to pictures, and talks like a book
- pays attention to print, identifying some words and inventing the rest to produce a meaningful version of the story
- pays attention to print, focusing primarily on word identification
- pays attention to both print and meaning cues, reading fluently.

All children do not go through all these stages, but it is clear that most begin by focusing on pictures and need to spend some time internalizing and telling stories before they are ready to profit from a heavy focus on print. David, whose miscues are shown in Exhibit 11.5, was paying attention to both print and meaning cues and approaching reading fluency.

Another way of analyzing running records is to code deviations from the text in relation to what type of information the child used to produce this deviation. Goodman (1969) coined the word **miscues** to refer to these deviations rather than the word *errors* because he believes that they provide us with a great deal of useful information about how children read. As children read, they are constantly using picture, print, and **context cues** to predict words; miscues provide insight into which cues children use. Miscue analysis basically involves looking at each miscue the child has made and asking why the

EXHIBIT 11.5

Taking a Running Record (two options)

Codes for running records

A stroke (/) indicates word read correctly
A substituted word is written above the text word
An omission is indicated with a circle around the word
T indicates the word was provided by the teacher
SC indicates that a miscue was self-corrected

Using a blank sheet of paper

Text (*Whistle, Mary, Whistle* by Bill Martin Jr.)	Coding
"Whistle, Mary, Whistle, and you shall have a trout."	/ / / / / / / / T
"I can't whistle, Mother, because my tooth is out."	/ / / / / / / *fell* / is
"Whistle, Mary, Whistle,	/ / /
and you shall have a rabbit."	/ / / / / / (used picture cue for rabbit)
"I can't whistle, Mother, because I've lost the habit."	/ / / / / I / *my* *tooth* I've the habit
"Whistle, Mary, Whistle, and you shall have a daisy."	/ / / / / / / / *dandy* daisy
"I can't whistle, Mother, because it looks so crazy."	/ / / / / / / / T

Making a copy of the text the child is reading

T
Whistle, Mary, Whistle, and you shall have a trout.

fell
I can't whistle, Mother, because my tooth is out.

"Whistle, Mary, Whistle, and you shall have a rabbit."

I *my tooth*
"I can't whistle, Mother, because I've lost the habit."

dandy
"Whistle, Mary, Whistle, and you shall have a daisy."

T
"I can't whistle, Mother, because it looks so crazy."

---

child said that. For classroom purposes, we recommend a simplified system for analyzing miscues although more sophisticated systems are necessary for children who have significant difficulty learning to read.

In Chapter 6, we indicated that children use two major sources of information as they read: print information and knowledge-based information. In order to become good readers, they need to integrate both sources of information so that what they read makes sense and is consistent with the print information. In our simplified miscue analysis, we recommend that you look at each miscue a child made and ask yourself two questions: Does the word the child said look like the word in the text (print cues)? Does the word the child said make sense (knowledge-based cues)? If the word the child said contains any of the letters in the text word, write the letter *P* above the word to indicate use of print cues. If the miscue makes sense up to that point, write the letter M above it to indicate use of meaning cues. Some miscues will have only a *P* above them, indicating that the child used print cues but did not rely on his or her knowledge to make a meaningful prediction. Others will have only an M above them, indicating that the child used his or her knowledge to predict a word that made sense but did not look carefully at the print. Finally, some miscues will have both a *P* and M above them, showing that the child made integrated use of both print-based and knowledge-based information. Exhibit 11.6 shows how David's miscues were coded using this simplified system of analysis.

A simple count of the number of miscues of each type shows that three were coded as meaningful, one as using print cues and two as using both print and meaning cues. In addition, David waited for help from the teacher on two words, indicating that he was focusing on print cues, even though he was unable to identify the words from these cues. Overall, this analysis of David's miscues shows that he is attending to both meaning and print cues but does not always use the cues together. He also does not correct any of his miscues, suggesting that he is either unaware that what he is reading doesn't make sense or look right or that he has not yet developed enough facility with using print and meaning cues to self-correct. In the actual classroom situation we would want to analyze a larger sample of David's miscues in order to confirm this interpretation. However, from both the running record in Exhibit 11.6 and his writing sample in Exhibit 11.4, it is clear that David has considerable knowledge about how books work, knows that written language is meaningful, and is developing strategies for encoding and decoding words on the basis of print and sound cues. He has achieved most of the learning goals expected of emergent reader–writers and is rapidly reaching independence in reading and writing.

EXHIBIT 11.6

Coding of David's Miscues on a Predictable Book

P: miscue contains at least one letter in the text word
M: miscue makes sense in relation to prior text

T
"Whistle, Mary, Whistle, and you shall have a trout."

M
fell
"I can't whistle, Mother, because my tooth is out."

"Whistle, Mary, Whistle, and you shall have a rabbit."

PM M PM
I my tooth
"I can't whistle, Mother, because I've lost the habit."

P
dandy
"Whistle, Mary, Whistle, and you shall have a daisy."

T
"I can't whistle, Mother, because it looks so crazy."

Inside **the Classroom**

Angela Ward is a faculty member in the Department of Curriculum Studies at the University of Saskatchewan. She describes what she has done with the parents of the children in her kindergarten to share information about their language and literacy development.

I remember my own mother, long ago, dreading parent–teacher interviews. Because she had only a limited education, she felt that teachers were talking down to her. A side-effect of this feeling can be a sense that somehow teachers are not sharing all the relevant information about the children. Since becoming a teacher myself, I have tried hard to involve parents in the assessment and reporting process. Parents have told me that this not only demystifies reporting for them, but also helps them understand classrooms better.

Early in September I have a meeting of parents of children in my kindergarten class and talk about the curriculum and planned activities. I show a video of last year's class in action, which demonstrates the informal literacy activities of children. They may be stapling books together and writing in them with felt markers, listening to books on tape, playing alphabet games, or sitting quietly in the old bathtub that is part of my reading corner. I then invite parents to come in and observe their own children. Most manage to come, even if they have to work through lunch hour to make up the time spent in the classroom. I ask parents and care-givers to observe reading behaviours, to collect samples of their child's writing, and to jot down examples of oral language and listening that they have noticed. Parents always enjoy doing this and appreciate the insights they gain into how their children are learning literacy.

After the observation, we briefly discuss what they've seen, and then I put their comments into the child's file. At interview time, I add my own observations of the same kinds of behaviours, so the discussion becomes a shared one. Parents have said that they like the chance to contribute to the interview. They also say they have more realistic views of their children after seeing for themselves how they behave in a classroom.

The key to the interactions between Angela Ward and the parents of the children in her kindergarten class is collaboration. The parents are an important source of information about their children's literacy development. However, equally important is the opportunity for the parents to obtain further insights into their children's literacy development. Reporting to parents will be considered in greater detail in the final section of this chapter.

Reading

Observing Reading Behaviour

As noted in the section on emergent literacy, teachers are continuously assessing the reading strategies of their students each time they interact with them. A checklist is provided (Exhibit 11.7) to help teachers focus on and interpret children's reading behaviours during daily classroom reading instruction.

The headings in the left-hand column reflect those used to organize teaching/learning techniques in Chapter 7. Hence, if a child does not display a particular reading behaviour listed in the middle column, the teacher can go directly to the appropriate section in Chapter 7 to select teaching/learning techniques to use with the child. For example, a child who is not yet able to include information from the setting, events, and endings of stories in retellings would benefit from work on narrative **text structure**. A child who is not yet representing most letters in inventive spellings and whose miscues bear little resemblance to words he or she is reading would benefit from work on letter sounds.

Interviews

Many of the same questions suggested for use with emergent reader–writers are appropriate for children beyond that stage as well. During classroom interactions, they can be encouraged to talk about what they read, why they read, and how they read. The interview schedule outlined in Exhibit 11.8 can be used by teachers as a source of possible questions to use to collect more specific information about a child's reading interests, habits, and knowledge about reading. A range of interview schedules were consulted in devising the list in Exhibit 11.8 (Atwell, 1987; Goodman, Watson, and Burke, 1987; Lipson and Wixson, 1991).

You will not likely ask any child all these questions in one sitting. Instead, you will think about what you need to know about a particular child and select those questions that might help gather this information. For example, if a child rarely seems to choose books to read independently, you might want to ask some of the questions about attitudes and interests. If a child appears to have few strategies for making meaning as he or she reads, you might want to ask the last four questions in the reading strategies section.

EXHIBIT 11.7

Reading Checklist

Area	Reading strategy	Comments
Positive attitude to reading	___ is able to name favourite books and authors ___ enjoys reading silently in class time ___ engages in extensive independent reading	
Integrates knowledge and text to construct meaning	___ is able to set a purpose for reading ___ is able to predict what a story or text will be about from the title ___ is able to predict what will happen next in a story ___ uses both knowledge and text information to answer inference questions ___ retellings include inferences as well as text information	
Uses story structure to construct meaning	___ is able to answer questions about the setting, characters, events, and ending of stories ___ includes information from setting, events, and ending in retellings of stories ___ retells stories in sequence	

continued

Uses expository text structure to construct meaning	___ is able to answer questions involving main idea, sequence, cause/effect, and comparison/contrast relationships ___ retellings reflect organizational patterns of informational texts (enumeration, cause/effect, sequence, comparison/contrast)	
Uses context cues to identify words	___ oral reading miscues make sense and sound right in relation to prior text ___ gives real word rather than nonsense word responses when reading ___ corrects miscues that do not make sense	
Uses print cues to identify words	___ oral reading miscues look and sound like the words in the text ___ most sounds are represented in inventive spellings ___ identifies words by processing letter groupings, syllables, or words within other words ___ corrects miscues that do not look right	
Integrates context and print cues to identify words	___ most miscues both make sense and sound right ___ corrects most miscues that change the author's meaning	

continued

Reads with automaticity	___ identifies high-frequency words immediately ___ reads fluently and at an appropriate rate ___ completes silent reading assignments in a reasonable time	

Reading Samples

As with emergent readers, you will want to save samples of children's reading throughout the school year to assess growth. Reading logs are one type of information commonly kept in children's reading portfolios. Children keep a list of books they have read during the year, including amount, genre, and level of material being read. Wiseman (1992) suggests recording in the log the date each book was selected and completed, along with the child's comments about the book. These logs help teachers determine children's growth in voluntary reading behaviour.

Another sample of children's reading is their written responses to literature. It is crucial in examining these responses that they be evaluated in terms of the child's ability to relate the text to his or her own life and to reflect on the text. Examples of children's responses to literature as well as interpretations of these responses were provided in Chapter 6. These responses illustrate how children interact with texts rather than their specific use of reading strategies or their level of reading achievement.

Information on strategies and achievement is best gathered by examining children's responses to reading comprehension assignments. Samples of written answers to questions can be included in the child's portfolio periodically throughout the school year. In addition, it is also useful to collect samples of children's oral reading to examine their growth in use of meaning and print cues to identify words. As with young children, running records can be kept of children reading stories from basal texts, books, or passages specifically designed for this purpose. While it is more authentic to gather running records of materials actually being used in the classroom, at times teachers may wish to use informal reading inventories.

Informal Reading Inventories

These consist of a series of word lists and passages at increasing levels of reading difficulty. Children are asked to read these passages both orally and silently and to answer questions about them to assess reading comprehension. Many teachers choose to use informal reading inventories because the passages and questions are all in one place and

EXHIBIT 11.8

Reading Interview

Area	Questions
Interests	• What kinds of things do you like to do in your spare time? • What is your favourite subject at school? Why? • What kinds of books do you like to read? • Name two books that you have read recently that you liked.
Attitudes	• If you could read a story or watch it on television, which would you choose? • How much time do you spend reading each day at home? At school? • How many books do you own? Do you go to the library to get books? • How do you feel about reading?
Knowledge about reading	
Functions of reading	• What is reading? • Why do people read?
Reading strategies	• Think of someone who is a good reader. How do you know he or she is a good reader? • How would you help someone who was having trouble reading? • What do you think about as you read? • What do you do when you are reading and come to a word you don't know? • What do you do when you are reading and something doesn't make sense?

continued

	• What do you do to help you remember what you read (for example, in social studies)? • Do you ever read something over again? Why? • Do you read some things faster than others? Why?
Self-appraisal	• How would you describe yourself as a reader? • Is learning to read easy or hard? Why? • What's the easiest thing about reading for you? What's the hardest thing? • What kind of help do you think you need with your reading?

the teacher does not have to search out a series of books at a range of reading levels and design tasks to assess comprehension of these books. Informal inventories are designed to be administered individually so they are used primarily with children the teacher is puzzled about and needs more information about in order to plan appropriate instruction. A wide range of informal inventories is available, including the *Informal Reading Inventory* (Burns and Roe, 1993), the *Classroom Reading Inventory* (Silvaroli, 1986) and the *Basic Reading Inventory* (Johns, 1991).

Word lists are included on informal reading inventories to estimate the level at which to begin administering reading passages. The level at which children identify all or most of the words is the level to begin at. This ensures that children do not spend time reading passages that are much too easy or much too difficult. The teacher then has the child read passages (both orally and silently) of increasing difficulty until the child is no longer able to identify 90 percent of the words or answer 70 percent of the questions correctly. As the child reads orally, the teacher keeps a running record of oral reading miscues and writes down the child's answers to comprehension questions. The coding system used for taking a running record with emergent readers is also appropriate for use with more independent readers.

Interpreting Informal Reading Inventories

The teacher gets two major types of information from an informal reading inventory: achievement and diagnostic information. The child's level of reading achievement is the highest level at which the child meets the criteria set in the test for **instructional reading level**. Although tests vary, the instructional reading level is generally the level at which the child is able to identify 90 percent or more of the words accurately *and* answer 70 percent or more of the comprehension questions correctly. The child is able to read material independently if word identification and comprehension are close to

100 percent. Material is too difficult for a child if he or she reads with less than 90 percent accuracy *or* 60 percent comprehension. It is important to keep in mind that informal inventories provide only a rough indication of the level of material children can handle. Children may be able to understand more difficult material if it is a topic they know a great deal about or are very interested in. On the other hand, if a topic is unfamiliar, children may have difficulty with a passage designated as being at their instructional reading level.

Two major sources of diagnostic data are available from informal reading inventories: oral reading miscues and question data.

Miscues

Oral reading miscues are analyzed in terms of the same two major **cueing systems** as for emergent readers: meaning and print. The major difference is that the criteria for coding miscues are more stringent. The criteria, as well as examples of miscues of a Grade 4 child, Paul, are in Exhibit 11.9. The passage in this example is from a goal-based **narrative** at the Grade 4 level from the *Qualitative Reading Inventory* (Leslie and Caldwell, 1990).

It is clear from the number of miscues on this passage that fourth-grade material is at Paul's instructional level. When asked to read material at the fifth-grade level, he made well over the acceptable number of miscues. When reading material at his instructional level, he showed that he was able to effectively use both print and **context cues** to predict words that made sense, sounded right, and checked out with the print. He was able to integrate print and knowledge-based cues to construct meaning as he read. Like many good readers, he corrected miscues when they did not make sense. He did not correct his substitution of *for* for *of* because this miscue was consistent with his meaning. It is not surprising that he was able to answer seven of the eight questions asked about this passage.

All children need to learn to use cues both in context and within words as they read. Miscues help teachers determine where to place the instructional focus at any point in time. If children focus almost exclusively on print cues in material at instructional level, they need less attention to cues within words for a while and a heavier focus on using context cues. If their miscues make sense but are not consistent with print cues, they need instruction on strategies for processing cues within words. As soon as children begin to show more effective use of the cueing system that is the focus of instruction, however, it is crucial to provide a balanced program so that children learn to use multiple sources of information to identify unfamiliar words. Paul is showing not only that he is able to use both print and meaning cues but that he can integrate them to construct a message consistent with that intended by the author.

Questions

Question data are examined to determine what types of questions a child is able to answer. If children are successful in answering factual questions, they are able to use text

EXHIBIT 11.9

Oral Reading Miscues of a Grade 4 Boy
(Excerpt from Fourth Reader Passage)

Coding system for miscues

M (meaning-based): miscue makes sense in relation to prior text and the rest of the sentence as the child reads it.

P (print-based): miscue contains half or more of the same letters as the text word.

I (integrative [both print and meaning]): miscue contains half or more of the same letters as the text word and makes sense in relation to prior text and the rest of the sentence.

I (Johnny) John first gathered bags I (for) of apple seeds. He got many of his seeds from farmers who squeezed apples to make a drink called cider. Then, in the spring, he left for the western P (front tire sc) frontier. He planted I (trees) seeds as he went along. Also, he gave them to people who knew how valuable apple trees were.

John walked many miles in all kinds of weather. He had to cross dangerous rivers and find his way through strange forests. Often he was hungry, I (cool) cold and wet. Sometimes he had to hide from unfriendly Indians. His clothes became ragged and torn.

From Lauren Leslie and JoAnne Caldwell, Qualitative Reading Inventory. *New York: HarperCollins, 1990.*

information to construct meaning. If they are successful in answering inferential questions, they are able to integrate their world knowledge with text information to construct meaning as they read.

Children who are able to answer factual but not inferential questions may think reading is a meaning-getting rather than meaning-making enterprise, or they may not know how to use their knowledge along with text to construct meaning. They would benefit from the teaching/learning strategies described in Chapter 7 under integrating knowledge-based and text-based information.

Children who are able to answer inferential questions better than factual ones may be relying too much on their background knowledge to construct meaning. Often, if they're asked to retell what they have read, they will demonstrate limited processing of text information. They would benefit from teaching/learning strategies designed to help children use the structure of narrative and expository texts to construct meaning.

Portfolios and Self-Assessment

All the assessment techniques in this section provide potential material for inclusion in children's reading portfolios. Reading logs are a record of what children have read. Responses to literature give an indication of how they have interacted with literature. Checklists record teacher observations for reflection and program planning. Informal inventories administered at regular intervals throughout the year provide an indication of reading progress. Some portfolios even include the results on standardized reading tests.

One of the arguments put forward for portfolio assessments has been their potential for involving children in the assessment process. This involves much more than a change in how assessment is done, however. Instead, it means making a fundamental change in the power relationships between teachers and children. Children need to participate in decisions not only about what goes into portfolios but about what counts as good reading. Are we prepared to give up our power over assessment to children? Even if we were prepared to do so, it's highly unlikely that administrators, politicians, and parents would let us.

However, we can at least invite children to talk with us about their reading. The kinds of questions included in the self-appraisal section on the reading interview presented in this chapter are a starting point. We can ask children to select some of the reading samples included in their portfolios. We can sit down with them periodically to look at and talk about their reading growth shown in their portfolio samples. The children can be invited to share their portfolios with their parents when they visit the school. When teaching a new reading strategy in the classroom, we can invite children to comment on whether the strategy works for them and why or why not. All these approaches are illustrated in the classroom vignette later in this chapter. However, these possibilities are only the beginning; we need to explore many others as we move toward a more democratic model of assessment.

Writing

Describing Good Writing

One of the greatest problems elementary school teachers face in assessing children's writing is their general lack of vocabulary for describing writing or assessing it. It is difficult for a teacher to describe a child's development in writing if that teacher does not possess explicit knowledge of what constitutes good writing, or what elements of writing might be assessed. At the elementary school level most teachers tend to focus on handwriting and the conventions of the language—the ability to write legibly and use the conventions of capitalization, spelling, and punctuation. There is no one way to evaluate children's writing and generate a mark that represents the child's level of development in writing as a whole.The primary focus of assessment should be on helping children to increase their learning and helping teachers to plan for it.

The publicity given to the deterioration of writing skills in the United States during the 1970s and 1980s led to a plethora of kits, cassettes, programs, and books designed to cure the perceived decline. Writing centres were established and thrived; the Bay Area Writing Project eventually led to the development of writing projects in many parts of the United States and Canada. Wide use of a process approach to writing helped many teachers to understand writing more fully. Yet, although most people have an internalized set of criteria that tells them when they have read a good piece of writing, they might have problems articulating *why* that particular piece could be described as good. The assessment strategies described in this chapter should help to alleviate that problem.

Evaluating or Responding

The method of assessment teachers choose is generally related to the purpose for the assessment and to the teachers' beliefs about their roles as teachers of language.

> *If one seeks to develop only the skills of writing, one chooses a marking scheme focusing on that. But if one is concerned with the growth of individuals, for whom language is a means to that end, then one's scheme of assessment is conceived to perceive that growth and to further it. (Wilkinson, Barnsley, Hanna, and Swan, 1983, 872)*

Searle and Dillon (1980) found that when teachers responded to student writing they focused on form, and their written comments to students consisted mainly of evaluative and instructional points. The teachers in the study generally attempted to correct all the mechanical errors themselves. This indicates that some fifteen years ago teachers did not focus on the meaning and purpose of language, but rather promoted the belief that what a child has to say matters less than how it is said. Since that time there have been enormous changes in the teaching of writing. We now know that the ways in which teachers respond to children's writing shape the children's writing behaviours by giving them indications of teacher expectations. How then can teachers teach good writing through their responses and through their assessment strategies? How do students view writing when responses from the teacher are generally negative and pertain mainly to conventions? "Learned terror" of the act of writing is one response, which can be seen in the apologies most adults make to each other when sharing a piece of writing (even in letters). Short words, short sentences, and short stories are another result. But teachers' responses to writing need not be evaluative. Writing is a creative act, and creativity involves risk-taking. It cannot be promoted in classrooms where errors are counted. In responding to writing, teachers must count the successes, not the failures, in order to encourage language maturation.

How can student writing be assessed so that growth can be recorded, parents can receive helpful and clear information on their children's progress, and students can discover the joy of language and develop as writers?

The assessment of writing ability can be completed through **direct assessment** of written language samples, and through standardized tests. Although objective tests have frequently been used in the past, direct assessment is increasingly being utilized, even in large-scale province-wide or statewide assessments.

Writing Samples

If actual writing samples are used to assess children's written language skills, many troublesome issues still have to be resolved. Writing is not a single skill: **syntax**, organization, and word choice vary according to purpose and audience. **Expressive writing** is writer-oriented—its purpose is to reveal feelings, attitudes, and perceptions. **Expository writing** is subject-oriented: it is meant to explain or present information on a subject. Persuasive writing is audience-oriented: the writer takes a position on a topic and tries to convince others. The stimulus, or prompt, for a writing task also frames the piece of writing and may influence the product considerably.

The development of writing in children progresses from simple to complex, from literal to metaphoric, and from a preoccupation with self to an awareness of the psychological characteristics of others (Wilkinson, Barnsley, Hanna, and Swan, 1983). Children differ in the concepts they have of other people, differences that become more apparent as they mature cognitively. Thus, their stories reflect growth in empathy, social cognition, personal perception, and self-awareness, as well as in language skills. It is therefore possible to see a developmental process in children's writing, and direct assessment focuses on children as communicative beings who are developing their abilities as writers. Taking account of the thinking and feeling involved in creating a story provides useful insights into children's cognitive processes and shows how young writers may use the world of imagination as a means of understanding their own reality. Learning to write is very much like learning to think, for only through writing can we examine the actual meaning of our words and the logic—or lack of it—that leads from one statement to another.

Holistic Scoring

> *Holistic evaluation of writing is a guided procedure for sorting and ranking written pieces. The rater takes a piece of writing and either 1) matches it with another piece in a graded series of pieces or, 2) scores it for prominence of certain features important to that kind of writing or, 3) assigns it a number or letter grade. The placing, scoring, or grading occurs very quickly and impressionistically, after the rater has practiced the procedure with other raters. (Cooper, 1977, 3)*

Such assessment assumes that writing is a complex interaction of many skills, and students are evaluated on what they do well rather than on what they fail to do. This method encourages teachers to focus on the specifics they have in mind for rating essays and stories before reading them. These specifics may include:

a. attention to purpose and audience, and the ability to organize ideas according to the needs of communicating with that audience, whether through poetic, persuasive, expressive, or informative modes

b. attention to the visual and verbal cues of the assignment (for example, "give at least one reason—")

c. developmental capabilities of the students, allowing for the general language characteristics of children of a similar age (for example, the invented spelling of children in the primary grades)

d. constraints of the evaluation situation, that is, the context or setting where the writing takes place; in many evaluative situations, for example, children do not have time to revise, edit, or ask for peer or teacher assistance.

General Impression Marking

This is one of the simplest forms of holistic assessment. The rater scores the paper by deciding where it fits in the range of papers produced for that assignment on that occasion. Although there is no analysis of specific features and no summary of scores, this method has high reliability (Cooper and Odell, 1977) because experienced raters use an implicit list of features in much the same way as classroom teachers. If teachers were to spread out in front of them a set of writing from all the children in their class, written on the same day and on the same topic, it would be fairly clear which were good pieces of writing and which were not. The middle-ranked pieces would be more difficult to arrange in some kind of order, but eventually a teacher would be able to make the decision based on an implicit or internalized set of criteria. This can be facilitated in a school setting by a second teacher working collaboratively on the assessment. On these occasions, the teachers' implicit criteria have to be made explicit as problematic pieces of writing are discussed.

Primary Trait Scoring

Many types of criteria-based scales are used in *holistic scoring*, and these can objectively identify the qualities of a specific type of writing and the levels of attainment by a student. They usually describe four or five levels of writing performance from weakest to strongest for a particular mode. This is often referred to as primary trait scoring since it focuses the rater's attention on just those aspects of a piece of writing relevant to that type of discourse. For example, a writer shows different levels of persuasiveness and audience awareness when writing to a friend than when writing a letter to a government agency (Walter, Kahn, and Johannessen, 1983).

Essay Scale

The essay scale is a series of complete pieces arranged according to quality. At one end of the scale is an exceptionally good example and at the other end, a totally inadequate one. A rater attempts to evaluate a new piece of writing by matching it on the scale with the piece of writing most like it. This is frequently undertaken in large-scale assessment projects, such as those at the state, provincial, or school district level.

Analytic Scales

Analytic scoring breaks the writing performance down into component parts, such as organization, wording, and ideas. It takes longer to accomplish than holistic scoring, but provides more specific information on the strengths and weaknesses of the writing. The list of features assessed may range from four to twelve, with each feature described in some detail and with high, mid, and low points identified and described along a scoring line for each feature.

Criteria-based assessment of writing has been used by the Alberta Department of Education since 1983 in the Grades 3, 6, and 9 provincial tests of written language.

A modified version of these criteria is still used in the provincial tests and has proven especially useful to teachers in developing a vocabulary for discussing and conducting writing assessment, and in developing an explicit sense of what might constitute good writing. In the provincial tests, the students are required to produce a writing sample from a story starter. In recent years the tests have allowed the children a large element of choice and have included planning time and discussion time with peers. The pieces of writing are then assessed according to five criteria: content (plausibility, details); organization (sequencing, closure); sentence structure (type, length); vocabulary (specific, image-creating); and language conventions (capitalization, spelling, and punctuation). The reporting categories of content and organization for Grade 6 are shown in Exhibits 11.10 and 11.11. Each category is scored from INS to five. Below are the Grade 6 descriptors for a piece of writing that approaches the standard of excellence.

Content

- The writer's purpose, whether stated or implied, is established and generally sustained.
- The events and/or actions are appropriate for the context established by the writer.
- Supporting details are specific and generally effective.
- The writing engages and generally holds the reader's interest.

Organization

- The introduction clearly establishes events, characters, and/or setting, and provides direction for the writing.
- Events and/or details are arranged in a purposeful order, and coherence is generally maintained.
- Connections and/or relationships between events, actions, details, and or characters are maintained.
- The ending provides an appropriate finish for events and/or actions.

Sentence Structure

- Sentence structure is generally controlled.
- Sentence type and length are usually effective and varied.

EXHIBIT 11.10

Reporting Category: Content

When marking **Content** appropriate for Grade Level 6 writing, the marker should consider how effectively the writer

- establishes a purpose
- develops a relationship between events and/or actions and his/her established context
- used specific detail
- considers the reader

Meets the Standard of Excellence **5**	• The writer's purpose, whether stated or implied, is clearly established and sustained. • The events and/or actions are consistently appropriate for the context established by the writer. • Supporting details are specific and consistently effective. • The writing captivates and holds the reader's interest and may be lively and/or imaginative.
Approaches the Standard of Excellence **4**	• The writer's purpose, whether stated or implied, is established and generally sustained. • The events and/or actions are appropriate for the context established by the writer. • Supporting details are specific and generally effective. • The writing engages and generally holds the reader's interest.
Clearly Meets the Acceptable Standard **3**	• The writer's purpose, whether stated or implied, is established but may not be sustained. • The majority of the events and/or actions are appropriate for the context established by the writer. • Supporting details are general and may be predictable but are appropriate. • The writing generally holds the reader's attention.

Note: content and organization are weighted to be worth twice as much as the other categories.

continued

Does Not Clearly Meet the Acceptable Standard **2**	• The writer's purpose, whether stated or implied, is vaguely established and may not be sustained. • Some of the events and/or actions are appropriate for the context established by the writer. • Supporting details are few and/or may be repetitive. • The writing does not hold the reader's interest.
Clearly Below the Acceptable Standard **1**	• The writer's purpose may be unclear; if a purpose is stated or implied, it is not sustained. • There are few events and/or actions. • Supporting details are scant. • The writing is confusing and/or frustrating for the reader.
INSUFFICIENT **INS**	• The student has written so little that it is not possible to assess the content.

Reprinted with the permission of the Minister of Education, Province of Alberta, Canada, 1995.

EXHIBIT 11.11

Reporting Category: Organization

When marking **Organization** appropriate for Grade Level 6 writing, the marker should consider how effectively the writer

- introduces the topic/subject
- follows a coherent order
- establishes connections and/or relationships between events, actions, details, and/or characters
- brings closure to the writing

Meets the Standard of Excellence **5**	• The introduction captures the reader's attention, clearly establishes events, character, and/or setting, and provides direction for the writing. • Events and/or details are arranged in a purposeful and effective order, and coherence is maintained.

continued

	• Connections and/or relationships between events, actions, details, and/or characters are consistently maintained. • The ending ties events and/or actions together.
Approaches the Standard of Excellence **4**	• The introduction clearly establishes events, characters, and/or setting, and provides direction for the writing. • Events and/or details are arranged in a purposeful order, and coherence is generally maintained. • Connections and/or relationships between events, actions, details, and/or characters are maintained. • The ending provides an appropriate finish for events and/or actions.
Clearly Meets the Acceptable Standard **3**	• The introduction directly presents information about events, characters, and/or setting. • Events and/or details are arranged in a discernible order, although coherence may falter from time to time. • Connections and/or relationships between events, actions, details, and/or characters are generally maintained. • The ending is predicable and/or contrived, and may not be connected to events and/or actions.
Does Not Clearly Meet the Acceptable Standard **2**	• The introduction provides little information. • Arrangement of events and/or details is not clearly discernible, and coherence falters frequently. • Connections and/or relationships between events, actions, details, and/or characters are unclear, and/or inconsistent or missing. • The ending is predictable and/or contrived, and may not be connected to events and/or actions.
Clearly Below the Acceptable Standard **1**	• The introduction may be confusing. • The arrangement of events and/or details is haphazard and incoherent. • Connections and/or relationships between events, actions, details, and/or characters are missing.

continued

	• The ending, if present, is unconnected to the events and/or actions.
INSUFFICIENT **INS**	• The writing has been awarded an INS for **Organization**.

Reprinted with the permission of the Minister of Education, Province of Alberta, Canada, 1995.

Vocabulary

- Specific words and expressions show some evidence of careful selection.
- Words are used accurately and often effectively.

Conventions

- The writing has few errors in spelling, punctuation, and grammar.
- Proportion of error to length and complexity of the response must be considered.

These criteria are used below in the analysis of the following excerpt from a piece of writing by a Grade 6 student. The piece is entitled *Zulu*.

> *They came over to me talking in soft mumbling sounds that I couldn't understand. I backed into the corner of the stall and watched as they brought out a small harness. The creature reached out a hand and stroked my neck.*
>
> *"He's a big one Alana, are ya still sure you want 'im?" One asked, odviously refering to me.*
>
> *"Yes, the bigger they are the higher they jump."*
>
> *The first speaker stepped forward and held out the soft leather thing, which they called a halter, for me to smell. It had no scent but I drew my head back and turned away. I looked for my mother, she was watching, but did nothing. The one they called Alana took the halter and slipped it over my head. I shook my head, not liking this thing tight on my face, I ran around the stall and rubbed my face on the rough wood of the wall.*
>
> *"He's a spirited one alright." Henry said (The first one)*
>
> *"Yeah, I don't intend to break that." Alana commented*
>
> *"What are you going to call him?"*
>
> *"Well his sire is Zulu Royaal and then his mother is Gotoit, so his name is Go to it Zulu. A pretty good name I think."*

Henry came over, took hold of the halter and rubbed my ears. His hands were strong and gentle, I now knew why my mother was kind to these creatures.

A week passed. I got used to the halter and lead rope. I saw Henry and Alana each day. I asked my mother about them. She told me that Alana was her master and mine too. She said that I was to do what Henry and Alana wished me do and never to kick or bite. They have big plans for you, she would say, you will become great one day, till then you must do as they say.

When they came into the stall I could tell that there was something different about them. Not as happy. Alana came over to me right away and rubbed my nose and ears. I sniffed at her pockets as I had seen my mother do. She patted my side and slipped the halter over my head. I had grown much stronger over the last few days and loved to play tug'a'war with the shank. I looked at my mother, who I still would not move far from, Henry had put a halter on her too. I knew something was different today.

Content. This piece of writing demonstrates a strong voice. Written as a first-person **narrative**, it has details and description that create an immediate engagement with the central character, a horse. The vivid description is enhanced by the use of dialogue. Rather than telling the reader that Zulu is a large horse, the writer demonstrates it in Henry's comment: "*He's a big one, Alana, are you still sure you want 'im?*" The reader is also forewarned of coming events through Alana's response: "*Yes, the bigger they are the higher they jump.*" The entire excerpt from the story is focused on the events in the stall, and the early breaking and introduction of the harness to the young horse. There are no extraneous details, no irrelevant content. The reader's interest is captivated and sustained.

Organization. The events of the story are arranged in a coherent sequence and are clearly connected, creating a cohesive piece of writing. The unfolding of events reveals the horse's character and situation.

Sentence structure. The sentence structure is mature and effective, with a variety of sentence lengths and types; from coordination (*I backed into the corner of the stall and watched as they brought out a small harness*), to subordination (*The first speaker stepped forward and held out the soft leather thing, which they called a halter, for me to smell*). There are no sentence fragments or run-on sentences.

Vocabulary. The vocabulary is varied and colourful. Words such as *mumbling, creative, scent,* and *spirited* create vivid images and add to the engagement the reader feels.

Conventions. In this piece of writing, the conventions of written language are generally a high standard. Quotation marks are used appropriately, as are question marks and periods. Paragraphs are well formed and the indentation of paragraphs and direct speech is formatted correctly. Occasionally **dialect** is used and appropriate punctuation is used to mark this (as in *'im*). There are numerous commas where periods or semicolons would have been more appropriate. This is an aspect of writing that has not yet been mastered by this student (*I looked for my mother, she was watching, but did nothing*), yet it is also connected to the reading the student has done. This student's favourite book was *Black Beauty* by Anna Sewell, originally published in 1877. *Black Beauty* uses a more old-fashioned style, with the frequent use of commas to break up the text, rather than periods or semicolons.

Process or Performance Assessment

The previous strategies have dealt with the assessment of written products only. The shift in teaching writing, however, from a product to a process orientation has created a similar shift in assessment strategies. Educators now realize that if children's writing is to be assessed, then an essential part of that assessment must consist of observations of the general writing behaviours of children, not just their written products. One of the most thorough and useful guides to this type of assessment is in the *English Profiles Handbook*, published by the Department of School Education in Victoria, Australia (1991).

In this book (1991, 65), nine "bands" of writing development have been identified to cover Grades 1 through 9. These bands range from a) *Knows that you say something when you write. Is curious about print and beginning to find out what it means* through e) *Able to plan, organize, and polish own writing. Can write in paragraphs using vocabulary and grammar suited to the topic. Writes convincing stories* to i) *is a skilled writer, able to produce text in many forms. Writing can be powerful and evocative.* Each band is then described in more detail, with suggestions as to how data can be collected through writing conferences, writing sessions, discussion with parents, samples in writing folders, written conversations, publishing and presenting writing, proofreading, editing, and taking notes. A collection of observations about each child can be organized under the headings of "what the writer does," "what the writing shows," and "use of writing." A companion volume and a most useful book to have in any professional library is *The English Language Framework P-10*, which clearly outlines growth points in writing.

Stephen Leppard undertook a similar endeavour in Canada, though his *Writing Continuum* (1991) goes only from kindergarten to Grade 3. A copy of the continuum for each child should be passed along from one class to the next as the child progresses through the grades. Each assessment period is noted in a different colour of highlighting pen. The list of descriptors can be read, and any that pertain to an individual child at that time can be highlighted. Thus, over a period of time, the child's progress is revealed as the different colours flow through the continuum. An excerpt from the continuum is in Exhibit 11.12. The continuum is easy to use and convenient for teachers, since the observations have only to be recorded by highlighting certain characteristics. Yet these characteristics are essential features of what it means to be a developing writer.

EXHIBIT 11.12

Individual Writing Stages

1. Take-off Stage	2. Independent Writing
• Can write name. • Excitement about writing. • Wants to write (stories, lists, letters or ideas). • Need not rely on patterning. • Invented (temporary) spelling becomes closer to standard. • Writing is more meaning-centered. • Can pick out words that are spelled incorrectly. • Understands that each letter is a representation of a sound (Phonetic understanding). • Use of characters is moving closer to standard form. • Sound correspondence more complete. • Sound features of words are represented according to the child's hearing and articulation (leads to omission of pre-consonant nasal) e.g., *NUBRS—numbers*. • Realizes that print can conserve a thought statement permanently.	• Write stories with some sense of story structure. • Awareness of grammar and language conventions. • Spelling is near standard OR spelling deteriorates because more complex words are being used. • Understands that vowels are included in every word. • Understands that vowels are included in every syllable. • Vowels may be used inappropriately, e.g., *MEAK—make*. • Developing a sense of punctuation. • Developing an ability and desire to self-edit some corrections (spelling, simple sentence structure) • Written work can begin to be carried over, or continued, the next day. • May begin to understand the inconsistencies within the English language.

From Program Continuity: The Positive Link. © ACCESS NETWORK. *Reprinted with permission.*

McKenzie and Tompkins (1984) developed a writing process checklist that covers all the phases of writing, shown in Exhibit 11.13. This checklist can be modified by individual teachers to reflect aspects of the writing process that they believe are important, or that better meet the needs of the children in their classrooms.

Portfolio Assessment

Portfolio assessment is one form of process or performance evaluation. The aim is not to take one piece of writing in isolation, but to look at a collection of children's writings in many forms and voices. A portfolio might include stories, poems, letters, journal entries, lists, idea trees or semantic maps, responses to literature, book reviews, artwork associated with the language arts, puppets, and writing from across the curriculum. In this way, children can see their writing as more than separate pieces in isolation from each other. Portfolios also give children the opportunity to self-evaluate in choosing what they wish to put into the portfolio. A portfolio is not the same as a writing folder. A writing folder contains work-in-progress, some finished work, and topics that might be the bases for future pieces. A portfolio should be carefully put together to show what a student can do. The portfolio might be a flat-bottomed paper bag that the child has decorated, or it might be a concertina folder that expands to accommodate objects other than sheets of paper. Published books and reports might go into the portfolio, as well as comments from peers who have read or heard pieces written by the student.

Farr and Tone (1994) provide many suggestions for developing and assessing portfolios. Among them is that teachers look at the volume of work in the portfolio, the interest and attitudes of the writers, and of course the development and growth of the writing. Here the criteria outlined earlier in this section on content, organization, vocabulary, sentence structure, and conventions will be useful. Farr and Tone also suggest how teachers can use portfolios to aid them in their instruction, as well as assess the portfolio. An example of one teacher's comments is shown in Exhibit 11.14.

A general assessment of the portfolio can also be made using the organizational outline adopted by the Ministry of Education in Victoria, Australia. An example of how this might be done follows.

> **What the writer does:** *Shaun edits work to a point where others can read it. He corrects common spelling errors, punctuation, and grammatical errors, especially when he reads his pieces aloud to peers. He develops ideas into paragraphs and uses a dictionary or thesaurus to extend and check his writing vocabulary.*
>
> **What the writing shows:** *Sentences have ideas that flow. Paragraphs have a cohesive structure. Shaun shows the ability to argue and persuade. The messages in his expository and persuasive writing can be identified by others, but some-*

EXHIBIT 11.13 Checklist of Writing Processes

Student	Dates					
Prewriting Can the student identify the specific audience to whom he/she will write?						
Does this awareness affect the choices the student makes as he/she writes?						
Can the student identify the purpose of the writing activity?						
Does the student write on a topic that grows out of his/her own experience?						
Does the student engage in rehearsal activities before writing?						
Drafting Does the student write rough drafts?						
Does the student place a greater emphasis on content than on mechanics in the rough drafts?						
Revising Does the student share his/her writing in conferences?						
Does the student participate in discussions about classmates' writing?						
In revising, does the student make changes to reflect the reactions and comments of both teacher and classmates?						
Between first and final drafts, does the student make substantive or only minor changes?						
Editing Does the student proofread his/her own papers?						
Does the student help proofread classmates' papers?						
Does the student increasingly identify his/her mechanical errors?						
Publishing Does the student publish his/her writing in an appropriate form?						
Does the student share this finished writing with an appropriate audience?						

From G. Tompkins, Teaching Writing: Balancing Process and Product, *2nd ed. New Jersey: Merrill, p. 211. Reprinted with permission. Originally published in L. McKenzie and G. Tompkins, "Evaluating Students' Writing: A Process Approach,"* Journal of Teaching Writing, *3, 201–202.*

EXHIBIT 11.14

What teacher notices in portfolio	What that suggests
Hillary has written comparing her little brother to the little brother in Judy Blume's *The Pain and the Great One.*	She likes stories that relate fairly directly to things that are happening in her life.
There is little fluency and connection in pieces of writing in Keith's portfolio.	There is very little evidence that Keith thinks much about a topic before he begins writing.
This fifth-grade boy reads one comic book after another and does not record them all on his logs. Most are the funny type; many are about Garfield.	I will look for some humorous stories about cats for him to read—perhaps with a character as ornery as Garfield.
Anders has a note attached to two mysteries he has written, saying they are his favourites. He also has indicated on his log that an adventure story he wrote is his best because "it is exciting." There is not a large amount of writing in the portfolio, though.	I need to develop more opportunities for Anders to write. The adventure is a good story; perhaps if he shared it with some fellow students and saw how they enjoyed it, he would be encouraged.
Tad doesn't write a lot, but he draws well and his classmates consider him the best artist in the class. His journal, which is spotty, is mainly about sports heroes. He also writes reviews about scary movies he has seen.	I will ask Tad if he wants to be the sports editor on the next issue of the class newspaper. He could also illustrate one of his friend Adam's stories and perhaps write a sequel to it. I will see if he might like to read *Joe Montana and Jerry Rice* by Richard J. Brenner and the mystery *Is Anybody There?* by Eve Bunting. Another book I can recommend to him is *Scary Stories to Chill Your Bones* by Alvin Schwartz. He could review the ones he reads for the paper and/or for the bulletin board.

continued

Heriyadi's story "A Pizzaman's Adventure" is a string of events that happen to a delivery person. It uses the same character names as in his story "The City Street." Both of these stories have stringy plots but are very rich in details that build and build offering the reader a complete picture of the character.	There is keen evidence that Heriyadi is thinking about what he writes and its impact on his reader. It's as if he keeps wanting to ensure that the picture is really complete enough for his viewers to see it as he does.
There are no obvious sources for Benny's writing about bats and Thanksgiving. There are numerous accurate details about bats. He details the familiar feast in describing Thanksgiving.	Benny appears to have used background knowledge in writing.
The student wrote "Ghost Story" about witches and cats because it was Halloween and he wanted something appropriate. He also has many cats at home.	The student uses familiar things.
Harold's "Snow Day" is about sledding, eating snow, and building a snowman. It ends with a question asking reader's what they remember about snowy days	He seems to be very audience-conscious in this piece. He anticipates that the things he likes about snow will also be what the audience likes, but he has to ask to check it out.

From Portfolio and Performance Assessment: Helping Students Evaluate their Progress as Readers and Writers *by Roger Farr, Bruce Tone, © 1994 by Harcourt Brace & Co. Reprinted by permission of the publisher.*

times information is omitted. Brief passages are written with clear meaning, accurate spelling, and appropriate punctuation. Shaun can shift appropriately from first to third person in his writing. He consistently uses the correct tense in his writing. He uses compound sentences with conjunctions. His vocabulary is appropriate for a familiar audience such as peers, younger children, or adults, but he occasionally chooses an inappropriate word. Shaun has a consistent handwriting style, and when using the word processor, he uses a variety of fonts and print styles appropriate for the task.

Use of writing: *Shaun creates characters from his imagination and makes appropriate use of narrative and other forms of writing. He writes properly sequenced narratives with convincing settings.*

Inside **the Classroom**

Robert Piccott, a Grade 6 teacher at Michael Wallace School in Dartmouth, Nova Scotia, describes how he uses portfolio assessment.

I use portfolio assessment in my classroom for many reasons. It assists me in evaluating student progress, but most importantly, it challenges students to research their own learning. The children keep a photocopy box, which they use to house their portfolios. These boxes are divided into subject areas. Each week we have a portfolio update time, when students are asked to select from their works and add to their portfolio. I developed a form that the children must complete before including selections in the portfolio. I also include other reading and writing inventories, which the children re-do from time to time so they can assess how their reading and writing behaviours are changing. Each box has a table on the cover showing all the different activities we do in our classroom. I ask the students to try to add a wide variety of items to their portfolios, and they use the table on the cover as a guide to insure they are doing this.

The children include only those items they feel are their best work. They may include anything, so long as they can justify why they chose it. Periodically I conference with each student to help them reflect and set goals for the coming weeks.

Twice each year I conduct parent–teacher–student conferences that last between thirty minutes and one hour. The onus is on the child to demonstrate progress through discussion of the work in the portfolio. At this time, we set goals for the coming months. These goals are specific in nature and based on what the student feels she or he needs to work on. The student must identify an assessment component so we can know how he or she has moved toward fulfilling the goals. Highly positive in nature, these conferences are a time to celebrate student-perceived successes. Again, I supply the students with a four-page handout that is a basis for discussion.

The children also keep a videotape as part of their portfolios. We do a lot of oral discussion and presenting in the classroom. I have access to a full-size video camera, which I use to tape each student on a regular basis. I ask children to review the videos periodically and write about what they see. For example, I may ask them to fill out a checklist on public speaking while they view a particular session. They are asked to write about what they do well and discuss what they can improve upon for the next

continued

public speaking session. Involving the children in their own assessment makes it more meaningful to them, and as a result, they are more willing to act upon their observations.

Through discussion, writing, and reflecting, portfolio assessment helps children become better thinkers and communicators. More important is the fact that they learn to take responsibility for their own learning.

The last sentence captures the essence of portfolio assessment. It is not something teachers do to children but rather with them. Portfolio assessment in Robert Piccott's classroom is a reflection of holistic, constructive language learning and teaching in action.

Reporting to Parents

With all of these asssessment methods at hand, a question that continues to challenge teachers is how to most effectively report student progress to parents. Parents have a right to know how their children are progressing in school, and they generally *want* to know. Report cards have changed greatly in the past fifteen years, and in addition, an increased range of alternatives to the report card are now being used. These include parent-teacher-student conferences, portfolios to demonstrate student achievement, and the use of student journals and anecdotal notes to show a record of student performance. Many of these strategies are used in conjunction with the more formal report card.

A number of issues arise to complicate the process of reporting to parents. For example, do parents want to know what their children can do, or do they want to know how their children stand in relation to the other students in the class? What is the role of effort and persistence with learning tasks, and what is the role of individual accomplishment and growth over a period of time? Do we regard reporting as the equivalent of creating a league table (with all the repercussions that has for children who turn out to be at the bottom), or do we consider it a matter of focusing on the development and learning needs of the individual children?

In general, *how* we assess children's growth reflects what we value. What is tested, recorded, and reported, in the end, becomes the focus of teaching. When teachers know that persuasive writing will be tested on the Grade 6 provincial achievement tests, then obviously they will teach persuasive writing. Not a bad thing. But what happens if the *emphasis* in testing is on grammar or spelling? Some people would think that, too, is not a bad thing, but we, along with many other educators, believe that it would not be helpful to the balanced nature of a language program, or to the development of children's writing skills.

Report Cards

Report cards usually require the teacher to make a judgment about the child's performance and rate it with a letter grade, number, or percentage. Most report cards also have room for teacher comments, and some also have a separate space for a grade for effort. Report cards are usually sent home three times each year in the elementary grades. Sometimes report cards are distributed to the children (especially the first one of the year) only when parents attend a parent–teacher–student conference at the school. This ensures that parents fully understand the report card, and that they also see evidence of what their child is doing in school. Parents find this much more helpful than simply receiving the report card at home in an informational vacuum.

Teachers accumulate data about the children throughout the weeks of schooling. A file might be kept on each child with notes about her or his progress. Samples of writing, reading checklists, and other such instruments can be kept in the file. At reporting time, the teacher must convert this information into a grading system. Most teachers struggle with this task for a long time. How do we best represent the efforts of children in their schooling? There is no simple and straightforward answer to this question, and most teachers find their own way to amalgamate the data. The problem, of course, is that descriptive data have to be converted to a numerical grading system. What does a percentage mark mean? If a child gets 75 percent in reading, what does it mean? A parent will know that 75 percent is a better mark than 60 percent but neither mark shows what a child can or cannot do, nor do they reflect individual student growth over time. Obviously, report cards need to be accompanied by other more descriptive reporting methods, as mentioned earlier, in order to have much value to parents.

Student-Led Conferences

A recent development in reporting to parents is the student-led conference. Here, the students are in charge, selecting the material to show the parents, and explaining what these materials mean in terms of the children's progress. Obviously, the teacher plays a crucial role in preparing the children and materials for the conference. The teacher must ensure that children are well prepared, have selected appropriate materials to share, and can say why these materials reflect their growth and achievement.

Portfolios

If portfolios are kept on an ongoing basis, then the conference will be much easier to facilitate. Student learning logs and journals can also be used to demonstrate a child's learning. Tests, special projects, and any other relevant materials can be put into the portfolio, and a selection of material from it can be used in the parent–child conference. Parents do not need to see everything their child has done. Students will have taken some work home on a daily or weekly basis before report time. Material selected from the portfolio is chosen for a particular reason, some of it by the child and some by the child and teacher together. Hopefully, the combination of report card, portfolio, and teacher–parent–student conference will give the parents a clear picture of what their children are accomplishing in school and what the children can successfully do as well as what they need in order to learn most effectively.

Chapter Summary

The major goal of language learning assessment is to improve instruction in order to maximize children's language growth. Two major types of assessment tools are used. Standardized tests measure a child's achievement in relation to others, and the primary purpose of this type of assessment is accountability. However, other information is needed to serve as a basis for daily planning, and informal techniques are widely employed for this purpose. There are four major types of informal assessment: observation, interviews, samples of work, and children's self-assessment. The focus of this assessment is on what children do as they talk, read, and write.

The assessment of oral communication relies on the ability of the teacher to listen to children and to talk with them. Most assessment strategies are descriptive and depend upon the teacher catching the salient features of the child's language in use. Since oral language is immediate, teachers can best observe it by being perceptive to the intentions of the students and the fluency and clarity with which children articulate their ideas, needs, and feelings. Recording these features in a checklist form is probably the most helpful way for teachers to complete an oral language assessment in the classroom. The checklist can then be used to create opportunities to enhance individual oral communication, and develop awareness among the children of what they need to do in order to be understood and to understand what others are saying to them.

We constantly observe young children as they interact with print, and when we want a more organized record of their emergent literacy development, a checklist can be helpful. By organizing the checklist according to learning contexts in the classroom, we directly link assessment and instruction. Interviews of both parents and children provide information on children's literacy experiences at home and on their understanding of why and how people read. More specific information is obtained by giving children a storybook and asking them to demonstrate their understanding of such concepts as how the book works, the importance of print, and the terms *letter* and *word*. Samples of children's reading and writing also provide important clues to their literacy development. Their early writing attempts are examined in relation to both form (e.g., drawing, scribbling, letters) and function. It is more difficult to collect samples of children's emergent reading, but running records can be taken to provide permanent records of their reading. The child reads orally and the teacher notes what the child says and does. These records are analyzed to describe children's use of picture, print, and meaning cues as they interact with print.

As with emergent readers, checklists and interviews are used to assess how children are using print-based and knowledge-based cues to construct meaning as they read. Reading logs are a record of what children have read, and response journals provide an indication of how children interpret and react to literature. Samples of children's oral and silent reading are collected on informal reading inventories or as children engage in daily reading in the classroom. Examining answers to comprehension questions and oral reading miscues reveals further information on children's use of print-based and knowledge-based cues as they read.

The assessment of writing is an area of evaluation that needs to be explored by classroom teachers in their day-to-day work with students, since teachers can adapt methods to meet their own classroom needs. If, indeed, direct and standardized evaluation techniques measure different tasks, then we need to focus increasingly on assessing children's writing itself and not on the peripheral skills of recall and recognition.

The focus of assessment in children's writing must be on children as developing writers and on the process of writing, as well as on the product and the mechanical skills required. Just as writing skills can be learned effectively in context, they can also be evaluated in context. As teachers, we must facilitate rather than judge student writing, emphasizing process as much as finished product and giving constant feedback. We can encourage children to write evaluative comments on their own papers to promote reflection and growth, and through this to develop a sense of an imagined external audience, and of themselves as both writer and audience. Process or performance evaluation ensures that the teacher's response to a piece of writing will be appropriate to its type, reasonably comprehensive, and concerned with substantive matters, that is, with communication and quality of language use.

A real challenge to teachers is how to most effectively report children's progress in language learning to parents. Report cards have changed and many alternative ways of reporting to parents are now being used in conjunction with the formal report card. Student-led conferences and sharing information in portfolios are two ways to help parents understand what their children can do and what they need to learn most effectively.

Selected Professional Resources

Alberta Education. (1994). *Information Bulletin: Grade Six English Language Arts 1994–95.* Edmonton, Alberta

Since 1984, the Student Evaluation Branch of Alberta Education has put together an annual booklet outlining the assessment formats and standards used that year for evaluating writing. The booklets include the story starter or prompt for the writing task, and the instructions teachers are to give students as the task is begun. Booklets are also available for Grades 3 and 9.

British Columbia Ministry of Education. (1988). *Enhancing and Evaluating Oral Communication in the Primary Grades: Teacher's Resource Package.* Victoria, B.C.: British Columbia Ministry of Education.

These materials were designed to provide a comprehensive resource for teachers, combining background information with specific, practical strategies. Resource packages are also available for the intermediate and secondary grades. The packages can be used to assist teachers in planning and monitoring oral language learning across the curriculum, in making decisions about the oral language development of their students, in planning instructional strategies, and in developing evaluation formats.

Centre for Language in Primary Education. (1988). *The Primary Language Record: Handbook for Teachers.* Markham, Ont.: Pembroke Publishers Ltd.

This handbook was developed in England to provide administrators with information about a child's work, to inform parents about their child's progress, and give teachers the information they need on a daily basis to plan language arts instruction.Various informal techniques are included, and both parents and children are involved in the assessment process.

Rhodes, L.K. (1993). *Literacy Assessment: A Handbook of Instruments.* Portsmouth, NH: Heinemann.

Rhodes pulls together informal assessment tools from a wide range of sources, including interview schedules, checklists, miscue analysis, self-assessments, and observation schedules, and focusing on emergent literacy, reading, and writing.

Glossary

Aesthetic response is a term coined by Louise Rosenblatt to describe the enjoyment or appreciation a reader feels while reading a text. An aesthetic response is not concerned with comprehension, word meanings, recall, or learning, but with the deep personal engagement of reader and text. Aesthetic responses are not necessarily pleasurable; some texts can be deeply moving and cause stress or discomfort rather than pleasure, but this is still an aesthetic response.

Automaticity is the ability to carry out a complex act rapidly and without conscious awareness or control. An important characteristic of automaticity is that an individual can perform a complex skill or act while at the same time performing another that may not be automatic. As readers become proficient and are able to identify most of the words in texts automatically, they are able to direct their mental resources to the construction of meaning. Most experts feel that children need to engage in extensive reading to achieve automaticity.

Basal reading series is a set of materials for teaching reading and language arts. These series generally consist of teacher guides, student anthologies, workbooks, and supplemental materials such as assessment materials, big books, correlated trade books, audiovisual aids, and computer software. Initially, basal series focused almost exclusively on reading, but in recent years, they have included other areas of language arts as well.

Basalization occurs when a trade book (i.e., published literature) is treated in a classroom in the same way as a basal reader. Trade books have different lessons to teach children than do basal readers. The objective of a basal reading series is to teach children how to read, and so a basal reading series is usually accompanied by sets of activities and suggestions for use with children. The objective of working with trade books is to teach children how to become readers. The ways in which texts work, and the enormous variety of text styles and formats become apparent to readers of trade books. The essence of working with trade books is that children enjoy the reading experience and learn about the vast range of books available, and the delight that reading can produce.

Challenged books are ones that groups or individuals have tried to have removed from the shelves of libraries, especially in schools. Not all challenges result in the removal of a book. Specific procedures are usually followed in dealing with a challenge to a book, and a committee of parents and teachers usually make the final decision about whether or not a book should be removed from a school library.

Classification of dramatic forms is based on the way drama is implemented: as part of dramatic play, as a way of interpreting text, as part of a performance for an audience, or as a way of creating a context for learning. Dramatic play, drama-as-interpretation of literature, contextual drama, and drama as theatre make different demands on students and teachers.

Constructive theory refers to reading and writing of texts as acts of construction in which individuals use their knowledge to build or make meaning. Texts are viewed as providing cues to possible meanings rather than as containing meaning themselves. Readers are viewed as active meaning makers rather than passive receivers of meaning, and because of variations in background knowledge, they construct variable meanings of the same text.

Context cues are knowledge and linguistic cues that help to construct meaning when reading. Linguistic cues involve both syntactic (grammar or word order) and semantic (meaning) aspects of language. When children use context cues, they make predictions and monitor their reading in terms of what sounds right and makes sense.

Critical literacy goes beyond providing students with conventional reading and writing skills to equipping them to critically examine how written language reflects power structures and inequalities. Temple refers to this as reading against the grain. Written language is shaped by how power is distributed in society. Critical literacy is seen as a necessary step in bringing about social change.

Cueing systems are the three systems of semantics, syntax, and grapho-phonics that are used by readers and writers to make meaning from printed symbols. Pictures, diagrams, charts, and so on also act as cues for readers to construct meaning. However, the term "cueing systems" usually refers to the text-based systems mentioned here.

Contextual drama often requires the teacher to work in role and to facilitate the drama from within the context. Rather than acting out a story with a defined beginning, middle, and end, this form of drama is more concerned with creating dramatic contexts within which teacher and students explore themes, issues, and relationships. As in dramatic play, the participants construct the meaning of the dramatic situation as opposed to re-presenting the ideas of an author or poet. Contextual drama has the spontaneous appearance of drama-as-play, but unlike it, contextual drama is carefully structured by the teacher to help students achieve new insights and understanding.

Cursive writing is handwriting where the letters are connected to each other with a continuous flow from one stroke to another. The most prevalent form of handwriting today is a combination of printing and cursive writing, with printed uppercase letters and cursive lowercase letters.

Dialect is a variety of a spoken language that is spoken in a geographic region or by members of a social class. Every dialect has distinctive patterns, rules, and features. Regional dialects are much less pronounced now than they were fifty years ago, but speech in the southeastern part of the United States, the north of England, the east coast of Australia, and maritime Canada are examples of dialects that remain distinct. The advent of radio, television, and movies has brought a more standard version of spoken language into our homes and schools.

Dialectic journals are learning journals that help children clarify ideas and develop new understandings. As they write for understanding, children reflect on, reshape, and redraft what they know. All areas of the curriculum (e.g., mathematics, science) can serve as the focus of children's writing in dialectic journals.

Direct assessment occurs when a sample of writing is used as a basis for writing assessment. Direct assessment takes longer to complete than indirect assessment (which consists of multiple-choice and short-answer questions that can be machine scored), and is more open to subjective judgment, but it is generally agreed that it is the only way to authentically assess a learner's writing ability.

Discourse is a linguistics term used to describe a continuous stretch of spoken or written language longer than one sentence. Frequently, *discourse* is reserved for spoken language and the term *text* for written language. Discourse is also used to refer to specific topics or types of language (e.g., the discourse of high-finance). Discourse can also be perceived as process, and text as product.

Dramatic forms include storytelling, puppetry, choric speech, choric drama, readers' theatre, dramatization, and story theatre (see classification of dramatic forms).

Efferent response is a term coined by Louise Rosenblatt to describe a response to literature where the intent is to focus upon what can be learned, observed, and taken away from the reading. Focused on gaining information, an efferent response is at the opposite end of the continuum from an aesthetic response.

Emergent literacy is a term developed during the early 1980s to refer to the literacy development of young children. Sulzby defines emergent literacy as the reading and writing concepts, attitudes, and behaviours that precede and develop into conventional literacy. Emergent literacy begins early in children's lives at home, involves interactions with print, and is part of, rather than separate from, reading and writing development.

Environmental print is print in the home and community, such as on McDonald's signs and cereal boxes. The term is also used to refer to print in the classroom such as labels, signs, calendars, charts, and lists used to organize the room.

Expressive writing is a term used by James Britton to describe one of the three voices of writing (the others being poetic and transactional). Expressive writing is found in diaries, journals, and personal letters, where the writer's intent is to share personal points of view, ideas, thoughts, and questions. Expressive writing aims to communicate the personal identity of the writer.

Expository writing is a form of writing that provides information, detailed explanations, and judgments, along with supporting examples. It may be persuasive or argumentative writing.

Genre refers to the different linguistic forms and functions of various texts. Narrative is different in form and function than expository text, which is different again from persuasive or descriptive text. Genre is also used to refer to categories of literature such as high fantasy and contemporary realistic fiction. Each of these meets different functions, and uses a variety of different forms to achieve the intentions of the text.

Grammar is an ambiguous term that has been largely replaced today by the term *syntax*. However, where grammar is used, it refers to three distinct perspectives on language: 1) **systemic-functional grammar** is a description of the choices made by language users based on context and intention in order to create meaning (e.g., Halliday's work); 2) **generative-transformational grammar** is a description of how language actually works as a process and is based on language universals (e.g., Chomsky's work); 3) and **prescriptive grammar** focuses on the rules of language and how language *should* work. Where most grammar taught in the first part of this century was prescriptive (frequently dealing with inappropriate usage as in *seed* and *saw*, most grammar taught today is descriptive and functional, and more like syntax.

Grapho-phonics refers to the print–sound relationship of text. **Graphic cues** generally include letters, letter clusters, words, and parts of words. **Phonics** refers to the relationships between graphic cues and sounds. Grapho-phonic cues are one of the cueing systems that help readers to identify words as they read. The reader identifies words by relating speech sounds to letters and letter clusters.

Heuristics—sometimes used to refer to educated guesses—are a process of discovery through exploration. M.A.K. Halliday labelled one of the seven functions of language he identified as being heuristic. Some instructional methodology is based on heuristics in an attempt to have learners make discoveries for themselves, and thus be more likely to have a more meaningful learning experience than by simply being told.

High fantasy usually involves a quest, elements of the mystical or magical, time travel, and time warps, and frequently takes place in a fictional setting and with a fictional language (e.g., *A Wizard of Earthsea* by Ursula LeGuin and *The Dark Is Rising* by Susan Cooper). High fantasy is based on mythology (frequently Celtic), and can be difficult for elementary school children to read if they are not introduced to it in the middle grades and if they do not have some familiarity with mythology.

Historical fiction is set in a specific place and time in the past. It requires a great deal of research, descriptive detail, and authentic language to be credible. Good historical fiction will be both an aesthetic and an efferent reading experience. The reader will learn history from it, and will also appreciate and identify with the lives and concerns of the characters.

Holistic scoring is assessing writing according to a set of criteria that are either explicitly stated or implicitly required (as in general impression marking), and which provide an overall impression of the piece. The writing has to be read and responded to quickly, and many features of the writing must be kept in mind at once. Holistic scoring is largely a matter of ranking and sorting. Holistic scoring does not focus on just one aspect of writing as do some other scoring procedures.

Instructional reading level is the level of reading instruction that a child needs in order to make maximum progress learning to read. The material must be just difficult enough to help children develop reading strategies with the support of instruction. On an informal reading inventory, this is the highest level at which a child is able to accurately identify 90 percent of the words and answer 70 percent of the comprehension questions.

Integration is the organization of language arts into a unified curriculum so that reading, writing, speaking, and listening are taught together rather than separately. Another level of integration involves teaching and learning language arts in other subject areas. A third level involves integration of experiences inside and outside of school.

Intertextual refers to the cues readers (and writers) use to relate one text with another. Each time we read a book we establish connections with others we have read. *The Jolly Postman* by Janet and Allen Ahlberg is a text that depends heavily upon intertextuality. Other texts are much less explicit. When reading Cora Taylor's book *The Doll*, the reader might see intertextual relationships with *A Handful of Time* by Kit Pearson, and other time-slip fantasies. *The Doll* might also create intertextual connections for the reader with many other events, books, or poems that relate to the characters, theme, setting, style, or plot of the book. It is largely through intertextual connections that we become better readers and continue that growth throughout our lives.

Invented spelling is the child's first attempts at transcribing spoken language into print symbols, before learning the conventions of standard spelling. Children pay particular attention to the sounds of language, and their first writing reflects this.

Literacy is a term generally associated with reading and writing but has been defined in many different ways. **Basic literacy** is the ability to read and write. **Functional literacy** is frequently defined as those reading and writing skills needed by people to do everyday tasks such as write cheques and read instructions on a medicine bottle. **Critical literacy** goes beyond conventional reading and writing to an awareness of how written language reflects power and inequalities in society.

Mainstreaming is the practice of integrating students with special needs into regular classrooms. Children with mild disabilities are often integrated into regular classrooms for their entire day while children with more severe disabilities are integrated for part of the day and receive specialized instruction for the remainder of the time.

Manuscript writing, more commonly called *printing*, is the first form of written language taught to children and consists of individual letters. There are a number of styles of manuscript writing, but all of them are plain, easy to recognize, and easy for children to learn.

Metacognition is awareness and control of the thinking processes involved in developing an ability. Metacognition in reading includes knowledge of factors that affect reading, of reading tasks, and of reading strategies. The regulative or control dimension of metacognition in reading involves planning and monitoring.

Metalinguistic awareness is the growing awareness and ability we have to think and talk about language as a formal code. With children, it refers to understanding terms such as *letter*, *word*, *sentence*, and *sound*.

Miscues are Goodman's term for errors during oral reading. Goodman believes that analyzing oral miscues gives insights into the reading process since miscues result from the same cues and processes as correct responses.

Morphology is the study of the structure of words, specifically the ways in which morphemes (the smallest units of meaning in a language) combine to create meanings. An example of a morpheme is *s*, which denotes plural in English. Hence *dog* means one creature and *dogs* means more than one. Suffixes and prefixes are also morphemes. Morphology is one of the essential cueing systems readers use in order to make sense of the printed word. Morphology is distinct from syntax in that syntax deals with the meaning of language at the level of sentences and phrases.

Narrative consists of a story or a succession of related events. These events are frequently organized according to cause and effect or chronology. Narratives include descriptions of settings, events, and characters, as well as comments and observations. Narratives can have the structure of a story or can have much looser structures without opening and closing sequences.

Native speaker ability is the ability to use language in many situations to accomplish a wide range of purposes. Idiomatic language, pragmatics, and dialect are all important in native speaker ability.

Newbery medal is awarded by the American Library Association each year for the best work of juvenile fiction published in the United States. Honour books are also named. The award is named after London publisher John Newbery, one of the first to publish books for children.

Performance assessment refers to assessment in which students demonstrate what they can do by actually doing it. Rather than using paper and pencil tests, teachers use their best judgment to evaluate performance along a continuum defined by increasingly demanding performance criteria. These criteria are written descriptions that capture quality performance at various levels of achievement. This form of assessment is frequently used for children's writing.

Phonetics refers to the way sounds are articulated and produced. The term *phonetics* is often used to describe the way children spell, sounding out a word so they can articulate individual sounds (phonemes) within a word and transcribe them into print symbols.

Phonics is the relationship between letters and their spoken sounds. Analytic or whole word phonics is the association of sounds with larger clusters of letters such as phonograms or word families (e.g., *ight*). Synthetic phonics is the association of sounds with individual letters or letter clusters and the blending of these sounds to identify words.

Phonological awareness is the ability to segment the language sounds, including words, syllables, and phonemes. **Phonemic awareness** means hearing sounds or phonemes in words. Research shows that performance on phonological awareness tasks is related to beginning reading acquisition.

Phonology, sometimes called **phonemics**, is the study of the patterns of sound that create meaning in language. In any one language, a number of sounds (**phonemes**) combine to produce words and meanings.

Picture books are books in which illustrations play an integral role in creating meaning. Picture books are not the same as illustrated books, where meaning is not dependent upon illustrations. In a picture book, text and pictures work together. Good examples of picture books are *Each Peach Pear Plum* by Janet and Allan Ahlberg, and *The Tunnel* by Anthony Browne, for older children.

Poetic writing is a term used by James Britton to describe one of the three voices of writing (the others being transactional and expressive). Meant to have an aesthetic element to it, poetic writing consists of poetry and also fictional writing, including narrative and description. The purpose of poetic writing is purely for pleasure or satisfaction on the part of the writer and audience. (Poetic writing is not necessarily pleasurable to read, but can, in fact, cause distress or discomfort for the reader).

Polysemic is a semantics term that describes words with more than one meaning. A polysemic text allows the reader to make inferences and judgments, and to interpret the text in several ways. Examples of polysemic texts are *Rosie's Walk* by Pat Hutchins and *Tuck Everlasting* by Natalie Babbit. A text that is not polysemic provides a narrower reading experience for accomplished readers.

Portfolio assessment uses a compilation of work done by a child over a period of time. Frequently, the portfolio items are selected by the learner or by the teacher and learner together. Items included in a portfolio are chosen with deliberation in order to demonstrate what a learner can do. Teachers find portfolios useful in demonstrating a child's learning to parents and administrators, and in explaining to children what they need to focus on and what learning must be accomplished next. Portfolios also give teachers an opportunity to reflect on their teaching and the learning their students are engaged in. Portfolios provide children with an opportunity to see the range of work they have done over time, and to assess what they are accomplishing.

Pragmatics is the study of how speakers create meaning. The emphasis in pragmatics is on the context of language use, and on the intentions and presuppositions of the speakers. The focus is on what an individual speaker means, and on how that meaning is communicated. Pragmatics examines relatively short stretches of language, compared with discourse analysis, which studies linguistic patterns in longer stretches of language.

Predictable books, a term coined by Goodman, are books that make reading easy for emergent readers. They have the following characteristics: the pictures support the text; large chunks of text are repeated; and the language has cadence, rhythm, or rhyme that supports the reading of the text. *Brown Bear, Brown Bear, What Do You See?* and *Each Peach Pear Plum* are examples of predictable books.

Realistic fiction is also called **contemporary realistic fiction** or **problem fiction**, although it does not have to be problem oriented. These stories deal with contemporary issues in the lives of children, and are books the readers can easily identify with. *The Great Gilly Hopkins* by Katherine Paterson and *Mama's Going to Buy You a Mockingbird* by Jean Little are examples of realistic fiction.

Schemata (singular **schema**) are organized mental frameworks that develop through repeated exposure to ritualized experiences such as playing baseball, eating in restaurants, singing on car trips. Schemata influence our expectations and impose structure on the information we receive.

Semantics is the meaning component of language. It does not simply refer to the denotational meanings of words, but to the ways in which words are used, in the actual choice of one word rather than another and in the connotations created by those words. It includes idioms and compound words, and the unique ways words are used in different situations.

Semantic map or web is a diagram that shows relationships among ideas. It consists of nodes containing key words with connecting lines between the nodes. Teachers and students use semantic maps or webs to organize ideas about concepts, texts, or units of study.

Standardized tests are norm-referenced tests comparing a student's performance with that of other students. These tests are developed by administering a test to a large number of students (the standardization group) to develop norms.

Syntax (what used to be called grammar) is a linguistic term that refers to the structure of sentences. In the English language syntax consists largely of word order. English is a non-inflected language. It does not depend upon specific inflectional word endings to denote the role of a word in a sentence.

Text structure is the pattern or organization of ideas in a text. There are two major types of texts: narrative (story) and expository (informational). Knowledge of text structure helps us to construct meaning for texts when reading and writing.

Thematic organization is a way of organizing learning matter around a central concept (such as courage), the work of a particular author, or a topic (such as farms). The theory is that learning will be facilitated and deepened by connecting ideas together. Thematic units may be organized within language arts or extend across other areas of the curriculum as well.

Time-slip fantasy is a genre of literature that involves the main character or protagonist in two eras. An object often enables the character to slip from one era to the other. In *Who is Francis Rain?* by Margaret Buffie, the object is a pair of spectacles. In *Playing Beatie Bow* by Ruth Park, the object is a piece of fabric on a dress. In time-slip fantasy, the protagonist explores issues in the past that lead to an understanding of current issues.

Trade books are books published by publishing companies as works of literature and not as educational texts. Books published as part of an educational program and intended for use in schools are usually referred to as textbooks.

Traditional stories are ones that were originally handed down from one generation to another orally. Traditional stories often have many versions, which developed in different regions.

For example, the story of *Cinderella* (originally French) is known as *Tattercoats* in parts of England, and has a slightly different plot. Traditional stories include fairy tales, folk stories, myths, legends, tall tales, and fables.

Transactional theory, also called **transactive theory**, is based on the work of Louise Rosenblatt and posits that meaning comes from a transaction between a reader and text in a specific context. Readers rely on the text itself and on their background knowledge, experiences, and world view to construct meaning while reading. The focus is on the reader's response to texts.

Transactional writing is a term used by James Britton to describe one of the three voices of writing (the others being poetic and expressive). Like expository writing, which it is often used interchangeably with, transactional writing is meant to accomplish a specific practical goal. Business letters, reports, term papers, report cards, recipes, and shopping lists are all examples of transactional writing.

Whole language is a philosophy about learning, language, and the nature of relationships between children and adults. Meaning is seen as the essence of language learning and children are viewed as learning language through using it. Language is also seen as indivisible and as personal, social, and cultural. Practices that have been associated with whole language include involving children in real reading and writing, immersing them in a print-rich environment including quality children's literature, and basing assessments on observation of children using language in the classroom.

Zone of proximal development is a term coined by Vygotsky to refer to a level of difficulty just beyond that which a child can handle independently but which he or she can handle with help from others. Providing children with the opportunity to work with others on problems or tasks at this level maximizes learning.

References

Adams, M.A. (1990). *Beginning to read: Thinking and learning about print*. Cambridge, MA: MIT Press.

Adams, M.J., Anderson, R.C., and Durkin, D. (1978). Beginning reading: Theory and practice. *Language Arts*, 55, 19–25.

Alberta Education. (1993). *Diagnostic teaching in a language learning framework 5*. Edmonton, AB: Student Evaluation Branch.

———. (1994). *Information bulletin: Grade 6 English language arts, 1994–95*. Edmonton, AB: Student Evaluation Branch.

Allen, V.G. (1991). Teaching bilingual and ESL children. In J. Flood, J.M. Jensen, D. Lapp, and J.R. Squire (Eds.), *Handbook of research on teaching the English language arts* (pp. 356–364). New York: Macmillan Publishing Company.

Altwerger, B., Edelsky, C., and Flores, B.M. (1987). Whole language: What's new? *Reading Teacher*, *41*, 144–154.

American Library Association. *Booklist*.

Anderson, R., Hiebert, E., Scott, J., and Wilkerson, I. (1985). *Becoming a nation of readers*. Washington, DC: National Institute of Education.

Applebee, A. (1978). *The child's concept of story*. Chicago: University of Chicago Press.

Arrasmith, D., Sheehan, D., and Applebaum, W. (1984). A comparison of the selected-response strategy and the constructed-response strategy for assessment of a third-grade writing task. *Journal of Educational Research*, 7(3), 172–177.

Atwell, N. (1987). *In the middle: Writing, reading, and learning with adolescents*. Portsmouth, NH: Heinemann.

———. (1990). *Coming to know: Writing to learn in the intermediate grades*. Portsmouth, NH: Heinemann.

Bachor, D.G., and Crealock, C. (1986). *Instructional strategies for students with special needs*. Scarborough, ON: Prentice-Hall Canada Inc.

Barnes, D. (1976). *From communication to curriculum*. Harmondsworth, Middlesex: Penguin Books.

Barr, R., and Dreeben, R. (1991). Grouping students for reading instruction. In R. Barr, R.L. Kamil, P.B. Mosenthal and P.D. Pearson (Eds.), *Handbook of reading research, Volume II* (pp. 885–910). New York: Longman.

Barton, B. (1980). *Tell me another*. Markham, ON: Pembroke Publishers Limited/Portsmouth.

Benterud, J.G. (1983). Four first-graders' use of reading time during the language arts period in their natural classroom setting. Unpublished master's thesis, University of Alberta, Edmonton.

Benton, M., and Fox, G. (1985). *Teaching literature 9–14*. London: Oxford University Press.

Bhola, H.S. (1981). Why literacy can't wait: Issues for the 1980s. *Convergence*, *14* (1), 6–22.

Bloom, B. (1956). *Taxonomy of educational objectives: Cognitive domain*. New York: McKay.

Bloome, D. (1991). Anthropology and research on teaching the English language arts. In J. Flood, J.M. Jensen, D. Lapp, and J.R. Squire (Eds.), *Handbook of research on teaching the English language arts* (pp. 46–56). New York: Macmillan Publishing Company.

———, and Green, J. (1984). Directions in the sociolinguistic study of reading. In R. Barr, M.L. Kamil, and P.B. Mosenthal (Eds.), *Handbook of reading research* (pp. 395–421). New York: Longman.

Bogdan, D., and Straw, S. (1993). Introduction. In S.B. Straw and D. Bogdan (Eds.), *Constructive reading: Teaching beyond communication* (pp. 1–14). Portsmouth, NH: Heinemann.

Bohm, D. (1990). *On dialogue*. Ojai, CA: David Bohm Seminars.

Bolton, G. (1979). *Towards a theory of drama in education*. London: Longman.

Bond, G.L., Tinker, M.A., Wasson, B.B., and Wasson, J.B. (1994). *Reading difficulties: Their diagnosis and correction*. Boston: Allyn and Bacon.

Booth, D. (1986). *Games for everyone*. Markham, ON: Pembroke Publishers Limited.

———. (1994). *Classroom voices: Language-based learning in the elementary school*. Toronto: Harcourt Brace & Company Canada.

Bowker, R.R. *School Library Journal*.

Braddock, R., Lloyd-Jones, R., and Shoer, L. (1963). *Research in written composition*. Champaign, IL: National Council of Teachers of English.

Brailsford, A. (1991). *Paired reading: Positive reading practice*. Edmonton, AB: Northern Alberta Reading Specialists Council.

British Columbia Ministry of Education. (1988). *Enhancing and evaluating oral communication in the primary grades*. Victoria, BC: British Columbia Ministry of Education.

Britton, J. (1970). *Language and learning*. Harmondsworth, Middlesex: Penguin Books.

———. (1982). *Prospect and retrospect: Selected essays of James Britton* (Ed. G. Pradl). New Jersey: Boynton Cook.

Britton, J., Burgess, G., Martin N., McLeod, A., and Rosen, H. (1975). *The development of writing abilities, 11–18*. London: MacMillan Education.

Brophy, J. (1985). Interactions of male and female students with male and female teachers. In L.C. Wilkinson and C.B. Marrett (Eds.), *Gender influences in classroom interaction*. Toronto: Academic Press.

Brown, A. (1980). Metacognitive development and reading. In R.J. Spiro, B.C. Bruce and W.F. Brewer (Eds.), *Theoretical issues in reading comprehension* (pp. 453–481). Hillsdale, NJ: Lawrence Erlbaum Associates.

Brown, R. (1973). *A first language*. Cambridge, MA: Harvard University Press.

Bruce, B. (1991). Roles for computers in teaching the English language arts. In J. Flood, J.M. Jensen, D. Lapp, and J.R. Squire (Eds.), *Handbook of research on teaching the English language arts* (pp. 536–541). New York: Macmillan Publishing Company.

Bruner, J. (1975). The ontogenesis of speech acts. *Journal of Child Language, 2*, 1–40.

Bruner, J.S. (1966). *Towards a theory of instruction*. Cambridge, MA: The Belknap Press of Harvard University.

Burns, P.C., and Roe, B.D. (1993). *Informal reading inventory*. Chicago: Rand McNally.

Calkins, L. (1986). *The art of teaching writing*. Portsmouth, NH: Heinemann.

———. (1994). *The art of teaching writing* (2nd ed.). Toronto: Irwin Publishing.

Cameron, I., and Mickelson, N. (1989). Whole language and basal readers. *Reading-Canada-Lecture, 7* (3), 267–271.

Canadian Children's Book Centre. *Children's Book News*. Toronto.

Carroll, J., Davies, P., and Richman, B. (1971). *Word frequency book*. Boston: Houghton Mifflin Company.

Carswell, R.J.B. (1988). Journals in a graduate curriculum course. *English Quarterly, 21* (2), 104–114.

Cazden, C.B. (1988). *Classroom discourse*. Portsmouth, NH: Heinemann.

Centre for Language in Primary Education. (1988). *The primary language record: Handbook for teachers*. Markham, ON: Pembroke Publishers Ltd.

Chall, J.S. (1967). *Learning to read: The great debate*. New York: McGraw-Hill.

———. (1983). *Stages of reading development*. New York: McGraw-Hill.

Chittenden, E., and Courtney, R. (1989). Assessment of young children's reading: Documentation as an alternative to testing. In D.S. Strickland and L.M. Morrow (Eds.), *Emerging literacy: Young children learn to read and write* (pp. 107–120). Newark, DL: International Reading Association.

Chomsky, N. (1957). *Syntactic structures*. The Hague: Mouton & Co.

Clark, H., and Clark, E.V. (1977). *Psychology and language*. New York: Harcourt Brace Jovanovich Inc.

Clarke, M.A. (1990). Some cautionary observations on liberation education. *Language Art, 67*, 388–398.

Clay, M.M. (1972). *Reading: The patterning of complex behaviour*. Auckland, NZ: Heinemann Educational Books.

———. (1975). *What did I write?* Portsmouth, NH: Heinemann.

———. (1985). *The early detection of reading difficulties*. Portsmouth NH: Heinemann.

Clymer, T. (1963). The utility of phonic generalizations in the primary grades. *Reading Teacher*, (4), 252–258.

Cochrane, O., Cochrane, D., Scalena, S., and Buchanan, E. (1984). *Reading, writing and caring*. Winnipeg: Whole Language Consultants Ltd.

Coles, G.S. (1987). *The learning mystique*. New York: Pantheon Books.

Commaire, A. (Ed.). *Something about the author*. Detroit: Gale Research.

Cooper, C.R. (1977). Holistic evaluation of writing. In C.R. Cooper and L. Odell (Eds.), *Evaluating writing: Describing, measuring, judging* (pp. 3–31). Urbana, IL: National Council of Teachers of English.

———, and Odell, L. (Eds.). (1977). Evaluating writing: *Describing, measuring, judging*. Urbana, IL: National Council of Teachers of English.

Corrigan, R.W. (1992). *The world of the theatre*. Dubuque, IO: Wm. C. Brown Publishers.

Cross, D.R., and Paris, S.G. (1988). Developmental and instructional analyses of children's metacognition and reading comprehension. *Journal of Educational Psychology, 80*, 131–142.

Cunningham, P.M. (1979). A compare/contrast theory of mediated word identification. *Reading Teacher, 32* (7), 774–778.

———, and Cunningham, J.W. (1992). Making words: Enhancing the invented spelling-decoding connection. *Reading Teacher*, 46 (2), 106–113.

D'Arcy, P. (1987). Writing to learn. In T. Fulwiler (Ed.), *The journal book* (pp. 41–46). Toronto: Boynton Cook.

———. (1989). *Making sense, shaping meaning: Writing in the context of a capacity-based approach to learning*. Portsmouth, NH: Heinemann.

deHirsch, K., Jansky, J.J., and Langford, W.S. (1966). *Predicting reading failure*. New York: Harper and Row.

Delpit, L. (1988). The silenced dialogue: Power and pedagogy in educating other people's children. *Harvard Educational Review, 58*, 280–298.

Department of Education and Science. (1990). *English in the national curriculum, 2*. London, UK: HMSO.

Department of Education and the Welsh Office. (1995). *English in the national curriculum*. London, UK: HMSO.

Department of School Education, Victoria. (1991). *English Profiles Handbook*. Melbourne, Australia: Victoria Department of School Education.

Derwing, T.M. (1990). Speech rate is no simple matter: Rate adjustment and NS-NNS interaction. *Studies in Second Language Acquisition, 12* (3), 303–313.

Dillon, D. (1985). Editorial. *Language Arts, 62* (1), 9.

Doake, D.B. (1981). *Book experience and emergent reading behaviour in preschool children*. Unpublished doctoral dissertation, University of Alberta, Edmonton, AB.

———. (1988). *Reading begins at birth*. Richmond Hill, ON: Scholastic-TAB Publications Ltd.

Donaldson, M. (1978). *Children's minds*. New York: W.W. Norton & Co.

Downing, J. (1979). *Reading and reasoning*. New York: Springer-Verlag.

———, Ayers, D., and Schaefer, B. (1983). *Linguistic awareness in reading readiness (LARR) test*. Windsor, Berks: NFER-Nelson Publishing Company Ltd.

Durkin, D. (1966). *Children who learn to read early*. New York: Teachers College Press.

———. (1978–79). What classroom observations reveal about reading comprehension instruction. *Reading Research Quarterly, 14* (4), 481–533.

———. (1983). *Teaching them to read* (4th ed.). Boston: Allyn and Bacon.

Dyer, P.C. (1992). Reading recovery: A cost-effectiveness and educational-outcomes analysis. *ERS Spectrum, 10* (1), 10–19.

Eco, U. (1978). *The role of the reader*. Bloomington: Indiana University Press.

Edelsky, C. (1994). Education for democracy. *Language Arts, 71* (4), 252–257.

Edwards, A.D. (1980). Patterns of power and authority in classroom talk. In P. Woods (Ed.), *Teacher strategies: Explorations in the sociology of the school* (pp. 237–253). London: Croom Helm.

Edwards, J. (1992). Dialogue journals in math: Grades two, four and six. *Reflections on Canadian Literacy, 10* (1), 2–12.

———, and Payne, P. (1994). A drama support group: Context for teacher change. *Youth Theatre, 8* (3), 19–23.

Egoff, S., and Saltman, J. (1990). *The new republic of childhood*. Don Mills, ON: Oxford University Press.

Elley, W., Barham, I., Lamb, H., and Wyllie, M. (1976). The role of grammar in a secondary school English curriculum. *Research in the Teaching of English, 10*, 5–21.

Farr, R., and Tone, B. (1994). *Portfolio and performance assessment*. Fort Worth, TX: Harcourt Brace College Publishers.

Farrell, E., and Squire, J. (Eds.). (1990). *Transactions with literature: A fifty-year perspective*. Urbana, IL: National Council of Teachers of English.

Ferreiro, E., and Teberosky, A. (1982). *Literacy before schooling*. Exeter, NH: Heinemann Educational Books.
Field, J.C. (1990). *Educators' perspectives on assessment: Tensions, contradictions and dilemmas*. Unpublished doctoral dissertation, University of Victoria, BC.
Fish, S. (1980). *Is there a text in this class? The authority of interpretive communities*. Cambridge, MA: Harvard University Press.
Flavell, J.H. (1979). Metacognition and cognitive monitoring: A new area of cognitive-developmental inquiry. *American Psychologist*, *34*, 906–911.
Freeman, E., and Person, D. (1992). *Using nonfiction trade books in the elementary classroom*. Urbana, IL: National Council of Teachers of English.
Freire, P. (1970). *Pedagogy of the oppressed*. New York: Herder and Herder.
Freshour, F., and Bartholomew, P. (1989) Let's start improving our own listening. *Florida Reading Quarterly*, *25* (4), 28–30.
Froese, V. (1991). *A language approach to reading*. Scarborough, ON: Nelson Canada.
———. (1990). *Whole language: Practice and theory*. Scarborough, ON: Prentice-Hall Canada Inc.
Fulwiler, T. (Ed.). (1987). *The journal book*. Toronto: Boynton/Cook.
Furner, B. (1969). Recommended instructional procedures in a method emphasizing the perceptual motor nature of learning in handwriting. *Elementary English*, 46 (8), 1021–1030.
Gates, A.I. (1937). The necessary mental age for beginning reading. *Elementary School Journal*, *37*, 497–508.
Gillespie-Silver, P. (1979). *Teaching reading to children with special needs*. Columbus: Charles E. Merrill Publishing Company.
Gillet, J.W., and Temple, C. (1994). *Understanding reading problems: Assessment and instruction*. New York: HarperCollins Publishers.
Glynn, T., Bethune, N., Crooks, T., Ballard, K., and Smith, J. (1992). Reading recovery in context: Implementation and outcome. *Educational Psychology*, *12*, 249–261.
Golub, J.N. (1994). Cooperative learning. In A.C. Purves (Ed.), *Encyclopedia of English studies and language arts* (pp. 298–299). New York: Scholastic.
Goodman, K. (1993). *Phonics Phacts*. Portsmouth, NH: Heinemann.
———. (1969). Analysis of oral reading miscues: Applied psycholinguistics. *Reading Research Quarterly*, 5 (1), 9–30.
———. (1970). Behind the eye: What happens in reading. In K.S. Goodman and O. Niles (Eds.), *Reading: Process and program* (pp. 3–38). Urbana, IL: National Council of Teachers of English.
———. (1986). *What's whole in whole language?* Richmond Hill, ON: Scholastic-TAB Publications Ltd.
———, Shannon, P., Freeman, Y.S., and Murphy, S. (1988). *Report card on basal readers*. Katonah, NY: Richard C. Owen Publishers.
Goodman, Y.M. (1991). Informal methods of evaluation. In J. Flood, J.M. Jensen, D. Lapp, and J.R. Squire (Eds.), *Handbook of research on teaching the English language arts* (pp. 502–509). New York: Macmillan Publishing Company.
———, Watson, D.J., and Burke, C.L. (1987). *Reading miscue inventory: Alternative procedures*. New York: Richard C. Owen Publishers, Inc.

Gordon, C.J. (1991). English language arts instruction and assessment in Canada. *Reflections on Canadian Literacy*, 9 (3 & 4), 153–158.

Gough, P.B. (1972). One second of reading. In J.F. Kavanagh and J.G. Mattingly (Eds.), *Language by ear and eye* (pp. 331–358). Cambridge, MA: MIT Press.

Graff, H. (1987). *The labyrinths of literacy: Reflections on literacy past and present*. London: Falmer.

Graves, D.H. (1983). *Writing: Teachers and children at work*. Exeter, NH: Heinemann Educational Books.

Great Britain Department of Education and Science. (1975). *A language for life*. London: Her Majesty's Stationery Office.

Hall, M. (1981). *Teaching reading as a language experience*. Columbus, OH: Charles E. Merrill.

Halliday, M.A.K. (1969). Relevant models of language. *Educational Review*, *22* (1), 26–37.

———. (1975a). *Explorations in the functions of language*. London: Edward Arnold.

———. (1975b). *Learning how to mean*. New York: Elsevier North-Holland Inc.

Hammill, D.D., and Larsen, S.C. (1988). *Test of written language-2*. Austin, TX: Pro-ed.

Hardy, B. (1975). *Tellers and listeners: The narrative imagination*. Dover, NH: Longwood.

Harker, W.J. (1991). The profession of literacy: Basal readers and whole language. *Reflections on Canadian Literacy*, 9 (3 & 4), 217–220.

Harste, J., Woodward, V., and Burke, C. (1984). *Language stories and literacy lessons*. Portsmouth, NH: Heinemann Educational Books.

Hayden, H.M.R. (1985). *Clarification strategies within joint book interactions*. Unpublished doctoral dissertation, University of Alberta, Edmonton, Alberta.

Heath, S.B. (1983). *Ways with words: Language, life and work in communities and classrooms*. Cambridge: Cambridge University Press.

Heathcote, D. (1972). *Three looms waiting: A BBC omnibus programme*. Ipswich, England: Concord Films.

Holdaway, D. (1979). *The foundations of literacy*. Gosford, NSW: Ashton Scholastic.

Hough, R.A., and Nurss, J.R. (1992). Language and literacy for the limited English proficient child. In L.O. Olilla and M.I. Mayfield (Eds.), *Emerging literacy: Preschool, kindergarten, and primary grades* (pp. 137–165). Toronto: Allyn and Bacon.

Huck, C., Hepler, S., and Hickman, J. (1993). *Children's literature in the elementary school*. (5th ed.). New York: Harcourt Brace Jovanovich College Publishers.

Huey, E.B. (1908). *The psychology and pedagogy of reading*. New York: Macmillan.

Hughes, M., and McInnes, J. (1983). *Reading and how*. Scarborough, ON: Nelson Canada.

Hunt, K. (1965). *Grammatical structures written at three grade levels*. NCTE Research Report Number 3. Urbana, IL: National Council of Teachers of English.

Hunt, L.C. (1970). The effect of self-selection, interest and motivation upon independent, instructional and frustration level. *The Reading Teacher*, *24* (2), 146–151.

Hunter, C., St. John, and Harman, D. (1979). *Adult illiteracy in the United States*. New York: McGraw-Hill.

Indrisano, R., and Paratore, J.R. (1991). Classroom contexts for literacy learning. In J. Flood, J.M. Jensen, D. Lapp, and J.R. Squire (Eds.), *Handbook of research on teaching the English language arts* (pp. 477–487). New York: Macmillan Publishing Company.

Jacobs, E., and Jordan, C. (1993). Understanding minority education: Framing the issues. In E. Jacob and C. Jordan (Eds.), *Minority education: Anthropological perspectives* (pp. 3–13). Norwood, NJ: Ablex Publishing Company.

Jacobs, J.E., and Paris, S.G. (1987). Children's metacognition about reading: Issues in definition, measurement, and instruction. *Educational Psychologist, 22* (3 & 4), 255–278.

Jobe, R., and Hart, P. (1991). The basalization of children's literature. *Reflections on Canadian Literacy*, 9 (3 & 4), 147–150.

John-Steiner, V., and Tatter, P. (1983). An Interactionist model of language development. In B. Bain (Ed.), *The sociogenesis of language and human conduct* (pp. 79–97). New York: Plenum Press.

Johns, J.L. (1991). *Basic reading inventory* (5th ed.). Dubuque, IA: Kendall/Hunt Publishing Company.

Johnston, P., and Allington, R. (1991). Remediation. In R. Barr, M.L. Kamil, P.B. Mosenthal, & P.D. Pearson (Eds.), *Handbook of reading research*, Volume 2 (pp. 984–1012). White Plains, NY: Longman.

Juliebö, M.F. (1985). *The literacy world of five young children*. Unpublished doctoral dissertation, University of Alberta, Edmonton, Alberta.

Kretovics, J.R. (1985). Critical literacy: Challenging the assumptions of mainstream educational theory. *Journal of Education*, *167*, 50–62.

King, E.M. (1976). *Canadian tests of basic skills*. Don Mills, ON: Thomas Nelson & Sons (Canada) Ltd.

Kozol, J. (1991). *Savage inequalities: Children in America's schools*. New York: Crown Publishers.

Laberge, D., and Samuels, S.J. (1974). Toward a theory of automatic information processing in reading. *Cognitive Psychology*, 6, 293–323.

Langer, J. (1994). Focus on research: A response-based approach to teaching literature. *Language Arts*, *71* (3), 203–211.

Lenneberg, E.H. (1964). The capacity for language acquisition. In J.A. Fodor and J.J. Katz (Eds.), *The Structure of Language* (pp. 580–605). Englewood Cliffs, NJ: Prentice-Hall, Inc.

Leppard, S. (1991). A reading–writing continuum. *Program continuity: The positive link*. Calgary, Alberta: Alberta Educational Communications Corporation.

Leroy, C. (1995). Opposition and literacy among girls in an inner-city classroom. Unpublished doctoral dissertation, University of Alberta, Edmonton.

Leslie, L., and Caldwell, J. (1990). *Qualitative reading inventory*. New York: HarperCollins Publishers.

Levine, K. (1986). *The social context of literacy*. London: Routledge & Kegan Paul.

Lewis, C. (1989). *Partnership writing: Ten-year-olds talking and writing together*. Unpublished masters thesis, University of Alberta, Edmonton.

Lewis, C. (1993). "Give people a chance": Acknowledging social differences in reading. *Language Arts*, *70* (6), 454–461.

Liberation education. An interview with Ira Shor. (1990). *Language Arts*, *67* (4), 342–352.

Lindfors, J.W. (1987). *Children's language and learning* (2nd ed.). Englewood Cliffs, NJ: Prentice-Hall, Inc.

Lipson, M.Y., and Wixson, K.K. (1991). *Assessment and instruction of reading disability: An interactive approach*. New York: HarperCollins Publishers.

Littledyke, M., and Baum, C. (1986). Structures for drama. *2D*, 5 (2), 72–78.

Loban, W. (1963). *The language of elementary school children*. NCTE Research Report Number One. Urbana, IL: National Council of Teachers of English.

Loomer, B. (1978). *Educators guide to spelling research and practice*. Iowa City: Iowa State Department of Public Instruction and Project Spelling.

MacAlister, S., Kydd, G., and Jones, G. (1988). *Writing and primary science*. Calgary: Calgary Board of Education.

MacGinitie, W.H., and MacGinitie, R.K. (1992). *Gates-MacGinitie reading tests* (2nd Canadian ed.). Scarborough, ON: Nelson Canada.

Malicky, G.V. (1991). Myths and assumptions of literacy education. *Alberta Journal of Educational Research, 37* (4), 333–347.

———, Juliebö, M.F., and Norman, C.A. (1994). *Metacognition of young readers in an early intervention program*. Paper presented at the 22nd Annual Conference of the Canadian Society for the Study of Education, June 16, 1994, Calgary, Alberta.

———, Purkiss, K., and Nugent, B. (1988–89). Early intervention: A collaborative holistic approach. *Alberta English, 27* (1), 21–29.

Mandler, J., and Johnson, N. (1977). Remembrance of things parsed: Story structure and recall. *Cognitive Psychology*, 9, 111–151.

Mason, J.M. (1984). Early reading from a developmental perspective. In P.D. Pearson (Ed.), *Handbook of reading research* (pp. 505–544). New York: Longman.

———, Peterman, C.L., and Kerr, B.M. (1989). Reading to kindergarten children. In D. Strickland and L.M. Morrow (Eds.), *Emerging literacy: Young children learn to read and write* (pp. 52–62). Newark, DL: International Reading Association.

Mathematical Association. (1987). *Math talk*. Portsmouth, NH: Heinemann.

Mayfield, M.I. (1992). Organizing for teaching and learning. In L.O. Ollila and M.I. Mayfield (Eds.), *Emerging literacy: Preschool, kindergarten and primary grades* (pp. 166–195). Boston: Allyn and Bacon.

McGuire, M.L., and Bumpus, M.J. (1973). *Croft skillpacks*. Old Greenwich, CT: Croft Educational Services.

McKay, R. (1993). Whole language: Defining our beliefs, examining our practices. In L.L. Stewin & S.J.H. McCann (Eds.), *Contemporary educational issues: The Canadian mosaic* (pp. 482–504). Toronto: Copp Clark Pitman Ltd.

McKenzie, L., and Tompkins, G. (1984). Evaluating students' writing: A process approach. *Journal of Teaching Writing*, 3, 201–212.

McKeown, M.G., and Curtis, M.E. (Eds.). (1987). *The nature of vocabulary acquisition*. Hillsdale, NJ: Lawrence Erlbaum Associates.

Meek, M. (1988). *How texts teach what readers learn*. Stroud, UK: Thimble Press.

Miller, G. (1977). *Spontaneous apprentices: Children and language*. New York: A Continuum Book. The Seabury Press.

Ministry of Education, Victoria. (1988). *English language framework, P-10: Language for living*. Melbourne, Australia: Victoria Ministry of Education.

Mitchell, C.A., and Cheverie, A.E. (1989). "Now that we've got them writing...": Addressing issues of ethics, aesthetics, taste, and sensibility within the content of student writing. *Reading-Canada-Lecture, 7* (3), 180–190.

Moffett, J. (1968). *Teaching the universe of discourse*. Boston: Houghton Mifflin.

———. (1979). Integrity in the teaching of writing. *Phi Delta Kappa, 61* (4), 276–279.

Moller, D. (1991). Scandal of Britain's illiterate kids. *Reader's Digest, 139*, 29–35.

Moray, N. (1969) *Listening and Attention*. Baltimore: Penguin Books.

Morphett, M.V., and Washburne, C. (1931). When should children begin to read? *Elementary School Journal, 31*, 496–508.

Morrow, L.M. (1989). Designing the classroom to promote literacy development. In D.S. Strickland and L.M. Morrow (Eds.), *Emerging literacy: Young children learn to read and write* (pp. 121–134). Newark: DL: International Reading Association.

Moss, P., Cole, N., and Khampalikit, C. (1982). A comparison of procedures to assess written language skills at grades 4, 7, and 10. *Journal of Educational Measurement, 19* (1), 37–47.

Mueller, S. (1983). An investigation in social competence using clinical and societal profiles. Unpublished master's thesis. University of California, Santa Barbara; as cited in Prutting, C., and Kirchner, D. (1987). A Clinical Appraisal of the Pragmatic Aspects of Language. *Journal of Speech and Hearing Disorders, 52*, 105–119.

Murphy, S. (1991). Authorship and discourse types in Canadian basal reading programs. *Reflections on Canadian Literacy*, 9 (3 & 4), 133–138.

National Anti-Poverty Organization. (1992). *Literacy and poverty: A view from the inside*. Ottawa, ON: Author.

Neelands, J. (1984). *Making sense of 'drama': A guide to classroom practice*. London: Heinemann.

———. (1992). *Learning through imagined experience*. New York: Cambridge University Press.

Neuman, S.B., and Roskos, K.A. (1993). *Language and literacy learning in the early years: An integrated approach*. New York: Harcourt Brace Jovanovich College Publishers.

Newkirk, T. (1987). The non-narrative writing of young children. *Research in the teaching of English, 21*, 121–145.

Newman, J.M., and Church, S.M. (1994). Myths of whole language. In J.E. DeCarlo (Ed.), *Perspectives in whole language* (pp. 24–31). Boston: Allyn and Bacon.

Ogbu, J.U. (1993). Variability in minority school performance: A problem in search of an explanation. In E. Jacob and C. Jordan (Eds.), *Minority education: Anthropological perspectives* (pp. 83–111). Norwood, NJ: Ablex Publishing Company.

Ogle, D.M. (1986). K-W-L: A teaching model that develops active reading of expository text. *Reading Teacher, 39* (6), 564–570.

Ohio State University. (1988). *Reading recovery in Ohio 1984–1987*. Columbus, OH: National Diffusion Network.

Olilla, L.O., and Mayfield, M.I. (1992). *Emerging literacy: Preschool, kindergarten and primary grades*. Toronto: Allyn and Bacon.

Olson, C.P., and Sullivan, E.V. (1993). Beyond the mania: Critical approaches to computers in education. In L.L. Stewin and S.J.H. McCann (Eds.), *Contemporary educational issues: The Canadian mosaic* (pp. 424–441). Toronto: Copp Clark Pitman Ltd.

Ondaatje, M. (1992). *The English patient*. Toronto: Vintage Books Canada.

O'Neill, C., Lambert, A., Linnell, R., and Warr-Wood, J. (1977). *Drama guidelines*. London: Heinemann Educational Books.

Ozdoba, A. (1992). *Writing to learn: Science journals in year one*. Unpublished masters thesis, University of Alberta, Edmonton.

Palincsar, A.S. (1986). Metacognitive strategy instruction. *Exceptional Children, 53* (2), 118–124.

Pantaleo, S. (1994). *Teacher influence on student response to literature*. Unpublished doctoral dissertation, University of Alberta, Edmonton.

Paris, S.G., Wasik, B.A., and Turner J.C. (1991). The development of strategic readers. In R. Barr, M.L. Kamil, P.B. Mosenthal and P.D. Pearson (Eds.), *Handbook of reading research*, Volume 2 (pp. 609–640). White Plains, N.Y: Longman.

Paterson, K. (1989). *The spying heart: More thoughts on reading and writing books*. NY: Lodestar Books.

Pearson, P.D. (1993). Teaching and learning reading: A research perspective. *Language Arts, 70* (6), 502–511.

———, and Johnson, D.D. (1978). *Teaching reading comprehension*. New York: Holt, Rinehart & Winston.

Petite Rivière Elementary School. (1993a). *History of Crousetown*. Lunenburg County, NS: Petite Rivière Publishing.

———. (1993b). *Tales of Crousetown*. Lunenburg County, NS: Petite Rivière Publishing.

Piaget, J. (1973). *The language and thought of the child*. New York: World.

Pica, T., Young, R., and Doughty, C. (1987). The impact of interaction on comprehension. *TESOL Quarterly, 21*, 737–758.

Pike, K., Compain, R., and Mumper, J. (1994). *New connections: An integrated approach to literacy*. New York: HarperCollins Publishers.

Polanyi, M. (1969). Knowing and being. In M. Grene (Ed), *Knowing and being: The essays of Michael Polanyi* (pp. 123–137). Chicago: University of Chicago Press.

Pressley, M., and Rankin, J. (1994). More about whole language methods of reading instruction for students at risk for early reading failure. *Learning Disabilities Research and Practice*, 9 (3), 157–168.

Preston, D. (1994) *Whole language: Novel studies for the intermediate grades*. Prince George, BC: Author.

Proctor, J.R. (1986). *The effect of teacher's theoretical orientations on the writing produced by grade one students*. Unpublished master's thesis, University of Alberta, Edmonton.

Purves, A. (1993). Toward a reevaluation of reader response and school literature. *Language Arts, 70* (5), 348–361.

———, and Rippere, V. (1968). *Elements of writing about a literary work: A study of response to literature*. Research Report No. 9. Urbana, IL: National Council of Teachers of English.

Raphael, T.E. (1986). Teaching question answer relationships. *Reading Teacher, 39* (6), 516–522.

Read, C. (1975). *Children's categorizations of speech sounds in English*. Urbana, IL: National Council of Teachers of English.

Reid, J. (1966). Learning to think about reading. *Educational Research*, 9, 56–62.

Rennie, J. (1990). Computers and literacy in schools. *Reflections on Canadian Literacy,* 8 (1), 50–52.

Rhodes, L.K. (1993). *Literacy assessment: A handbook of instruments*. Portsmouth, NH: Heinemann.

Robinson, F. (1961). *Effective study*. New York: Harper & Row.

Roderick, J.A., and Berman, L.M. (1984). Dialoguing about dialogue journals. *Language Arts*, (61) 7, 686–692.

Rosen, H. (1984). *The importance of story*. Sheffield, England: National Association for the Teaching of English.

Rosenblatt, L. (1978). *The reader, the text, the poem: The transactional theory of the literary work*. Carbondale, IL: Southern Illinois University Press.

———. (1989). Writing and reading: The transactional theory. In J.M. Mason (Ed.), *Reading and Writing Connections* (pp. 153–176). Boston: Allyn and Bacon.

Rossman, A.D. (1987). Reading automaticity: The essential element of academic success. *Principal*, 28–32.

Rumelhart, D.E. (1980). Schemata: The building blocks of cognition. In R.J. Spiro, B.C. Bruce, and W.F. Brewer (Eds.), *Theoretical issues in reading comprehension* (pp. 33–58). Hillsdale, NJ: Lawrence Erlbaum Associates.

———. (1977). *Introduction to human information processing theory*. New York: John Wiley & Sons.

Rymer, R. (1992). Annals of science: A silent childhood (1 & 2). *The New Yorker*, 68, 41–81, April 13 and 69, 43–77, April 20.

Schaffner, M. (1985). Drama and language. *2D*, *4* (2),35–44.

Schickendanz, J. (1989). The place of specific skills in preschool and kindergarten. In D.S. Strickland and L.M. Morrow (Eds.), *Emerging literacy: Young children learn to reading and write* (pp. 96–106). Newark, DL: International Reading Association.

Schwartz, L. (1988). *Drama themes: A practical guide for teaching drama*. Markham, ON: Pembroke Publishers Ltd.

Searle, D. (1984). Scaffolding: Who's building whose building? *Language Arts*, *61* (5), 480–483.

———, and Dillon, D. (1980). The message of marking: Teacher written responses to student writing at intermediate grade levels. *Research in the Teaching of English*, *14* (3), 233–242.

Shannon, P. (1989). The struggle for control of literacy lessons. *Language Arts*, 66 (6), 625–634.

Shuy, R. (1987). Research currents: Dialogue as the heart of learning. *Language Arts*, *64* (8), 890–897.

Silvaroli, N.J. (1986). *Classroom reading inventory*. Dubuque, IO: Wm. C. Brown Company Publishers.

Simmons, J. (1994). *Censorship: A threat to reading, learning, thinking*. Newark, DL: International Reading Association.

Simner, M.L. (1993). A position paper on beginning reading instruction in Canadian schools. *Canadian Journal of School Psychology*, 9 (1), 96–99.

Simpson, C. (1980). *The Scott, Foresman word study for spelling*. Glenview, IL: Scott, Foresman and Company.

Skinner, B. (1957). *Verbal behavior*. Englewood Cliffs, NJ: Prentice Hall.

Slavin, R.E. (1980). Cooperative learning. *Review of Educational Research*, *50*, 315–342.

Smith, F. (1975). *Comprehension in learning*. New York: Holt, Rinehart and Winston.

———. (1983). Reading like a writer. *Language Arts*, *60*, 558–567.

———. (1988). *Joining the literacy club: Further essays into education*. London: Heinemann.

Smith, N.B. (1965). *American reading instruction*. Newark, DL: International Reading Association (First published in 1934 by Silver Burdett and Co.).

Southam News. (1987). *Literacy in Canada: A research report*. Toronto: The Creative Research Group Ltd.

Staats, A.W. (1971). Child learning, intelligence, and personality: Principles of a behavioral interaction approach. New York: Harper & Row.

Standal, T.C., and Betza, R.E. (1990). *Content area reading: Teachers, texts, students*. New York: Prentice-Hall.

Stanovich, K.E. (1986). Matthew effects in reading: Some consequences of individual differences in the acquisition of literacy. *Reading Research Quarterly, 21* (4), 360–406.

Stauffer, R.G. (1975). *Directing the reading-thinking process*. New York: Harper & Row.

Stewig, J.W. (1983). *Informal drama in the elementary language arts program*. New York: Teachers College Press.

Straw, S.B. (1990). The actualization of reading and writing: Public policy and conceptualizations of literacy. In S.P. Norris and L.M. Phillips (Eds.), *Literacy policy in Canada* (pp. 165–181). Calgary, AB: Detselig Enterprises Ltd.

Strickland, D.S., Feeley, J.T., and Wepner, S.B. (1987). *Using computers in the teaching of reading*. New York: Teachers College Press.

———, and Morrow, L.M. (Eds.). (1989). *Emerging literacy: Young children learn to read and write*. Newark, DL: International Reading Association.

Sulzby, E. (1985). Children's emergent reading of favorite storybooks: A developmental study. *Reading Research Quarterly, 20*, 458–481.

———. (1991). The development of the young child and the emergence of literacy. In J. Flood, J.M. Jensen, D. Lapp, and J.R. Squire (Eds.), *Handbook of research on teaching the English language arts* (pp. 273–285). New York: Macmillan Publishing Company.

———, Teale, W.H., and Kamberelis, G. (1989). Emergent writing in the classroom: Home and school connections. In D. Strickland and L.M. Morrow (Eds.), *Emerging literacy: Young children learn to read and write* (pp. 52–62). Newark, DL: International Reading Association.

Tarlington, C., and Verriour, P. (1983). *Offstage: Elementary education through drama*. Toronto: Oxford University Press.

Teale, W.H., Hiebert, E.H., and Chittenden, E.A. (1987). Assessing young children's literacy development. *Reading Teacher, 40* (8), 772–777.

Temple, C. (1993). Suppose Beauty had been ugly? Reading against the grain of gender bias in children's books. *Language Arts, 60* (2), 89-93.

———, and Gillet, J.W. (1989). *Language arts: Learning processes and teaching practices*. (2nd ed.). Glenview, IL: Scott, Foresman & Company.

Terrace, H.S. (1979). How Nim Chimpsky changed my mind. *Psychology Today, 13* (6), 65–76.

The Horn Book Inc. *The Horn Book Magazine*.

Thomas, V. (1979). *Teaching Spelling: Canadian word lists and instructional techniques*. Toronto: Gage Publishing.

Thomson, J. (1987). *Understanding teenagers' reading: Reading processes and the teaching of literature*. Norwood, SA: Australian Association for the Teaching of English.

Tierney, R.J., Readence, J.E., and Dishner, E.K. (1995). *Reading strategies and practices: A compendium* (4th ed.). Boston: Allyn and Bacon.

Tizard, B., and Hughes, M. (1984). *Young children learning*. Cambridge, MA: Harvard University Press.

Topping, K. (1989). Peer tutoring and paired reading: Combining two powerful techniques. *Reading Teacher, 42* (7), 488–494.

Torrey, J. (1969). Learning to read without a teacher: A case study. *Elementary English*, 46, 550–556.

Tough, J. (1976). *Listening to children talking: A guide to the appraisal of children's language use*. Portsmouth, NH: Heinemann.

Vacca, J.L., Vacca, R.T., and Gove, M.K. (1991). *Reading and learning to read* (2nd ed.). New York: HarperCollins Publishers.

Valencia, S. (1990). A portfolio approach to classroom reading assessment: The whys, whats, and hows. *Reading Teacher, 43* (4), 338–340.

Vygotsky, L.S. (1962). *Thought and language*. Cambridge, MA: MIT Press.

———. (1978). *Mind in society: The development of higher psychological processes* (Eds.: M. Cole, V. John-Steiner, S. Scribner, and E. Souberman). Cambridge, MA: Harvard University Press.

Wagner, B.J. (1976). *Dorothy Heathcote: Drama as a learning medium*. Washington: National Educational Association of the United States.

Walter, C., Kahn, E., and Johannessen, L. (1983). If you can teach it, you can test it. *Curriculum Review, 22* (3), 11–14.

Wason-Ellam, L. (1987). Writing across the curriculum. *Canadian Journal of English Language Arts, 11* (3), 5–23.

Wells, G. (1986). *The Meaning Makers*. Portsmouth, NH: Heinemann.

Wilkinson, A., Barnsley, G., Hanna, P., and Swan, M. (1983). More comprehensive assessment of writing development. *Language Arts*, 60 (7), 871–881.

Wilkinson, L.C., and Marrett, C.B. (1985). *Gender influences in classroom interactions*. Toronto: Academic Press.

Wilson, R.M., and Cleland, C.J. (1985). *Diagnostic and remedial reading for classroom and clinic*. Columbus: Charles E. Merrill Publishing Company.

Wiseman, D.L. (1992). *Learning to read with literature*. Boston: Allyn and Bacon.

Wolvin, A., and Croakley, C. (1985). *Listening instruction* (TRIP Booklet). Urbana, IL: ERIC Clearinghouse on Reading and Communication Skills and the National Council of Teachers of English.

Yaden, D.B. (1984). Reading research in metalinguistic awareness: Findings, problems and classroom applications. *Visible Language*, 28, 5–47.

Index

To the owner of this book

We hope that you have enjoyed *Constructing Meaning: Integrating Elementary Language Arts*, and we would like to know as much about your experiences with this text as you would care to offer. Only through your comments and those of others can we learn how to make this a better text for future readers.

School ________________ Your instructor's name ______________________

Course ___________ Was the text required? _______ Recommended? _____

1. What did you like the most about *Constructing Meaning?*

____

____

____

2. How useful was this text for your course?

____

____

____

3. Do you have any recommendations for ways to improve the next edition of this text?

____

____

____

4. In the space below or in a separate letter, please write any other comments you have about the book. (For example, please feel free to comment on reading level, writing style, terminology, design features, and learning aids.)

____

____

____

____

Optional

Your name ______________________________ Date __________________

May Nelson Canada quote you, either in promotion for *Constructing Meaning* or in future publishing ventures?

Yes _______ No _______

Thanks!

FOLD HERE

Canada Post Corporation / Société canadienne des postes

Postage paid
if mailed in Canada

Port payé
si posté au Canada

Business Reply

Réponse d'affaires

0107077099 01

TAPE SHUT

0107077099-M1K5G4-BR01

Nelson Canada
Market and Product Development
1120 Birchmount Rd.
Scarborough, ON M1K 9Z9

PLEASE TAPE SHUT. DO NOT STAPLE.